POST-IMPERIAL POSSIBILITIES

Post-Imperial Possibilities

EURASIA, EURAFRICA, AFROASIA

Jane Burbank
& Frederick Cooper

PRINCETON UNIVERSITY PRESS
PRINCETON & OXFORD

Copyright © 2023 by Princeton University Press

Princeton University Press is committed to the protection of copyright and the intellectual property our authors entrust to us. Copyright promotes the progress and integrity of knowledge. Thank you for supporting free speech and the global exchange of ideas by purchasing an authorized edition of this book. If you wish to reproduce or distribute any part of it in any form, please obtain permission.

Requests for permission to reproduce material from this work should be sent to permissions@press.princeton.edu

Published by Princeton University Press
41 William Street, Princeton, New Jersey 08540
99 Banbury Road, Oxford OX2 6JX

press.princeton.edu

All Rights Reserved

ISBN 978-0-691-25037-3
ISBN (e-book) 978-0-691-25150-9

British Library Cataloging-in-Publication Data is available

Editorial: Priya Nelson and Emma Wagh
Production Editorial: Jill Harris
Jacket Design: Chris Ferrante
Production: Danielle Amatucci
Publicity: William Pagdatoon
Copyeditor: Karen Verde

Jacket art: World map courtesy of Vemaps.com

This book has been composed in Miller

Printed on acid-free paper. ∞

Printed in the United States of America

10 9 8 7 6 5 4 3 2 1

To the people of Ukraine

There is no inevitability; there is possibility. Only by means of intense creativity, without fear of confessing mistakes and acknowledging weaknesses, only at the price of uninterrupted efforts, carried out within the limits of a world that is plastic and open to will, can the possible become real.

—PETR SAVITSKII, "PIVOT TO THE EAST,"
ISKHOD K VOSTOKU: PREDCHUVSTVIIA I SVERSHENIIA:
UTVERZHDENIE EVRAZIITSEV (SOFIIA, 1921)

CONTENTS

List of Maps · xi
List of Illustrations · xiii

INTRODUCTION
1

CHAPTER 1
Eurasia
45

CHAPTER 2
Eurafrica
89

CHAPTER 3
Afroasia
153

CHAPTER 4
Eurasia Redux
221

CHAPTER 5
Reflections
262

Acknowledgments · 283
Index · 287

MAPS

2.1. World regions, after Richard von Coudenhove
 Kalergi, 1923 — 92
3.1. Countries participating in the Afro-Asian
 Conference, Bandung, 1955 — 173
3.2. Countries participating in the first conference of
 the Non-Aligned Movement, Belgrade, 1961 — 185
4.1. "Russia as a Eurasian Empire," after Alexander Dugin — 242
4.2. "Geopolitical revolution," after Alexander Dugin — 244

ILLUSTRATIONS

0.1.	Mackinder's "Natural Seats of Power"	16
1.1.	Prince Nikolai Trubetskoi	52
1.2.	Exodus to the East	60
2.1.	Léopold Sédar Senghor, 1949	96
2.2.	"Eurafrique," *Abidjan-Matin*, 1959	135
3.1.	Afro-Asian Conference, Bandung, 1955	175
3.2.	Non-Aligned Movement Conference, Belgrade, 1961	186
3.3.	Tricontinental Conference, Havana, 1966	206
4.1.	Monument to Lev Gumilev in Kazan	251
4.2.	Vladimir Putin and Nursultan Nazarbaev, 2017	253

POST-IMPERIAL POSSIBILITIES

Introduction

ON FEBRUARY 24, 2022, troops and tanks of the Russian Federation crossed the border of Ukraine, launching an all-out effort to conquer a sovereign state. President Vladimir Putin declared that the invasion would free the people of Ukraine from their "nazi" oppressors and restore their historic unity with Russia. To accomplish this liberation, Putin ordered the terror bombing of apartment buildings, hospitals, power plants, and cultural institutions, killing thousands. In his furious speech on the eve of the assault, Putin described Ukraine as an artificial creation of Soviet politics, an area that had never had its own "real statehood." Ukraine's corrupt leaders had made Ukraine into a "colony," from which NATO was preparing an attack on Russia.[1] Putin did not mention that Ukraine's people had voted for independence in 1991 and had exercised sovereignty for more than three decades.

Putin's tirade of February 2022 explicitly repudiated what had been vaunted as a major achievement of the Soviet Union—its multinational composition—as well as that structure's origins in Leninism and communist rule. Putin cited Lenin as the "author and architect" of Ukraine as a political entity, its first borders

---

[1]. For Putin's speech on the eve of the invasion, see "Obrashchenie Prezidenta Rossiiskoi Federatsii," February 21, 2022, http://kremlin.ru/events/president/news/67828, accessed February 11, 2023. Months before the beginning of the war, Putin had proclaimed that Ukrainians and Russians were a single nation: "Stat'ia Vladimira Putina 'Ob istoricheskom edinstve russkikh i ukraintsev,'" July 12, 2021, http://kremlin.ru/events/president/news/66181, accessed February 11, 2023.

established when Bolshevik leaders configured the USSR as a union of nationally based republics. In Putin's perspective, this federalism had been a terrible mistake, an unnecessary "lordly gift" to nationalists that left a "land-mine"—the constitutional right to secede—waiting for its moment to explode. And explode it did in 1990 and 1991, bringing down the Soviet Union with it. This argument—Putin presented it as "historical fact"—called into question the sovereignty of all the states that had emerged from the dissolution of the USSR. Further, Putin's condemnation of NATO and its putative threat to Russia's security implied that the states of eastern Europe that had been under Soviet domination until 1989 had no right, even as sovereign entities, to choose their own means of defense.[2] Putin's speech was an assertion of Russia's return, not as a bastion of communism, but as an empire that straddled the continents of Europe and Asia.

One of the most eloquent critiques of Putin's arguments was made at the time by Kenya's ambassador to the United Nations, Martin Kimani. On the eve of Russia's assault, Kimani explained to the Security Council that just as Ukraine had once been part of a large empire, African countries had been parts of colonial empires. European empires had often drawn territorial boundaries in Africa that divided people with a common language, culture, and sense of belonging or grouped people of unlike cultures and affiliations within a single political unit. But when African colonies became independent states, Kimani observed, they did not fight each other to remake the past but accepted existing boundaries in order to insure peace on the continent. African leaders had agreed that the decolonized states, however their frontiers had been defined, had become sovereign polities.[3] He had a point. For all the challenges that Africa has faced since the era of independence in the 1950s and 1960s, wars between states and the redrawing of boundaries have been rare. Only two new states, Eritrea and South Sudan, have been carved out from the borders designed during colonial rule.

---

2. "Obrashchenie Prezidenta Rossiiskoi Federatsii," February 21, 2022, http://kremlin.ru/events/president/news/67828, accessed February 11, 2023.

3. https://www.un.int/kenya/statements_speeches/statement-amb-martin-kimani-during-security-council-urgent-meeting-situation, accessed February 24, 2023.

Kimani's thoughtful response made a case for accepting the statehood of former colonies. Yet the institutions designed to safeguard the sovereignty of states have not always had the strength and motivation to fulfill this goal—not in the case of Russia's invasion of Ukraine, not when the United States invaded Iraq in 2003.[4] Nor has a world order based on nation-states provided sufficient means to counter the extreme inequalities that emerged between former colonies like Kenya and states in Europe and North America. Were other ways of governing relations among different peoples, replacing those of empires, imaginable?

In this book, we turn back to twentieth-century moments of imperial dissolution to explore questions of political imagination and reconfiguration. We focus on three efforts to create large-scale, transcontinental projects that could unite peoples of different origins in productive, attractive, and strong political units: Eurasia, Eurafrica, and Afroasia. All three concepts were both influential and controversial in their times. Projecting political linkages across states and continents could inspire a quest for equality and justice but could also provide a rationale for imperialist aggression. We focus on both context and consequence—on situations in which these projects flourished, foundered, or were transformed, as well as on their impacts on the configuration of power in the world.

After the collapse of the Russian empire in 1917, the idea of uniting peoples across Eurasia was proposed as a counter both to western claims to civilizational superiority and to the Bolsheviks' version of nations united under communist rule. Eurasianism reappeared in the 1990s after a second imperial breakdown, this time of the Soviet Union, as a rejection of the purported triumph of liberal democracy and capitalism over communism. Eurafrica and Afroasia also emerged first in the 1920s, the former as an effort to replace rivalry among European empires with cooperation in the exploitation of Africa, the latter as a challenge to the global reach of European empires. Both concepts took on new forms in the 1950s as anti-imperial activists and political leaders worried

---

4. The United States did not intend to incorporate Iraq into its polity, as Russia intends with regard to Ukraine, but the United States did clearly violate Iraqi sovereignty on grounds that were largely bogus.

that nation-states created after the deprivations of colonial empire would have difficulty making their way in a world of concentrated economic, military, and political power.

Eurasia, Eurafrica, and Afroasia shared an emphatic rejection of Eurocentric approaches to politics and culture but did not propose the development of national cultures and self-contained national politics as the only or best way forward. They were not the only initiatives created in the twentieth century to overcome the confines of both empire and nation-state. Some political leaders and intellectuals in the early decades of the century thought that the world would soon divide itself into a small number of geographical blocs. The Bolsheviks chose the word "Union" to describe their reconfiguration of Russian empire; France would choose the same word in 1945; Britain thought of Commonwealth as a complement or a successor to empire. After World War II, the world appeared to be divided into two blocs, led by the United States and the Soviet Union, but from the 1950s, scholars and activists invoked a "third world" that asserted its independence from both. After the implosion of the second world in 1989-91, pundits thought the three worlds had been reduced to one. In the early twenty-first century, some claim that the world is multipolar; others say it is fragmented.

This book focuses on three post-imperial possibilities raised by people looking beyond national and continental boundaries to reconfigure world space. For these activists and intellectuals, space was not shaped just by landmasses, oceans, mountains, and rivers but by political relationships that could be made and remade.[5] Imagined futures in each of our cases were challenged by the constraints of institutional, economic, and cultural realities and were, fatefully, transformed by them.

Let us briefly introduce the three projects, beginning with Eurasia.

After the fall of Russia's Romanov dynasty in 1917, politically minded intellectuals sought ways to reorganize sovereignty across the huge space of the former empire. Some were engaged in wars of independence for regions and peoples that had been incorporated into the tsarist empire. Two intertwined projects challenged both

---

5. Henri Lefebvre, *The Production of Space* (Oxford: Blackwell, 1991).

the old imperial system and the nation-state alternative. The more visible one was the reconstruction of much of the former empire as a communist federation. The Union of Soviet Socialist Republics served as a model or an anti-model for state remaking for much of the twentieth century. The other plan existed in the creative imaginations of intellectuals, most of them émigrés and opponents of Soviet power. This idea, emerging in the 1920s, was Eurasianism—the notion that people across the great space once criss-crossed by Mongol and Turkic conquerors and inhabited by groups with different ethnic origins and religions shared a historically conditioned capacity for alliance in a multinational polity.

A number of influential intellectuals and political leaders in African and Asian countries also sought alternatives to both colonial empire and nation-state. As the possibility that imperial rule was vulnerable to challenge became stronger in the years after World War II, some worried that territorial independence would separate African or Asian people from each other as well as from a colonizing power. Two of these alternatives for a post-imperial future will be examined here: Eurafrica and Afroasia. The polities emerging out of colonial empire were often small or fragmented, lacking resources and in some cases population, largely resulting from the ways that empires had divvied up their overseas territories. Many of the new states had been impoverished by their imperial pasts—their wealth expropriated, their people made to work in demeaning conditions, their leaders disparaged. The doubts expressed by African leaders from Kwame Nkrumah to Léopold Sédar Senghor in the heat of anticolonial struggles of the 1950s anticipated some of today's concerns that the end of colonial rule has not brought about economic and social equality on a global scale.

The goals of advocates of Eurafrica in French Africa overlapped with those of political leaders in France who sought integration with the other states of Europe without giving up France's overseas territories. Both African and French leaders realized that in the new situation the former colonizer and the former colonized would have to become more equal partners in an overarching political structure organized along federal or confederal lines. Advocates of Afroasia, in contrast, sought to break with just such connections, reminiscent as they were of European dominance. They sought instead to devise mechanisms for cooperation among former colonies to contest the ways in which the former colonial states, as well as the United States and the USSR, were exercising economic and political power around the world.

Eurafrica and Afroasia were the focus of vigorous political contestation—from the late 1940s to the late 1950s in the case of Eurafrica, from the mid-1950s to the late 1970s in the case of Afroasia. Both projects confronted on the one hand the opposition of wealthy states to any political structure that would pressure them to redistribute their resources and on the other hand the vested interest that elites in decolonizing states acquired in the constituencies they were riding to power (chapters 2 and 3). Eurasia, however, took on a new life in the 1990s. What for a time seemed to be a post-imperial array of independent states formed by the breakup of the Soviet Union set a Eurasian stage for advocates of a restored Russian empire (chapter 4).

The leading figures behind these three projects gave them names that emphasized their cross-continental assertiveness, but their continental visions were political constructions, not strictly geographic ones according to the conventions of today's maps. Eurasia did not include India, China, Southeast Asia, or most of Europe; its spatial configuration was defined by the expansion of Russian empire and by the fusion of Turkic, Mongol, and Slavic heritages. The European component of 1950s Eurafrica embraced only the six aspiring members of the European Economic Community and its Africa was French and Belgian, although leaders on both sides of the Mediterranean thought Eurafrica could eventually become more inclusive. The Afro-Asian Conference of 1955, bringing together representatives of twenty-nine states, defined itself as a political project of formerly colonized states, attracting the interest of more countries as they liberated themselves. The Afroasian effort to redefine a world economic order eventually brought in countries of Latin America to create a coalition that called itself the Group of 77, keeping that name even as the number of member states grew to 120.

China, following upon the triumph of communist revolution in 1949, was present at the 1955 Conference and sought to expand its influence on the Afroasian movement. China's brand of communism appealed to some militants in Africa and Asia, but ruling elites were more likely to see it as a threat. In the early 1960s, China became embroiled in conflict with India and the USSR. By the 1990s, when China was becoming a global economic power, the Afroasian movement had lost its steam; China—with its Belt and Road and other initiatives—became a source of investment capital and aid, eagerly sought by some, regarded by others as a neocolonial power like those of the west. Its ambiguous position as an imperial, post-imperial, and anti-imperial polity put China in awkward and shifting relations with Afroasia. China was looked at askance by Eurasianists and not envisioned as part of their projects.

All three movements were spearheaded by intellectuals and political elites, and none of them became a full-fledged mass movement able to bring people across the spaces they claimed into sustained and collective mobilization. Eurasianism began among Russian exiles in the 1920s and stood no chance of penetrating the closed and repressive Soviet polity; its reemergence in the 1990s and 2000s attracted discontented university, political, and military elites. The leading advocates of Eurafrica and Afroasia were cosmopolitan intellectuals and political activists engaged in transnational circuits that crossed the line between colony and metropole. They sought to mobilize people in widely varying localities and circumstances, to channel people's anger over colonial repression and exploitation into electoral campaigns, street demonstrations, general strikes, and in some cases armed struggle. Making the connection to popular masses required boundary-crossing elites to develop local networks and constituencies—a goal that was widely recognized but difficult to accomplish. As we shall see, the very success of movements in obtaining national independence—starting with India in 1947 and Indonesia in 1949—pushed new ruling elites to focus on national politics even as their status as heads of recognized states gave them a platform to criticize imperialism and global inequality.

Post-Imperial Opportunities

All three movements gained ascendancy from crises of empire. Dissolutions of empire, peaceful or violent, reconfigured France, Great Britain, and Belgium in the 1950s and 1960s and Portugal in the

1970s. Russian empire collapsed twice, first in 1917 and a second time with the breakup of the Soviet system in 1989–91. A world of about fifty states at the end of World War II became a world of nearly two hundred states at the end of the century, each claiming to govern a territory and the exclusive power to represent that territory's population.

The Eurafrica that influential leaders in French Africa advocated from the late 1940s to the late 1950s offered one approach to confronting economic inequality between colonizer and colonies. After the war, advocates for Eurafrica built on France's insistence that the people of its African colonies were an integral part of the French population to turn prewar assumptions upside down: Europe's claim to exploit African resources would become Africa's claim for resources it needed to develop. For their part, the leaders of France were seeking economic and political integration within Europe but feared that incorporating France without its African colonies into a European entity would split France in two. By the 1950s, African political movements were strongly challenging colonial rule, and they were in a position to insist that if Eurafrican political institutions were to be created, Africans must have a voice in them. The overlapping goals of political elites in African and European France meant that the aftermath of colonialism became a much-debated issue in the politics of constructing Europe. The European side of the Eurafrican project blinked first, pushing aside the voices and demands of France's African citizens while remaining open to supranational structures integrating the relatively affluent states of Europe.

Afroasian possibilities seemed to open up as Eurafrican ones were shutting down. Whereas both Eurafrica and Eurasia posited a continued relation with what had been an imperial center—Paris or Moscow—Afroasian advocates insisted that as states became liberated from colonial rule they should focus on cooperation with each other. Afroasian politics had emerged first in early twentieth-century circuits of anticolonial militants through London, Paris, Hamburg, Moscow, Singapore, Beijing, and other cities. Many opponents of colonial rule were influenced by communism and other strands of socialism and attracted by the European left's explicit condemnation of imperialism; these activists acquired a powerful patron after the Russian Revolution of 1917. Anticolonialism took other forms—liberal, pan-Arab, pan-Islamic, pan-African, Christian—in the first decades of the twentieth century. Over time, the USSR, following its own strategic and ideological course, became a force that divided as well as brought together the enemies of colonial rule. World War II produced both a crisis of empire in western Europe and the expansion of the Soviet sphere into eastern Europe. Which territories could aspire to sovereignty and what sort of future that sovereignty would entail was in question for the subsequent decades.

The Afro-Asian Conference held in Bandung, Indonesia, in 1955 brought together the rulers of ex-colonial states that had by then become independent. Attendees broached the possibility of acting collectively as a bloc while retaining individual sovereignty. As more colonies became independent, other organizations with differing memberships took up the challenge laid down at Bandung, among them the Afro-Asian Peoples Solidarity Organization (1957), the Non-Aligned Movement (1961), and the Tricontinental Conference of Solidarity of the Peoples of Africa, Asia, and Latin America (1966). Meanwhile, intellectuals, artists, and activists made efforts—through such organizations as the Afro-Asian Writers Bureau—to work together to combat Eurocentrism, to enhance people's pride in their cultural heritages, and to make clear to the world the contribution of African and Asian civilizations to humanity.

There was a tension between an Afroasianism of people and political movements and an Afroasianism of states. The sovereignty of the national state proved to be both a strength and a weakness of the new states' drive for global reform. By the mid-1960s, it was becoming clear that the ruling elites of newly independent countries were following different trajectories in economic and social policy, in ideological development, and in their relationships with the rich and powerful states of the world. The ruling elites of each state were—indeed had to be—most concerned with maintaining their own power against internal and external challenges. An attempt to hold a successor conference to Bandung in Algiers in 1965 ended in a fiasco.

There followed other attempts to use the architecture of interstate relations, particularly the United Nations and its affiliated organizations, to develop cooperation among the states of Asia, Africa, and—increasingly—Latin America. The wealthy states' reaction to proposals to reform global economic structures was to refuse not only specific proposals but also their underlying premises, denying that either a past of colonial exploitation or a present of poverty and hunger constituted a basis for reorganizing global economic relations and insisting instead that all states make what they could of their "freedom."

Unlike Eurafrica and Afroasia, Eurasia has a present as well as a past. The Eurasianists of the 1920s underscored the shared cultural attributes that linked the myriad peoples in this vast region and advocated both political and economic integration across the reimagined continent. Their theories were not welcomed by communists in Russia, who were embarking on a new kind of multinational politics. In the USSR, nationality was recognized in the units and subunits of its formally federalized polity, while centralized control was maintained through a political innovation—the one-party state. But when communist authority collapsed many decades later, intellectuals revived the Eurasian idea as a successor ideology to what had been the defining purpose of the Union of Soviet Socialist Republics.

As Sharad Chari and Katherine Verdery have argued, there are parallels between the "post-socialism" of 1989–91 and the "postcolonialism" of the 1960s, when states faced the task of "becoming something other than socialist or other than colonized" in a global context in which most economic resources and international rules governing economic life were shaped by the great powers.[6] During the implosion of the partly self-contained economic and political structure of the Soviet bloc and consequent ideological void, Eurasianism seemed to offer possibilities for a post-Soviet future for Russia. After Vladimir Putin consolidated his control over the Russian Federation in the 2000s, Eurasianism became a frankly imperial ideology. Prominent advocates of Eurasianism called for a new "geopolitics" to counter the new west—Europe and the United States. Russia

---

6. Sharad Chari and Katherine Verdery, "Thinking between the Posts: Postcolonialism, Postsocialism, and Ethnography after the Cold War," *Comparative Studies in Society and History* 51, 1 (2009): 6–34, 11 quoted.

should recover its historical Eurasian territory and develop affiliations with other areas to create a "multi-polar world."[7]

Both the resurgence of an imperial Eurasia and the inability of advocates of Eurafrica and Afroasia to achieve their desired structural changes expose the limitations and constraints of the international order that was supposed to make the world less unequal and more stable. The radical shifts in formal sovereignty of the last half of the twentieth century did not produce equality or stability.

Sovereignty in Question

All three post-imperial projects both asserted and nuanced concepts of sovereignty, countering the legitimacy of forces seen as external to a given population but leaving open the means by which political power should be exercised and legitimated. The conventional notion of sovereignty as an all-or-nothing proposition corresponds poorly to the complexities of power relations in world history. As James Sheehan argues, "As a doctrine, sovereignty is usually regarded as unified and inseparable; as an activity, however, it is plural and divisible." It is a bundle of claims "by those seeking or wielding power, claims about the superiority and autonomy of their authority." Claiming sovereignty depends to varying degrees and particular circumstances on law, force, political culture, and external recognition. It is not fully located in "the people" of a particular state or in the person of a sovereign; it is not separable from normative and institutional structures among the states of the world. Sovereignty can be crosscut by non-territorial networks and institutions that assert power in certain domains—the World Trade Organization's regulation of international commerce for instance. Empires, generally, could recognize a degree of sovereignty in a subordinated polity, what political theorists call layered or shared sovereignty.[8]

---

7. The emphasis on geopolitics in this latter version of Eurasianism figures in the title of an influential book by Alexander Dugin, "The Foundations of Geopolitics": Aleksandr Dugin, *Osnovy geopolitiki: geopoliticheskoe budeshchee Rossii* (Moscow: Arktogeia, 1997). See chapter 4. We use Dugin's first name in its English variant in the text and his Russian first name for his Russian publications.

8. James Sheehan, "The Problem of Sovereignty in European History," *American Historical Review* 111, 1 (2006): 1–15, 2, 3 quoted; Hent Kalmo and Quentin Skinner, eds.,

Advocates of Eurasia, Eurafrica, and Afroasia had experienced the layered dimensions of imperial formations and could both envision independence from imperial rule and look beyond the nation-state. They sought overarching institutions to express—and possibly enforce—common projects while recognizing national difference and varying degrees of political autonomy within a larger structure. In the last half of the twentieth century, advocates for Eurafrica, Afroasia, and Eurasia had to make their way in an international scene that both reified the division of the world into national states (expressed in membership in the United Nations) and intruded—through UN agencies, the World Bank, and the International Monetary Fund—on those states' control over economic and social life. The debates over Eurafrica and Afroasia in the 1950s and 1960s were about shaping untried forms of post-imperial sovereignty. In the 1990s, the relationship between Moscow and the fourteen ex-Soviet states as well as with the component parts of the Russian Federation itself were in question. In each case, the would-be makers of new social possibilities were constrained by already constituted and self-interested political and economic actors.

Military violations of sovereignty, like Russia's invasion of Ukraine, are not the only problematic aspect of the post-imperial world order. The boundedness of the sovereign state implies that the welfare of the people of each state is a matter for that state alone; by "freeing" their colonies, imperial leaders freed themselves from responsibility for the social conditions and civil rights of the people they used to rule. Paralleling the idea of autonomous state sovereignty, theories of economic behavior stress individual autonomy—of the person, the corporation, or state—each of which is free to sink or swim in the waters of global commerce. During struggles against colonialism, advocates of independence pushed for support from international institutions committed to global justice, but once independence was achieved, poor states could only *appeal* to

---

Sovereignty in Fragments: The Past, Present and Future of a Contested Concept (Cambridge: Cambridge University Press, 2010); John Agnew, *Globalization and Sovereignty* (Lanham, MD: Rowan & Littlefield, 2009); Lauren Benton, *A Search for Sovereignty: Law and Geography in European Empires, 1400–1900* (Cambridge: Cambridge University Press, 2010).

richer states to redistribute some of their resources. At the same time, people within a sovereign country had limited means to enlist support beyond their borders for injustices or deprivations, whether caused by external forces or the rulers of their own countries.

Connections and Disconnections

The three projects for political reconfiguration examined in this book expressed aspirations to make connections—political, economic, and cultural—across land and sea and to respond to the challenges of both empire and narrow nationalism. They did so in different ways and without strong or consistent connections to each other.

The example of communist modernization in Central Asia appealed to some Asian radicals, and the USSR provided aid and connections to activists in the countries involved in the Afroasian movement.[9] China was also in position to play the Afroasian card. But both Soviet and Chinese initiatives did as much to divide as to unite Afroasian states, with their various ideological postures and relations with western powers (chapter 3).

Eurasianists situated themselves first against western Europe and later, targeting the United States as well, against "the Atlantic," while Eurafrica was a project that brought Europe and Africa together. Both concepts emphasized culture, but to different ends. Léopold Sédar Senghor, a major theorist of Eurafrica, imagined a shared "African" culture that embraced variations within the continent; N. S. Trubetskoi's "Eurasia" focused on cultural affinity across a linguistically varied landscape. Senghor continually emphasized the complementarity of unlike civilizations, African and European, while Trubetskoi and other Eurasianists stressed the divergence of large-scale world cultures—Eurasian versus European. Trubetskoi was radically hostile to European "civilization," and, while an agile operator in international social science, he acknowledged no European sources for his arguments in the 1920s and 1930s. In

---

9. Masha Kirasirova, "Sons of Muslims in Moscow: Soviet Central Asian Mediators to the Foreign East, 1955–62," *Ab Imperio* 2011, 4: 106–32; Marek Eby, "Global Tashkent: Transnational Visions of a Soviet City in the Postcolonial World, 1953–1966," *Ab Imperio* 2021, 4: 238–64.

the 1990s, the neo-Eurasianist Alexander Dugin drew on European sources of political theory and engaged in the politics of the European far right, but his goal was the rejection of what he saw as European social norms. Dugin bound the North Atlantic powers—Europe and North America—into a single hostile camp. His Russia-centered Eurasia did not overlap Afroasia or Eurafrica, although he did envision a Russian-led alliance with the "Poor South" against the "Rich West."

Before World War II, anticolonial activists in Asia and Africa paid attention to cultural affinity within each continent. This cultural complex created the possibility for political relationships that would allow for both autonomy and cooperation. But what galvanized Afroasian movements was not so much cultural likeness as the struggle against imperialism and its aftermaths, notable in the continent-crossing connections forged by, among other groups, the League against Imperialism (1927–37) and the Bandung Conference of 1955. Some theorists and activists developed what might be termed an "anticolonial culture," whose contents, as in the writing of Frantz Fanon, were defined by common struggle.[10] The emerging Afroasian movements of the 1950s stood in opposition to calls for Eurafrica; anticolonial culture presented a direct challenge to Senghorian ideals of civilizational complementarity.

The point of juxtaposing Eurasia, Eurafrica, and Afroasia in this book is that all three concepts addressed a critical political issue of their times—the power of the world's great empires and the uncertainty of how to escape and supersede them.

Eurasia and Eurafrica, in their manifestations in the 1920s and 1930s, reflected geopolitical awareness generated in the context of inter-imperial rivalry in the early twentieth century. They grew out of a widespread interest among political theorists as well as activists in organizing political relations around large blocs, transcending both imperial and national states. Among these endeavors were Pan-Africanism, Pan-Asianism, Pan-Slavism, and Pan-Arabism—movements that brought together people who claimed to have

10. Frantz Fanon, *Toward the African Revolution: Political Essays* (New York: Grove Press, 1967); Frantz Fanon, *Les damnés de la terre* (Paris: Maspero, 1961); Ismay Milford, *African Activists in a Decolonising World: The Making of an Anticolonial Culture, 1952–1966* (Cambridge: Cambridge University Press, 2023).

common cultural roots across vast tracts of land and in some cases oceans. Activists believed these connections could lead to collective action, perhaps trans-territorial governance but at least some form of alliance and cooperation.

Another impulse for thinking in large geographical terms was exemplified by the British scholar Halford John Mackinder. In an influential article published in 1904, Mackinder argued that mobility across the steppes and marshes of what he called "Euro-Asia" made that region into a "pivot" of history. The volatile politics of nomadic populations had led to the crystallization of imperial power, until countered by the "oceanic" strategies of the western European empires. Euro-Asia, he predicted, would revive in the age of railways.[11] Visions of world politics organized around blocs, such as those of Mackinder, had considerable influence before and after World War I, both among imperial leaders eager to extend their web of power and intellectuals hoping that federal relations among states within a large geopolitical sphere would produce a more stable order than competition among empires.[12]

Eurasian and Eurafrican projects took shape in Russian and French imperial settings, but they looked beyond empire to a political formation that would override rivalries within it. Afroasian politics posited a new kind of power bloc of independent states that had overcome western imperialism. As the challenge to European empires grew more compelling in the years after World War II, Afroasian movements shifted back and forth between a revolutionary current directed against the United States and the states of western Europe but open to cooperation with the communist

11. Halford John Mackinder, "The Geographical Pivot of History," *Geographical Journal* 23 (1904): 421–44.

12. On the importance of variants on the theme of blocs in Germany, the United States, and Great Britain, see Charles Maier, *Once Within Borders: Territories of Power, Wealth, and Belonging since 1500* (Cambridge, MA: Harvard University Press, 2016), Gerard Kearns, *Geopolitics and Empire: The Legacy of Halford Mackinder* (Oxford: Oxford University Press, 2009), and Liane Hewitt, "The World in Blocs: Leo Amery, the British Empire and Regionalist Anti-internationalism, 1903–1947," *Journal of Global History* 2022, doi:10.1017/S1740022822000262. Trubetskoi did not cite Mackinder but was well aware and appreciative of Oswald Spengler's related arguments in his *Decline of the West* (first published in 1922). Sergey Glebov, *From Empire to Eurasia: Politics, Scholarship, and Ideology in Russian Eurasianism, 1920s–1930s* (De Kalb: Northern Illinois University Press, 2017), 82.

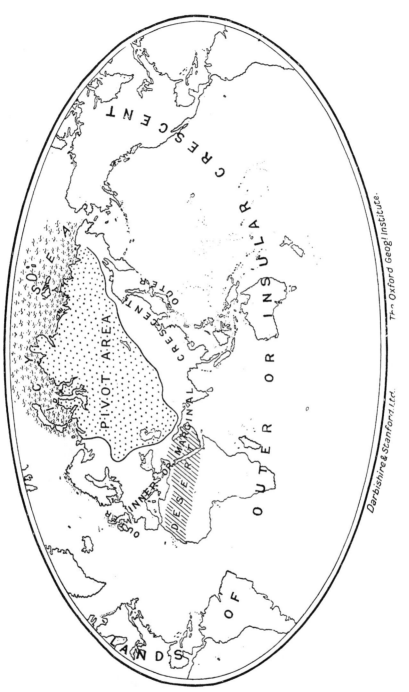

FIGURE 0.1. Halford Mackinder's map "The Natural Seats of Power," showing what he considered "the pivot of history," 1904.
Source: Halford John Mackinder, "The Geographical Pivot of History," *Geographical Journal* 23 (1904): 436.

world (complicated by the Sino-Soviet split) and a "third worldist" viewpoint that favored the creation of a bloc capable of collective political and economic cooperation that could stand up to both the first and the second worlds.

Although the term "third world" was coined by a French geographer in 1952,[13] it appealed to political elites who saw the need to act collectively and did not want to get trapped in a world divided into two blocs. Afroasia could be imagined as a megabloc, but more compact regional groupings of like-minded ex-colonial states also emerged, for example the socialist-oriented "Casablanca Group" (Ghana, Guinea, Algeria, Libya, Egypt, Mali, and Morocco) and the more conservative "Monrovia Group" (Liberia, Ethiopia, Nigeria, and other English-speaking African countries). The initiatives of these new leaders signaled that the newly won status of nation-state was an insufficient foundation for their aspirations.

Imperial Origins

Eurasia, Eurafrica, and Afroasia each emerged out of empire and in opposition to western European claims to civilizational superiority. The three possibilities did not derive from preset concepts of an ideal polity, of a single people ruling themselves or otherwise, but from people's experience of empire and their interest in transforming it.

Empires had devised ways to address the multiple and unlike peoples they ruled. Violence was fundamental to building and maintaining empires, but imperial polities, if they were to endure, had to intervene in a variety of ways in the lives of their subjects. Rulers of empire tried to ensure that components of the polity would form closer relationships with the imperial overlord than with each

13. Alfred Sauvy, "Trois mondes, une planète," *L'Observateur*, 118 (1952), reprinted in *Vingtième Siècle. Revue d'histoire* 12 (1986): 81–83. Sauvy argued that the Third World was "ignored, exploited, despised like the Third Estate" (of revolutionary France) and emphasized that "what matters to each of the two worlds is to conquer the third, or at least to have it on their side." A less-known usage of the term came from the British High Commissioner to India describing speeches made at the Asian Relations Conference of 1947 calling on Asian territories to assert themselves and avoid dependence on either the United States or the USSR. Vineet Thakur, "An Asian Drama: The Asian Relations Conference, 1947," *International History Review* 41, 3 (2019): 673.

other. At the same time, empires needed intermediaries—sent out from the center, co-opted from incorporated societies, or recruited through exclusive ties to the rulers—who could connect their disparate lands to the faraway imperial authorities. Intermediaries were necessary but dangerous; they had to be kept loyal. Empires were held together not just through rewards and coercion, but through cultural and ideological representations that portrayed their power as in the nature of things, as systems of relations that gave people a place in a powerful entity, even if that place turned out to be on the lower level of a hierarchy.[14]

The imperial powers considered in this book followed different politics of difference at the turn of the twentieth century. France proclaimed the principle of equality for all its citizens but defined the vast majority of the inhabitants of its expanding overseas territories as "subjects," excluded from citizens' rights and vulnerable to forced labor, land seizures, or arbitrary punishments. Such invidious distinctions and deviations from principles of republican governance disturbed some members of the political establishment and were challenged by many colonial subjects, but French governments stuck to their practices of governing different people differently for decades.[15] Russia, in contrast, was ruled by an autocracy. Rather than a dichotomy between a rights-bearing and a rights-less population, the differential allocation of rights and privileges among the diverse peoples of the empire was legally the prerogative of the Russian emperor. No one was a rights-bearing citizen.[16]

These were two strategies for imperial rule among many others. At the beginning of the twentieth century, much of the world's population lived in or within the reach of some kind of imperial polity: in the long-standing but troubled Chinese empire, the durable Ottoman empire, the vast and still spreading Russian empire, or the

---

14. Jane Burbank and Frederick Cooper, *Empires in World History: Power and the Politics of Difference* (Princeton, NJ: Princeton University Press, 2010). The literature on particular empires and the interactions among them is now vast.

15. For an overview of struggles over citizenship and colonialism, see Lorelle Semley, *To Be Free and French: Citizenship in France's Atlantic Empire* (Cambridge: Cambridge University Press, 2017).

16. Jane Burbank, "An Imperial Rights Regime: Law and Citizenship in the Russian Empire," *Kritika: Explorations in Russian and Eurasian History* 7, 3 (Summer 2006): 397–431.

colonial empires of western Europe and Japan. In each of these settings, the forceful incorporation of people had led to the subordination and exploitation of ethnic, racial, and religious groups, their differences defined in multiple ways.

Empire, in colonial and other forms, had long been subject to challenges from multiple sources: intermediaries who sought autonomy or the takeover of the empire, rival empires that tried to weaken their rivals by supporting subordinated religious or ethnic groups in someone else's empire, and political movements that rejected the principle of imperial rule altogether. Starting with the revolutions in North and South America in the late eighteenth and early nineteenth centuries, nations had been carved out of empires. But the societies that resulted from these revolutions were highly unequal and far from homogeneous. Making them more homogeneous—closer to the ideal-type of the nation-state—entailed violence and exclusion. And some of those nations had empire-building ambitions themselves.

Imperial ambitions intersected explosively in the early twentieth century. The most powerful empires of that time—Germany, France, Britain, Austria-Hungary, Russia, the Ottomans—drew each other into a war that mobilized and devastated subject peoples in many parts of the world and eventually brought in the United States and Japan. As the states that had dominated so much of the world threatened and undermined each other, what alternatives to the fractured and entangled assemblages of the unlike and the unequal were imaginable?

In the 1920s and 1930s, the three spatially and humanly ambitious projects of Eurasia, Eurafrica, and Afroasia coexisted with empires that had emerged victorious in 1918 as well as with new and expanding empires—Japan, the Soviet Union, fascist Italy, Nazi Germany. The idea that the nation-state should be the basic building block of global politics was not hegemonic in these decades. What sovereignty would mean in a post-imperial world had to be worked out; it was not a given to which all anticolonial activists aspired. None of the projects we examine leapt straight from the national to the global, and they did not necessarily claim that the principles on which they were based were universal. They each took a relational and regional view of connection and affinity, while remaining tensely aware of the wider context of economic and political power.

We are not negating the importance of nationalism in the history of the twentieth century, especially the power of claims to national autonomy coming from people subordinated by colonial regimes. These histories have received dedicated attention from scholars of history, politics, and international relations.[17] Eurasia, Eurafrica, and Afroasia should be seen in relation to contemporaneous assertions of national identification. Eurasia, in both Trubetskoi's and Dugin's formulations, posited imperial rule, but recognized the diversity of the Eurasian polity; Senghor's Eurafrica was confederal, with a layer of collective governance over French and African polities that were internally self-governing and reflecting their own notions of "nation"; the Afroasia of Bandung was an alliance of nation-states, building solidarity based on a long-term goal of transforming the world.

This book does not exhaust the possibilities of political relationships that cross large spaces without recreating the hierarchies of empire. The "pan" movements mentioned above—pan-African, pan-Slavic, pan-Arab—attempted trans- and post- imperial association. Devotees of Esperanto hoped that a new language could overcome national animosities.[18] Religion cut across imperial lines: Britain, France, the Netherlands, and Russia claimed authority at various points over some of the largest populations of Muslims in the world, and they constantly feared that Islamic connections would threaten imperial ones—a fear recently revived in the face of networks advocating "jihad" across national and continental boundaries. World communism was also seen by many as an alternative to capitalist imperialism. The projects of the USSR intersected all three—Eurasian, Eurafrican, and Afroasian—possibilities.[19]

---

17. For a recent forum presenting different scholarly views on the place of nationalism in world history, see *American Historical Review* 127, 1 (2022): 311–71. See also John Breuilly, ed., *The Oxford Handbook of the History of Nationalism* (Oxford: Oxford University Press, 2013).

18. Brigid O'Keeffe, *Esperanto and Languages of Internationalism in Revolutionary Russia* (London: Bloomsbury, 2021).

19. See the references to pan movements and communist internationalism in chapter 3.

The British Commonwealth, measured against other supranational and transcontinental possibilities, was in an ambiguous position. It was constructed more as an imperial than a post-imperial project.[20] The Commonwealth was initially a very white enterprise, in which settlers from the British Isles living in places where indigenous populations had been subordinated—Canada, Australia, New Zealand, South Africa—gradually acquired the capacity to govern themselves in most respects while remaining subjects of the king or queen of England. In India beginning in the nineteenth century and later in parts of Africa, activists well-versed in British practices of governance at home and abroad laid claim to "imperial citizenship," demanding rights and political voice in a transcontinental polity, something the British government had no intention of conceding. In the early twentieth century, Canada, Australia, and other dominions refused to allow Indians a right to immigrate into these parts of the British empire. This racially motivated rejection of a rights regime across spaces identified as "British" was instrumental in pushing the Indian National Congress to demand full independence rather than reform of the British empire.[21]

As most parts of the British Empire in Africa and Asia acquired independence from the 1940s through 1960s, the Commonwealth became a post-imperial umbrella for former British territories, but it was a weak structure unable to act on major issues. It did not stop

20. On the ideas behind the "white" vision of Empire and Commonwealth, see Duncan Bell, *The Idea of Greater Britain: Empire and the Future of World Order, 1860–1900* (Princeton, NJ: Princeton University Press, 2007). In the aftermath of World War II, the British government looked to the Commonwealth to maintain British economic and political power, softening the transition from an imperial to a post-imperial project. But both the "white" and the "non-white" Commonwealth proved impossible to control—not least because of tension between the two. Daniel Haines, "A 'Commonwealth Moment' in South Asian Decolonization," in Leslie James and Elisabeth Leake, eds., *Decolonization and the Cold War: Negotiating Independence* (London: Bloomsbury, 2015), 185–202; John Darwin, *The Empire Project: The Rise and Fall of British World-System, 1830–1970* (Cambridge: Cambridge University Press, 2009), 569–73.

21. When India did become independent in 1947, its new status meant that the Indian state achieved formal equality with the other states of the former empire, but overseas Indians were left in limbo between their host countries and India. Raphaëlle Khan, "Sovereignty after Empire and the Search for a New Order: India's Attempt to Negotiate a Common Citizenship in the Commonwealth (1947–1949)," *Journal of Imperial and Commonwealth History* 49, 6 (2021): 1141–74.

the repression of African nationalism by a white minority government in Rhodesia in the 1960s, and it did not give rise to a citizenship that could be exercised anywhere in the Commonwealth.[22]

What had united the United States in the 1780s was preserving its post-imperial existence from the threat of the powerful empires of that time. After independence the United States asserted that its defensive perimeter extended to the rest of the Americas even as territories in much of the region acquired sovereignty in their own right. Over time, the United States developed its own imperial reach. Some elites around the world found utility in an American connection, however unequal, while others hoped to find an antidote to American economic, political, and military power in connections among themselves—including, as we will see, the solidarity offered by Eurasia, Eurafrica, and Afroasia.

The range of post-imperial possibilities proposed over the twentieth century gave different meanings to "sovereignty," not necessarily congruent with a singular people living in a defined space.[23] Afroasia posited a close cooperative relationship among sovereign states, Eurafrica a layering of sovereignty, Eurasia a singular authority but a multi-ethnic society, its distinctive social groups connected by cultural affinities and historical linkages.

Each of these projects had a relationship—an uneasy one—to questions of human rights and hence to the idea that certain principles were "universal." Human rights discourse posited a set of values that was supposed to apply to all human beings irrespective of membership in a political unit. It presumed that sovereignty was not absolute. The difficulty was the absence or weakness of

22. Philip Murphy, *The Empire's New Clothes: The Myth of the Commonwealth* (Oxford: Oxford University Press, 2018). Even the Nationality Act of 1948, which conveyed a form of British citizenship to the subjects of dominions and colonies—including the right to enter and live in the United Kingdom—was undermined by the refusal of much of the "white" Commonwealth to allow nonwhites to exercise such rights in their countries, and once Great Britain gave up most of its colonies, it began to erode the rights that the Act had provided within the United Kingdom. The empire-wide citizenship provisions enacted by France in 1946 were more far-reaching and became part of the debate over Eurafrica in the 1950s (chapter 2).

23. On the uncertain nature of sovereignty in a decolonizing world, see Adom Getachew, *Worldmaking after Empire: The Rise and Fall of Self-Determination* (Princeton, NJ: Princeton University Press, 2019), and the discussions of the topic based on her book in *Comparative Studies of South Asia, Africa, and the Middle East* 40, 3 (2020): 597–635.

enforcement mechanisms beyond the jurisdiction of any state. The International Court of Justice (established in 1946), the European Court of Justice (1952), and the International Criminal Court (2002) were attempts to regulate behavior at a global or regional level, but their jurisdiction and power were limited. The absence of enforcement mechanisms erased much of the practical significance of the Universal Declaration of Human Rights that emerged from long discussions at the United Nations in 1948.

There was also considerable ambiguity about the relation of human rights to the colonial question as it played out in Africa and Asia. In the 1950s, African and Asian leaders used the language of rights to protest the violence, racial degradation, and exploitation that colonial regimes inflicted on inhabitants of their territories but left open the question of what rights formerly colonized people would have in their new states. That the ability of "a people" to govern itself should be considered a human right is a relatively new norm; it was only recognized by the United Nations in a resolution of December 1960. Scholars debate the importance of human rights arguments to anticolonial activism, but there is considerable agreement on what happened next. As political leaders of anticolonial movements established themselves in power, they became increasingly wary of the idea of universal rights; the kind of arguments that they had used against colonial regimes might be turned against them.[24] A small number of African leaders have been brought before international jurisdictions for human rights violations with varying degrees of success, while many Africans wonder why it is Africans who are most often brought before these bodies.

To argue, as do some African leaders, that criticism of human rights violations in African states in the name of human rights

24. Samuel Moyn sees arguments for independence and for human rights as quite distinct. *The Last Utopia: Human Rights in History* (Cambridge, MA: Harvard University Press, 2010). Roland Burke stresses the importance of human rights arguments to the decolonization process. *Decolonization and the Evolution of International Human Rights* (Philadelphia: University of Pennsylvania Press, 2010). Both scholars agree that after acquiring independence, ex-colonial states tended to consider arguments based on universal human rights to be an intrusion on their sovereignty. See also Meredith Terretta, "From Below and to the Left? Human Rights and Liberation Politics in Africa's Postcolonial Age," *Journal of World History* 24, 2 (2013): 389–416.

constitutes a neocolonial intrusion is to make a claim about the inviolate nature of sovereignty. It is the flip side of the argument that once independent, ex-colonial states have no claim on the resources of the former colonizer.[25] The individual state, like the individual person, is in such conceptions a free and autonomous actor interacting with other actors in equivalent positions. These assertions are the object of dispute today.

Both appeals to the universality of rights and assertions of national sovereignty raised the difficult question of where the defense of rights could be located. Some advocates of Eurafrica thought that the ideals of the Declaration of the Rights of Man and of the Citizen might be best protected by institutions above the give-and-take of politics in the individual territory. The Afroasian movement argued that the rights of sovereignty gave each state control over natural resources that superseded multinational corporations' rights to property; some asserted that the people of poor states had a "right to development." Eurasianists were never concerned about rights, and in their more recent incarnations Eurasianist theorists explicitly rejected values declared to be universal and castigated them as western, decadent, and perverse.

What was at stake for the projects of Eurasia, Eurafrica, and Afroasia was the possibility of constructing institutions beyond the territorially bounded state that could offer protection and provide needed resources to people across large areas of the globe. In multiple sites, political thinkers and activists attempted to rethink political space in terms that were bigger than nationally bounded territories and smaller than global or universal scales. Their historical experiences had made clear to them both the dangers and the possibilities of connections across space.

---

25. Christian Olaf Christiansen and Steven L. B. Jensen conclude that ending colonial rule both freed colonizing states from historic responsibility for their effect on the economic, social, and political rights of colonized people and freed newly independent states from scrutiny for their violation of rights: "Decolonisation—owing to its sovereignty emphasis—would over time prove to be the perfect storm for rights denial." "The Road from 1966: Social and Economic Rights after the International Covenant," in Steven L. B. Jensen and Charles Walton, eds., *Social Rights and the Politics of Obligation in History* (Cambridge: Cambridge University Press, 2022), 293.

Themes

Several themes run through our account of the histories of Eurasia, Eurafrica, and Afroasia.

VERTICAL AND HORIZONTAL SOLIDARITIES

A conceptual anchor of our analysis comes from the writings of the Senegalese politician, philosopher, and poet Léopold Sédar Senghor. In the late 1940s and 1950s, Senghor argued that there were two forms of political association, "vertical solidarity"—the relationship of the poor and weak with the rich and powerful—and "horizontal solidarity," by which he meant a relationship of equals among the formerly colonized.[26] For Senghor, horizontal solidarity without vertical connections was unity in poverty; it risked perpetuating the inequalities to which colonialism had given rise. Vertical solidarity without horizontal ties was another version of colonial domination. However, horizontal solidarity combined with vertical solidarity would give the poor the collective strength to make demands on the rich.

When Senghor introduced these concepts, the conjugation of horizontal and vertical soldarities seemed a promising possibility. France, weakened by World War II and striving to hold on to its overseas territories, had to respond to the demands of its overseas peoples, first for citizenship, then for equality among citizens.[27] Senghor's strategy became the basis for making claims within what had been the French empire, renamed the French Union in 1946 and the Community in 1958. Efforts to obtain equal wages, benefits, and rights to representation for all of France's citizens, in African territories as well as European France, achieved a measure of success, enough to push French leaders to ask whether France could afford to keep its overseas territories.

Senghor's schema is relevant to other political settings and projects. For the proponents of Eurasia, Eurafrica, and Afroasia, the

---

26. One of his earliest expressions of the horizontal-vertical dialectic was in the newspaper he edited, *La Condition Humaine,* July 11, 1948. Senghor's views will be discussed more fully in chapter 2.

27. Frederick Cooper, *Citizenship between Empire and Nation: Remaking France and French Africa, 1945–1960* (Princeton, NJ: Princeton University Press, 2014).

interplay of vertical and horizontal ties was critical. The idea of a Eurasian connection between Slavic regions and the huge landmass to their east was supposed to affirm civilizational affinities under the oversight of the Russian state. Most Eurasianists postulated that groups on this vast terrain influenced each other's cultural practices, but that political connections ran vertically from each group to the overall ruler. Advocates of Eurafrica argued that the horizontal affinity of Africans within a Eurafrican polity would allow them access to the resources needed to close the gap between colonizer and colonized and thus to overcome a history of oppression and exploitation. Afroasianists wanted to replace the vertical structures of empire with horizontal connections among the formerly colonized, enabling them to challenge the power of former colonizers in western Europe, the United States, and, for some, the Soviet Union. All three movements promised to change the relationship of space and power and to overcome the economic and cultural superiority of "the west," either by operating within asymmetrical structures to reduce their inequities or by challenging them head-on.

But the very reasoning that made these concepts so attractive was also an obstacle to their success: extremes of inequality meant that the poor needed the help and patronage of the rich. Collective efforts to challenge inequality between Europe and North America and Africa and Asia did not necessarily address political and economic inequality within the states that had emerged from colonization. After 1991 many of the states that had been Soviet republics remained dependent upon economic connections and resources of the Russian Federation. The multiple pathways out of empire led the former components of French, British, and Russian empires to unanticipated futures.

POLITICAL IMAGINATION

The most durable contribution of Benedict Anderson's *Imagined Communities* has not been his analysis of nationalism but his emphasis on the political significance of imagination.[28] Imagination, even

---

28. Benedict Anderson, *Imagined Communities: Reflections on the Origin and Spread of Nationalism* (London: Verso, 1983); Max Bergholz, "AHR Reappraisal: Thinking the

in what is sometimes considered the age of nationalism in the nineteenth and twentieth centuries, went beyond a national focus. Intellectuals and activists focused their thoughts and efforts at popular mobilization on a variety of potential units, from the provincial to the transcontinental. Activists, as Anderson pointed out, traveled in different circuits; contacts made inside, across, and outside state borders helped to shape conceptions of what kinds of political entities were possible—Eurasia, Eurafrica, and Afroasia among them.

National projects were beset by tensions and conflicts that threatened their coherence and attractiveness. Anderson insists that nationalism is a "horizontal" construct, positing a common identification with a singular nation. Yet his foundational example—the nationalism of creole societies of the Americas in the early nineteenth century—emerged in the condition of vertically organized power. The societies of South America were highly stratified, with a small landlord class of European origin at the top, commanding the services and labor of peasants of indigenous origin and of slaves and their descendants. Tensions between the opposing pulls of vertical and horizontal solidarity produced both defenses of hierarchy and demands for equality and inclusion.[29]

AFFINITY

A third theme is social affinity, imagined or experienced. Although there has been a strong tendency in history and the social sciences to emphasize like-to-like relationships and to see them as constituting collective actors—the proletariat, African Americans, the LGBTQ community—relationships between the unlike and the unequal have also shaped history and inhabit the present. Eurasia, Eurafrica, and Afroasia were projects based on affinity among

---

Nation: *Imagined Communities: Reflections on the Origin and Spread of Nationalism*, by Benedict Anderson," *American Historical Review* 123, 2 (2018): 518–28, esp. 519.

29. Anderson, *Imagined Communities*, 16; Jeremy Adelman, *Sovereignty and Revolution in the Iberian Atlantic* (Princeton, NJ: Princeton University Press, 2006); Hilda Sabato, *Republics of the New World: The Revolutionary Political Experiment in Nineteenth-century Latin America* (Princeton, NJ: Princeton University Press, 2018); Marcela Echeverri, *Indian and Slave Royalists in the Age of Revolution: Reform, Revolution, and Royalism in the Northern Andes, 1780–1825* (Cambridge: Cambridge University Press, 2016).

people, not identity.[30] Different types of affinity presented different possibilities for collective action. A person in Senegal under French rule might self-describe as a member of the Serer ethnic group, a speaker of the Wolof language, an inhabitant of the colony of Senegal, an African, a subject or perhaps a citizen of the French empire, a member of a religious confraternity, and a person sharing racial and cultural connections to people of African descent in the Americas. Such a person might "be" male, female, a youth, an elder, a person of high or low status. Affinity could be territorial or cosmopolitan.

The advocates of Eurasia emphasized elements of a shared history, based on environmental pressures and social responses across a vast space. Eurasian conditions meant that widely dispersed peoples were expected to have developed distinctive social behaviors, yet still share assumptions about how political life should be conducted. Senghor and other advocates of Eurafrica argued that what could connect people was not just cultural commonality but cultural complementarity. In their view, the rationalistic attitudes of Europeans and the more intuitive, familial notions of Africans enabled two-way interactions and contributed to the richness of humanity. In contrast, the politics of Afroasian activists was less about cultural foundations for affinity than the experience of colonial oppression and the ongoing need to combat European imperialism and end economic exploitation.

These projects for affinities across large spaces constituted challenges to the politics of identification that in various forms asserted likeness as the basis for allegiance and drew sharp lines between those included in a group and outsiders—defined by nationalism, ethnic politics, or racial identification. The promoters of Eurasia, Eurafrica, and Afroasia did not exclude other forms of affinity or collective action, but they were trying to get people to situate themselves and their aspirations in wider frameworks, at a time when other political entrepreneurs were advocating affiliations that were defined more narrowly.

30. Rogers Brubaker and Frederick Cooper, "Beyond 'Identity,'" *Theory and Society* 29, 1 (2000): 1–47. Scholarship has tended to emphasize either the power of "identity politics" or else the politics of connectivity and inclusivity, but both positions are claims, assertions that exist in relation to each other, in a contradictory or perhaps complementary manner.

Advocates of Eurafrica had to build a bridge across the racial divide that decades of European colonialism had fostered and that persisted even when the French government claimed to repudiate invidious distinctions among its citizens. Eurasianism began in the 1920s by celebrating multiplicity of cultures and revived in the 1990s under the influence of the Soviet ideology of the "friendship of peoples." That same regime, however, had claimed that some ethnic groups harbored "enemies of the people." Moreover, despite official recognition of multiple ethnicities within the Soviet Union and the Russian Federation, hierarchical distinctions between Russians and non-Russians as well as racist stereotyping remained salient elements in social life.[31] Afroasianists were themselves divided over whether their project was anti-European or anti-imperialist, and attempts to forge unity among the "darker nations" faced different forms of division, prejudice, and conflict within the Afroasian universe.[32] Despite the widespread repudiation since World War II of the kind of white supremacist ideology that underpinned colonialism, racialized distinction keeps resurfacing in many world areas, inflecting social possibilities for well-being and political participation.[33]

RECONFIGURING SPACE

The advocates of Eurasia, Eurafrica, and Afroasia did not presume that political space was neatly bounded by linguistic or cultural frontiers or by a long common history.[34] The concepts of space they deployed were dynamic, shaped by both imagination and political action. Eurafrica started with a spatial configuration created by

---

31. David Rainbow, ed., *Ideologies of Race: Imperial Russia and the Soviet Union in Global Context* (Montreal: McGill-Queen's University Press, 2019). For comparative perspectives, see Sarga Moussa and Serge Zenkine, eds., *L'imaginaire raciologique en France et en Russie, xixe-xxe siècle* (Lyon: Presses universitaires de Lyon, 2019).

32. Vijay Prashad, *The Darker Nations: A People's History of the Third World* (New York: New Press, 2007).

33. See Chari and Verdery, "Thinking between the Posts," 26.

34. Alternative ways of conceiving of space, whether in terms of defining regions or connections across regions, has become a major preoccupation of scholars. For a recent compendium of different issues and approaches, see Matthias Middell, ed., *The Routledge Handbook of Transregional Studies* (London: Routledge, 2019).

French empire-building. This geography was combined with the project of European integration to create a complex political unity, in which different European states (six were in play at the time) and former French and Belgian colonies in Africa would exercise certain functions within their established boundaries while ceding others to common institutions. Just who would have political voice and how and where it would be exercised was disputed for a decade, a time when the space of the French Union and of Europe were both in question.

Eurasianists emerged from a space that had been configured by the world's largest empire. Tsarist rulers changed the internal map of the territory multiple times, and Soviet leaders followed suit.[35] Eurasianist attempts to found the geography of power on acceptance of diversity, overlapping cultures, and civilizational attributes have contributed to recent ideological initiatives in the Russian Federation. In Putin's version of a Eurasian polity, adherence is not a matter of choice but an historical necessity: Russia must defend its "great space" against other geopolitical actors.[36]

The politics of Afroasia involved a rethinking of space at a global level, severing the asymmetrical connection of south to north. It linked independent states more through a common project than in common institutions. The insistence on the part of ex-colonial leaders like Kwame Nkrumah that a world divided into sovereign nation-states did not have to be a world in which each state pursued only its own political destiny was a break with conventional theories of nationalism and of international relations.[37] But that project sat uneasily with the way decolonization was proceeding in the 1950s and 1960s, territory by territory, through negotiation or revolution. The nation-state may not have been what Nkrumah and others most wanted, but it was what they could get.

---

35. Jane Burbank, "All under the Tsar: Russia's Eurasian Trajectory," in Yuri Pines, Michal Biran, Jörg Rüpke, and Eva Cancik-Kirschbaum, eds., *The Limits of Universal Rule: Eurasian Empires Compared* (Cambridge: Cambridge University Press, 2021), 342–75.

36. The most influential theorist of Russian "great space" politics is Alexander Dugin. See among his many publications, Aleksandr Dugin, *Geopolitika postmoderna: Vremena novykh imperii. Ocherki geopolitika XXI veka* (St. Petersburg: Amfora, 2007) and chapter 4 in this volume.

37. Getachew, *Worldmaking after Empire*.

Afroasianism ran into a double problem: how to institutionalize a common project when sovereignty was configured in terms of bounded spaces and how to manage the cross-cutting effects of global capitalism. Capital is highly mobile. Workers can move only with difficulty, and states can't move at all. Moreover, states do not act as abstract entities. They have rulers and elites who act to obtain and maintain power, making connections inside and outside state borders in their own interests and in line with their own conceptions, against those of other claimants to power and voice within the societies leaders claim to represent.

The re-imaginings of spacial affiliations considered in this book derived much of their proposed strength by explicitly crossing continental divides. The continental identification with which most of the world operates has been shaped more by human history than by physical geography.[38] That we divide Europe, Asia, and Africa from each other, rather than, to take one example, considering all the lands around the Mediterranean as a geographical unit, reflects both Eurocentrism and the imperialism it fostered. "Europe" is as much a claim to power or to civilizational superiority as to a spatial unit. "Africa" and "Asia"—and Eurafrica, Eurasia, and Afroasia—represent counterclaims, with their own histories. Spatial identifications do not necessarily resonate throughout the areas in question. People on either side of the Sahara Desert do not necessarily think of being "African" the same way; Tanzanians and Indians may make connections across the Indian Ocean and recall their history of subordination within the British Empire but do not always see themselves occupying the same position in the world order.[39]

---

38. Martin Lewis and Kären Wigen, *The Myth of Continents: A Critique of Metageography* (Berkeley: University of California Press, 1997); Jeffrey James Byrne, "Beyond Continents, Colours, and the Cold War: Yugoslavia, Algeria, and the Struggle for Non-Alignment," *International History Review* 37, 5 (2015): 912–32. On the idea of a "historical meta-region"—defined by the connections that people forge rather than geographical conventions—see Cyrus Schayegh, *The Middle East and the Making of the Modern World* (Cambridge, MA: Harvard University Press, 2017).

39. Christian Grataloup and Vincent Capdepuy, "Continents et océans: le pavage européen du globe," *Monde(s)* 3 (2013): 29–51. At times the three continents examined here were considered a single contiguous unit, and of course some have argued that the Mediterranean *should* be considered a framework for analysis. Oceans as historical units have been given more weight in recent decades. David Armitage, Alison Bashford, and Sujit Sivasundaram, eds., *Oceanic Histories* (Cambridge: Cambridge University Press, 2018).

POLITICAL INSTITUTIONS

As the Eurasian example suggests, concepts can become politically salient if they find an anchorage in institutions capable of shaping action within a spatial domain. Both Eurasia and Eurafrica developed when a particular kind of alternative to empire had attracted the attention of political theorists and statesmen—federalism. Like empire, federalism presumes a heterogeneous polity, with political authority shared between component parts and an overarching structure. Unlike empire, federalism does not naturalize strict hierarchy but presumes shared governance, which in practice may be more—or less—democratic.

In India and parts of Africa in the early and mid-twentieth century, political leaders often looked to federalism as an exit from empire that could take into account the diversity of the regions concerned. Early in the twentieth century, these arguments usually implied a continued imperial connection, federalism within federalism one might say. A federation of a region of Africa or South Asia would become part of a British polity that allowed internal autonomy to each federated unit and a measure of political voice—how much was rarely clear—at the center.[40]

In India, variants on imperial federalism, including citizenship rights in the British Empire, were the most influential current within the Indian National Congress until the late 1920s, when the party's goals shifted to complete independence.[41] Among the political parties of French Africa, one of the two positions that had the most sway until the 1960s was Senghor's call for a federation of African territories that as a single unit would participate in a French

---

40. As early as 1903, a leading lawyer and journalist from the British colony of the Gold Coast, J. E. Casely-Hayford, argued that the indigenous communities of the region could formalize their relationship to each other into a federation, which in turn could take its place in the British Empire: *Gold Coast Native Institutions with Thoughts upon a Healthy Imperial Policy for the Gold Coast and Ashanti* (London: Cass, 1970 [1903]). On the importance of federalism to thinking about the future of colonial empires in the post–World War II era, see Michael Collins, "Decolonisation and the 'Federal Moment,'" *Diplomacy and Statecraft* 24, 1 (2013): 21–40.

41. Mrinalini Sinha, "Whatever Happened to the Third British Empire? Empire, Nation Redux," in Andrew Thompson, ed., *Writing Imperial Histories* (Manchester: Manchester University Press, 2013), 168–87.

confederation in which all people would exercise the rights of the citizen. Félix Houphouët-Boigny's alternative proposal was for direct membership of each individual territory, such as his Côte d'Ivoire, in a French federation that would also entail equal citizenship rights for all.

These rival ideas for a Eurafrican polity point to the fundamental problem that the activists we consider addressed: how to constitute political institutions that can recognize cultural difference at the same time as associating people with a common project. If looking beyond the territorial state toward a federation of diverse components posed difficult questions, so too did the existence of cultural and regional difference within a supposedly unitary polity. Advocates of supranational federalism in both Africa and Asia often opposed subnational federalism within their respective state structures.[42]

Federalism had long been a topic for discussion in the Russian empire, as reformers with different political goals considered new ways to rule the multiethnic polity.[43] After the revolutions of 1917, both communists and leaders of other parties proposed federal structures to replace dynastic rule.[44] In the early 1920s, the communist winners of the civil war created the Union of Soviet Socialist Republics, an institutional structure that recognized national differences, while binding the whole together through the party's disciplined leadership of each unit. The culturally oriented Eurasianists active in the 1920s were not focused on institutional arrangements, although Trubetskoi articulated the need for interactive personalized connections between the "top" and "bottom" levels of a multicultured realm (chapter 1). After the Soviet collapse in 1991, the rump but still huge and multinational Russian republic

---

42. Lydia Walker, "Decolonization in the 1960s: On Legitimate and Illegitimate Nationalist Claims-making," *Past & Present* 242 (2019): 227–64; Séverine Awenengo Dalberto, "Hidden Debates over the Status of the Casamance during the Decolonization Process in Senegal: Regionalism, Territorialism, and Federalism at a Crossroads, 1946–62," *Journal of African History* 61, 1 (2020): 67–88.

43. Mark von Hagen, "Federalisms and Pan-movements: Re-imagining Empire," in Jane Burbank, Mark von Hagen, and Anatolyi Remnev, eds., *Russian Empire: Space, People, Power, 1700–1930* (Bloomington: Indiana University Press, 2007), 494–510.

44. Jane Burbank, "Eurasian Sovereignty: The Case of Kazan," *Problems of Post-Communism* 62 (2015): 10–21.

retained the USSR's composite structure and took a second name, the Russian Federation. With Putin's consolidation of power, however, Russian federalism turned more authoritarian, centralized, and imperial.

Afroasian movements were rarely clear on how to embody their efforts at political and economic cooperation, although the UN and its agencies offered possibilities for institution-building at a global level. Institutionalizing Afroasia was constrained both by the opposition of the world's most powerful and wealthy states and by the entrenchment of the elites of the first Afroasian states within the global structure of national sovereignty.

Constraints and Cleavages

The advocates for Eurasia, Eurafrica, and Afroasia were proposing change; they were not themselves in charge of the political entities they designed. Bringing their imagined projects to life posed a series of challenges: how to reconcile the quest for equality within a political body with the heterogeneity of the population, how to shift from the current basis of an elite's power to the foundations of an enlarged spatial and social polity, how to make vertical and horizontal solidarities work together.

Even in formal democracies, political power is rarely if ever purely horizontal. In theory, voters pick their representatives, but in practice, leaders recruit followers through a variety of particularistic relationships with personal clients, fellow ethnics, union members, and so on. Federated states and unitary states both provide a base for politicians to work with. The challenge of turning an idea like Eurafrica or Afroasia into a politically viable institution was to persuade elites in each territory to look beyond their political base and accept the allocation of power to structures they could not themselves control. The national framework for politics need not be interpreted as either the natural inclination of people to attach themselves to units of likeness (nation or ethnic group) or as the instrumentalist actions of rulers or would-be rulers who self-interestedly create and manipulate sentiments of identification. The relationship between these motivations is dialectical: politicians manipulate particularistic sentiments; particularistic sentiments allow politicians to recruit followers. The upshot was that vertical ties of political mobilization inside the subunits of complex political "communities" were an obstacle to implementing the horizontal solidarities that advocates of Afroasia and Eurafrica were pressing.

The problem of democratic mobilization was not of concern to advocates of Eurasia; they were working with a frankly imperial structure. Verticality was a deeply entrenched principle of Russian politics, softened but not fundamentally challenged by a horizontal element—the carefully supervised elections of both Soviet and post-Soviet times.

The possibilities and limitations of supranational integration played out in a world in which economic power was highly concentrated. This was not a closed system; the transformation of China into an economic powerhouse beginning in the 1980s as well as the industrialization of the Asian "tigers" showed that Asia was hardly the singular ex-colonial space some activists asserted it to be. The rulers of fledgling national economies faced immediate pressure to get what they could from relations with corporations, financial institutions, and development agencies in the capitalist world economy—or with the socialist bloc—even if they thought that horizontal solidarity among ex-colonial states offered better long-range opportunities.[45] Oil-producing states developed their common interest, while oil-consuming states had other concerns. Export manufacturing and agricultural exports implied different strategies and different connections. The collapse of the Soviet Union and the increasing involvement of China in Africa and the rest of Asia changed earlier equations. The post-colonial world—more than a world divided up by a small number of empires—offered corporations a wide choice about where to invest and what to write off. It was in the context of highly unequal economic relations that advocates of cross-continental integration tried to find their way.

---

45. On divisions and tensions within Asia in the context of capitalism and uneven development, see Marc Frey and Nicola Spakowski, "Introduction" to their edited volume, *Asianisms: Regionalist Interactions and Asian Integration* (Singapore: NUS Press, 2016), 1–18.

A Starting Point: Reconfiguring and Combating Empire after World War I

With these concerns in mind, we turn to the historical setting where the ideas discussed in this book developed. Eurasian, Eurafrican, and Afroasian projects first emerged out of the shakeup of the world of empires at the end of World War I. The contents of these visions would undergo major changes in the ensuing decades. They would contribute to fundamental questioning of existing political structures, but their impact was conditioned by both the tenacity and the adaptability of those structures. Empires presented moving targets to advocates for change.

A range of alternative conceptions of state, nation, sovereignty, and political belonging was in play in the aftermath of the war of 1914-18.[46] Our perspective is different from the conventional narrative that draws a direct line from the enunciation of the doctrine of self-determination during the Paris peace talks of 1919 to the emergence of states claiming nationhood from colonial empires. The concept of a singular nation on a singular territory with its own government was certainly available after 1919, and it acquired prominence as a consequence of the rearranged map of Europe after the war. But it was not evident that empires—at least those on the winning side of the war—were tottering and that their demise was only a matter of time. New forms of empire were emerging and other forms of political organization, including those described here, captured people's imagination.

As Glenda Sluga, Patricia Clavin, and others have argued, the supposed age of nationalism was also characterized by internationalism, a belief that, however important the integrity of each national body, cooperative relations among them were essential to economic and social progress. Individuals and associations were

---

46. Margaret Macmillan, *Paris 1919: Six Months that Changed the World* (New York: Random House, 2002). For recent reassessments of the impact of the postwar settlements on different parts of the world, see Marcus Payk and Roberta Pergher, eds., *Beyond Versailles: Sovereignty, Legitimacy, and the Formation of New Polities after the Great War* (Bloomington: Indiana University Press, 2019), and the special issue "World Politics 100 Years after the Paris Peace Conference," *International Affairs* 95, 1 (2019), including Jane Burbank and Frederick Cooper, "Empires after 1919: Old, New, Transformed," 81–100.

developing linkages and common modes of action that crossed borders, while insisting that world peace demanded the strengthening of institutions above those of individual states.[47] Many intellectuals and political elites in Europe were sensitive to the dangers and fragilities of a nationalized state order, and they were aware of challenges to European power coming from other parts of the world.

Internationalist thinking in Europe had deeper historical roots. As early as 1815, the major powers of Europe, in the wake of the Napoleonic Wars, had met to regulate their competition with each other, adjusting borders after Napoleon's defeat, then trying to limit the horrors of war.[48] Later in the century, at two conferences in Berlin, one focused on the Balkans in 1878, the other on Africa in 1884–85, diplomats attempted to settle or avoid disputes among European empires over territorial claims. Building on the 1815 conference's gestures toward stopping the slave trade, the conference of 1884–85 pledged conquering powers to abolish it altogether. At a subsequent conference in Brussels in 1890–91, the powers portrayed themselves collectively as civilizing agents acting in the interest of Africans by suppressing trade in slaves, arms, and liquor. The conferees promoted their vision of Europe as the embodiment of civilization and not just power even as they engaged in brutal conquest and in the exploitative extraction of resources from the colonies.

In August 1914, the attempt to regulate inter-empire conflict failed spectacularly and tragically.[49] European empires, each with the possibility of mobilizing resources in people and materials beyond any single national site, formed alliances and rivalries that demolished what little stability the prewar configuration had offered. The horrors of World War I led to still other attempts to prevent future conflagrations, a key tactic of which was stripping the losing imperial powers—Germany, Austria-Hungary, and the

47. Glenda Sluga and Patricia Clavin, eds., *Internationalisms: A Twentieth-Century History* (Cambridge: Cambridge University Press, 2017); Glenda Sluga, *Internationalism in the Age of Nationalism* (Philadelphia: University of Pennsylvania Press, 2013).

48. Beatrice de Graaf, Ido de Haan, Brian Vick, and Susanne Keesman, eds., *Securing Europe after Napoleon: 1815 and the New European Security Culture* (Cambridge: Cambridge University Press, 2019).

49. It can be argued that the breakdown began in 1912, with the wars in the Balkans. See Mark Mazower, *The Balkans: A Short History* (New York: Modern Library, 2000).

Ottomans—of extra-national territories and populations. In Europe, postwar strategy was founded on the hope that having multiple national states in the middle of Europe would make it more difficult for any single power to put together an alliance against the others. Outside of Europe, what the victorious states sought amounted to an inter-empire redistribution of dependent territories. The Paris-drawn map of the Middle East was challenged by large-scale revolts in Iraq, Syria, and elsewhere, claims for recognition as a national group by Kurds and others, arguments over boundaries, assertions of dynastic power, and resistance to day-to-day administration of mandated territories.[50]

There was tension between inter-*national* and inter-*empire* thinking.[51] The League of Nations included as members not only the major European empires, but also states in Latin America, eastern Europe, and the Balkans, China, Siam, Persia, Ethiopia, and Liberia, among others. The treaties distributed some of the territories that had been ruled by Germany and the Ottoman Empire to France, Britain, Belgium, South Africa, and Australia, creating a new category in the imperial repertoire, the mandate.

As Susan Pedersen has shown, the Permanent Mandates Commission, intended to provide a layer of international supervision over mandated territories, was a kind of colonialists' club. The information the Commission received and the responsibility for implementing its recommendations depended on the mandatory powers, and the most influential members of the Commission had long had the habit of ruling Africans and Asians. However, petitions to the commission could come from individuals or associations, a process that established the precedent of bringing issues of governance in mandated territories before an international audience. There resulted an escalation of claims-making in the interwar period, although such claims were rarely met or even taken seriously.[52]

---

50. Jonathan Wyrtzen, *Worldmaking in the Long Great War: How Local and Colonial Struggles Shaped the Modern Middle East* (New York: Columbia University Press, 2022), 17, 21–22.

51. Daniel Hedinger and Nadin Heé, "Transimperial History: Connectivity, Cooperation and Competition," *Journal of Modern European History* 16, 4 (2018): 429–52.

52. Susan Pedersen, *The Guardians: The League of Nations and the Crisis of Empire* (New York: Oxford University Press, 2015); Miguel Bandeira Jerónimo, "Imperial

Outside of League institutions, elites with an interest in colonies—business operators as well as colonial administrators—talked with each other in organizations like the International Colonial Institute. Their conversations spelled out what might be termed best practices for colonial administration, including scientific understanding of medical issues, resources, and colonial labor, and ways of justifying colonial enterprises. Missionaries and humanitarian organizations also took an interest in the conditions of colonized people and sometimes instigated scandals over the abuses of colonial power in places like the Belgian Congo or Portuguese Africa.[53] In the patchwork of colonies, mandates, and new and old states, banks and business associations intervened in questions of tariffs and taxes, especially where local authorities were considered weak, in ways that compromised the fledgling norms of sovereignty.[54]

The empires that had emerged victorious in World War I faced challenges within their respective domains and in internationalist circles, but in the 1920s and 1930s they had the means to counter those challenges. The British government in India reneged on its wartime promises to give Indians a measure of self-government after the war; this led to an escalation of conflict that persisted despite both repression and concessions of power at the provincial (but not central) level in the 1930s. The French in Indochina and the Dutch in Indonesia faced active anti-imperial movements but kept them in check until the Japanese takeover in the 1940s. Anti-imperial activists from the British, French, and Dutch empires in Asia circulated among colonial capitals, with stops in London, Paris, Berlin, Moscow, Beijing, and Tokyo as well as Bombay, Cairo,

---

Internationalisms in the 1920s: The Shaping of Colonial Affairs at the League of Nations," *Journal of Imperial and Commonwealth History* 48, 5 (2020): 866–91; Meredith Terretta and Benjamin Lawrance, "'Sons of the Soil': Cause Lawyers, the Togo-Cameroun Mandates, and the Origins of Decolonization," *American Historical Review* 124, 5 (2019): 1709 14; Natasha Wheatley, "Mandatory Interpretation: Legal Hermeneutics and the New International Order in Arab and Jewish Petitions to the League of Nations," *Past and Present* 227, 1 (2015): 205–48.

53. Florian Wagner, *Colonial Internationalism and the Governmentality of Empire, 1893-1982* (Cambridge: Cambridge University Press, 2022).

54. Jamie Martin, *The Meddlers: Sovereignty, Empire, and the Birth of Global Economic Governance* (Cambridge, MA: Harvard University Press, 2022).

and Singapore, attracting surveillance by the secret services of the imperial powers (chapter 3).

In Africa, British and French rule became, in some ways, more conservative in the aftermath of World War I. Officials in both regimes considered and backed away from plans for more interventionist approaches to economic development of the colonies, not just because they preferred to invest elsewhere, but because they feared upsetting the delicate structures of cooperation with indigenous elites that had allowed for control at minimum cost. In the French case, the extensive use of colonial troops from across the empire in the trenches of northeastern France during the war had given rise to demands from political activists for extending citizenship rights to colonial subjects. Those demands were firmly rejected, and the government in the 1920s, as in British Africa, put more emphasis than before on preserving the "traditional" nature of African societies. Africans were expected—often forced—to contribute labor and export crops to the imperial economy, but were still treated as members of "tribes" and not as participants in wider economic, social, and political structures.[55] As we will see in chapter 3, African and Asian activists were engaged throughout the interwar period in multiple contests with colonial regimes, both as particular "peoples" seeking to shape their own destiny and as part of a broader struggle against imperialism.

The world of empires in the interwar period was not limited to the overseas projects of western European powers. Japan had made its mark in global power relations with its defeat of China in 1895 and the resulting acquisition of Taiwan and other territories, its victory over Russia in 1905, and the formal annexation of Korea in 1910 (after years of exercising de facto control). Its imperial reach was extended to Manchuria and other parts of China in the 1930s and—at the expense of European empires and the United States—to Southeast Asia in the 1940s.[56]

---

55. Dónal Hassett, *Mobilizing Memory: The Great War and the Language of Politics in Colonial Algeria, 1918-39* (Oxford: Oxford University Press, 2019); Alice Conklin, *A Mission to Civilize: The Republican Idea of Empire in France and West Africa, 1895-1930* (Stanford, CA: Stanford University Press, 1997).

56. On Japanese empire, see the pioneering work of Louise Young, *Japan's Total Empire: Manchuria and the Culture of Wartime Imperialism* (Berkeley: University of

The most radical transformation of empire in the early twentieth century was accomplished in Russia, which was convulsed by a vast anti-Russian rebellion in Central Asia in 1916, followed by two revolutions in February and October 1917.[57] The Bolsheviks' victory in the subsequent and devastating "civil" wars meant that Lenin and his renamed Communist Party could redefine the goals and institutions of the reconstituted state. The Bolsheviks' ideology was explicitly universalist—world revolution in the name of the world's proletarians—but the party was forced by military losses in borderlands and by the failure of revolutions in other countries to concentrate on building a socialist society on the successfully reconquered spaces of the Romanovs' empire. Crucial to the recovery of centralized power in Russia was the creation of a new kind of empire—one that could attract or at least constrain people who had been trying before 1914 to enhance the power of "their" ethnic or religious community. The communist state was structured as a federation of national republics, each purportedly the homeland of a different ethnic group. The creation of nominally national republics in Central Asia, and the incorporation of multiple Turkic, Mongol, and Altaic peoples into the enormous Russian Soviet Federal Socialist Republic (RSFSR) as "autonomous Soviet republics," expressed a turn to the east in Soviet domestic politics.[58] The break with Eurocentrism, however, was far from complete. While Soviet policies directed at the "Asian" parts of the USSR referred to overcoming colonial exploitation, they retained the civilizational assumptions of the overturned empire: the "west" would teach the "east" how to be communist.[59]

California Press, 1999), and Ryūta Itagaki, Satoshi Mizutani, and Hideaki Tobe, "Japanese Empire," in Phillipa Levine and John Marriott, eds., *The Ashgate Research Companion to Modern Imperial Histories* (Farnham, UK: Ashgate, 2012), 273–99.

57. Joshua A. Sanborn, *Imperial Apocalypse: The Great War and the Destruction of the Russian Empire* (Oxford: Oxford University Press, 2014); Aminat Chokobaeva, Cloé Drieu, and Alexander Morrison, eds., *The Central Asian Revolt of 1916: A Collapsing Empire in the Age of War and Revolution* (Manchester: Manchester University Press, 2020).

58. Francine Hirsch, *Empire of Nations: Ethnographic Knowledge and the Making of the Soviet Union* (Ithaca, NY: Cornell University Press, 2005); Tatiana Linkhoeva, *Revolution Goes East: Imperial Japan and Soviet Communism* (Ithaca, NY: Cornell University Press, 2020).

59. Masha Kirasirova, "The 'East' as a Category of Bolshevik Ideology and Comintern Administration: The Arab Section of the University of the Toilers of the East," *Kritika:*

In 1919, with the civil war still raging, the Bolsheviks convened the first meeting of the Comintern (the Communist International) in Moscow. This new alliance of Marxist parties was created to replace the socialist Second International as the leader of world revolution and to counter hostile alliances emerging from the war. Anti-imperialism became an explicit principle of Soviet foreign policy, as Bolshevik Russia took up the task—a time-honored imperial strategy—of mobilizing people in other empires against their overseers. Soviet party leaders asserted their own inalienable hold over the tactics and resources of "international" communism.[60]

It was not clear in the 1920s what the future of empires and other states would be. A new set of states supposedly based on the congruence of a national population and a state boundary had appeared, but that kind of transition was for white people only. Moreover, the one-to-one relationship of state to nation in Central Europe was deeply problematic; it had been sought by nationalists in different territories, but it threatened people who became defined as "minorities" inside borders imposed by the great powers under the Versailles treaties. The "unmixing" of peoples, as one of the statesmen who helped to bring it about described the strategy, was coercive.[61] The state defined the nation more than the nation the state. Outside of Europe, the people subordinated to European and Japanese rule were shuffled, but not liberated.

The presumption of the mandate system was that some people—mainly in the Middle East—were en route to becoming national and then to having a state, at some unspecified point in time. In Africa and Oceania, the future of mandated territories was

---

Explorations in Russian and Eurasian History 18, 1 (2017): 7–34; Adeeb Khalid, "Central Asia between the Ottoman and the Soviet Worlds," *Kritika: Explorations in Russian and Eurasian History* 12 (2011): 451–76.

60. Branko Lazić and Milorad Drachkovitch, eds., *Lenin and the Comintern* (Stanford, CA: Hoover Institution Press, 1972), 1: 50–88. On Soviet foreign policy and tactics, see Sabine Dullin, *La frontière épaisse: Aux origines des politiques soviétiques (1920–1940)* (Paris: Editions de l'EHESS, 2014).

61. The phrase is from Lord Curzon. Among books presenting a critical view of the effects of the self-determination doctrine are Eric Weitz, *A World Divided: The Global Struggle for Human Rights in the Age of Nation-States* (Princeton, NJ: Princeton University Press, 2019); Philipp Ther, *The Dark Side of Nation States: Ethnic Cleansing in Modern Europe* (New York: Berghahn Books, 2014).

even more distant and not at all clear. Outside of the mandates, the colonies and protectorates of European powers and Japan were not even nominally under any form of international supervision. Their status, in the eyes of their rulers, was likely to remain unchanged for years, decades, or centuries.

Inside a European empire, one territory pulled itself out of imperial subordination in the immediate aftermath of World War I: Ireland. A powerful independence movement had emerged before the war, but its example was ambiguous. People of Irish origin had fought on both sides of the Anglo-Boer war, some serving in the British army, others leaving Ireland to join rebel armies to fight against the British Empire. During World War I, Irish people fought for and against the empire. That the confrontation in Ireland escalated during the war, continued afterward, and led to the negotiated independence of the Irish Republic was conditioned by the density of relations within the United Kingdom. The cultural gap between colonizer and colonized was not as wide there as in Africa or Asia.[62]

Ireland's exodus from empire left uneasy compromises and tensions in place, including the division of the territory in two, one of which remained within the British orbit. Violent conflict, particularly over the status of Northern Ireland, reemerged periodically and the possibility of its revival persists to this day. Despite their early victory against a powerful empire, Ireland's new rulers did not see themselves as obliged to take on the mantle of leading Africans and Asians to independence; Africans and Asians had often seen Irish officials and soldiers on the other side of the colonial divide.

The map of the colonial world in 1939 differed only slightly from that of 1919. Ireland was an exception, and the formal independence of Iraq (1932) and Egypt (1922) was more than nominal and less than actual. Defiant Ethiopia had succumbed to Italian imperialism. Colonial rule had never gone unopposed: its imposition was resisted; its authority often ignored or deflected if not overtly contested; its ideological basis challenged on the colonizers' own terms by people educated to use them or in frameworks based

---

62. Shereen Ilahi, *Imperial Violence and the Path to Independence: India, Ireland and the Crisis of Empire* (London: Bloomsbury, 2020).

on other religious and political concepts. World War I had revealed that inter-empire conflict could overturn or weaken the capacity of once-powerful empires. The peace process had introduced expectations that had not been met; these in some cases inspired direct challenges to the legitimacy of the status quo. The postwar period gave rise not only to new forms of imperial power but also, as we shall see, to anti-imperial mobilization with multiple goals, based on new patterns of affiliation and cooperation.

Empires crossed over continents; this raised the possibility that long-distance linkages could be managed and altered to preserve the unity of the imperial polity. But the critique of empire also traveled beyond continents' edges. Many people opposed to imperial rule realized that they were not alone and that their struggles entailed confronting not just "their" empire but a trans-imperial edifice. Similarly, European empires might be rivals but they also asserted a shared civilizational superiority. While some political activists strove to break up empires into separate, ethnically homogenous states, others could imagine themselves into a future that would incorporate people who were culturally different into new kinds of political community. The future of political organization after World War I was not set in advance. In the chapters that follow, we engage with three visions of post-imperial societies that transcended territorial limits and challenged the world Europeans thought they had made.

CHAPTER ONE

Eurasia

LET'S BEGIN WITH EURASIA. The enormous landmass extending between what we today call the North Atlantic and the North Pacific oceans would appear to be a single continent, but humans, who until recently did not have a bird's eye view, saw things differently as they discovered each other over time in this space. The ancient Greeks imagined the world divided into Europe, Asia, and Africa. The Nile sufficed to set Africa apart, but what constituted the European-Asian divide? The questions of where to draw this boundary, and what Europe and Asia meant, would engage scholars, artists, and politicians for the next two thousand plus years.[1]

Russia's Case of Europeanitis

Nowhere was this division into Europe and Asia more troublesome than in Russia. The Russian state took shape in the fourteenth century as a princely clan, descendants of the Riurikid dynasty and clients of the Mongol khan, began to establish their control over small towns and territories that had earlier been part of Kievan

---

1. On ancient divisions of the "world" and various ideas of Europe, see Chris Haan, "Europe in Eurasia," in Ullrich Kockel, Máiréad Nic Craith, and Jonas Frykman, eds., *A Companion to the Anthropology of Europe* (Chichester: John Wiley and Sons, 2012), 88–102. On contentions among anthropologists over the meanings and uses of Eurasia in contemporary social science, see Chris Haan, "A Concept of Eurasia," *Current Anthropology* 57, 1 (February 2016): 1–27.

Rus'.[2] The Grand Princedom of Moscow was geophysically "Eurasian" from at least 1552, when the tsar's troops conquered Kazan on the Volga River; by 1639, Russian explorers had reached the Pacific. But this was not how Russian leaders, when they thought about it, interpreted their empire's position. They were dead set on belonging to Europe.

Europe offered useful symbolism to Russia's leaders. Christianity signaled a break with Moscow's Mongol connection and offered the Grand Princes a handy ideology for their multiple campaigns against the mostly Muslim khanates to the east and south. In the sixteenth century, Russia's chroniclers rewrote the dynasty's past. The politically corrected version was that Riurik, the legendary founder of Kiev, was a descendant of the Roman emperor Augustus. Indulging in Christian/Byzantine regalia, the Muscovite princes gave themselves a Roman title. In 1547, Ivan IV became "tsar" (Caesar).[3] This fixation on a Roman and Christian genealogy evolved into a fascination with Russia's European rivals. By the end of the seventeenth century, European states were turning their overseas and contiguous conquests into domestic profit and global hegemony. The way to become a real empire, a great power, was to latch onto the European bandwagon—culturally, militarily, diplomatically.[4]

Peter the Great (ruled 1689–1725) took this lesson to heart, with his demand for the reeducation of state servitors, his assault on the authority of the Russian (Eastern) Orthodox Church, and his insistence on European styles in architecture, clothing, and social life. He gave himself the European-style title of "Emperor" in 1721. Over the course of the eighteenth century, European fashion, arts, and sciences became the obsession of Russian elites. Asia served as an anti-model of barbarism and exotic decadence, as Russians

---

2. On the relation of the Muscovite princes to Kiev, see Serhii Plokhy, *Lost Kingdom: A History of Russian Nationalism from Ivan the Great to Vladimir Putin* (London: Penguin Books, 2018), 3–17.

3. On the re-interpretation of the Mongol past, and the transformation of the rulers' images, see Donald Ostrowski, *Muscovy and the Mongols: Cross Cultural Influences on the Steppe Frontier, 1304–1589* (Cambridge: Cambridge University Press, 1998), 164–98. For the rewriting of the Muscovite princes' genealogy, see Plokhy, *Lost Kingdom*, 14–16.

4. Jan Hennings, *Russia and Courtly Europe: Ritual and the Culture of Diplomacy, 1648–1725* (Cambridge: Cambridge University Press, 2016).

sought to define their place in the new world of imperial competition.[5] Historians created a populist version of their deep past. The Slavs of ancient times were fearsome warriors. The word "slav" was linked to *"slava,"* the word for glory, not to the ignominious "slave." The lack of written evidence for this heroic past was explained by the early Slavs' priorities: there were no scholars among them because this warrior people was too busy being glorious to have time to write its own history.[6]

As the empire's reach extended into the Caucasus in the nineteenth century, association with Europe became a cultural mission. Commentators and officials declared that Russia's destiny was to spread European civilization to its new subjects.[7] After Russia with great sacrifice rescued its western allies from Napoleon's imperial over-reach, Alexander I set the stage for the "concert of Europe" with his Holy Alliance, signaling Christianity as the common core of European culture. But as Russia became a more powerful player in inter-imperial politics, it became clearer that Europeans did not regard Russia as one of their kind.[8]

What had gone wrong? Some Russian writers sounded the note of victimization: Russia had been attacked from the west more than once. Others, Russia's domestic critics, had a different, civilizational answer. Russia was not "western" or "contemporary"

5. Tat'iana Artem'eva, "'Osoblivaia chast' sveta': Formirovannie gosudarstvennoi identichnosti Rossii v XVIII veke," in Aleksandr Etkind, Dirk Uffel'mann, Il'ia Kukulin, eds., *Tam, Vnutri: Praktiki vnutrennei kolonizatsii v kul'turnoi istorii Rossii* (Moscow: Novoe literaturnoe obozrenie, 2012), 159–63.

6. Olga Maiorova, "A Revolutionary and the Empire: Alexander Herzen and Russian Discourse on Asia," in Mark Bassin, Sergey Glebov, and Marlène Laruelle, eds., *Between Europe and Asia: The Origins, Theories, and Legacies of Russian Eurasianism* (Pittsburgh, PA: University of Pittsburgh Press, 2015), 15; Wladimir Berelowitch, "Les origines de la Russie dans l'historiographie russe au XVIIIe siècle," *Annales* HSS 58, 1 (janvier–février 2003): 63–84; Hans Rogger, *National Consciousness in Eighteenth-Century Russia* (Cambridge, MA: Harvard University Press, 1960), 186–252; Valeriia Sobol, "'Komu ot chuzhikh, a nam ot svoikh': prizvanie variagov v russkoi literature kontsa XVIII veka" in Etkind et al., eds., *Tam, Vnutri*, 186–216.

7. On historians' perspectives on Russia's imperial destiny, see Seymour Becker, "Contributions to a Nationalist Ideology: Historians of Russia in the First Half of the Nineteenth Century," *Russian History/Histoire Russe*, 13, 4 (Winter 1986): 331–53.

8. For Europeans' perspectives on Russia, see Larry Wolff, *Inventing Eastern Europe: The Map of Civilization on the Mind of the Enlightenment* (Stanford, CA: Stanford University Press, 1994).

because its politics and culture were retrograde; Russian values and behaviors provided no foundation for the superior forms of social organization in the dynamic European empires. Still other commentators lifted the problem to a higher plane. Russia was "better," morally, than its European rivals and neighbors *because* it was different: Slavic roots, Eastern Orthodoxy, supposedly communal traditions—these all set Russia apart from, and above, Europe.

Both "westernizer" and "Slavophile" variants of Russian self-assessment validated the Europe versus Asia dichotomy.[9] Disillusion with European-style progress typically set in when Russians lived among Europeans, but even for critics of the "west," Asia remained the standard of what not to become.[10]

Russia Goes Asian

In the 1880s and 1890s, the East began to look different. By this time, Russia had extended its physical empire still further, consolidating its earlier gains in the Caucasus, incorporating the huge region we now call Central Asia, and vying with Japan for the best parts of vulnerable Chinese territories and ports. Some of Russia's philosophers, writers, and artists were drawn eastward toward a different conception of Russia's past and her place on the globe.[11] Viktor Rozen, Dean of Oriental Studies at St. Petersburg University, the art historian Nikodim Kondakov, and their followers emphasized the synthetic dynamism of the empire's multiplex composition: the "East" was essential to the composite whole.[12] The steppe, the Mongols, the ancient civilizations of the oases and the silk routes,

9. On Slavophiles and Westernizers, see, as part of a vast literature, Andrzej Walicki, *The Slavophile Controversy: History of a Conservative Utopia in Nineteenth-Century Russian Thought* (1975, Oxford University Press; reprint ed., Notre Dame, IN: University of Notre Dame Press, 1989).

10. See Maiorova, "A Revolutionary and the Empire," on Herzen's change of heart in the mid-nineteenth century, pp. 13–16 in *Between Europe and Asia*.

11. Vera Tolz, "The Eurasians and Liberal Scholarship of the Late Imperial Period: Continuity and Change across the 1917 Divide," pp. 27–47 in *Between Europe and Asia*. The major figure in this transition was Vladimir Soloviev. For Soloviev's writings on "Eastern" themes, see Vladimir Wozniuk, *Enemies from the East? V. S. Soloviev on Paganism, Asian Civilizations, and Islam* (Evanston, IL: Northwestern University Press, 2007).

12. V. V. Bartol'd's students at St. Petersburg University were taught the constructed nature of the very categories east and west. On the forerunners of post-1917 Eurasianism,

holistic religions, ancient cultic sculpture inspired novels, poetry, mystic visions, and paintings.[13] Imperial Russia had sponsored "Oriental" and Islamic studies and projects since the time of Catherine the Great,[14] but it was only in the early twentieth century that the empire's "east" became a civilizational attribute.

This fascination with "Russia's Orient"[15] persisted through the First World War, the 1917 revolutions, and the ensuing civil war. The Bolshevik seizure of power inspired an outburst of Eastern-themed artistic and literary productions, most shockingly with Aleksandr Blok's blustery poem, "Scythians," published in 1918. The poem began with Vladimir Soloviev's provocation—"PanMongolism! It's a savage name, but it caresses my ears"—and continued in the same bloody vein. Addressing specifically "you"—Europeans, the "old world," the poet declares, "yes, we are Scythians. Yes, we are Asians." The poem ends with a threat:

> Come to us! From the terrors of war
> Come to our peaceful embraces!
> While it's not too late—the old sword in its sheath,
> Comrades! We'll become—brothers!
> But if not—we have nothing to lose,
> And we can be treacherous!
> . . .
> We'll trample all over the thickets and forests
> of pretty Europe!

---

see Tolz, "The Eurasians and Liberal Scholarship of the Late Imperial Period: Continuity and Change across the 1917 Divide," pp. 27–47.

13. See Michael Kunichka, "'The Scythians Were Here . . .': On Nomadic Archaeology, Modernist Form, and Early Soviet Modernity," *Ab Imperio* 2012, 2: 229–57. For the long-term and differentiated impact of Russia's empire on its writers and their creations, consult Harsha Ram, *The Imperial Sublime: A Russian Poetics of Empire* (Madison: University of Wisconsin Press, 2003) and Susan Layton, *Russian Literature and Empire: Conquest of the Caucasus from Pushkin to Tolstoy* (Cambridge: Cambridge University Press, 1994).

14. On imperial Russia's approach to its "east," see Robert D. Crews, *For Prophet and Tsar: Islam and Empire in Russia and Central Asia* (Cambridge, MA: Harvard University Press, 2006), Robert Geraci, *Window on the East: National and Imperial Identities in Late Tsarist Russia* (Ithaca, NY: Cornell University Press, 2001), and Daniel R. Brower and Edward J. Lazzerini, eds., *Russia's Orient: Imperial Borderlands and Peoples, 1700–1917* (Bloomington: University of Indiana Press, 1997).

15. For a recent use of the concept, see Brower and Lazzerini, *Russia's Orient*.

We'll turn toward you
our Asian mug!
. . .

We won't move, when the fierce Hun empties the pockets of corpses,
burns cities, drives herds into the church,
and grills the meat of white brothers!
For the last time, wake up, old world!
To the brotherly feast of labor and peace,
For the last time the barbarian lyre
calls you to the light-filled brotherly feast.[16]

The poem can sustain endless commentaries.[17] We cite it here in evidence of the bravado and delight in Orientalist identification played back at Europe by one of Russia's most elegant poets during the uncertain years after 1917. Russia was "Asian," and to join the new brotherhood, Europe had to come to "the Urals."

"Scythians" was a Eurasian offer in poetic form. In the 1920s, an explicitly "Eurasianist" group of theorists and commentators emerged in the Russian emigration. They were not the first to use the term, which may have been coined by British administrators in India in quite a different sense, to describe people of "mixed" European and Indian heritage.[18] Ideas promoted by these émigrés had

16. Aleksandr Blok, "Skify," in Aleksandr Blok, *Stikhotvoreniia Poemy Teatr. V dvukh tomakh*, Vol. 2, 1908-1921 (Leningrad: Khudozhestvennaia literatura, 1972), 196-98.

17. Sergey Glebov, *From Empire to Eurasia: Politics, Scholarship, and Ideology in Russian Eurasianism, 1920s-1930s* (DeKalb: Northern Illinois University Press, 2017), 55-57. According to Harsha Ram, the poem abolishes the dichotomy between east and west that had earlier structured so much of Russian literature: Ram, *Imperial Sublime*, 230-31.

18. The first usage of the word "Eurasia" is a matter of both dispute and unconnected scholarly environments. Mischa Gabowitsch claims that the "first verifiable occurrence" of the term was in a geographical handbook, published in Stuttgart in 1858, but also refers to its colonial origins: Mischa Gabowitsch, "'Eurasie': Eléments pour une histoire conceptuelle et sémantique comparée du terme," in Wanda Dressler, ed., *Eurasie: Espace mythique ou realité en construction?* (Brussels: Etablissements Emile Bruylant, 2009), 15. On Eurasia identified as a continent, Leonid Savin references both Eduard Suess's three-volume geological study, *Das antlitz der erde* (1885-1909) and the Russian ethnographer Vladimir Lamanskii's 1892 book, *Tri mira aziisko-evropeiskogo materika*: Leonid Savin, "Introduction: the Genesis of the Eurasian Theory," in Jafe Arnold and John Stachelski, eds., *Foundations of Eurasianism*, Vol. I, (n.p.: PRAV Publishing, 2020), 24. In "western" scholarship, Halford Mackinder is often credited with the invention of Eurasia as a geopolitical unity: See his "The Geographical Pivot of History," *Geographical Journal* 23, 4 (1904): 421-37. On the multiple uses of the term in contemporary scholarship and politics, see the succinct summary in Glebov, *From Empire to Eurasia*, 1.

been introduced earlier, but their aggressive appropriation of the term Eurasia, the post-revolutionary timing of their publications, and their targeted political claims turned them into the founders of a "Eurasian" movement.[19]

Europe vs. Humanity

The Eurasianists' foremost theorist was Prince Nikolai Sergeevich Trubetskoi, a brilliant young linguist who had been evacuated from war-torn Crimea in 1920. The scion of an ancient Russian family prominent in both politics and scholarship, Trubetskoi later acquired world renown as a founder of the Prague school of linguistics.[20] Before 1917 he had been a professor at the University of Moscow and a specialist on Finno-Ugric folklore, Sanskrit and comparative linguistics.[21] In 1920 from his exile in Sofia, where he had obtained a university appointment, Trubetskoi published a small book that precipitated the Eurasian movement and offered a seminal critique of Eurocentrism. Its suggestive title was *Europe and Humanity*.[22]

Europe *and* humanity. Europe was not part of humanity, but counterposed to it. The book was a direct attack on European universalism and a defense of the multiplicity of civilizations. Written in a positivist vein, Trubetskoi denied that there was any objective basis for considering "Romano-Germanic" culture superior to other cultures. Moreover, according to Trubetskoi's theory of cultural

---

19. On the Eurasianist movement of the 1920s, see among many studies: Glebov, *From Empire to Eurasia*; Jane Burbank, *Intelligentsia and Revolution: Russian Views of Bolshevism 1917-1922* (New York: Oxford University Press, 1986), 208-22; Nicholas V. Riasanovsky, "The Emergence of Eurasianism," *California Slavic Studies* 4 (1967): 39-72; Otto Böss, *Die Lehre der Eurasier: Ein Beitrag zur russischen Ideengeschichte des 20. Jahrhunderts* (Wiesbaden: Otto Harrasowitz, 1961).

20. Jindřich Toman, *The Magic of a Common Language: Jakobson, Mathesius, Trubetzkoy, and the Prague Linguistic Circle* (Cambridge, MA: MIT Press, 1995).

21. On Trubetskoi's life, see Anatoly Liberman, "Postscript: N. S. Trubetzkoy and His Works on History and Politics," in Nikolai Sergeevich Trubetzkoy, *The Legacy of Genghis Khan and Other Essays on Russia's Identity*, ed. Anatoly Liberman (Ann Arbor: Michigan Slavic Publications, 1991), 295-337; Glebov, *From Empire to Eurasia*, 13-19; Toman, *The Magic of a Common Language*, 186-211. Toman proposes a strong connection between Trubetskoi's political context, his cultural attitudes, and his linguistic theory.

22. Nikolai Sergeevich Trubetskoi, *Evropa i chelovechestvo* (Sofiia: Rossiisko-bulgarskoe isdatel'stvo, 1920).

FIGURE 1.1. Prince Nikolai Trubetskoi. *Source:* https://commons.wikimedia.org/wiki/File:Nikolay_Trubezkoy.jpg.

transfers—premised on the idea of organic and distinctive civilizations—it was impossible for one culture ever to become the same as another, and not desirable. The borrowing culture would always be behind. As non-European societies tried to make "sporadic historical leaps" toward European standards and practices, they would become exhausted by their immense efforts and fall back into a period of "apparent (from the European point of view) stagnation."[23]

The root of this predicament, in Trubetskoi's analysis, was not capitalism or socialism. If Europe ever became socialist, he averred, it would apply this European idea to the world with ruthless violence, exploiting its colonies to indulge privileged Romano-German

23. Trubetskoi, *Evropa i chelovechestvo*, 68–69.

aristocrats, turning everyone else into their "slaves," and eradicating cultural differences by demanding uniform ways of life and identical political structures everywhere. The problem was more basic: "unsatisfied greed, lodged in the very nature of the international plunderers—the Romano-Germans, and ... egocentrism, which has permeated their whole notorious 'civilization'." The only way out was an uprising of "real humanity"—"its majority composed of the Slavs, Chinese, the Indians, the Arabs, the Negroes and other tribes, all those who without regard to the color of their skin languish under the heavy yoke of the Romano-Germans."[24]

Europe and Humanity sketched out in ruthless clarity the case for what we now call cultural relativism. There were no universal cultural values, Trubetskoi insisted. Europeans' "cosmopolitanism" was a product of their formation as an "ethnic group," created by the merger of Roman and German peoples and nourished on the ideals of classical antiquity. To Europeans, the idea of universal values came naturally, but in fact it was just one more myth derived from their "Romano-Germanic chauvinism."[25] As European values were differentially diffused, they created generational, class, and other divides within the assaulted society. Those who tried to Europeanize themselves looked down on those who did not, but also lost their own self-respect.[26]

A first step toward any effective rebellion against European domination was conceptual. Intellectuals had to free themselves from the mystique cast by the Romano-Germans, begin to appreciate their own culture, and expose the "naked deception" and "unconditional evil" of Europeanization. Knocking down "certain idols" was essential to Trubetskoi's goal—a "revolution in consciousness."[27]

Eurasia vs. Europe

The 1920 publication of *Europe and Humanity* sent a shock wave through the Russian emigration in Europe and Asia, where many had fled to escape from the violence, persecution, and multiple

24. Ibid., 72–76.
25. Ibid., 2–3, 5–6.
26. Ibid., 64–70.
27. Ibid., 79–82; *N. S. Trubetzkoy's Letters and Notes*, ed. Roman Jakobson (The Hague: Mouton, 1975), 12–13.

wars that had engulfed the former empire. Three years after the 1917 revolutions, politically minded émigrés were agonizing over the ever more conclusive failures of liberal, social democratic, monarchist, and anarchist oppositions to Bolshevik power.[28] Whatever their commitments, most Russian exiles considered themselves participants in one or another expression of European culture; to them Trubetskoi's assaults were reprehensible. An exception was another young émigré, Petr Savitskii, who took up with verve the challenges posed by Trubetskoi's text. In a tough-minded response published in the prestigious journal *Russian Thought*,[29] Savitskii gave Eurasia a definable location and a practical politics.

By birth Savitskii was a member of the Ukrainian gentry.[30] He studied economics and geography in St. Petersburg and served in the Russian diplomatic corps before the outbreak of the world war. After the Bolshevik revolution, he returned to Ukraine, lived and fought on several fronts of the military campaigns there, and in 1920 became an advisor to General Wrangel's ill-fated government in the Crimea.[31] When Wrangel, facing defeat, evacuated his troops, Savitskii left for a property his family had acquired near Istanbul.[32] He signed his review of Trubetskoi's book, "From the farm Narli on the Asian bank of the Bosphorus, January 8, 1921."[33]

---

28. On the conditions in which the book appeared, see N. I. Tolstoi, "N. S. Trubetskoi i evraziistvo," in N. S. Trubetskoi, *Istoriia. Kul'tura. Iazyk*, ed. V. M. Zhivov (Moscow: Izdatel'skiai gruppa "Progress-Univers," 1995), 6–7. The various responses of Russian intellectuals to the Bolsheviks' success are the subject of Burbank, *Intelligentsia and Revolution*.

29. The pre-revolutionary periodical was revived in the emigration by its prolific editor, Petr Struve: Richard Pipes, *Struve: Liberal on the Right, 1905–1944* (Cambridge, MA: Harvard University Press, 1980), 335.

30. Martin Beisswenger explores Savitskii's early interest and activism in Ukrainian culture and its connection to his later defense of Russian imperialism: "Was Lev Gumilev a 'Eurasianist?': A New Look at His Postwar Contacts with Petr Savitskii," *Ab Imperio* 2013, 1: 91–92.

31. On Savitskii's origins and education, see Glebov, *From Empire to Eurasia*, 26–31, and K. B. Ermishina, "Petr Nikolaevich Savitskii: zhiznennyi i tvorcheskii put'," in P. N. Savitskii, *Nauchnye zadachi evraziistva: Stat'i i pis'ma* (Moscow: Dom russkogo zarubezh'ia im. A. Solzhenitsyna Vikmo-M, 2018), 7–61.

32. Glebov, *From Empire to Eurasia*, 30. The Crimean government, which included several prominent liberal advisors, collapsed with the defeat of Wrangel's army in November 1920. See Jonathan D. Smele, *The "Russian" Civil Wars 1916–1926: Ten Years that Shook the World* (New York: Oxford University Press, 2017), 166–71.

33. Petr Savitskii, "Evropa i evraziia (Po povodu broshiura N. S. Trubetskogo 'Evropa i chelovechstvo')," *Russkaia mysl'* no. I–II (January–February 1921): 138. An English

The title of Savitskii's article, "Europe and Eurasia (On Trubetskoi's Brochure 'Europe and Humanity')," signaled a fateful transformation of the binaries of global confrontation. Eurasia, not all of mankind, was the counter to European power. Savitskii both called out what he saw as major flaws in Trubetskoi's argument and responded to Trubetskoi's demand for rethinking with a plan for action.

Trubetskoi's claim that his analysis was founded on incontrovertible logic ignored the Romano-Germanic origins of this very method, Savitskii wryly observed. Trubetskoi had offered no "new nonRomano-Germanic logic" in its stead, and in any case Savitskii disputed the possibility of defining cultures "objectively." The notion of a "culture" was "subjective" and any assessment of a "cultural value"—including the Europeans' supposed universalism— was a philosophical, not a scientific, project.[34]

Savitskii did not reject the concept of distinctive cultures, nor the particularity of their material products. What he decried was Trubetskoi's complete relativism. Savitskii distinguished two "orders of cultural values"—ideological and technical—and insisted that it was possible and even essential to evaluate technological aspects of culture. Wouldn't "every homo sapiens recognize that the rifle was 'more perfect' than the boomerang as an arm for attack and defense?"[35]

This provocation signaled Savitskii's major worry: Trubetskoi had left in dangerous abeyance the question of power in a world of competing cultural formations. For a culture to survive, appreciated or not, it had to sustain itself. In Savitskii's words: "Only those cultures that in contact with others prove themselves strong enough to defend their existence in . . . either military-political or cultural influence or both will survive and acquire historical significance."[36]

Savitskii confronted the organization of power directly. The peoples of the world had never lived in equivalent conditions; they were situated "more on a 'staircase' than on a 'horizontal surface'." Trubetskoi's call for emancipation of all humanity from the

---

translation can be found in Arnold and Stachelski, eds., *Foundations of Eurasianism*, Vol. 1, 91–113.

34. Savitskii, "Evropa i evraziia," 119–21.
35. Ibid., 121.
36. Ibid., 121, 125–26.

"Romano-German yoke" was pure mysticism. It lacked any plan for implementation; furthermore, not all peoples were equipped to defend themselves against the Europeans. Still, Savitskii intuited, behind Trubetskoi's fanciful calls for cultural emancipation and his opposition of Europe and humanity, stood a crucial "reality"—"the opposition between Europe and Russia." Russia—rather than inchoate humanity—had the capacity to confront European power.[37]

Savitskii singled out two decisive developments that gave Russia an advantage over its opponent. First, Russia had not been weakened, as Trubetskoi would have it, but rather made "self-confident" through its centuries of contact with European cultures. Russia's "exports" in literature and the arts were no less significant than its "spiritual imports." Second, Bolshevism, and here Savitskii echoed Trubetskoi, had shaken up the world order. Russia's new leaders had taken hold of European Marxism and given it a Russian essence and a new world headquarters. Bolshevism itself would be replaced "sooner or later," but whatever regime came next would inherit this significant "change in the cultural-historical relationships between Europe and Russia."[38]

Savitskii's argument transformed Trubetskoi's grand anti-European humanism into a dichotomous power struggle between Europe and Russia. This nomenclature, he acknowledged, might raise questions; wasn't Russia part of Europe? Turning back to his earlier studies of geography, Savitskii pointed out the critical impact of Russia's location on its history and cultural development. Russia was a "continent in itself," defined by three "plains"—the White Sea to the Caspian, the Siberian plain, the Turkestan plain. This region, with its uniformity in climate, absence of natural borders, and multiple peoples, was different from Europe to its west and Asia to the east. Physical location defined many aspects of the cultural life of what Savitskii called Russia-Eurasia. For one thing, the extreme spans of seasonal temperatures across the region had prepared people to produce and accept radically different kinds of cultural expression. The "Russian-Eurasian spirit" could accommodate

37. Ibid., 126–28.
38. Ibid., 129–30.

"darkness and baseness" as well as "enlightenment and impulse" in ways that were inaccessible to Europeans who lived in the confines of their narrow, divided spaces in less demanding climate zones.[39]

Although in later publications Savitskii developed these sketchy suggestions into a full-blown theory of "place-development,"[40] in "Europe and Eurasia" he emphasized the pragmatic possibilities of this political formation. He ruminated on just which people might eventually be drawn into Russia-Eurasia's opposition to Europe. The "whole circle" of "Turanian,[41] Mongol, Aryan, Iverian, and Finnish peoples" had contributed with the Slavs to Eurasian culture and belonged with Russia in the "ideological and military" struggle. Peoples beyond Russia's borders might join in as well, since the climate zones of parts of Iran and northwest China resembled those of Eurasia. But Savitskii drew a racist line based on very un-Trubetskoi-like stages of development. Not all of "humanity" could be drawn into the "opposition of Europe and Eurasia," because "the Indians or Chinese, in the sense of their potential for cultural-historical opposition, are not at all identical to, for example, the Negroes, Australians, or Papuans."[42]

Unlike Trubetskoi, Savitskii confronted the prospect of a revived Russian imperialism openly. Would drawing non-Russian peoples into the opposition to Europe mean that they would just be exchanging the Romano-Germanic "yoke" for a Russian one? Savitskii had a split-level answer. Referring again and without apology to hierarchies of cultural achievement, he declared that "life is cruel,

---

39. Ibid., 130–33.

40. P. N. Savitskii, *Mestorazvitie russkoi promyshlennosti* (Berlin: Izdanie Evraziitsev, 1932).

41. Savitskii refers to the theory of a Turanian language group, thought to describe the languages of the nomads of the Eurasian steppe, including Turkic, Mongol, Finno-Ugric and other non-Indo-European languages. Trubetskoi developed his version of this theory and its significance in Russian history in his essay, "O turanskom elemente v russkoi kul'ture," available in English translation as Nikolai Trubetskoi, "On the Turanian Element in Russian Culture," *Anthropology & Archeology of Eurasia* 37, 1 (Summer 1998): 8–29. The concept originated in Europe and was initially deployed to deny Russia a European heritage. It was later turned on its head by Russian intellectuals who appropriated Asian-ness for their own purposes: see Marlène Laruelle's article, "La question du 'touranisme' des Russes: Contribution à une histoire des échanges intellectuels Allemagne-France-Russie au XIXe siècle," *Cahiers du monde russe*, 45, 1–2 (2004): 241–66.

42. Savitskii, "Evropa i evraziia," 134–35.

and a Russian yoke could hang as heavily as the Romano-Germanic one on the weakest people of Eurasia." But there was a crucial difference: Russia's relations with the non-Russian peoples of Eurasia were qualitatively different from those of Europeans with people they had colonized. This was because "Eurasia is a region of a certain kind of equality and brotherhood of nations." Such "cultural commonality" across the steppe was "unthinkable" for Romano-Germans with "for example, the Bantu negroes or Malayans."[43]

The main thrust of Savitskii's seminal article was the proposal of "real forms" that Trubetskoi's "revolution in psychology" could take. His emphasis was material and technical: Eurasians had to use the Romano-Germans' science and technology if they wanted to escape the "hated yoke" of European imperialism. But the ideological struggle also mattered. Savitskii converted Trubetskoi's condemnation of European universalism into a recipe for aggression. In *Europe and Humanity*, Trubetskoi had declared that Romano-German culture was saturated with "egocentrism," enabling its fallacious claim to universalism. Savitskii insisted that all peoples had their egocentrisms and that any practical application of Trubetskoi's project would require an ideology, one that appealed to Eurasia's particular cultural makeup with values that Eurasian peoples recognized as their own and regarded as "higher and more complete." The "cultural emancipation of Russia-Eurasia" could not be founded on mystical protests and condemnations of European egocentrism alone. Instead its promise was in the "creation, consciously and unconsciously, of a real and creative 'egocentrism' of Eurasia that would rally together our forces and push them forward toward a sacrificial feat."[44]

This bombastic conclusion to Savitskii's review echoed Trubetskoi's fervor while transforming his assault on Europeans' presumptuous universalism into a call for Eurasian militancy. Meanwhile Savitskii had given the cause a name. Or two names: he deployed Eurasia and Eurasia-Russia interchangeably without any comment. Savitskii's personal fate was tragic, and his environmental theory of place-development was ignored for decades, but his conversion of Trubetskoi's anti-imperialism into what he liked to call "real"

43. Ibid., 135–36.
44. Ibid., 136–38.

projects, both material and ideological, would live into the next century (see chapter 4). Eurasia had become a political plan.

Eurasianism Declares Itself

Eurasia acquired a collective voice in 1921 when Trubetskoi, Savitskii, and two other Russian émigrés (the theologian G. V. Florinskii and P. P. Suvchinskii, an aspiring musician and entrepreneur) issued the first manifesto of the Eurasian movement.[45]

Graced with a constructivist cover by Petr Chelishchev, the slim book entitled *Exodus to the East* proclaimed that Russian culture was moving eastward and thereby transforming itself and the world order. "The introduction of... Eastern European and Asiatic peoples into the conceptual sphere of Russian world culture stemmed," they argued, from an "affinity of souls" that made "Russian culture understandable and close to these peoples and, conversely, determines the fruitfulness of their participation in Russian affairs" as well as from a "community of economic interest." In this geocultural perspective, Russian people were "neither European, nor Asians." Instead, the contributors argued, "merging with our kinfolk and with the elemental force of culture and of life surrounding us, we are not afraid to pronounce ourselves Eurasians."[46]

The contributors to the first Eurasian miscellany were far from united in their elaborations of this initiative, but they agreed that the world was undergoing a "great historical spasm." After the debacle of the Bolshevik revolution, the "epoch of science" would give way to the "epoch of faith." Russia's great "truth" was "the repudiation of socialism and the affirmation of the Church."[47] These mystical affirmations would become tenacious elements in the Eurasian repertoire.

Savitskii wrote three of the ten articles in the collection. In "Pivot to the East"—the title echoed Mackinder (see introduction)—he elaborated on Russia's potential to combine "East" and "West,"

---

45. For biographies of the first Eurasianists, see Glebov, *From Empire to Eurasia*, 13–32.

46. *Iskhod k vostoku: Predchuvstviia i sversheniia: Utverzhdenie evraziitsev* (Sofiia: Rossiisko-bolgarskoe knigoizdatel'svo, 1921), VII.

47. *Iskhod k vostoku*, III–VI.

FIGURE 1.2. *Exodus to the East*, the manifesto of the Eurasianists. Cover by P. F. Chelishchev. Sofiia: Rossiiko-Bulgarskoi knigoizdatel'stvo, 1921. *Source:* Elmer Holmes Bobst Library, New York University.

Orthodoxy, Islam, and Buddhism.[48] "The Migration of Culture" sketched out his theory that civilizations moved north, to colder climates, over thousands of years. At the end of the second millennium AD, the hegemony of European culture was ceding to the more

48. Petr Savitskii, "Povorot k vostoku," in *Iskhod k vostoku*, 1–3. The Russian word for "pivot" could be a calque of Mackinder's term. Glebov comments on Mackinder's influence on Savitskii's theories: Glebov, *From Empire to Eurasia*, 133.

northern spaces of North America and Russia-Eurasia. Of these two regions, Russia was the more promising. North America, after all, was populated and dominated by emigrants from Europe, while Russia-Eurasia with its multiple peoples and its multiple cultural traditions was creating a more complex and richer "new world."[49]

In "Continent-Ocean (Russia and the World Market)" Savitskii took up the distinction, proposed earlier by Mackinder, between oceanic and continental powers. Savitskii focused on the possibilities and limitations of Russia's physical location. One of his points, elaborated in later works, was that the requirements for transportation and exchange on Russia's continental space were fundamentally different from those of oceanic competitors. Russia should focus on developing an "intracontinental" economy across Eurasia, exploiting its diversity of resources and products. Russia's industrial regions should be linked to the steppes and to the cotton- and rice-producing regions of Afghanistan, China, and Turkestan. The enormous military efforts of the past to gain an "outlet to the open [not frozen] sea" had been a huge historical mistake, although Russia did need to protect the Black Sea coast from its enemies and perhaps try to gain access to the Persian Gulf. Savitskii concluded, "the economic future of Russia lies not in copying the oceanic politics of others . . . but in the recognition of its continentality and in accommodation to it."[50]

It is difficult to read Savitskii's formulations without leaping forward to the end of the century when these issues and terminology would take hold of both political imagination and strategy with a vengeance (chapter 4). But let's stay in 1921 with Trubetskoi's contributions to the Eurasians' manifesto.

Recombinant Culture

In *Exodus to the East*, Trubetskoii continued his assault on European universalism with two essays on nationalist ideas. In "On True and False Nationalism," Trubetskoi introduced, perhaps originally, the concept of "Eurocentrism,"[51] and savaged it. In the same vein,

49. Petr Savitskii, "Migratsiia kul'tury," in *Iskhod k vostoku*, 40–51.
50. Petr Savitskii, "Kontinent-Okean (Rossiia i mirovoi rynok)," in *Iskhod k vostoku*, 117–21, 124–25.
51. N. S. Trubetskoi, "Ob istinnom i lozhnom natsionalizme," in *Iskhod k vostoku*, 72.

he undermined nationalism, as conventionally defined, as a counter to imperialism. He proposed instead a theory of how affiliation could be reconstructed in Eurasian space.

Trubetskoi insisted on the multiplicity of cultures, each expressive of the "individuality" of a people, and necessarily different from the cultures of other peoples. When non-Europeans adopt European culture with its fallacious claims, these imitators suffer from "exocentrism, or more accurately, Eurocentrism." The duty of each non-Romano-German people was to overcome both egocentrism—a belief that one's own culture was superior, and exocentrism—the European conceit of "universal human civilization."[52]

Trubetskoi combined his critique of Eurocentrism with an assertive and novel analysis of nationalism. He used the word, but in the plural. There were good—"true"—nationalisms, and wrongheaded—"false"—ones. "True nationalism" was not about being recognized by "great powers" and trying to be like the other "big peoples." "Self-determination" of nations was just an attempt to play the Europeans' own game and would have disastrous results. The "national" cultures of emergent states would be sacrificed to their leaders' efforts to emulate the Europeans. After independence, even the local languages on which political activists had staked their claims would become distorted by a "huge quantity of Romano-Germanisms and awkward neologisms" and become "almost incomprehensible" for the "real people, who had not yet been denationalized and depersonalized by 'democracy for all.'"[53]

Another false nationalism was cultural conservativism—defining the national culture according to the values and practices of some earlier era, even when these do not fit with contemporary sensibilities. This position violates the "living tie of culture with the psyche of its bearers at any given moment." Yet another nationalist error was to try to impose one's culture on other people.[54] The Romanov empire's policy of Russification was mere mimicry of German-style

---

52. "The Romano-Germans have always been so naively convinced that only they are people that they call themselves 'humanity' and their culture 'universal-human civilization' and . . . their chauvinism 'cosmopolitanism.'" Trubetskoi, "Ob istinnom i lozhnom natsionalizme," 71–73.

53. Ibid., 79–80.

54. Ibid., 81–82.

nationalism, with its egotistical claims to cultural creativity and its projects of compulsory language education and ethnicized unification. Slavophilism, too, was false nationalism, expressed in idealization of a mythic past, exaggerated claims for Russian originality, and aggressive pan-Slavic posturing.[55]

Trubetskoi was no democrat, but like many other Russian intellectuals in the aftermath of 1917, he lauded the values of the authentic "people" over those of the corrupt elite.[56] Most educated Russians did not want to "be themselves," they wanted to be "real Europeans," he averred. Trubetskoi called for a radical "reversal" in the consciousness of the Russian intelligentsia. True nationalism—"based entirely on self-awareness and . . . the restructuring [*perestroika*] of Russian culture in the spirit of its originality"—had no roots in earlier social movements; it would have to be created in the future.[57]

Russian intellectuals had been deformed by Europeanization, but were there ways to bring people and elites together on a new basis? Trubetskoi offered readers a novel proposal—and a suggestive image—for how multicultured peoples could be linked to each other in an inclusive structure. In his article "Heights and Depths of Russian Culture," Trubetskoi proposed that each cultural formation possessed a "top" and "bottom." The whole ensemble was a building in his metaphor. The bottom floor was a "store of cultural values that satisfy the needs of the widest layers of the national whole, the so-called popular masses." The top floor contained cultural elements that were more "refined," the collective product of individuals who bring values from the bottom and adjust them to the more complex tastes of those in dominant positions. A "normal culture" fosters an ongoing exchange and interaction between the bottom and the top.[58]

---

55. For a sense of Trubetskoi's rhetoric: "Since the Germans base their nationalist arrogance on the service of the German race to the creation of culture, our nationalists also try to speak of some kind of original Russian culture of the nineteenth century, blowing up to half-cosmic dimensions the significance of the work of a Russian or a Russian subject that deviates in the smallest way from the Western European mold and declaring this creation 'an invaluable contribution to world civilization.'" Trubetskoi, "Ob istinnom i lozhnom natsionalizme," 83–84.

56. See Burbank, *Intelligentsia and Revolution*, 249–53.

57. Trubetskoi, "Ob istinnom i lozhnom natsionalizme," 85.

58. N. S. Trubetskoi, "Verkhi i nizy russkoi kul'tury (Etnicheskaia osnova russkoi kul'tury)," in *Iskhod k vostoku*, 86–87.

At the top story, cultural creations are taken in, sorted out, and harmonized. Phenomena from outside the building altogether can be absorbed, but this process can impact the top and the bottom layers equally or differently. If an import from a foreign culture causes a rift between the top and the bottom, this means that the "source of the foreign influence is too alien to the given national psyche." The top layer is not static or permanent in content or membership. Talented individuals from the lower stories can enter it. And if the occupants of the top story damage its "prestige"—its capacity to inspire imitation—another social group, closer to the bottom, can take their place, bringing with them values from the lower story's reserves.[59]

Trubetskoi's overtly hierarchical construction accommodated both populist and princely perspectives. It addressed the issue of vertical and horizontal relations of unlike civilizations that concerned Léopold Sédar Senghor in a different post-imperial setting (introduction and chapter 2). But what were the elements of the "Russian" culture that could find expression in Trubetskoi's building?

Consonant with his critique of the intelligentsia's malignant Eurocentrism, Trubetskoi sought an answer in the pre-contact past of the "depths." From ancient times, Slavs had been intermediaries between East and West. Their "soul" tended East, to the "Indo-Iranians," while their "body" had been drawn by geographical and material conditions to the West, to the "western Indo-Europeans."[60] The Eastern imprint on the early Slavs had been preserved in words for religious ideas, in ornamentation, in music, dance, and tales. The five-tone scale of folk music recalled the Slavs' connections to Turkic and Mongol peoples. The attraction of the East was visible in the choice of eastern Christianity and Byzantine variants in architecture and art. Contacts with the West did not produce the same psychological impact: western goods were imported, but they were just used, "not reproduced." Russians felt an "instinctive feeling of repulsion from the Romano-Germanic

59. Ibid., 87.
60. Ibid., 88–92.

spirit." This was why Peter I's reforms had shattered the national community.⁶¹

As he explored the contents of his building, Trubetskoi offered a general theory of how cultures take shape over space and time. Russia's culture, he argued, was created at the geographical intersections with other cultural formations. The ethnic foundation of the bottom culture was the "special zone" where Slavs, Finno-Ugric, Turkic, and Mongol peoples had encountered each other over centuries.⁶² More generally, what took hold in any cultural arena was a blend of elements that was psychically satisfying and hence lasting. There was no "national" kernel that produced one kind of fruit. Instead there were proclivities and affinities that were allowed to develop over time into an absorptive, diversified, yet strong cultural sphere.

Change came from proximity to new practices, both outside and inside the cultural zone. In a healthily interactive culture, innovations introduced in the "heights" could penetrate to the "depths." An example was the Russian church: Byzantine Christianity, introduced from outside, had been absorbed by Russian culture, transformed and enracinated in the people. Similarly, Russian people admired heroes who displayed "daring, . . . a pure steppe virtue, understood by the Turks, but not by the Romano-Germans or the Slavs."⁶³

Geography and history together thus set limits and possibilities for creating the new Russian culture of Trubetskoi's hopes. The upper story had to take the lower story's "specific psychological and ethnographic shape" into account or calamity would follow. Trubetskoi elaborated his architectural metaphor:

> As long as the building of Russian culture was topped off with a Byzantine cupola, it was sturdy. But from the time when that cupola was replaced with a top story of Romano-Germanic construction, all stability and proportionality of the parts of the building were lost. The top started to tilt further and further and finally fell down, and we, Russian *intelligenty*, having wasted so much work and strength on propping up

---

61. Ibid., 89–92, 94, 97–101.
62. Ibid., 100–101.
63. Ibid. Daring translated from *udal'*.

the Romano-Germanic roof that is dangling unattached from the Russian walls, stand in amazement before this gigantic ruin and everyone thinks about how to rebuild a new roof again on the same Romano-Germanic model. These plans should be firmly rejected.[64]

But how should rebuilders proceed? It was impossible to go back to original Byzantine principles, Trubetskoi argued. A church reform purportedly based on Byzantine models had already been tried in the seventeeth century: Russian people found it alien and broke with the church. Their dedication to the "Old Belief" morphed over time into a "protest against Europeanization." Pugachev, the leader of an immense rebellion in the eighteenth century, had attracted the dissident Old Believers with his repudiation of "pagan Latins and Lutherans," and had "found nothing wrong in allying with Bashkirs and other nonOrthodox and even non-Christian peoples of the Turanian East."[65]

This positive gloss on the vast revolt that had threatened the empire under Catherine the Great presaged Trubetskoi's idea for a new Russian covenant. A new culture must unite "in one cultural whole tribes of different origins, historically tied to the fate of the Russian people." Trubetskoi was vague about the contents of this mélange: it was "impossible to predict and prescribe [its] concrete forms." He assured skeptics that the alignment of culture with the values of the depths did not mean that bast sandals and the five-tone scale would become basic ingredients of Russia's high culture. (Stravinsky proved otherwise in music.) What was essential was an organic linkage of the top with the bottom, a "reworking and detailing of the elements of a single culture."[66]

Linguistic diversity presented no problems for Trubetskoi; it was a playing field for the exploration of affinities. But where religion was concerned, Trubetskoi introduced what may seem insurmountably contradictory positions—his commitment to Orthodoxy alongside the vision of multiple "Eastern" peoples, most not Orthodox, united by a shared history and space. The question of confessional compatibility was fudged. Trubetskoi noted tersely that previous efforts

64. Ibid., 101.
65. Ibid., 102.
66. Ibid., 102–103.

at conversion to Christianity had failed, but that other affiliations in the depths nonetheless made possible a "single culture" for all in the zone.[67]

Trubetskoi's essays in the Eurasian manifesto combined dazzling displays of ethnographic and linguistic evidence with confident, completely unverified assertions about the capabilities of the Russian/Turanian/Eurasian "depths," not to mention people's actual desires. He focused on what the depths did *not* want—Europeanization—but even this was not backed up with any investigation of the "psyche" he so eloquently invoked. Somehow salvation was to be found in the innate force of the Russian people, expressed in the untranslatable notion of *stikhiia*—spontaneous, elemental being. If only the heights could reunite with the depths, a great new Russian-Eurasian culture could be built, on old and new, but not western, foundations.

Setting aside this exuberant vision, we pause to engage from a sociological perspective Trubetskoi's model for how cultures form and transform over time. His emphasis, like Savitskii's, was on geography, on the physical proximity of groups of humans, each with inherently dissimilar habits, who then interact with their neighbors, sharing activities, language, music, techniques of daily living, and in so doing create larger identifiable cultural worlds. He rejected the notion of fixed national cultures, with distinctive starting points, well defended boundaries, and assimilating extensions over time.

Internal to any cultural formation were differences in values. Trubetskoi proposed a variant of what we now call "high and low" culture[68] and brought attention to the vitality of the popular sphere. The distinctions between the "top" and the "bottom" need not be fatal or disruptive, he insisted, as long as there is communication and interchange between the two levels. Those at work in the high culture are supposed to absorb, refine, and make choices about cultural values; they should accept talented individuals from the "depths" into their ranks. Problems arise when the two levels

---

67. Ibid., 102–103.

68. Lawrence W. Levine, *Highbrow/lowbrow:The Emergence of Cultural Hierarchy in America* (Cambridge, MA: Harvard University Press, 1988).

are out of touch, and when the top's values do not click with those of the bottom. This can bring down the building.

Eurasianism vs. Bolshevism

Trubetskoi's vision maps nicely onto the particular imperial condition in which he grew up. His elite—very elite—youth had been spent in a society deeply divided by education and resources, although the mobility of individuals across social estates was much more extensive than he from his princely perch may have been able to see.[69] The multiethnic nature of the empire was part of everyone's reality at the time; the "Eastern" components and their meaning had taken on new urgency during the world war and revolution. The empire had indeed collapsed, imploding on itself when Central Asians rebelled against Russian settlers in 1916,[70] and a year later when two revolutions brought down the Byzantine cupola and seemingly everything else with it.

The question of how to put Russia back together was acute for many in the top stories. Outside Russia activists and intellectuals strove for several, unlike, and increasingly unlikely outcomes to the crisis of the state. Some wanted to escape from empire; others to rebuild it on various political foundations—socialist, liberal, monarchist.[71] As the Communist Party in Russia consolidated the former empire's fragments into a functioning state, the Eurasian exiles in Europe managed to publish their manifestos, find jobs and financing, quarrel with each other, and, by the late 1920s, fall prey to the Soviet secret police. The "movement" was no more than a few argumentative individuals, and the readers of their newspapers, serials, and miscellanies were probably only in the hundreds.[72] But their ideas did matter, and not just to Moscow's

---

69. On mobility across estates, see Elise Kimerling Wirtschafter, *Social Identity in Imperial Russia* (DeKalb: Northern Illinois Press, 1997), esp. 164–69.

70. Joshua A. Sanborn, *Imperial Apocalypse: The Great War and the Destruction of the Russian Empire* (Oxford: Oxford University Press, 2014), 175–83; Aminat Chokobaeva, Cloé Drieu, and Alexander Morrison, eds., *The Central Asian Revolt of 1916: A Collapsing Empire in the Age of War and Revolution* (Manchester: Manchester University Press, 2020).

71. Burbank, *Intelligentsia and Revolution*.

72. On the practical composition of the movement, estimates of its output, and the fate of individual Eurasianists, see Glebov, *From Empire to Eurasia*, 175–88.

agents. Eurasian concepts inspired historians, linguists, musicians, and artists in what turned out to be the first wave of "Russian" post-revolutionary emigration.

The works of the most scholarly of the Eurasian founders, Savitskii and Trubetskoi, influenced structuralist theories, notably those of the linguist Roman Jakobson.[73] Jakobson had been an intellectual companion of Trubetskoi since their university days; he continued to collaborate with his friend on linguistic theory in the emigration and corresponded enthusiastically with Savitskii. Jakobson's structuralist theory became highly regarded in the west without much acknowledgment of its Eurasian roots.[74]

Savitskii elaborated his theory of place-development in his 1927 study, *Geographical Specificities of Russia*.[75] In this work, a forerunner of environmental science, Savitskii argued that distinct morphological situations—Europe's segmented geography versus Russia's un-mountained, west-east sweep—gave rise to different ways of thinking about geography. Russia's unbordered territories demanded the study not just of separate objects, but of relationships between humans, territory, plants, and animals.[76] Jakobson and Savitskii both emphasized connections between geographical location and the formation of distinctive cultural phenomena—vocabulary and grammar, and even unlike methods of scientific inquiry.[77]

---

73. On the Eurasianists' input into structuralist theory, see Toman, *The Magic of a Common Language* and Glebov, *From Empire to Eurasia*, 148–74.

74. An exception is Toman, *The Magic of a Common Language*.

75. P. N. Savitskii, *Geograficheskie osobennosti Rossii* (Prague: Evraziiskoe knigoizdatel'stvo, 1927).

76. Savitskii's work and life have attracted scholarly and polemical attention in Russia recently. See the attentive editing of his lesser-known works and correspondence in Savitskii, *Nauchnye zadachi evraziistva*. Alexander Dugin (chapter 4) published Savitskii's Eurasian texts in Petr Savitskii, *Kontinent Evraziia* (Moscow: Agraf, 1997). Social scientists in the "west" do not seem to recognize Savitskii as a kindred spirit if not a progenitor of contextualist and environmentalist theories of scientific production.

77. With their insistence on holistic approaches to knowledge and their emphasis on the impact of geography, Jakobson and Savitskii could be considered forerunners and creative theorists of what later became known in the west as area studies. Neither scholar is credited or recognized in the recent scholarly spats outside Russia over this field. In Russia itself, area approaches had been firmly embedded in a variety of institutions since the nineteenth century. Glebov, *From Empire to Eurasia*, 157–62.

As the Eurasian movement, tiny as it was, fizzled out, the Bolshevik leadership was claiming Russia's place as a civilizer in a communist mode. Soviet officials fostered "native" languages, schools, and other cultural projects as the USSR re-incorporated, in many cases violently, the former "east" of the tsars. Students from the Middle East and North Africa joined their purported peers from Central Asia at the "Communist University for the Toilers of the East" set up in Moscow in 1921.[78] Perhaps surprising the Bolsheviks themselves, communism turned out to be attractive to colonized peoples in many parts of the world, even as it failed to produce the anticipated revolutions in Europe.

Trubetskoi was not surprised. Hostile to Bolshevism, he nonetheless appreciated the revolution's anticolonial potential. In 1921, he had pointed out that the "red mask of Marxism" on Russia's "Asiatic or half-Asiatic face" could mobilize "the despised against the despisers."[79] Eurasianism as explicit ideology was unacceptable in the USSR, but Trubetskoi had identified an unexpected capacity of the communist revolution—its appeal to defenders of national cultures against western cultural and economic domination.

The Legacy of Chinggis Khan

Writing from his European exile, Trubetskoi developed a fuller explanation for communism's ideological success. He produced a personal manifesto—a sixty-page booklet, published in Berlin in 1925, boldly entitled *The Legacy of Chinggis Khan: A Perspective on Russian History Not from the West, But from the East.*[80] The deliberately awkward subtitle signaled Trubetskoi's revisionist perspective, but the volume did more than rewrite Russian history. It contained a theory of how Eurasian-style government should

---

78. Masha Kirasirova, "The 'East' as a Category of Bolshevik Ideology and Comintern Administration: The Arab Section of the Communist University of the Toilers of the East," *Kritika: Explorations in Russian and Eurasian History* 18, 1 (Winter 2017): 7–34.

79. N. S. Trubetskoi, "Predislovie," in G. D. Uel's *Rossiia v mgle* (Sofiia: Rossiiskobulgarskoe knigoizdatel'stvo, 1921), xv–xvi. This is Trubetskoi's introduction to a translation of H. G. Wells's *Russia in the Shadows*, published in 1920 in London by Hodder and Stoughton Limited.

80. N. S. Trubetskoi, *Nasledie Chingiskhana: Vzgliad na russkuiu istoriiu ne s zapada, a s vostoka* (Berlin: Evraziiskoe knigoizdatel'stvo, 1925).

be organized and what its foundational principles and strategies should be. These proposals included Trubetskoi's answers to the tricky question of Russian Orthodoxy's relation to a confessionally inclusive Eurasian state.

The Legacy of Chinggis Khan turned the anti-Mongol narrative of Russian history on its head. There was no "Mongol yoke" responsible for holding Russia back from European-style development. Instead, the Mongol conquest had stimulated the formation of the Russian state and provided its rulers with the tools to govern. The Mongols had united Eurasia into a single political space that was the natural terrain for a diverse and inclusive polity.

Conventional histories designated Kiev as Russia's progenitor, but Kievan Rus' had failed its geographical "task," Trubetskoi asserted. Surrounded by nomads, Kiev had not kept a secure hold on the route from the Baltic to the Black Sea. Kiev's princes had not been able to overcome their quarrels and unite their lands into a single state.[81] The Mongols on the other hand had fully lived up to their geographical circumstances. Echoing Savitskii, Trubetskoi termed the Mongols' terrain a "special continent, a special part of the world," not Europe, not Asia, but an economically self-sufficient region where populations were dispersed yet connected to each other. Eurasia was "by its very nature, . . . historically destined for the establishment of a state entity."[82] It was Chinggis Khan who had fulfilled this destiny, putting Eurasia together under Mongol rule.

Mongol rule also offered lessons in how to govern this space, principles that Trubetskoi turned into a theory of political structure and strategy. For Trubetskoi, Chinggis was not just a great conqueror, but a great organizer, who acted according to a "system" of ideals and principles.[83] True, these principles were nowhere articulated for posterity, but Trubetskoi alleged,

> As a typical representative of the Turanian race, he [Chinggis] was not capable himself of clearly formulating this system in abstract philosophical expressions, but all the same [he] felt and recognized this

81. Ibid., 4.
82. Ibid., 6.
83. Ibid., 9.

system, was completely imbued with it, and every one of his actions, every step or order flowed logically from this system.[84]

Note the replay here of an older theme in Russian historical myth-making: a life of action left glorious heroes no time for philosophizing. But what, according to Trubetskoi, were the elements of Chinggis's unarticulated "system"?

A primary concern of the great leader was morality. Chinggis valued "truth, loyalty and hardiness," and despised "betrayal, treason, and cowardice." In Trubetskoi's account the first set of values were evidence of an "internal moral law," of respect for a "world order in which all have their established place, defined by God's will, bound together by duty and obligation." This attitude was to be found among the nomads, while most settled peoples were only concerned for their material well-being and safety. For this reason, Chinggis chose nomads as his military-administrative officers.[85]

Chinggis's highest officials did not necessarily descend from the nomad aristocracy. The critical value for him was not origin or class position but "psychological type." Nomads of the right type were made into his commanders and "organized into a strong hierarchical system," with Chinggis at the apex. He used only a few *"spetsy"* (Soviet slang for specialists, technicians) from the settled peoples for financial and office work.[86]

Chinggis's system of personalized command based on honor and loyalty was suffused with religious spirit. In Trubetskoi's interpretation, Chinggis was "a deeply religious man, continuously aware of his personal tie to the divine," who chose as his subordinates people who believed that "[their] personal fate, like the fate of other people and the whole world, were in the hands of a eternal, higher and unassailable being." What mattered was belief in a God-given order, not in a particular religion. Chinggis did not institute a state religion, and his tolerance of different religions was not a sign of indifference or passivity: "he actively supported" the multiple religions of his

84. Ibid.
85. Ibid., 9–14.
86. Ibid.

subjects. His administrators came from Mongol and Turkic tribes that belonged to different confessions.[87]

How did this system relate to Russia's historical development? Trubetskoi had an ingenious answer, or a few of them. A first effect of the Mongol conquest had been a kind of religious shock therapy: The Mongol conquest jolted the conscience of early Russians. Before the Mongols arrived, Russians had only "primitive" notions about the state; the Mongols brought to their aid not only techniques of rule, but the very idea of a great state based on a religious principle. Reacting to the religious, but foreign, ideals of the Mongol rulers, Russians sought inspiration in their own religious past, in Byzantine Christianity. The "yoke" produced an outburst of "creative work in all areas of religious art." Thus occurred the "miraculous transformation of the Mongol state concept into the Orthodox-Russian idea."[88]

From this "miracle"—certainly a wrenching twist to the usual narrative—came the beginnings of Russian statehood. Under the guidance of their Mongol overlords, the Moscow princes took on the task of administrative and financial unification of the "Russian lands"; later, by conquering other territories of the Mongol empire, they became rulers of a new state. Revitalized Christianity was an essential element in this transfer of statehood. The Mongols' eclectic Shamanism proved incapable of competing with the other great religions on their territories, particularly Islam and Buddhism.[89] But under Russian rule the Mongol state ideal could be anchored in a powerful and compatible religion. The Russian incarnation of Mongol values was facilitated by Tatars who converted to Orthodoxy and entered the Russian "ruling class." (Trubetskoi used Tatar in the conventional way to refer to Mongol and Turkic people of the Golden Horde.) They brought with them Mongol traditions of statehood and "personally sealed the inherited connection between Mongol and Russian state traditions."[90]

---

87. Ibid., 13-15.

88. Ibid., 15-20.

89. Trubetskoi argued that Islamic law was incompatible with Mongol law and that the Buddhist way of life was difficult to adapt to nomadism and could not support the "spirit of state and military activity": *Nasledie Chingiskhana*, 24-26.

90. Ibid., 21-27.

Trubetskoi's account addressed what he saw as the social, spiritual, and institutional foundations of the post-Mongol "Russian state system."[91] It was a state in which all shared the same moral and religious culture: "Russian faith and Russian lifeways are inseparable." The Tsar, at the head of this state, was the representative of the "national will." The Tsar in turn deemed himself responsible for all his subjects before God; his service was a "special kind of moral heroic feat." Trubetskoi specified the ideal organization of government. The Tsar rules best when he has unlimited power, is fully informed about conditions in the state, and listens attentively to the clergy.[92]

The Legacy of Chinggis Khan seemed to solve puzzles invoked by the Eurasians' earlier proposals. Russia was the inheritor of Chinggis's empire, because Russia leaders, learning from the Mongols, had built a state of their own on the space of the Mongol empire. Why Russia among the other candidates for power on this space? There was a gap between the "great size" of the Mongol state and "primitive formless Shamanism." The Russians had not only imbibed the religious spirit of the Mongol empire, they could rely on their own reinforced version of Orthodoxy, a suitable religion for a great Eurasian polity.[93]

Trubetskoi took pains to explicate the differences and connections between the Mongol and Russian state systems. The Russian state was superior to that of the Mongols because Russia had Orthodoxy as its motivating ideal, but this commitment did not mean exclusion of other religions. In the place of the Mongols' "full confessional tolerance" that could potentially "undermine the religious basis of the whole state-ideological system," the Russian state practiced "limited religious tolerance." Russian policy was "cautious" toward those whose faiths were "not founded on the old and new testaments." Believers in these religions were not to be "insulted"; care should be taken to make "Orthodoxy appear in a more worthy form than their own religion."[94] Trubetskoi's strategy

---

91. "*Russkaia gosudarstvennost*" is the term Trubetskoi uses; see an example in ibid., 27.
92. Ibid., 28–30. Moral heroic feat from *nravstvennyi podvig*. The word *podvig* and the concept reappears in Eurasian texts in the 1990s; chapter 4.
93. Ibid., 33.
94. Ibid., 31–33.

signaled inclusion of Muslims and Buddhists, but left the door wide open for incautious treatment of Jews and non-Orthodox Christians, whose faiths were indeed founded on the testaments.

Trubetskoi insisted upon the "internal kinship" of the Mongol and Russian states, both in spiritual inspiration and political form. At the head of both systems was a "pure and ideal representative of their way of life," nomadic or Orthodox. "State discipline" was attained in both cases by the "general subordination of all subjects and the monarch to a heavenly, godly principle, the subordination of one person to another and all to the monarch," who is the "earthly tool" of this godly principle. In both systems, civic virtue was expressed in "absence of attachment to earthly goods, freedom from the drive for material prosperity, and devotion to religiously inspired duty."[95]

But Moscow had succeeded as a state, where the Mongols ultimately failed. This was because Russian statehood was a closer fit to Eurasian geographic, cultural space, and because Orthodoxy was a better religious foundation than Shamanism, especially as nomadism faded away. In addition, the Mongols had been mistaken in trying to conquer China and Persia. What Trubetskoi called Chinggis's "Pan-Asian imperialism" had led to the cultural subordination of the core of his empire to the alien cultures of the conquered but venerable empires. This produced an "incoherence between the centers of power and the centers of culture." Moscow, on the contrary, had confined its extension to the "Eurasian world," which possessed "cultural self-satisfaction comparable to that of the old Asian realms."[96]

Trubetskoi's caution in regard to China and Persia recalls Savitskii's similar warnings and presaged later Eurasianist hesitations (see chapter 4). In their definitions, Eurasia did not embrace all of Asia and Europe: it was a spatial configuration shaped by a shared history and environment. By limiting their terrain to Eurasia, Russia's leaders had shored up their statehood in contrast to the overreaching Mongols.

On their western borders, however, the Russians had gone too far and the result was the self-inflicted damages Trubetskoi had

95. Ibid., 32–33.
96. Ibid., 33–34.

castigated earlier. He still held Peter the Great at fault for the moral and physical destruction of Russian society: "External power was bought at the price of complete cultural and spiritual enslavement of Russia to Europe."[97] Trubetskoi was equally bitter about Russia's foreign policy, the repeated attempts to play "senseless" European power games. In accord with Savitskii's continentalist theory, Trubetskoi regarded the long-term effort to expand into the Mediterranean region as a costly mistake for a state whose real geographical destiny was to connect east with west across Eurasia. The partitions of Catholic Poland had also been egregious errors; they strengthened Russia's European enemies and the influence of Catholicism.[98]

Russia's more recent conquests in Central Asia or the Caucasus did not figure in Trubetskoi's critique, presumably because these were Eurasian spaces ripe for Russian rule. But not for Russification. Trubetskoi reiterated his opposition to forcing assimilation: the "effort to culturally destroy . . . conquered peoples" was what Europeans did in their colonies. In Eurasian space peoples were mixing naturally, creating a "unique, new, whole, national Russian type." This "Slavic-Turanian" people was a result of the "fraternization" of Russians with other peoples.[99]

Did this glimpse at ongoing Eurasian cultural construction offer any hope for Russia's future? Trubetskoi extended his analysis to explain how the revolutions of 1917 had come about and what Chinggis's legacy might portend.

Once Russia's leaders started down the path of "reshaping Russian material into a mighty European power," the state had been doomed. The pursuit of western-style imperialism, militarism, chauvinism, and "state-worship"[100] had produced an intermediate group, between Europeanized elites and the common people. These "half intellectuals" hated both the old Russia and the new. The world war led to revolution as the people joined the opposition to

97. Ibid., 35.
98. Ibid., 37–41.
99. Ibid., 41–42.
100. By "state-worship" Trubetskoi referred to secularization of government. He condemned the Russian state's long-term effort to bureaucratize the Orthodox Church, bring it under state control, and consequently make it unpopular. Ibid., 42–43.

the state, and the intellectuals fought to reestablish it. The winning party was the one that stood for "the European ideal that was the hardest to put into practice and at the same time the most seductive." The result was a "new period" in Russian history, "the period of Soviet order and the rule of communism."[101]

Trubetskoi still liked several aspects of Bolshevik Russia, especially its anti-imperial ethos, rejection of Slavophilism and pan-Slavism, and overt eastward turn. "For the first time in relations with the East, Russia takes the right tone," he enthused. Russia "recognized herself as a true ally of Asian countries in their battle with the imperialist countries of European (Romano-Germanic) civilization." The Soviets were talking with Asians "as equals, as comrades in misfortune."[102] In domestic politics, Trubetskoi welcomed the recognition of national rights of all the peoples of "Russia-Eurasia" and the granting of "wide degrees of autonomy while keeping the unity of the state entity." These policies corresponded to the "historical essence of the Russian state tradition." Bringing in new "layers" of the population to cultural and administrative work was an attempt to destroy the "cultural gap" opened up by Europeanization.[103]

What Trubetskoi did not like was that the Bolshevik party was led by a Europeanized intelligentsia, and that once again, Russia was going to be "material" for a European plan—socialism. With this new goal, Russia was back in the European game, subsidizing communist parties and unions, spending wildly on communist propaganda. International proletarian solidarity was as much an illusion as Alexander I's Holy Alliance. As in the past, foreigners were flocking to Moscow to assist the state; earlier it was German barons, now it was Latvian communists. The novelty was that communists were trying to turn the masses away from the Orthodox Church.[104] Communism had turned out to be Peter the Great in a

---

101. Ibid., 43–47. "Rule" translated from *gospodstvo*, which also suggests "lordship."

102. Ibid., 47. Equality was not how many Asians, even those on the left, saw their relations with the Bolsheviks. See Tatiana Linkhoeva, *Revolution Goes East: Imperial Japan and Soviet Communism* (Ithaca, NY: Cornell University Press, 2020), for the multiple trajectories of Bolshevik policies and ideas in Japanese politics.

103. Trubetskoi, *Nasledie Chingiskhana*, 47.

104. Ibid., 48–50.

new version; instead of freeing Russia from the European yoke, "it had only worked to strengthen that yoke."[105]

The reference to a European "yoke" nicely wrapped up Trubetskoi's inversion of conventional Russian history: There was no Tatar yoke, instead the Mongols had essentially created the Russian state. The real yoke was European culture, that had, with the help of Russia's misguided leaders, turned Russian-Eurasian-Orthodox society into mere material for Romano-Germanic experiments and pan-European imperialism.

Trubetskoi concluded his account of Russia's present situation with a vision of a Russian-Eurasian future. The annexation of Crimea, the conquest of the Caucasus, Turkestan, Siberia under the tsars—these had been steps on the way to gathering the pieces of "the Eurasian *ulus* of Chinggis Khan's empire." The Russian masses instinctively understood this process. They fraternized with the natives and willingly adopted their technologies. In the newly reunited areas, new "special, mixed" practices were appearing, the "foundation for a whole rainbow of Eurasian cultures."[106] Tatars, Kirghiz, Bashkirs, Chuvash, Iakuts, Buriats, and Mongols were taking part in the rebuilding of the state. Some "new sound-combinations, also 'barbarian,' also Turanian," could be heard in the Russian language.

> All over Russia, again, as seven hundred years ago, wafts the odor of burning horse dung, horse sweat, camel hair—Turanian camps. And over Russia falls the shadow of the great Chinggis Khan, the unifier of Russia.[107]

It is hard to resist the sheer bravado of Trubetskoi's text—clever, shocking, and manipulative, and extremely irritating to those who wanted Russia to be more European, not less. Trubetskoi's account of Russia's trajectory both predicted an inclusionary, pluralistic society (the "rainbow of Eurasian cultures") and established Russia as the worthy ruler of all of Eurasia. Mongol "full confessional tolerance" morphed into "limited religious tolerance," while the

---

105. Ibid., 52.
106. Ibid., 56.
107. Ibid., 55.

principles of unlimited power invested in the state leader and strict hierarchical discipline were retained. Trubetskoi's post-imperial possibility was founded on the repudiation of European imperialism, but it envisioned the revival of a purportedly authentic Russian way of rule, without the despised and westernized communists, but with all Eurasia, it seemed, ready to join in.

Recombinant Nationalisms and the Ukrainian "Problem"

In the late 1920s, as the Eurasianist team in Europe was self-destructing with help from Soviet espionage,[108] Trubetskoi took up the question of affiliation in a multiethnic state. He proposed a general theory of dually located nationalisms and applied his analysis to the delicate question of Ukrainian culture inside a Russian-Eurasian polity.

By this time, the Soviet Union had officially taken on a federated form.[109] The communist leadership recognized and even cultivated the distinctions among nations in its population, a policy that Trubetskoi favored. This "especially many peopled nation" had its own nationalism, which Trubetskoi gave a new name: "This nation we call Eurasian, its territory Eurasia and its nationalism Eurasianism."[110]

Looking beyond or over Soviet policies, Trubetskoi envisioned an entity based on layered and mutually constituted national affiliations. He made the case for an "all-Eurasian nationalism,"[111] a concept that

---

108. Glebov, *From Empire to Eurasia*, 182–87.

109. The constitution of the Union of Soviet Socialist Republics was ratified on January 31, 1924. See Richard Pipes, *The Formation of the Soviet Union: Communism and Nationalism, 1917–1923*, rev. ed. (Cambridge, MA: Harvard University Press, 1964), and Francine Hirsch, *Empire of Nations: Ethnographic Knowledge & the Making of the Soviet Union* (Ithaca, NY: Cornell University Press, 2005) on the processes leading to the new state's composition.

110. N. S. Trubetskoi, "Obshcheevraziiskii natsionalizm," *Evraziiskaia khronika* 9 (1927): 28.

111. Trubetskoi, "Obshcheevraziiskii natsionalizm." Portions of this article by Trubetskoi have been edited out from a recent Russian edition of his writings; see the website "Gumilevica," http://gumilevica.kulichki.net/TNS/tns14.htm, accessed February 13, 2023. The meaning of the Russian word "*obshcheevraziiskii*," translated here as "all-Eurasian," is difficult to capture in English. Translators have used "Pan-Eurasian," but Trubetskoi hated

anticipated notions of political belonging promoted by Eurafricanists (chapter 2) and advocates of other supranational formations, such as the European Union.

Two variants of nationalism could imbue a single person's loyalties, Trubetskoi insisted.

> Each citizen of the Eurasian state must recognize not only that he belongs to a certain people (or to some variety of that people) but also that this same people belongs to the Eurasian nation. And the national pride of that citizen must find satisfaction in both of these recognitions.... All-Eurasian nationalism must appear as a widening of the nationalism of each of the peoples of Eurasia, a kind of merging of these particular nationalisms into a whole.[112]

As we have seen, Trubetskoi had earlier condemned "false nationalism," especially its European expressions in fabricated histories, fixed territoriality, and divisive state-based politics. Now he used the term, but insisted that it need not be based on loyalty to a single ethnic group. Instead, he argued, there were multiple types of nationalisms with different origins and valences.

Nationalism derived from "an intense sensation of the individuality of the nature of a given ethnic unit and therefore, above all, confirms the organic *unity* and *uniqueness* of this ethnic unit (a people, a group of peoples, or a part of a people)." Such groups, though, were never completely unified, for there were always differences—in customs, language, or other qualities within any group. And groups were unlikely to be completely unique, because peoples interact with each other. Peoples may enter a "group of nations," or some members of a nation might join a larger group while other members of the same nation could join another large collective. "The unity of an ethnic unit is inversely proportional and the uniqueness of an ethnic unit is directly proportional to the size of that

---

pan-Slavism, pan-Turkism, and the other "pans" of his time and rejected them as narrow and artificial ideologies. Trubetskoi may have wanted to avoid the Russian word for "all" (*vse*), which was part of many Russian and Soviet institutional names: *vse-sovetskii*, *vse-rossiiskii* (all-Soviet, all-Russian) used as an adjective. *Obshche*, "general," while awkward in English captures Trubetskoi's point that this was a nationalism that was common and shared.

112. Trubetskoi, "Obshcheevraziiskii natsionalizm," 29.

unit." Only very small units of people ("a tribal subgroup within a people") can be truly homogeneous, while large entities, with their different combinations of peoples "approach total uniqueness."[113]

Trubetskoi's emphasis was on affinity and its multiple possibilities, not identity with a fixed point of reference. His formula suggested that there can be many kinds of nationalism, deriving both from diversity within units and distinctive ways that units are associated in larger groupings. Taken together, these conditions— the particularity of peoples and the particular ways that they are brought together—produce the "uniqueness" of a large unit that is heterogeneous in composition. Nationalisms can be "included" within one another, and they can be combined.

Trubetskoi gave all-Eurasian nationalism a past. The history of Eurasian peoples had woven them together into a "massive tangle that can no longer be unraveled." The present and future of the idea were less certain. He felt that Eurasians needed to become conscious of their "brotherhood." Russian people had a special responsibility in this ideological project. Not only did they have to reject their earlier fixation on Europe, Russians, as the most numerous people of Eurasia and the former "masters" of the whole territory, had to set a good example for others.[114]

Prospects were dim for such a revival in the near future. Eurasianism was not tolerated in the USSR, but even more disheartening was its reception in the emigration. Most émigrés were Russian nationalists or Europeanized secularists, and neither party understood that citizens must feel themselves a part of a single "organic unity." Trubetskoi concluded that there were only two possibilities for such an overarching commitment at present. These were class (the Soviet version) or multiethnic solidarity (his version)—the "dictatorship of the proletariat or the recognition of the unity and uniqueness of the multinational Eurasian nation and all-Eurasian nationalism."[115]

Trubetskoi, as we have seen, was no fan of the proletarian solution—the worst of Europe's impositions on the world—but he realized that all-Eurasian nationalism was a hard sell. Ever one to

113. Ibid., 28.
114. Ibid., 29–30.
115. Ibid., 31.

take up a challenging counter-argument, he provided a specific example of his theory of combined nationalism in his 1927 article "On the Ukrainian Problem."[116] Ukrainian separatism posed an obvious threat to the prospect of Eurasian unity, but Trubetskoi managed to define a way forward.

Trubetskoi traced a long-term relationship between Ukrainian and Russian cultures. In his account, their paths had diverged from common Byzantine roots in the fifteenth century, but their interactions had transformed both cultures more than once since then. The "western Rus'" variant of Orthodox Christianity had been integrated into Russian church culture in the seventeenth and eighteenth centuries, a pragmatic choice of the Muscovite state as it worked to absorb Ukraine. This "Ukrainianization" of Russian high culture had prepared the way for the westward turn under Peter the Great and for another period of bifurcation and fragmentation. Ambitious and creative individuals had been drawn to the dynamic culture of the capital cities, while the "concrete ethnographic popular foundation" had been cut off from the metropoles and reappeared in regional variants. Both Ukrainian ("Little Russian") and "Great Russian" culture became localized in reaction to the Europeanized culture of the elites.[117]

This account of the interaction and intertwining of Russian and Ukrainian cultures corresponded to Trubetskoi's insistence on cultural fluidity. The breaking off of high culture from its "concrete" foundation harked back to his theory of the high and low stories of any culture. Writing on Ukraine, Trubetskoi proposed that there were many different "lower stories" in the Russian building. The "Russian people in general" was an "abstraction," he wrote. "Concretely there exist Great Russians (also with their varieties—northern Great Russians, southern Great Russians, coastal Russians, Bolgars, Siberians, Cossacks and so on), White Russians, Little-Russian Ukrainians (also with their varieties)." The task was not to overcome these differences, but to recognize them.

---

116. N. S. Trubetskoi, "K ukrainskoi probleme," *Evraziiskii vremennik* 5 (Paris, 1927): 165–84. The title of the journal roughly translates as *Eurasian Annals*.

117. Ibid., 165–74.

"Russian culture in the future must expressly be differentiated by separate territories and regions, and in place of the earlier abstract impersonal uniformed one-rootedness must appear a rainbow of brightly expressed local hues."[118]

Here was Trubetskoi's "rainbow" again—a multi-colored array of recognized and unlike localized cultural realms. The "lower story" of Russian culture would have many suites. But what about the upper story? It was essential to have only one, Trubetskoi insisted. Furthermore, any great culture must have a unifying upper story, otherwise it will fall prey to a foreign culture. A large-scale polity depended on a wide range of talents, the more talented people, the better. The top story in Russia must be open to people from "all the Russian tribes" who could work together to cultivate the "spiritual values" of the whole.[119]

This construction had implications for Ukraine. In the lower stories of Russian culture, diversity should be recognized and celebrated, while in the upper story localized or other particularities were limiting and obstructive. An effort to unite top and bottom in an ethnicized fashion would produce an inferior, provincialized upper story, unable to attract the most talented intellectuals. Creative, artistic people would prefer the dynamism of a great, open-to-all culture to a narrow, ethnicized one. It would not be wise, then, for Ukrainians to repudiate Russian culture and try to replace it with their own. A chauvinistic culture would be "tendentious" and "imitative." Instead, Ukrainian culture had a place as a unique expression of an all-Russian culture, one of its many hues.[120] That is, a place in the bottom story.

The new values of the higher story would guide the direction of cultural work in the lower story, and "conversely the cultural creations of the local individualizations of Russia, added together, neutralizing their specific, local, private characteristics, but emphasizing the general [ones], would define the spirit of the cultural work of the upper story."[121] Synthesized Russian culture

118. Ibid., 180.
119. Ibid.
120. Ibid., 178, 181, 184.
121. Ibid., 181.

would have to be based on a single "organizing principle" that was "native to every tribal individualization of the Russian people" as well as shared by those elevated to the upper story. What could serve this role? The answer, obvious to Trubetskoi, was the Orthodox faith.[122]

This blunt insistence on the unifying power of Orthodoxy undergirded Trubetskoi's solution to the "Ukrainian problem." A common faith had allowed western Rus' and Muscovite variants to be united in a single culture, before Peter spoiled everything with his Europeanization. Communism both completed the state's assault on religion and promoted cultural differentiation. Together these policies were provoking "distorted" expressions of Ukrainian culture, Trubetskoi complained. The worst were the initiatives of the Galician intelligentsia, perverted by the impact of their Catholic and Polish past and the "provincial-separatist nationalism typical of Austro-Hungary."[123]

But all was not lost: these misunderstandings and excesses could be overcome in the future through the "correct development of national self-understanding." Ukrainian culture would then take its place as a recognized and distinctive expression of all-Russian culture. Culture, not "egoistic instinct and naked self-affirmation of biological being," should be the basis for national life in Ukraine as in all other areas of "Russia-Eurasia." Trubetskoi concluded his article with a call, in the name of Eurasianism, to all "Russians, both Great Russians and Belorussians and Ukrainians," to join the "struggle" for the "primacy of culture, and both personal and national self-knowledge."[124]

Trubetskoi wove the threads of Ukrainian culture into his rainbow and tied them up in an elegant knot of historical connection to Russia's spiritual being. He recognized and celebrated the multiplicity of differentiated cultures, while insisting on the fluidity of the ways that they could change, combine, transform in interaction with each other. Nationality was not fixed at any point in time, but nationalisms did have histories that impacted their indeterminate futures. Nations could be reconfigured, and they could combine in

122. Ibid., 181–82.
123. Ibid., 182–83.
124. Ibid., 184.

large units without losing their particularity. Rather than accepting the convention that a great state must homogenize its subjects into nationhood, Trubetskoi drew the opposite conclusion. A great state would bring together different nations, celebrate their distinctive qualities, and be the more "unique" precisely because of its multiple components.

The trick was somehow to achieve the emotional identification of such a polity's subjects with the arch of its rainbow. Hostile to secular versions of state authority, Trubetskoi recognized the power of emotion: inspirational ideals were essential to holding a polity together. At the same time, he did not conceive of all subjects as equals or alike in their beliefs; each person should have an "individual" (one of his favorite words) connection to the greater culture; self-knowledge was essential to identification with groups, nations, or supranational bodies. He identified two spaces for cultural creativity: the bottom story of daily life with all its particularities and the top story of refinement that attracted talent from below. His explicit designation of "lower" and "upper" stories flew in the face of nationalist, democratic, and demagogic conceptions of "the" people. Trubetskoi placed the responsibility for ideology with elites and blamed them, not the bottom story, for failures of vertical solidarity (using Senghor's term retrospectively).

Each element in this theory of culture—its origins in difference, its transformations in interaction, its layerability—was an assault on nationalist conceptions of political organization and legitimacy. Trubetskoi insisted that people could have two kinds of loyalties—to their particular cultural sphere and to a larger polity that recognized the diversity of its population. This capacity was set forth as a general principle, designed to counter Europeans' universalistic pretensions and presented in a rationalist, proto-structuralist narrative. But when Trubetskoi explicated what his theory meant for Russia-Eurasia, his strident assertion of the primacy of Orthodox faith undermined his logical constructions. How could Orthodoxy speak to those peoples of Eurasia who were not even Christian, let alone the Christians who were not Orthodox? Nationalities could be recombinant—this word was Trubetskoi's contribution to political and cultural theory—but, for Russia-Eurasia, they would have to be combined in his own way.

Conclusion, or So It Seemed

Trubetskoi broke off in a huff with the already fractured émigré Eurasianists in 1929, rejecting all pro-Soviet nuances and denouncing the movement's "disorganization."[125] In the 1930s, he focused purposefully on scholarship. A founder of the subsequently renowned Prague Circle of linguistic theorists, he lived in Vienna where he held the Slavic Chair at the university. Combative, sensitive to European condescension, intolerant of inferior minds, in poor health, and depressed, Trubetskoi published occasional articles on politics and political theory in these years.[126] His essay "On racism," which analyzed and condemned German and Russian anti-Semitism and praised Eurasian rejection of Germans' "anthropological materialism," may have been a cause of his arrest in March 1938.[127] Trubetskoi was interrogated at length by the Gestapo. His papers were seized and he died in a Vienna hospital on June 25, 1938.[128]

Savitskii published regularly on Eurasianism into the 1930s. His perspectives on the cultural foundation of the project accorded closely with those of Trubetskoi. Savitskii similarly decried the "provincialization" of Ukrainian culture in the second half of the nineteenth century while praising Ukraine's many earlier contributions to Russian art, language, and literature.[129] He shared Trubetskoi's views on Russian Orthodoxy and embellished them in essays on faith and metaphysics,[130] but he also kept his feet on the ground

---

125. See his bitter letter to Suvchinskii, March 10, 1928, extracted in Trubetskoi, *Istoriia. Kul'tura. Iazyk*, 777–78.

126. One could argue, as Toman does, that his scholarship was prefigured by his political commitments. Toman describes Trubetskoi as working on a major political work on "ideocracy"; his papers on this topic were lost after his interrogation in 1938: Toman, *Magic of a Common Language*, 191, 200–201. For an example and interpretation of Trubetskoi's scholarly combativeness, see Stefanos Geroulanos and Jamie Phillips, "Eurasianism versus IndoGermanism: Linguistics and Mythology in the 1930s' Controversies over European Prehistory," *History of Science* 56, 3 (2018): 343–78.

127. The essay is published in Trubetskoi, *Istoriia. Kul'tura. Iazyk*, 449–57.

128. For more on Tribetskoi's life in the 1930s, see Liberman, "Postscript," 316–337; Toman, *The Magic of a Common Language*, 207–11.

129. P. N. Savitskii, "Velikorossiia i Ukraina v russkoi kul'tury," in Savitskii, *Nauchnye zadachi evraziistva*, 89–93, originally published in *Rodnoe slovo* 1926, no. 8, 10–14.

130. See the essays collected and published in Savitskii, *Nauchnye zadachi evraziistva*, whose editors stress his philosophical and cultural contributions to Eurasianism: Ermishina, "Petr Nikolaevich Savitskii: zhiznennyi i tvorcheskii put'," 7–8.

with publications elaborating his geographical description of Eurasia as a "continent." Frequently Savitskii combined his scientific and spiritual commitments, as in his essay on the dissident priest Avvakum, exiled to Siberia in the seventeenth century.[131] Both Savitski's rehabilitation of the "old belief" variant on Orthodoxy and his pathbreaking work in environmental studies would find a place in latter-day Eurasianism (chapter 4).

In the late 1930s, Eurasianism vanished into the graves and camps of Nazi terror and Stalin's Russia or sublimed into artistry and historical scholarship in the "west." Savitskii survived the war working as the principal of the Russian gymnasium in Prague, only to be arrested by the Soviets in 1945. He spent ten years in the Gulag, returned to communist Czechoslovakia, was arrested again in 1961, and put back in Soviet labor camps. He was released in 1964, and died in 1968.[132] This turned out not to be the end of the Eurasian story, but let us point out some salient qualities of its dramatic beginning.

The early twentieth-century version of Eurasianism broke out of what Trubetskoi would call the Romano-Germans' purported universalism. *Europe and Humanity* was a seminal critique of Eurocentrism—in politics, in scholarship, and in society. It was likewise a harsh indictment of imperialism: the imposition of European culture would divide colonized societies and these divisions would destroy any chance of catching up with the colonizers. Savitskii pushed Trubetskoi's negation of European achievements in a positive direction: the counter to European domination was not an idealized humanity, but Eurasianism with its very real potential for large-scale political organization.

Eurasianism in the 1920s offered a new way of thinking about politics; its proponents emphatically rejected conventional nationalism. Political imagination did not have to be limited to the nation;

---

131. "'Zhitie' protopopa Avvakuma kak geograficheskii pervoistochnik," in Savitskii, *Nauchnye zadachi evraziistva*, 94–105. This article was written in honor of the Russian geographer and botanist G. I. Tanfil'ev, whose studies inspired interest in the "Russian" east.

132. Glebov, *From Empire to Eurasia*, 26–32, 155–60; Ermishina, "Petr Nikolaevich Savitskii: zhiznennyi i tvorcheskii put'," 55–61. Among the other Eurasianists who returned to the USSR was the great literary critic, Prince Sviatopolk-Mirskii, executed in 1939: Gerald Stanton Smith, *D.S. Mirsky. A Russian-English Life, 1890–1939* (Oxford, UK: Oxford University Press, 2000), 295–96.

political loyalty was not reserved for those who think and speak alike. Instead, people could find satisfaction in a great overarching polity that recognized unlikeness and celebrated it. National feeling could be both local and transcontinental, and the two could augment each other. The foundation for this vision of a manifold politics was the existence of large geophysical units, where over time peoples had interacted to produce shared, but specific, civilizational conditions. Their past was one of interaction and transformation, not of the fixity of groups. Both history and environment shaped the possibilities for future configurations of allegiance and daily life.

What kinds of possibilities? Trubetskoi's writings analyzed the cultural foundations for expansive affiliation across Eurasia and provocatively lauded the structure and spirit of Chinggis Khan's empire. Savitskii introduced another approach—what he called "geopolitics." Writing from Prague, he emphasized that Russia had better grounds than China to be called "the middle kingdom" of Eurasia. The "geographical structure of Russia-Eurasia" offered the possibility to link and unify people across the landmass. Eurasians with their capacity for "brotherhood" could even draw other peoples—Indo-European, Iranian, East Asian—into a "great new world of the future."[133]

Applied to Eurasia, this transcontinental imaginary rejected European rules, put a positive accent on Asia, and, conveniently for Russia, explained this state's potential to unite and communicate over a wide cultural and economic terrain. After centuries of elite concern about not being sufficiently European, the Eurasianists insisted that Russia was *more* than Europe and that its Asian component was an essential element of its past, present, and future. Eurasianism emerged from the Russian empire's collapse as a civilizational argument, but it could be redirected and transformed, even into a recipe for a new imperialism.

---

133. Petr Savitskii, "Geograficheskie i geopoliticheskie osnovy evraziistva," in Savitskii, *Kontinent Evraziia*, 295, 301–303. According to the editor (p. 457), this text is a translation from a manuscript in the Russian archives; the article had been published in German in *Orient und Occident* 17 (Leipzig, 1934).

CHAPTER TWO

Eurafrica

THE STORY OF EURAFRICA is different from that of Eurasia.[1] It points to cultural complementarity rather than affinity and it is concerned above all with restructuring a political relationship of extreme inequality between Europe and Africa. When the term first appeared in the 1920s, it represented Europe's claim on Africa, an argument that European states, instead of pursuing their rivalry over Africa's material and human resources, should cooperate in rational exploitation of the continent. When the term reappeared in the late 1940s, after the second catastrophic clash of European empires in the twentieth century, its significance changed. By then, the very existence of colonial empires was under threat. Eurafrica reemerged in a specifically French context, aligned with France's

---

1. There is now a substantial literature in French on Eurafrica, including Yves Montarsolo, *L'Eurafrique contrepoint de l'idée de l'Europe: Le cas français de la fin de la deuxième guerre mondiale aux négociations des Traités de Rome* (Aix-en-Provence: Publications de l'Université de Provence, 2010); Guia Migani, *La France et l'Afrique sub-saharienne, 1957–1963: Histoire d'une decolonisation entre idéaux eurafricians et politique de puissance* (Brussels: PIE Peter Lang, 2008); Marie-Thérèse Bitsch and Gérard Bossuat, eds., *L'Europe Unie et l'Afrqiue: de l'idée d'Eurafrique à la Convention de Lomé I* (Brussels: Bruylant, 2005); and Papa Dramé and Samir Saul, "Le Projet d'Eurafrique en France (1946–1960): Quête de puissance ou atavisme colonial?" *Guerres Mondiales et Conflits Contemporains*, 216 (2004): 95–114. The first English-language book on the subject is Peo Hansen and Stefan Jonsson, *Eurafrica: The Untold History of European Integration and Colonialism* (London: Bloomsbury, 2014). It paints a vivid portrait of some of the ideas of Eurafricanists, going back to the early roots of the concept and explains the debates in Europe over Africa's place in the economic integration process, but gives less attention to the African side of the picture.

interest in European integration while retaining control over its overseas territories.[2] It represented an effort by French and African leaders—with quite different motivations—to devise some kind of post-imperial order that neither preserved colonial rule in its current form nor dissolved the asymmetrical ties of colonizer and colonized into states wholly independent of each other. African elites, well aware of how much the war had weakened the European empires, wanted to turn Europe's claim on Africa into Africa's claim on Europe, into a demand for resources to improve the well-being of African people and, at least as important, for a voice in allocating those resources.

Europe, Africa, and the Reconfiguration of Eurafrica

French leaders in the late 1940s and 1950s looked to Eurafrica to resolve a dilemma. France needed its overseas resources more than ever to boost economic recovery, and French leaders also wanted to transform France's relationship with its European neighbors, most importantly its long-time enemy, Germany. Whether the country had the means to accomplish either objective was not apparent to the more thoughtful members of its political elite. France quickly got into a colonial war in Indochina, which it would eventually lose, and it faced challenges from rapidly growing political and social movements in North and sub-Saharan Africa and the Caribbean. Its African colonies—mostly dating to the late nineteenth century (parts of Senegal to the seventeenth)—took on new importance as control over southeast Asian territories was threatened. Eurafrica promised to be the solution to France's double ambition by bringing its African colonies into whatever form of European community could be devised.

Meanwhile, political activists in sub-Saharan French Africa were achieving some success in their demands for political and civil rights as well as development programs within the imperial system. As France reconstituted itself after the war, renewing its claim to the ideals of republican governance, it gave up the invidious

2. Great Britain kept its distance from negotiations on European integration in the 1940s and 1950s, and only joined the European Economic Community in 1973. British elites had their own ideas about connections to other parts of the world, focused on the Commonwealth, as discussed in the introduction to this book.

distinction in its overseas territories between French citizens, who had rights, and French subjects, who lacked those rights but were told they were *French* and should not dream of being anything else. Whether Africans could turn citizenship rights into an effective capacity to make claims on behalf of all French citizens or whether elites in metropolitan France could control and limit the implications of a more inclusive version of empire was very much in question in the years after the war.

When, in 1948, African leaders became aware that the French government was talking with its neighbors about the possibility of political integration in Europe, they faced the possibility that their newly won gains in the French system might be submerged in a larger European political body. The issue could be resolved only if Africans could exercise voice in whatever institutional entity France could negotiate with its European partners.

The reconfigured idea of Eurafrica thus emerged from a convergence of different goals and imaginaries in the years after World War II. But we need to step back to examine how European and African elites first envisioned the possibilities for their future relations. Intellectuals on both sides of the Mediterranean shared a starting perspective with Eurasianists: they were looking beyond national boxes.

The European intellectuals who first used the term Eurafrica were thinking within a frankly colonialist framework: European mastery of technique and management through inter-empire cooperation would combine with African raw materials and raw labor power. One of the more ambitious projects came from an intriguing figure, Richard von Coudenhove-Kalergi, of Austrian, Greek, and Japanese ancestry, with claims to noble titles. In a book published in 1923, he looked to a world divided into five regional blocs, each exercising some kind of federal authority standing above the individual countries. One of these blocs he called "Pan-Europa," but it was in fact Eurafrica, since it took the colonies of Africa to be an annex of Europe.[3]

---

3. Richard von Coudenhove-Kalergi, *Pan-Europa* (Vienna: Pan-Europa Verlag, 1923); Richard Coudenhove-Kalergi, "The Pan-European Outlook," *International Affairs* 10 (1931): 638–51; Hansen and Jonnson, *Eurafrica*.

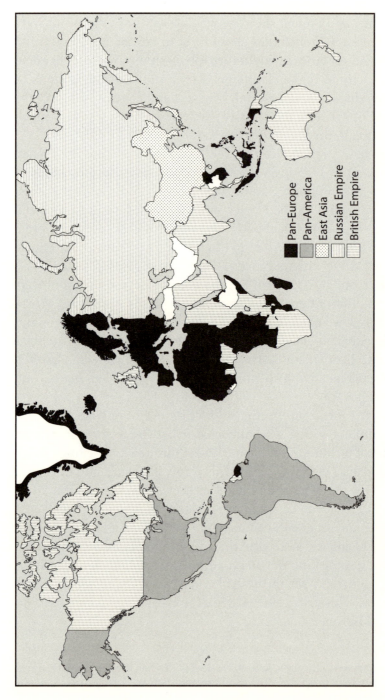

MAP 2.1. World regions, after Richard von Coudenhove-Kalergi's division of the world into blocs, 1923

Thorsten Botz-Bornstein has compared Coudenhove's perspective to that of Trubetskoi.⁴ They shared a distrust of nationalism and a willingness to devise new ways of thinking about political affinity. But while Trubetskoi thought of Eurasia as a complex cultural mosaic set against western Europe, Coudenhove had no interest in African culture. His idea was for Eurafrica to be an autarkic space, surrounded by a customs wall. He favored a kind of "supranationalism" in which Europe would act as "one big nation." Eurafrica would be a "joint project of the white race," a cooperative and systematic effort to extract mineral and agricultural resources for the benefit of Europe. Some European elites took up Coudenhove's conception as a counterweight to the United States, whose large size and rich resources made it a threat to Europe's economic status.⁵ Coudenhove's Pan-Europa had no place for the Soviet Union and in some ways anticipated long-term tensions between western Europe and Russia over the territories in between.⁶

The spirit of 1930s Eurafrica was captured in the title of a book by one of its French apostles, Eugène Léonard Guernier: *L'Afrique: Champ d'expansion de l'Europe* (Africa: Europe's Field of Expansion). Guernier envisioned the migration of 15–20 million Europeans to Africa, bringing about peace and prosperity. Similar arguments

---

4. Thorsten Botz-Bornstein, "European Transfigurations—Eurafrica and Eurasia: Coudenhove and Trubetskoi Revisited," *European Legacy* 12, 5 (2007): 565–75. Coudenhove-Kalergi is remembered more for his influence on European integration than for his ideas about Eurafrica. Richard Nicolaus Coudenhove-Kalergi, *Eine Idee erobert Europa, meine Lebenserinnerungen* (Munich: K. Desch, 1958); Fondation Charles de Gaulle, *Coudenhove-Kalergi, De Gaulle, Une certaine idée de l'Europe* (Colloquium held in Nancy, November 14, 1998), Cahier de la Fondation Charles de Gaulle, no. 6 (1999).

5. Sven Beckert, "American Danger: United States Empire, Eurafrica, and the Territorialization of Industrial Capitalism, 1870–1950," *American Historical Review* 122, 4 (2017): 1137–70, 1162 quoted; Botz-Bornstein, "European Transfigurations," 571.

6. Coudenhove-Kalergi, "The Pan-European Outlook," 649–50. Coudenhove's article (640) also refers to the plan presented to the League of Nations—but not adopted—by French statesman Aristide Briand for a "European Union." British statesman Leo Amery was also thinking about a European "bloc" with which the British Empire could have cooperative relations, and his positive commentary on Coudenhove's proposals are included in the published version (644–46, 650–51). On the importance of this line of thinking, see Katherine Sorrels, *Cosmopolitan Outsiders: Imperial Inclusion, National Exclusion, and the Pan-European Idea, 1900–1930* (New York: Palgrave Macmillan, 2016).

were advanced by Georges Valois in *Notes sur l'Afrique, chantier de l'Europe* (Notes on Africa, Europe's Workshop).[7]

Eurafrica at this time was a Eurocentric concept, a call for cooperation in exploitation. Relatively liberal European elites as well as Nazis, and especially Mussolini, saw something for themselves in Eurafrica. During the war, France's collaborationist Vichy regime also found Eurafrica an attractive idea. It appealed to the right's conviction of the superiority of European society as well as to the possibility of developing a rational organization of economic relations; it appealed to some on the left who hoped to fashion a European entity with the raw materials and manpower resources essential to standing up to the United States.[8] Throughout the interwar period and wartime, details of what Eurafrica would be were vague and common institutions were not developed, although elites from the different European powers did talk to each other and exchange information about their strategies and practices.[9]

This kind of thinking complicates viewing twentieth-century Europe through the prism of nationalist politics. So too does the development of institutions intended to foster international—or inter-empire—cooperation, including the League of Nations and the International Labour Office, as well as informal contacts among colonial administrators, business elites, and missionary societies. In their own ways, fascists, communists, socialists, and liberals looked beyond their borders for advancing political causes and economic interests, whether to sustain the world order as it stood or to advance alternatives to it. Both world wars led to internationalist initiatives in reaction to the devastation the wars brought about.[10]

---

7. Eugène Léonard Guernier, *L'Afrique: Champ d'expansion de l'Europe* (Paris: Colin, 1933); Georges Valois, *Notes sur l'Afrique, chantier de l'Europe* (Brussels: Institut d'économie européenne, 1932); Liliana Ellena, "Political Imagination, Sexuality, and Love in the Eurafrican Debate," *European Review of History* 11, 2 (2004): 241–72.

8. Charles-Robert Ageron, "L'idée d'Eurafrique et le débat franco-allemand de l'entre-deux-guerres," *Revue d'histoire moderne et contemporaine*, 22, 3 (1975): 446–75.

9. Florian Wagner, *Colonial Internationalism and the Governmentality of Empire, 1893-1982* (Cambridge: Cambridge University Press, 2022).

10. Glenda Sluga, *Internationalism in the Age of Nationalism* (Philadelphia: University of Pennsylvania Press, 2013); Glenda Sluga and Patricia Clavin, eds., *Internationalisms: A Twentieth-century History* (Cambridge: Cambridge University Press, 2017); Talbot Imlay, *The Practice of Socialist Internationalism: European Socialists and International Politics, 1914-1960* (New York: Oxford University Press, 2018); Sandrine Kott,

African leaders came to the political give-and-take following World War II with both ambitions and ideas that enabled them to imagine political space in a form that was neither imperial nor national. In this matter, the ideas of Léopold Sédar Senghor bear comparison with those of Trubetzkoi and Coudenhove. Senghor's layered view of political belonging allowed him to envision a future political organization that extended from an intimate community all the way to Eurafrica.

Senghor was born a subject in Senegal in 1906, but became a citizen thanks to his educational attainments and the patronage of officials who recognized his acute intelligence. He completed his studies at the prestigious French university, the Sorbonne, taught at a lycée in France, and was recognized as an accomplished poet in the French language. Along with his fellow writer and political activist from the Antilles, Aimé Césaire, Senghor helped to found during the interwar years the *négritude* movement, a literary and political effort to promote the unity of people of African descent around the world. During the war, he served in the French military and was a prisoner of war of Germany.[11]

Like Trubetskoi—and unlike Coudenhove—Senghor thought a lot about culture, notably what he called "Negro-African" civilization. Both intellectuals were critical of western European pretensions to represent a universal civilization. Whereas Trubetskoi denounced the negative impact of imported European ideas and practices, Senghor emphasized the complementarity of European and African cultures. Senghor remained faithful to basic tenets of the négritude movement throughout the time he was engaged in the nitty-gritty of politics, indeed well after he became president of an independent Senegal in 1960.

Organiser le Monde: Une autre histoire de la guerre froide (Paris: Seuil, 2021); Michele Louro, Carolien Stolte, Heather Streets-Salter, and Sana Tannoury-Karam, eds., *The League Against Imperialism: Lives and Afterlives* (Leiden: Leiden University Press, 2020). The relationship of internationalist thinking and organizing to African-Asian connections will be taken up in chapter 3.

11. On the ideas of Senghor and Césaire, see Gary Wilder, *Freedom Time: Negritude, Decolonization, and the Future of the World* (Durham, NC: Duke University Press, 2015), and Janet Vaillant, *Black, French, and African: A Life of Léopold Sédar Senghor* (Cambridge, MA: Harvard University Press, 1990).

FIGURE 2.1. Portrait of Léopold Sédar Senghor, 1949.
Source: Photo by Felix Man/Picture post/Hulton Archive, Getty Images.

Senghor believed that there was a "Negro culture" (*une culture nègre*), found from the southern edge of the Sahara desert to central Africa and in the African diaspora as well. Africans' "intuitive" way of reasoning differed from the rationalistic or discursive version of Europeans. African social life centered on the family, and family ideals extended in concentric circles to wider groupings, including tribes, kingdoms, and even empires. Senghor is sometimes accused of presenting an essentialized, homogenized vision of African culture, but his vision was not that of a walled-in cultural entity. Africa's civilization was interacting with, shaping, and being shaped by connections with European, Arab-Berber, Chinese, and other civilizations. As such African civilization contributed to the unity of humankind.¹² It is far from clear that Senghor's views of the complementarity of African and European civilizations were accepted by much of the French elite, but his engagement with French political institutions and media helped to promote rethinking of Franco-African connections.

Senghor's relational perspective on civilizations was intertwined with his ideas about political organization. He looked toward a post-colonial France governed, as he wrote in 1945, by an "imperial parliament" in which Africans would be fully represented, giving recognition both to the particularity of each component part and to the unity of the ensemble: "Far from weakening the unity of the Empire, it would solidify it, just as the orchestra conductor would have for his mission, not to stifle, in covering the voices of different instruments with his, but to direct them in unity and to permit the least important country flute to play its role."¹³

Beginning in 1948, Senghor began to delineate two forms of political affinity (as highlighted in the introduction). On the one hand, he described the horizontal solidarity of people who shared geographical space and cultural affinity; this kind of solidarity was the basis for his call for Africans to act together and build Africa-wide institutions. On the other hand, he made clear the importance of the "vertical solidarity" of people linked historically through colonization and who therefore had claims on each other. This conception imbued his argument for a continued relationship of France and Africa. Vertical solidarity implied a frank acknowledgment of

---

12. An extended presentation of Senghor's vision of négritude, written shortly before the war, can be found in his "Ce que l'homme noir apporte," a chapter in a collective book by the group "Présences," with an introduction by Cardinal Verdier, *L'homme de couleur* (Paris: Plon, 1939), 292–314. For some of his postwar thinking along similar lines, see "L'Afrique noire: La civilisation négro-africaine," reprinted from "Les plus beaux écrits de l'Union française et du Maghreb," La Colombe, 1947, in the collection of Senghor's speeches and writings, *Liberté I Négritude et Humanisme* (Paris; Seuil, 1964), 70–82. For his interventions after Senegal's independence, see Senghor's "Francité et Négritude," presentation to Colloque sur la littérature africaine d'expression française, March 26, 1963, in *Liberté III Négritude et civilisation de l'universel* (Paris: Seuil, 1977), 18–22.

13. Senghor, "Vues sur l'Afrique noire, ou assimiler non être assimilé," in Robert Lemaignen, Léopold Sédar Senghor, and Prince Sisonath Youtévong, *La communauté impériale française* (Paris: Alsatia, 1945), 57–98, 58 quoted.

inequality—in wealth, in scientific and technological knowledge, in experience in democratic institutions—but with the goal of making the relationship more equal.[14]

In the midst of intense political activities after the war, Senghor continued to elaborate his concept of solidarity. In 1955, he described different forms of affinity. At the most intimate level was what he called the "petite patrie," a natal community, by which Senghor meant an ethnic group or tribe, such as his own Serer (or the provinces of France). "Nation," in contrast, was a constructed entity, put together by men and women who sought a wider grouping capable of collective action. "State" was the agent that transformed patriotic sentiment into a coherent nation.[15] Having earlier compared "nationalism" to "an old hunting rifle" and looked skeptically at "independence," Senghor thought the twentieth century was characterized by interdependence—including his two forms of solidarity.[16]

Over the 1950s, Senghor gave increasing attention to the task of national construction. It was an *African* nation he wanted to construct, not a Senegalese one. He proposed that political belonging could be given institutional coherence by dividing administrative and political structures into three layers, each of which should have legislative and executive institutions: the individual territory (Senegal, Côte d'Ivoire, Dahomey, etc.), a primary federation (French Africa as a whole, potentially expanding to all of sub-Saharan Africa), and a confederation in which European France and the African federation would join as equals along with any other part of the former French empire that wished to participate. The horizontal strength of the African federation would give it the possibility of using its vertical relationship with the more affluent part of the confederation to push for using resources to promote both equality and recognition of cultural difference. At this time and later, Senghor emphasized the mixture (*métissage*) of African and French

14. One of his earliest expressions of the horizontal-vertical dialectic was in the newspaper he edited, *La Condition Humaine*, July 11, 1948.

15. Léopold Senghor, "Pour une solution fédéraliste," *La Nef* Cahier 9 (June 1955), 148–61. See also Etienne Smith, "'Senghor voulait qu'on soit tous des Senghor': Parcours nostalgiques d'une génération de lettrés," *Vingtième Siècle. Revue d'Histoire* 118 (2013): 87–100.

16. Senghor, "Rapport sur le méthode du Parti," to Congress of Bloc Démocratique Sénégalais, April 15–17, 1949, *La Condition Humaine*, April 26, 1949.

heritages in a polity that would respect the familial ethos of Africa, the democratic institutions of France, and the larger framework of a humanity of multiple civilizations interacting with each other. His views on the layering of sovereignty and governance, linking the petite patrie to a Franco-African confederation, pointed to the possibility of adding another layer: Eurafrica.[17]

Senghor had the unusual capacity of being able both to talk about political principles at a high level of abstraction and, in his role as leader of an African political party and a member of the French National Assembly, to propose specific institutional mechanisms for implementing these ideals. It was possible for him to look beyond colonial empire, beyond his native Senegal, and beyond Africa to entertain the possibility of a Eurafrican connection. In practical terms, Senghor and other African leaders had to make their way through contested political terrains, where the nature of France and Africa, of sovereignty and autonomy, were uncertain.

Beyond Empire in Europe and Africa

World War II shook up the world of empires—not just the empires of the losers—much more decisively than had World War I. France's need to rethink its own imperial system and its relationship to other European empires was particularly acute because of its defeat in 1940 and its subsequent collaboration with the Nazis.[18]

After the Nazi and Japanese regimes fell, France was presented with a challenge and a rare possibility: to remake itself and, along with other states also in the process of renewing themselves, to remake Europe. France faced this challenge weakened by material, moral, and human losses in the war. In Southeast Asia, nationalist and communist forces moved into the vacuum left by the sequence

---

17. Senghor's scalar view of political organization, extending from the petite patrie to Eurafrica, might be compared to Trubetskoi's metaphor of the multistoried house: a Eurasian nation built upon diverse nations. Senghor's nation, unlike Trubetskoi's, would be governed by democratic principles at all levels, so the top story as well as the bottom would be pluralistic.

18. The collaborationist regime controlled the colonies, except for French Equatorial Africa, where one of few colonial officials of color, Félix Éboué, led the region to side with the resistance led by Charles de Gaulle. Eric Jennings, *Free French Africa in World War II: The African Resistance* (New York: Cambridge University Press, 2015).

of French and Japanese defeats. France (like the Netherlands in the Dutch East Indies) tried to recolonize Vietnam, its most lucrative overseas territory, and failed. The possibilities as well as problems of a postwar world were discussed intensively by the French elite, while, on a global scale, diplomats and state officials were considering how to construct international institutions on more solid foundations than those of the League of Nations.

A new but still extended France needed a new name. The term empire had been sullied by the wartime actions of Nazi Germany, Japan, and France's collaborationist regime. Even before deliberations over a new French constitution began in late 1945, the state was renamed the French Union. The concept of union was vague enough to avoid commitment to any political form. Its appeal was the idea of uniting diverse elements, and even anti-communists did not seem to mind its echo of the Union of Soviet Socialist Republics. Colonies were renamed "Overseas Territories." The problem facing the political elite of France was holding the whole thing together.

The French Union combined non-equivalent elements in a complex and uncertain structure. It included European France; Algeria; the Overseas Territories, in turn divided into what had been the "old colonies" mostly in the Caribbean and the "new" ones in Africa and Asia; the protectorates (renamed Associated States) including most of Indochina, Tunisia, and Morocco; and the territories of Togo and Cameroon mandated to France by the League of Nations.

Algeria, like European France, was divided into departments. Its population included both citizens, largely of European origin, who had the same political and civil rights as the citizens of metropolitan France, and subjects, mostly Muslim, who had limited civil rights and participated only in local elections of minor significance. Like Algeria, the "new" Overseas Territories were considered part of the French Republic, but the overwhelming majority of their inhabitants were subjects without political rights.[19] Unlike Algeria, where

---

19. Among recent entries into the large literature on Algeria, of particular relevance to the present study are Megan Brown, *The Seventh Member State: Algeria, France, and the European Community* (Cambridge, MA: Harvard University Press, 2022), and Muriam Haleh Davis, *Markets of Civilization: Islam and Racial Capitalism in Algeria* (Durham, NC: Duke University Press, 2022).

settlers had considerable power, and a few cities that had elected local councils, territorial administration in sub-Saharan Africa was largely in the hands of the appointees of the ministry in Paris, with almost no role for democratic governance.

In 1946, the former old colonies—Guadeloupe, Martinique, Guyana, and Réunion—whose inhabitants had been citizens since 1848—were given the status of Overseas Departments, supposedly equivalent to that of the departments that made up European France, although the actual conditions of governance came up well short of equality.[20] Protectorates had been acquired by treaty (however imbalanced the power relations behind the treaty), and they retained their formal nationality and sovereignty and in some cases their hereditary monarchs. The mandated territories had been nominally under League (later United Nations) supervision, but in most respects were governed like colonies.

Like other imperial polities, the French Union was a complex structure in which different components were governed differently. Since the advent of the Third Republic in 1870, some pesky politicians in France—as well as activists in Algeria, the colonies, protectorates, and mandates—had raised the question of whether republican principles demanded that anyone considered French or under French rule be treated equally. That was not the way of empire, and despite periodic questioning, the norms and practices of unequal rights held sway throughout the Third Republic.

But after the war, a new republic was born. It required a constitution and hence debate over the nature of the new polity.[21] This discussion took place in a political institution whose name echoed that used by the people who wrote the constitutions of the first

---

20. Silyane Larcher, *L'autre citoyen: L'idéal républicain et les Antilles après l'esclavage* (Paris: Colin, 2014); Kristen Stromberg Childers, *Seeking Imperialism's Embrace: National Identity, Decolonization, and Assimilation in the French Caribbean* (New York: Oxford University Press, 2016); Yarimar Bonilla, *Non-Sovereign Futures: French Caribbean Politics in the Wake of Disenchantment* (Chicago: University of Chicago Press, 2015). Other French territories, mainly islands in the Pacific, Atlantic, and Indian Oceans, later acquired departmental status.

21. This and the following paragraphs are based on Frederick Cooper, *Citizenship between Empire and Nation: Remaking France and French Africa, 1945–1960* (Princeton, NJ: Princeton University Press, 2014).

republic of the 1790s, the National Constituent Assembly (Assemblée nationale constituante).

The debates in the assembly and the opinions expressed by jurists and others revealed a basic uncertainty. What exactly constituted the state and where was sovereignty located? Some participants in the debates asserted that France did not *have* an empire. It *was* an empire. The state was the entire entity—not just European France— and its component parts could be reconfigured in the interests of the whole.[22] The National Constituent Assembly included a small number of deputies, among them a handful from Africa and a few Muslim Algerians, who were elected not by citizens, but by subjects voting in a separate electoral college with a limited franchise. Despite jurists' arguments that the status of protectorates could only be regulated by treaty, the politicians in the assembly and officials in the ministries were intent on organizing the whole polity via a constitution.

The new constitution has been discussed at length elsewhere; here we highlight its results and some of the conceptual schemes that were in question.[23] The preamble to the constitution declared that the French Union consisted of "nations and peoples," in the plural. All the inhabitants of the Overseas Territories and Algeria were declared to be citizens of the French Republic, but the National Assembly would later decide how they would participate in the electoral process. They would be represented in the National Assembly. The protectorates, rebaptized "Associated States," would be part of the French Union but not the Republic and would not be represented in the National Assembly.

Even before the constitutional drafting began, the possibility that empire could give way to federalism was on the table. The word federation had been used (or abused) before: French West Africa and French Equatorial Africa were referred to as federations because they consolidated different colonies, even though they were only administrative units. The federal model seemed to

---

22. For the way an influential member of the colonial establishment thought about empire at the end of the war, see Robert Delavignette, "L'Union française à l'échelle du Monde, à la mesure de l'homme," *Esprit* 112 (July 1945): 214–36. Others advanced a similar conception of France as empire. See Brown, *Seventh Member State*, 39.

23. Cooper, *Citizenship between Empire and Nation*.

offer a solution in Indochina, where Ho Chi Minh had proclaimed a republic of Vietnam in September 1945. Until the situation degenerated, French officials thought Vietnam, along with Laos and Cambodia, could be part of a Federation of Indochina, with some measure of self-government for each component part, all folded into the French Union.[24]

Officials of the British and Dutch empires also considered federation—in the Dutch East Indies or British Malaya for instance—as a means of reaffirming the incorporation of diverse societies into an overarching Dutch or British political entity, allowing for a measure of controlled autonomy and partial democratization—a concept partway between an imperial and a post-imperial polity. These plans raised the possibility that empire could be made a little less colonial, accommodating a degree of political participation by colonized people without the metropole giving up its power over the ensemble.[25]

In France at the beginning of the constitution writing process, two influential leaders argued for a federalist route out of empire. One was Charles de Gaulle, hero of the resistance to Nazi Germany and head of the government until he quit in a huff over not getting his way on the structure of political institutions. De Gaulle's federalism was muscular, acknowledging the diversity of what had been the French empire, retaining most power and all claims to sovereignty at the center while allowing institutions in each territory to have political voice and autonomy over a limited range of internal questions.

The other leading advocate of federalism was Léopold Sédar Senghor, elected in the fall of 1945 as a deputy to the National

---

24. Vietnam itself had three components, the protectorates of Tonkin and Annam and the colony of Cochinchina, but after World War II it was treated as a single Associated State. On the descent into war, see Christopher Goscha, *The Road to Dien Bien Phu: A History of the First War for Vietnam* (Princeton, NJ: Princeton University Press, 2022).

25. Jennifer Foray, "A Unified Empire of Equal Parts: The Dutch Commonwealth Schemes of the 1920s–1940s," *Journal of Imperial and Commonwealth History* 41, 2 (2013): 259–84; Michael Collins, "Decolonisation and the 'Federal Moment'," *Diplomacy and Statecraft* 24, 1 (2013): 21–40. Or Rosenboim points to a variety of federalist visions circulating in Europe at the end of World War II, but they did not necessarily address the problem of the colonized world. *The Emergence of Globalism: Visions of World Order in Britain and the United States, 1939–1950* (Princeton, NJ: Princeton University Press, 2017).

Constituent Assembly by the noncitizen electors of Senegal in a vote limited to a couple of thousand people. Senghor's federalism was at the other end of the spectrum from de Gaulle's. He sought a high degree of autonomy for each territory and equal participation of those territories in the institutions of the French Union. The foundation of this version of post-imperial federalism was citizenship: all inhabitants of overseas France would have the rights of the citizen, just as the inhabitants of Provence or Brittany had within the historic Republic. Moreover, Senghor and the other deputies from Africa thought that the overseas citizens should be able to exercise these rights without having to come under the French Civil Code. Citizens could continue to regulate affairs of marriage, filiation, and inheritance under the regulations of personal status of their own society—Islamic law for Muslims, what was called customary law for other Africans. In Senghor's conception, a post-imperial federal France would be both multicultural and egalitarian.

These proposals aroused fierce opposition both from deputies who could not imagine people who were culturally different acting as citizens and from defenders of business interests who feared reform. The debates in the assembly were strenuous and heated. The outcome was a compromise that gestured to federalism without its substance, but which included the bottom-line demand of the deputies from the colonies who would otherwise have opposed the constitution. The category of subject was abolished. All inhabitants of the Overseas Territories (as well as Algeria) obtained the quality of citizen of the French Republic. Inhabitants of the associated states, on the grounds that they had their own nationalities, did not become citizens of the French Republic but of the French Union, a status whose significance was unclear to most people concerned.[26]

Real power remained in the hands of the National Assembly in Paris, in which the former colonies would be represented but not

---

26. Pierre Lampué, "La citoyenneté de l'Union française," *Revue Juridique et Politique de l'Union Française* 4 (1950): 305–36. The people of the French mandates in Africa—Togo and Cameroon—were unlike those of the overseas territories not considered French nationals and for this reason should not, in theory, have been represented in the National Assembly. They were, however, allowed to elect representatives on the grounds that in establishing the mandates the League of Nations (taken over by the United Nations) had insisted that their inhabitants should be treated as well as those of colonies.

in proportion to their population. That assembly would be charged with passing laws to determine voting rights; the new citizenship remained a diminished one until universal suffrage was implemented in sub-Saharan French Africa a decade later. The National Assembly could decide the powers to be entrusted to legislative assemblies in each territory and whether the territories in any region—French West Africa for instance—could federate among themselves. The principal gesture to post-imperial federalism was the creation of the Assembly of the French Union (Assemblée de l'Union française), in which half the members came from the different categories of overseas France, half from the metropole. That assembly had no legislative power itself, but the National Assembly was obliged to consult it on matters concerning overseas France. The institutions of the Fourth Republic were neither federal nor egalitarian, and they did not put an end to cultural denigration or racial discrimination. But as citizens, French Africans had gained a platform from which to make demands.

For Senghor and his allies, the battle for post-imperial federalism had only begun. They aimed to fulfill the promise of citizenship first by expanding voting rights to universal suffrage, then by devolving more powers to elected legislatures in the territories and giving real decision-making authority to the Assembly of the French Union. The deputies from Africa in the National Assembly were often a frustrated minority, but wiser heads among metropolitan politicians realized that on some matters the Africans' acquiescence was necessary to give the French government any legitimacy overseas. The wars in Vietnam (1946–54) and Algeria (1954–62) underscored the dangers of closing off ways to make African interests and desires part of the political process. So too did the largely peaceful but nonetheless militant mobilizations in the African territories—workers and trade unions for equal pay and benefits, ex-soldiers for equal treatment and payments, the earliest women's organizations for gender equality.[27] In this context, Senghor continued to elaborate his federalist concept into specific institutional proposals for restructuring the French

---

27. Frederick Cooper, *Decolonization and African Society: The Labor Question in French and British Africa* (Cambridge: Cambridge University Press, 1996); Gregory Mann, *Native Sons: West African Veterans and France in the Twentieth Century* (Durham, NC: Duke University Press, 2006); Emmanuelle Bouilly and Ophélie Rillon, eds., "Femmes africaines et mobilisations collectives (années 1940–1970)," special issue of *Le Mouvement*

Union in ways that would promote both equality and recognition of the diversity of its composition.

In Algeria, settlers, with their connections to the military, the civil administration, and the metropolitan political parties, used their citizenship rights to ensure that Muslim Algerians could not exercise theirs. Whatever possibilities had existed for meeting the aspirations of the Algerian people within the French Union were lost, putting Algeria on the path to violent confrontation.[28] In sub-Saharan Africa, there was more room to maneuver. Almost all major political parties in sub-Saharan French Africa, up to 1957, made their claims within the framework of the French Union rather than seeking independence.[29]

A salient component of African claim-making concerned labor. Trade unionists as well as political leaders argued from 1946 onward that as citizens Africans were entitled to equal pay for equal work and to the same social protections as other citizens. In metropolitan France, benefits were in those years being consolidated into what came to be considered social entitlements: pensions, family allowances, paid vacations, and accident insurance, as well as access to medical care and education. Overseas, the major achievement of the movement for social citizenship was the Labor Code, passed by the National Assembly in 1952. The Code treated wage workers in regular employment in the overseas territories on the same basis as workers of metropolitan origin. The extension of the labor code and later family allowances overseas alarmed politicians on the right and center of French politics; these policies opened up the possibility of a welfare state on an imperial scale

---

Social 255 (2016); Pascale Barthélémy, *Sororité et colonialisme: Françaises et Africaines au temps de la guerre froide (1944-1962)* (Paris: Editions de la Sorbonne, 2022).

28. On the ways in which the French government tried to reconceptualize the place of Algeria in the polity over the course of the Algerian war, see Todd Shepard, *The Invention of Decolonization: The Algerian War and the Remaking of France* (Ithaca, NY: Cornell University Press, 2006).

29. The notable exception before 1957 was the Union des Populations du Cameroun, which became increasingly radical in the late 1940s and demanded independence. It was driven underground by the French administration and carried out a guerilla effort that was kept in check. France eventually accepted that Cameroon would become independent under the rule of a political party more compliant to French wishes. See Meredith Terretta, *Nation of Outlaws, State of Violence: Nationalism, Grassfields Tradition, and State Building in Cameroon* (Athens: Ohio University Press, 2014).

whose cost—given the poverty and relatively low productivity of the African territories—could drag down the French economy.

One response of French leaders to this problem was to advocate sharing the burden of financing economic development in Africa with European partners; this idea, as we shall see, was a major motivation behind the later push for Eurafrica. At the same time, escalating social costs led to a shift in thinking about the relationship of France and Africa, which up to this point had been characterized by the French tendency toward political centralization. French leaders from the center-left to the center-right began to think that the only way to get African political and social movements to move away from their claims to economic and social equivalence among all citizens was to devolve power to political actors in the territories—a policy that became known as "territorialization."

Territorialization was the key element in the *loi cadre*—"framework law"—of 1956. This law instituted universal suffrage for all citizens in French Africa and provided that elected governments—territory by territory—would control their own budgets, including responsibility for the civil service, whose cost had become one of the main concerns of French leaders. The law was a victory for African political leaders who had sought, ever since the constitution of 1946, to put meaningful political power in the hands of elected governments in African territories and to ensure that all citizens in Africa, like those of European France, had the right to vote. But this victory came at a high cost: crystallizing power at the territorial level raised the stakes for political parties to mobilize voters at the level of the individual territory, thus creating obstacles to Africans uniting on a larger scale. Senghor referred to this process as the "Balkanization" of Africa, an allusion to an earlier post-imperial trajectory that had carved weak and sometimes antagonistic states out of the Ottoman and Austro-Hungarian empires.

In the early and mid-1950s, the costs of maintaining a socially egalitarian empire were being questioned in confidential reports within the French bureaucracy and in public.[30] An incisive version

---

30. Particularly influential in questioning whether maintaining empire was worth the costs was Raymond Cartier, "En France noire avec Raymond Cartier," *Paris-Match* 383 (August 11, 1956): 38–41, 384 (August 18, 1946): 34–37, and 386 (September 1, 1956): 39–41.

of the argument came before the National Assembly from one of the principal authors of the *loi cadre*, Pierre-Henri Teitgen:

> Whether you like it or not, whether you think they are right or wrong, in fact, when you speak of assimilation to our compatriots in the overseas territories, they understand it, first and foremost, as economic and social assimilation and assimilation in regard to standard of living. And if you say to them that France wants to realize assimilation overseas, they reply: Well, give us immediately equality in wages, equality in labor legislation, in social security benefits, equality in family allowances, in brief, equality in standard of living.
>
> . . .
>
> Attaining this goal would require that the totality of French people accept a decrease of their standard of living by 25 to 30 per cent for the benefit of their compatriots of the overseas territories.[31]

A goal of the *loi cadre* was precisely to blunt the momentum for equalizing the standard of living between overseas and metropolitan France. As the largest employer of wage labor (rather than of family farmers and other non-waged workers), the civil service was at the heart of the labor question in French Africa. By making the civil service a responsibility of the elected government in each African territory, the law would confront African politicians with the requirement of asking their own voters to pay more taxes to improve the wages and benefits of civil servants. Similar arguments could be made about the costs of education or medical care. The principle of equal citizenship across the French Union was not being questioned, but the implementation of such policies was

---

31. Assemblée Nationale, *Débats*, March 20, 1956, 1072–73. One need not take Teitgen's figures literally, but his point is clear. Denis Cogneau has shown that the French empire—including its African components—was not much of a burden on the French taxpayer up to 1945, largely because the government was able to make Africans pay the costs of their own exploitation. But after 1945, funding of development costs, paying higher salaries to a larger civil service, and responding to African trade unions' demands for more equal pay made for a quite significant increase in the metropole's expenditures. Military costs, especially for the wars in Vietnam and Algeria, climbed rapidly. These expenditures were still not a large percentage of the French GNP, but the direction and rate of change suggested ever-growing expenses for the future. *Un empire bon marché: Histoire et économie politique de la colonisation française, XIXe–XXIe siècle* (Paris: Seuil, 2023), 414–16.

being shifted in the direction of the territories, with their unequal resources and delicate political situations.[32]

The *loi cadre* went into effect in the summer of 1956, while French officials were negotiating with their would-be partners in re-making Europe and simultaneously escalating efforts to repress revolution in Algeria. French policy in the mid-1950s turned in two directions: toward devolving a measure of power and responsibility away from Paris and toward the African territories, and toward sharing African markets as well as the burden of promoting economic development with European partners. Having at the end of World War II attempted to hold the empire together by tying Africans into a web of citizenship, the French government was now trying to lessen the costs of their social inclusion. Eurafrica seemed to offer a way to diffuse that burden without abandoning the effort to maintain the integration of former subjects into a reconfigured polity that would remain, in at least some ways, French.

Eurafrica in a Post-Imperial World?

When conversations among France, Germany, Belgium, the Netherlands, Luxembourg, and Italy (at times including Great Britain) about Europe's future began in 1948, French politicians had to consider Europe in relation to Africa. After the transformations that had turned the French empire into the French Union, Eurafrica could no longer be considered in the same terms as before the war. Some referred to "Young Eurafrica."[33]

Old Eurafricanists were still around after the war, including Guernier himself, who participated in a number of associations and

---

32. These issues are discussed extensively in Cooper, *Decolonization and African Society*, and *Citizenship between Empire and Nation*.

33. Luisa Claire Rice, "Reframing Imperialism: France, West Africa, and Colonial Culture in the Era of Decolonization, 1944–1968," PhD dissertation, Rutgers University, 2006, 20–34. Rice points out that "Eurafrican" had a second meaning: people of mixed race. They too had their associations, concerned more with issues of personal status and discrimination than with economic relations, but the two Eurafricas overlapped in their concern with linkages across lines of difference. See also Owen White, *Children of the French Empire: Miscegenation and Colonial Society in French West Africa, 1895–1960* (Oxford: Oxford University Press, 1999), and Rachel Jean-Baptiste, *Multiracial Identities in Colonial French Africa: Race, Childhood and Citizenship* (Cambridge: Cambridge University Press, 2023).

argued as before for a more cooperative and rational exploitation of the African continent.³⁴ Similar arguments came from an influential official who had served in North Africa, Eirik Labonne, who had been advocating European economic interests in Africa since the 1930s, and proposed, as a counselor to the French president in 1950, the creation of "zones of African industrial organization." Labonne made a Eurasian comparison, arguing that "for the French Union, for the European Union, the Atlas Mountains should be our Ural and Africa our Siberia." Over the next few years, several books and influential journals took up the theme of Europe's need for Africa, expressed most crassly in the 1955 book of Pierre Nord, *L'Eurafrique, notre dernière chance* (Eurafrica, our last chance).³⁵

Meanwhile, the question of European political and economic integration was getting attention in high places. Although there is a tendency to write the history of constructing Europe along an upward trajectory from the European Coal and Steel Community (ECSC) of 1951 through the Common Market of 1958 to the European Union of 1993, there was a strong movement for political—not just economic—integration in the late 1940s. The ECSC represented a scaling back of ambitions in the face of disagreements over the extent and form of supranational institutions.

No less a figure than Winston Churchill in a speech in Zurich in 1946 broached the possibility of creating a "United States of Europe," admitting that he was building on the notion of "Pan-Europa," which "owes so much to Count Coudenhove-Kalergi." His Europe might include a "common citizenship." Including Germany within this structure was, he thought, particularly important to insuring peace. Churchill's proposal contributed to a conservative "Europeanism."³⁶

---

34. Rice, "Reframing Imperialism," 24.

35. Eirik Labonne, 1948, cited in Hansen and Jonsson, *Eurafrica*, 98; Pierre Nord, *L'Eurafrique, notre dernière chance* (Paris: Arthème Fayard, 1955). On this current, see Thomas Deltombe, "'Eurafrique', ou comment penser le colonialisme du futur," in Thomas Borrel, Amzat Boukari-Yabara, Benoît Collombat, and Thomas Deltombe, eds., *L'Empire qui ne veut pas mourir. Une histoire de la Françafrique* (Paris: Seuil, 2021), 93–104. Deltombe calls Eirik Labonne the "prophet of Eurafrica." Ibid., 105–107.

36. Winston Churchill, speech at University of Zurich, "The Tragedy of Europe," September 19, 1946, on website "Churchill in Zürich," https://www.churchill-in-zurich.ch/en/churchill/en-churchills-zurcher-rede/, accessed February 17, 2023. On Churchill and

The French Socialist party after the war hoped to see a federal, socialist Europe. One of its most important leaders, Guy Mollet, who would become a key actor in the story of Eurafrica in the mid-1950s, argued strongly in 1948 for the development of federal institutions for Europe, even if this meant abandoning some elements of French sovereignty. There was German support for these ideas, but opposition from the Labour Party then in control of the British government. In 1948, socialists from different countries and continents organized a "Congress of European, Asiatic and African Peoples" in Paris, attended by some 300 people. It had little impact and socialist internationalism was weakened by arguments over whether to give priority to socialist transformation or to liberation from colonial rule.[37]

This opening to federal institutions governing Europe inevitably posed the question of the colonies held by European powers. On the left were organizations like the Socialist Movement for a United States of Europe, which linked up with critics of colonialism to advocate internationalist alternatives to a Europe of rival empires. On the right, well-established business interests had their own vision of Eurafrica, one more like the prewar version with its emphasis on commercial interests and insistence on European control of the project. The European Union of Federalists advocated the inclusion of colonies in European political institutions.[38] Diplomats gingerly explored possible forms of political integration.

---

conservative arguments for Europeanism, see Marco Duranti, *The Conservative Human Rights Revolution: European Identity, Transnational Politics, and the Origins of the European Convention* (Oxford: Oxford University Press, 2017), 96–163.

37. Imlay, *Practice of Socialist Internationalism*, 321–22, 422–27. The most powerful British socialists (in the Labour Party) were rarely more than lukewarm about European integration and considered that they already had a framework for relations with colonies and former colonies—the Commonwealth—although its institutions gave the formerly colonized little if any power over the entity as a whole. Ibid., 346, 432; Philip Murphy, *The Empire's New Clothes: The Myth of the Commonwealth* (Oxford: Oxford University Press, 2018). The input of different organizations to this phase of the debates on European integration may be found in Walter Lipgens and Wilfried Loth, eds., *Documents on the History of European Integration. Vol. 4, Transnational Organizations of Political Parties and Pressure Groups in the Struggle for European Union, 1945–1950* (Berlin: De Gruyter, 1991).

38. Jean-Marie Palayret, "Les mouvements proeuropéens et la question de l'Eurafrique du Congrès de la Haye à la Convention de Yaoundé (1948–1963)," in Bitsch and Bossuat, *L'Europe unie et l'Afrique*, 189–200.

Meanwhile, in the late 1940s, France, Britain, and the Netherlands faced militant anticolonial movements in parts of their empires. The Asian rebellions raised the stakes in Africa, as the one region where a relationship between European states and African territories might be maintained, if enough decision-makers could be convinced that it could be of mutual benefit.

The Eurafrica project took hold during international meetings of leading European politicians in the Hague in May 1948 and in Strasbourg in September 1952, followed by the formation of an "ad hoc" assembly in October. At these venues, diplomats discussed the possibility of forming a "European Union" with decision-making bodies of elected representatives from the states that chose to join. As soon as such possibilities were mentioned—however tentatively—concerns arose among Europeans as well as Africans who feared that Eurafrica might in effect Europeanize—or worse Germanize—France's African territories. Some politicians insisted that preserving the reconfigured French Union should take precedence over European dreams.[39]

By 1949, African leaders were aware that their French compatriots were talking with other European leaders about common institutions. Senghor had to remind the National Assembly that "in terms of the Constitution, the French Republic is not just composed of the metropole, but also of overseas departments and territories." France was not, in short, a European country. On this point, government officials agreed: "France is not a European power. It is a world power."[40] Senghor and most of his African colleagues shared the double goal sought by advocates of European integration: "on the one hand European Union, on the other the French Union," as Senghor put it in 1952.[41]

In the midst of their efforts to turn their citizenship status into a measure of political power within the French Union, African

---

39. On the divergent views at the beginning of the debate, see Montarsolo, *L'Eurafrique*.

40. Senghor, Intervention in Assemblée Nationale, September 18, 1949, reprinted in *Liberté II : Nation et voie africaine du socialisme* (Paris : Seuil, 1971), 60 ; Directeur Général des Affaires Politiques, "Note sur la position des territoires d'outre-mer dans la question de l'intégration européenne," October 14, 1952, K.Afrique 1944–1952/Généralités/ L'Europe et l'Afrique, Archives Diplomatiques, La Courneuve.

41. Assemblée Nationale, *Débats*, January 17, 1952, 260.

political actors did not want to be left out if France ceded a measure of its power to Europe. In 1950, the group of deputies that Senghor headed, the Indépendants d'Outre Mer (Overseas Independents), expressed to the Minister of Overseas France their concern that negotiations over Europe were taking place over their heads and that French African territories risked becoming "an international colony." Instead, they insisted,

> Eurafrica, notably, which we believe to be necessary and possible, should be conceived of only as a form of economic association, freely conceived on the basis of equality, where the present and future interests of Africa will be protected under the same conditions as those of Europe.

Africans did not want their continent to become a "reservoir of primary material and an outlet for [Europe's] excessive production." The Minister replied by claiming that the presence of Africans in the French legislature assured that African interests would be represented and that access to a larger European market would benefit Africa.[42] Senghor was not convinced, asking later in the National Assembly how Africans could believe that the government would "better defend us inside the European political community in our absence?"[43]

Connections—interdependence—could and should be beneficial to Africa, Senghor argued in 1950. Some form of federation—bringing together disparate political units under agreed-upon collective institutions—offered a possible conceptual framework:

> The only efficacious solution thus lies in federation.... In my opinion this federation must be made along two axes of solidarity. On the one hand, vertical solidarity between the overseas peoples and those of Europe on the model of the French Union. On the other hand, horizontal solidarity among the peoples of the same continent.... This is the only chance for Europe and Africa to save themselves, for these

---

42. "Resolution du Groupe Interparlementaire des Indépendants d'Outre-Mer à propos des décisions de la conférence de Londres," enclosed Senghor to Minister, May 16, 1950, and Minister (Jean Letourneau) to Senghor, June 9, 1950, AP 219/3, Archives d'Outre-Mer, Aix-en-Provence (hereafter AOM).

43. Assemblée Nationale, *Débats*, November 18, 1953, 5249.

complementary continents, united by the same destiny, by history and geography. . . . Neither nationalist nor racist, I continue with men of good will the fight for Eurafrica.[44]

Senghor was turning the old idea of Eurafrica around. Eurafrican federal institutions would give Africans a place in which to bring vertical and horizontal solidarities together. The issue was practical, but also civilizational, based on the complementarity between European and African modes of being—the former rationalist, the latter intuitive, in his formulation. The richness of humankind was made up of difference and interdependence. But if cultural difference was a positive feature of humanity, economic difference—between rich and poor, those with access to education and those without it—was dangerous. The difficulty of integrating France's African territories into a European community was also the reason for doing so. The gap between the standard of living on opposite sides of the Mediterranean led to the hope of allocating resources to bring about greater equality and more balanced forms of economic interaction. This was a way to ensure that all people had the resources they needed for their social and cultural fulfillment.[45] The implication of Senghor's long-argued and deeply felt philosophical position was that political mechanisms had to be found to make sure that interdependence benefitted all concerned. As a politician, Senghor had to work out these practicalities.

The integrating dynamic would work to Africa's benefit only if Africans could have their say. European states in the late 1940s and 1950s were trying to bring themselves together economically and politically; Africa had to do the same; and the cause of Africa could best be advanced by Africans exercising political voice, in the French Union and Eurafrica.

Both Senghor's grouping of African political parties, the Indépendants d'Outre-Mer, and the other most important party in French Africa, the Rassemblement Démocratique Africain (African Democratic Assembly), led by Félix Houphouët-Boigny, supported a Eurafrica in which Africans could have their part in decision-making. Opposition to this idea came from youth, student, and

44. *Le Monde*, August 15, 26, 1950.
45. For more detail on Senghor's thinking, see Wilder, *Freedom Time*.

leftist movements, who opposed these parties' advocacy of continued relations with France. Europe was only indirectly an issue.[46] The evidence we have, mainly from elections held during the 1950s, suggests that voters supported the major parties, who advocated close association with France and hence involvement in negotiations of Eurafrica.[47] African political leaders, whether sitting in the Paris legislature or in the capitals of French territories, were confronted with policy-making at multiple levels, but they could draw on their own experience of multilayered politics in their communities, the colonial territories, and the French empire.

Some of Senghor's ideas were shared by Africans generally regarded as more radical than he, notably Sékou Touré of Guinea, who often used the phrase "Franco-African community."[48] Like Senghor, Sékou Touré favored the idea of a primary federation that was African and would join European France as an equal partner in a confederation. On this point, both he and Senghor differed

---

46. On the most important student movement of the 1950s, see Amady Aly Dieng, *Les premiers pas de la Fédération des étudiants d'Afrique noire en France (FEANF) (1950–1955) (de l'Union française à Bandoung)* (Paris: L'Harmattan, 2003), 250–68; Amady Aly Dieng, *Les Grands combats de la Fédération des étudiants d'Afrique noire* (Paris: L'Harmattan, 2009), 28–36; Charles Diané, *Les Grandes heures de la F.E.A.N.F.* (Paris: Editions Chaka, 1990), 83–99, 111–15. The Fédération campaigned for African unity (but against a federal relationship with France) as well as independence and associated itself with the spirit of Bandung without elaborating on the connection. It was only in 1957, aside from Cameroon, that leftist opposition to the major parties crystallized into a political party, the Parti Africain de l'Indépendance.

47. Elizabeth Fink, "Elections and the Politics of Mobilization in the Time of Decolonization: Voting in Postwar French West Africa," PhD dissertation, New York University, 2015; Ruth Schachter Morgenthau, *Political Parties in French-Speaking West Africa* (Oxford: Clarendon Press, 1964). Aristide Zolberg has argued that political parties in West Africa were less the mass mobilizing agents of Leninist dreams than political machines that worked through brokers—trade union leaders, local elites, farmers' organizations, religious leaders—to enroll members and bring out voters. The importance of party leadership was underscored in the referendum on a new French constitution in 1958, in which voters in Guinea backed their leader in voting no and voters in all other territories backed the major party leaders in voting yes. That said, there is increasing evidence of strong party activism in getting new citizens to register to vote and evidence that the intermediaries—unions, women's organizations—could bring pressure on leaders as well as the other way around. Aristide Zolberg, *Creating Political Order: The Party-States of West Africa* (Chicago: Rand McNally, 1966); Elizabeth Schmidt, *Mobilizing the Masses: Gender, Ethnicity, and Class in the Nationalist Movement in Guinea, 1939–1958* (Portsmouth, NH: Heinemann, 2005).

48. For example, *Afrique Nouvelle*, October 1, 1957.

from the other most influential figure of the politics of French West Africa, Félix Houphouët-Boigny of the Côte d'Ivoire. Houphouët-Boigny wanted to omit the middle layer and incorporate each African territory separately into a federation with France, in which the former metropole and the former colonies would all have equal status. The conflict between these two visions of a Franco-African polity became known in the African press as the battle of federation and confederation. The dispute continued throughout the 1950s.[49]

As discussions of European integration moved back and forth between 1950 and 1953, Africans expressed both hopes and fears concerning the extension of their federalist or confederalist aspirations beyond the French Union toward Eurafrica. Senghor in 1952 favored a "realistic" approach, seeing Eurafrica as in part a response to a "Eurasia in fact obedient to the USSR" and a southeast Asia looking to the United States. Europe—and he meant western Europe—could not be brought together without France, but a France of 42 million people (European France) would be in a weaker position among its partners than a France of 88 million, including the human resources of Africa. The French Union could not be subordinated to Europe any more than Europe could be subordinated to the French Union. But he wanted assurance from government leaders that Eurafrica would be "une Eurafrique à la française" and not a "Eurafrika à l'allemande" (French-style Eurafrica vs German style Eurafrica). He and his colleagues were in a position to make claims within French institutions and feared this possibility might be lost in negotiations between French and other European leaders.[50]

Senghor recognized that creating a Eurafrican political entity implied an "abandonment, a transfer of sovereignty." But since

---

49. Cooper, *Citizenship between Empire and Nation*. In most interpretations, confederation is distinguished from federation by the former's recognition of the national status of the component parts. Confederations are organized by treaties, federations by constitutions. As Jean Cohen points out, there is considerable overlap between the two and a range of ways of conjugating partial autonomy and partial unity. Jean Cohen, *Globalization and Sovereignty: Rethinking Legality, Legitimacy, and Constitutionalism* (Cambridge: Cambridge University Press, 2012). The distinction, however, mattered to Senghor, who explicitly distinguished the African federation from the confederation that would include both France and the African federation, and it mattered to Houphouët-Boigny, who advocated a Franco-African federation.

50. Senghor, Assemblée Nationale, *Débats*, January 17, 1953, 260.

under the Constitution sovereignty resided in the French people, and the French people included the citizens of French Africa, French Africans had to be heard in regard to any decisions in regard to Europe. Senghor's take on sovereignty was consistent with his vision of political structure as layered, both within the French Union and potentially between the French Union and Europe.[51]

African advocates of Eurafrica realized that the promises of "development" that the French government had made in 1946 were difficult to realize because of France's own economic weakness. They hoped that a larger economic community would entail more investment, more aid, and larger markets. As Sourou Migan Apithy of Dahomey told the National Assembly, Europe needed Africa, "and reciprocally we know that to attain their full evolution, the countries of Africa need Europe, and that the development of the resources that are found there require the mobilization of powerful financial means that are often more on a European scale than on that of the metropole."[52] But depending on the rules of a common market, Africa might lose the advantages of existing arrangements with France—which provided guaranteed markets for important African products—in exchange for trading advantages with other European states that might not materialize because those states had established relationships with suppliers elsewhere, with Latin America for example.[53]

To protect their interests, Africans therefore had to have a voice in European institutions. The parliamentary group, Indépendants d'Outre-Mer, in 1951 issued a manifesto (building on statements from the previous year) insisting that the entry of French Africa into "an expanded European union ... cannot be imagined without

---

51. Senghor, Assemblée Nationale, *Débats*, November 18, 1953, 5249. He was not so keen on layering beneath the level of Senegal. Initially willing to seek the support of a regional party, he soon insisted on unity in Senegal as it engaged with other territories of French West Africa and the French Union. Séverine Awenengo Dalberto, "Hidden Debates over the Status of the Casamance During the Decolonization Process in Senegal: Regionalism, Territorialism, and Federalism at a Crossroads, 1946–62," *Journal of African History* 61, 1 (2020): 67–88.

52. See the remarks of Sourou Migan Apithy and Abbas Guèye, Assemblée Nationale, *Débats*, November 24, 1953, 5478, 5487.

53. These doubts would become more explicit as the economic propositions became more concrete in the debate over the Common Market in 1957. See below.

the consent of Africans, nor at the price of economic or industrial stagnation of their territories, nor without the active participation of Africa in the advantages of the system." Senghor told the National Assembly in 1952, "Eurafrica will not be built without the consent of Africans."[54] In January 1953, he declared to the Ad Hoc Assembly, one of several inter-European meetings to discuss European integration, that Africans supported the European Community, notably the reconciliation of Germany and France, but that they refused to be "the pages that carry the bride's veil, we refuse to be the wedding presents or the china" of the new household.[55]

Apithy, the deputy from Dahomey, noted how much French Africans had gained by acquiring the rights of the citizen equivalent to those of the French citizens of Europe. He wondered if Europeans outside of France would recognize them. He worried in particular about Belgium, which denied similar rights to its subjects in the Congo.[56] Conversely, as French jurists noted, European integration implied a European "common citizenship" in which Africans would have to be included, giving them rights in all member countries.[57] That such a possibility would be acceptable to France's partners was not self-evident.

The French government faced the reality that there were multiple French voices that would have to be heard.[58] At the Ad Hoc Assembly in January 1953, delegates from French Africa asked for twenty delegates from African territories to be added to the French delegation to the European assembly that was to embody European

54. Statement of IOM at opening of session of Assemblée Nationale, *Débats*, July 6, 1951, 5909; Senghor to Assemblée Nationale, January 17, 1952, 260.

55. Senghor's interventions before Assemblée Ad Hoc chargée d'élaborer un projet de Traité instituant une Communauté Politique Européenne, Strasbourg, January 8–9, 1953, AP 219/3, AOM. Later that year, Senghor worried that French officials were trying to construct "a resolutely European Europe." Speech in Assemblée Nationale, November 18, 1953, cited in *La Condition Humaine*, December 10, 1953. Senghor's rejection of providing the wedding china for the marriage of France and Germany likely took off from the remark from 1950 of Robert Schuman, one of the principal architects of European integration, cited later in this section.

56. Apithy, Assemblée Nationale, *Débats*, November 24, 1953, 5477–78.

57. Juriconsulte of the Ministry of Overseas France, Note pour M. le Directeur des Affaires Politiques, February 9, 1953, AP 219/3, AOM.

58. Directeur des Affaires Politiques, "Note: La République française et la Fédération Européenne," January 28, 1953, AP 219/3, AOM.

political integration; the Ad Hoc Assembly agreed to seven. In principle, the idea of Eurafrica was receiving recognition and given possible institutional substance, but the entire program, European or Eurafrican, was still up in the air.[59]

It is important, if from today's vantage point counterintuitive, to make clear where this project was coming from. It did not derive from an ideal-type, such as the concept of the nation-state. On both sides of the Mediterranean, political elites had for a long time pushed and pulled on the complex and unequal structure of empire to make it suit their interests and ideals.

From the perspective of political activists in different parts of the French empire, earlier episodes of demands entertained and demands rejected underscored both the need for action and the possibility that citizenship could be won within an imperial system. African political parties and social movements had seized the opportunities that followed World War II to demand what amounted to imperial citizenship and then to make claims in the name of the equality of all citizens.[60] Eurafrica represented a scaling upward of this framing, opening new possibilities to Europeans for an expanded space in which to envision economic, social, and political action and to Africans for a larger space in which to lay claim to resources and to political inclusion.

French advocates of European cooperation did not want to be seen as jettisoning Africa in favor of Europe. Some of them saw Eurafrica as a way of extending social democracy over much of the world; others were more interested in Europe's access to Africa's raw materials.[61] Some saw a federal Eurafrica as a rival to the Soviet and American blocs. But some French politicians doubted that France's European partners would be willing to assume their share of the costs of development or that they would be willing to listen to Africans' opinions.[62] Some thought that integrating

59. Montarsolo, *L'Eurafrique*, 117–18.

60. Frederick Cooper, *Citizenship, Inequality, and Difference: Historical Perspectives* (Princeton, NJ: Princeton University Press, 2018), 66–75, 110–20

61. Palayret, "Les mouvements proeuropéens et la question de l'Eurafrique," 193–200, 205.

62. The economist Jacques Lecaillon emphasized that France lacked the means to respond to the "growing demands" of the Overseas Territories. But the thrust of his analysis was that he could not imagine France without the Overseas Territories or Europe without

Africa into Europe would give Africans incentives to remain tied to France; others feared that creating Eurafrica would allow African politicians to cooperate with European politicians whose interests diverged from those of the metropole.[63]

African deputies, discussing the stance the government was to take in negotiations over European integration, pointed to the constitution's clear statement that sovereignty lay in the people, and Africans were among the people. They emphasized the need to maintain the "integrity" of the French Union, which they wanted to preserve even if France became part of a European union. They worried that European integration might transfer control of African territories from the French government, where they had influence and where they were fighting for more, to European institutions in which their voices would not be heard.[64] As Senghor put it, "The best means of defending overseas departments and territories in the European political community is to allow them to be represented there, for in defending themselves, they defend France at the same time."[65]

One of the most influential socialist leaders, future Minister of Overseas France Gaston Defferre, grasped the stakes, telling the National Assembly in 1953, "The exclusion of the overseas countries . . . in the event of the integration of the metropole into a European community could only be considered by the peoples of these countries as an act of discrimination of a colonial, even racial,

---

France. "L'intégration de l'Union française dans l'Union européenne et les enseignements de la théorie économique," *Annales Africaines 1954*, 19–48, 19 quoted.

63. On the arguments coming from politicians in France, see Montarsolo, *L'Eurafrique*, and Migani, *La France et l'Afrique sub-saharienne*.

64. Senghor, November 18, 1953, 5249, Abbas Guèye, November 24, 1953, 5487, and Jean-Hilaire Aubame, Assemblée Nationale, *Débats*, November 27, 1953, 5629–30. Aubame repeated Senghor's image of Africans' refusal to be "the wedding present made to a community constituted without them." Ibid., 5630. See also Senghor, "L'intégration des pays d'outre-mer dans la Communauté européene," *Le Monde*, October 6, 1953. Gaston Monnerville, Senator from Guyana and one of the few people of color in that body, also warned of the dangers of the secession if African territories were not given full voice in Eurafrica. Speech in Brussels, March 1, 1954, 4AG 528, Dossier II, Archives Nationales de France. The argument for inclusion of overseas territories as a requirement of constitutional law was also put forward by the jurist P.-F. Gonidec, "L'Union française et l'Europe," *Union Française et Parlement* 52 (July 1954): 6–10.

65. Senghor, Assemblée Nationale, *Débats*, November 18, 1953, 5249.

character."⁶⁶ A convinced Europeanist, Defferre argued for making the new community more inclusive but less ambitious in its initial goals, focusing on strictly economic goals rather than political unification.

Eurafrica was not the only reason why European leaders opted for a more gradualist approach to integration. Each of the six would-be initial partners (with Great Britain keeping its distance) worried that control of national economies could be in jeopardy, that Germany, or France, might dominate the other partners, and that sharply differentiated tariffs between European partners and the rest of the world could jeopardize relations with the global economy. The first concrete step toward economic integration was the European Coal and Steel Community created by a treaty of 1951 that brought into being a common market for coal and steel, under a joint High Authority, including France, West Germany, Italy, Belgium, the Netherlands, and Luxembourg. Overseas France was not part of the ECSC on the presumption that it did not have such industries.

The ECSC, for all its limitations, looked to greater economic cooperation in the future while fulfilling a political purpose. Common production and marketing of steel, advocates contended, would make it impossible for either France or Germany to threaten each other militarily. It was in this context that the question of Eurafrica continued to be discussed, even as the prospect of a European Union as a political body was for the time being set aside.⁶⁷

When in May 1950 the French Foreign Minister, Robert Schuman, put forth a proposal that became the basis of the ECSC, he included an argument that a stronger European economy would enable the partners "to pursue the realization of one of its essential tasks: the development of the African continent."⁶⁸ Some days later, he seemed to reverse the priorities in an expression that made some

66. Gaston Defferre, Assemblée Nationale, *Débats*, November 17, 1953, 5210–11.
67. On the European side of the story, see for example Michael Sutton, *France and the Construction of Europe, 1944–2007: The Geopolitical Imperative* (Oxford: Berghahn Books, 2011), and Herrick Chapman, *France's Long Reconstruction: In Search of the Modern Republic* (Cambridge, MA: Harvard University Press, 2018).
68. Declaration of May 9, 1950, https://www.robert-schuman.eu/fr/questions-d-europe/0595-la-declaration-du-9-mai-1950, accessed October 21, 2021.

African leaders think that the new Eurafrica wasn't entirely new, telling an audience in Nantes that France could bring to Germany "as a 'dowry' not only its equipment but also the African market."[69]

As we have already seen (and will see again), it was precisely this evocation of Africa as a dowry given by France to Germany that led African leaders to insist that they had to be full participants in decision-making about Eurafrica. Ousmanne Socé Diop, Senator from Senegal, reacted to Schuman's remarks on the ECSC by insisting that what Africans wanted was not to be considered a wedding gift but to be the best man, hence having a seat at the table. Some Algerian leaders objected to the ECSC on the grounds that they were excluded from it. "We don't understand," said the Senator from Algeria Abdennour Tamzali, "why Italy, which provides neither iron nor coal but only labor that competes with ours, is included when Algeria is not."[70]

African politicians working within French institutions were engaging with the project of European economic integration but making clear that they might oppose these measures altogether if they were not satisfied with the way in which Africa was or was not included. When the French legislature considered in the summer of 1954 a treaty creating a European Defense Community to share military responsibilities with European partners, the Dahomean deputy Sourou Migan Apithy objected that the Community would conflict with the constitution's provision for the French Union to pool its resources for its defense. Apithy observed that the treaty writers considered overseas territories as "annexes of the metropole," as if they were being "given as dowry" to France's European partners. For Apithy, the choice between Europe and the French Union was between two systems of layered sovereignty, and when advocates of the defense community termed one of them "European," he assumed they meant what they said.[71]

---

69. "Entre la France et l'Allemagne une rivalité ruineuse doit faire place à l'intérêt commun déclare à Nantes M. Schuman," *Le Monde*, May 2, 1950.

70. Tamzali, Conseil de la République, *Débats*, April 1, 1952, 799. Diop's remarks, made to a meeting of the Conseil d'Europe in Strasbourg in August 1950, are quoted in Brown, *Seventh Member State*, 75–76.

71. Assemblée Nationale, *Débats*, August 29, 1954, 4419–4422. On the relation between the European Defense Community debate and the Algerian war, see Brown, *Seventh Member State*, 81–91.

A number of deputies from European France questioned the defense treaty for related reasons: Europeanizing defense might compromise France's ability to make decisions for the use of force in the territories of the French Union—a subject of acute concern because of active military conflicts in Vietnam and later Algeria and Cameroon. Others were concerned that insuring control over the defense apparatus would mean creating European political institutions that might undermine sovereignty. The National Assembly refused to consider ratifying the European Defense Treaty. Senghor and Apithy were on opposite sides of the vote.[72]

Europe was not about to be constructed overnight. But the flurry of arguments over the French Union and European integration in the early 1950s draws our attention to the two intertwined federalizing ideas, which—together or separately—constituted a historical break with the notion of France as a unitary, sharply bounded state.

A Eurafrican or European Economic Community?

African leaders were intervening in these critical debates at a time of great uncertainty about French institutions and their future reconfigurations. The French government in the early and mid-1950s was trying neither to simply maintain the colonial status quo nor to write off Africa in favor of Europe. It wanted simultaneously to maintain and reform—in a manner it could control—the French Union and develop closer relations with other European countries.[73] France wanted to have its cake and eat it too.

The ideas of civilizational complementarity that Senghor had long been advocating were echoed in different circles in the mid-1950s. A "European Youth Campaign" in 1955, for example, sought to mobilize young people for the cause of European integration,

72. Assemblée Nationale, *Débats*, August 30, 1954, 4471; Brian Shaev, "The Algerian War, European Integration, and the Decolonization of French Socialism," *French Historical Studies* 41 (2018): 76; Renata Dwan, "Jean Monnet and the European Defense Community, 1950–1954," *Cold War History* 1, 3 (2001): 141–60.

73. Gaston Defferre wrote to an official in the Foreign Ministry in May 1956 that France "cannot sacrifice its African vocation for its European vocation." Quoted in Brown, *Seventh Member State*, 115.

and it included an "Overseas Group" with African participation that organized a series of dinner discussions in France about the possibilities of Eurafrica. African Catholics were among those engaged in the debates, some of whom were trying to balance French elites' interest in education, conversion, and assimilation with many Africans' wishes to defend their own cultural practices. French advocates of Eurafrica were encouraged by Senghor's enthusiastic support for the interplay of civilizations; they hoped that Eurafrica would provide an alternative to Pan-African, Pan-Islamic, or Afroasian movements among young Africans. Officials hoped for closer connections with Africa and feared, especially because of the Algerian war, that the cultural and political gap between French citizens in Africa and Europe might be too wide.[74]

Implementation of a Eurafrican—or even a European—program in the mid-1950s was, in any case, not happening quickly. By the mid-1950s, the idea of integrating Europe politically into some kind of federation or confederation had been put on hold and the question was redefined as economic integration, building on the European Coal and Steel Community.

When the possibility of more far-reaching moves toward European economic integration returned, so too did the question of Eurafrica.[75] In 1956, the French government had come under the direction of the socialist Guy Mollet, who had long advocated an internationalist posture for France, open to the idea of building supranational institutions within Europe, including the expansion of the ECSC into a full-fledged common market. The equally internationalist Gaston Defferre, now Minister of Overseas France, persuaded Mollet to make the inclusion of France's overseas territories and departments a condition for France's acceptance of the European Economic Community. Mollet promised that Africa would

---

74. Emily Marker, *Black France, White Europe: Youth, Race, and Belonging in the Postwar Era* (Ithaca, NY: Cornell University Press, 2022); Elizabeth Foster, *African Catholic: Decolonization and the Transformation of the Church* (Cambridge, MA: Harvard University Press, 2019).

75. In the wake of the defeat of the European Defense Community, some proponents of integration reemphasized the economic side of Eurafrica, particularly the contribution that Africa could make to European revival and competition with the United States. Rice, "Reframing Imperialism," 38, 48.

have its place in the new Europe being negotiated with Germany, Italy, Belgium, the Netherlands, and Luxemburg.[76]

Mollet's Eurafrican vision played into his decision to escalate the repression of the revolt in Algeria even though many of his fellow socialists had their doubts about continuing to prosecute the Algerian war begun in 1954. He and some of his colleagues believed that if they could get their would-be partners in the European Economic Community to include Algeria in its purview, they would be recognizing his government's claim that Algeria was and would remain French. Mollet thought a socialist France in a progressive Europe could do more for social progress in Algeria than independence and conversely that including Algeria in Eurafrica would give Algerians a sense of inclusion in a large ensemble of considerable economic promise.[77] The position of Algerian nationalists in regard to Europe was not a simple rejection of everything that was European. The Front de Libération Nationale (FLN), the leading force in the war for independence, wanted nothing to do with the Eurafrica that Mollet had in mind, but it did not believe that the end of French domination would end Algeria's need for economic relations with wealthier states. This position recalls Senghor's vertical solidarity, although Algerian leaders would not have used such an expression. Eurafrica might have its uses for Algerians, not least because it wasn't specifically French.[78]

A significant part of the French political spectrum that favored European integration was also favorable toward Eurafrica. Robert Schuman reversed his earlier skepticism about an inclusive Eurafrica as well as his willingness to offer Africa as a dowry to

76. Mollet's promise (dated December 20, 1956) was conveyed in the statement of Georges Monnet in Assemblée de l'Union française, *Débats*, January 15, 1957, 13. The assembly wanted the overseas departments and territories to be included in the common market. Ibid., January 24, 1957, 58-76, 80-92, 95-107. See also Montarsolo, *L'Eurafrique*, 203-5, and Anne-Laure Ollivier, "Entre Europe et Afrique: Gaston Defferre et les débuts de la construction européenne," *Terrains & Travaux* 8 (2005): 14-33.

77. "What would Algeria amount to by itself?" Mollet asked rhetorically in January 1957. Quoted in Martin Evans, *Algeria: France's Undeclared War* (Oxford: Oxford University Press, 2012), 194. Evans concludes that "no theme was more insistent than 'Eurafrica' in justifying government action in Algeria." Ibid., 195.

78. Indeed, after Algeria gained independence in 1962, it continued to receive aid from the EEC and from France. Brown, *Seventh Member State*; Davis, *Markets of Civilization*, 146-49; Hansen and Jonsson, *Eurafrica*, 182-83.

Germany; he began to advocate Eurafrica rather than a narrowly defined Europe as the unit of economic integration.[79] Writing in January 1957, Schuman called the combination of European and Eurafrican unity "revolutionary." It implied more than providing aid, rather, the "constitution of an economic ensemble, a true association in the interior of which would be practiced reciprocity in benefits in a common politics of development." Any "colonialist exploitation" would be eliminated, and the common market would bring lower import costs and lower production costs for African exports as well as protection for new industries. Europe would help France finance the project. That same year, the influential economist Pierra Moussa published a book that stressed France's contribution to the economic development of Africa but looked beyond France to wider sources of investment and assistance to raise the standard of living of Africa. Schuman and Moussa were recognizing that the cause of economic development in former French territories, where France still had an interest, required cooperation beyond the French state.[80]

The arguments about Eurafrica within France and between France and its would-be partners in Europe in 1956 and early 1957 were occurring amidst multiple crises in the imperial order. In February 1956, shortly after Mollet became Prime Minister, he was confronted in Algiers by a violent demonstration of settlers who feared he would make concessions to the FLN. His worries about the consequences to his fragile political coalition of anything less than a vigorous defense of "Algérie française" and his own convictions in favor of a socialist French Union in which Algeria would remain led him in March to demand and obtain from the National Assembly full power to conduct the war

79. Robert Schuman, "Unité européenne et Eurafrique: Politique révolutionnaire. Aperçu d'ensemble," *Union Française et Parlementaire* 79 (January 1957): 1–3. On Schuman's change from advocating a strictly European Europe to promoting Eurafrica, see Montarsolo, *L'Eurafrique*, 72–73, 228.

80. Pierre Moussa, *Les chances économiques de la communauté Franco-Africaine* (Paris: Librairie Armand Colin, 1957). Another figure (and a friend of Moussa's) who was making related arguments at the time is Alexandre Kojève, whose talk in German of 1957 was recently translated as "Colonialism from a European Perspective," *Interpretation* 29, 1 (2001): 115–30. This was an argument—obviously highly problematic—for a "giving colonialism," through which the vertical relations of colonialism can be transformed into something that was then becoming known as development. For an overview of the history of the development concept and development practices, see Corinna Unger, *International Development: A Postwar History* (London: Bloomsbury, 2018).

in Algeria. This escalation entrenched France in a conflict that gave the FLN no alternative to victory or surrender.[81] Yet in that same month, years of both violence and negotiations ended with the independence of Morocco and Tunisia. That both these territories were Associated States and not an integral part of the French Republic facilitated these outcomes, despite the presence of French settlers in both states and a history that included repressive action by the French state. A territory's status under international law had consequences.[82]

In October 1956 another crisis both reflected and exacerbated the changing nature of imperial power on a global scale. President Gamal Abdel Nasser, who had been part of a group of army officers that seized power in Egypt in 1952, was seeking to give substantive meaning to his country's sovereignty, long compromised by interventions into its financial and foreign affairs by Great Britain and to a lesser extent France. Nasser's decision to nationalize the Suez Canal—a passageway in the midst of Egyptian territory under the control of a foreign corporation and foreign governments—led to the armed intervention in the canal region by Britain and France along with Israel. But the United States—with its capacity to exercise financial imperialism—pressured these countries to abort their invasion, to the great embarrassment of their governments. The Americans' struggle against the communist bloc was not to be compromised by defense of European imperialism.[83]

---

81. Mollet in the mid-1950s was critical of European oppression of Muslims in Algeria, but fearful that independence would mean Muslims would oppress Europeans. Only when decolonization was a fait accompli around 1960 did Mollet accept "more from resignation than from enthusiasm," the right of self-determination. Talbot Imlay, "International Socialism and Decolonization during the 1950s: Competing Rights and the Postcolonial Order," *American Historical Review* 118, 4 (2013): 1105–32, 1125 quoted.

82. For an overview that covers North Africa, see Daniel Rivet, *Le Maghreb à l'épreuve de la colonisation* (Paris: Hachette, 2002), and Muriam Haleh Davis and Thomas Serres, eds., *North Africa and the Making of Europe: Governance, Institutions and Culture* (London: Bloomsbury, 2018). On Morocco, see Adria Lawrence, *Imperial Rule and the Politics of Nationalism: Anti-colonial Protest in the French Empire* (Cambridge: Cambridge University Press, 2013), and Jonathan Wyrtzen, *Making Morocco: Colonial Intervention and the Politics of Identity* (Ithaca, NY: Cornell University Press, 2015). See also Ryo Ikeda, *The Imperialism of French Decolonisaton: French Policy and the Anglo-American Response in Tunisia and Morocco* (Basingstoke, UK: Palgrave Macmillan, 2015).

83. Wm. Roger Louis and Roger Owen, eds., *Suez 1956: The Crisis and Its Consequences* (Oxford: Oxford University Press, 1989); Odd Arne Westad, *The Global Cold War: Third*

If the imprint that European empire-building had placed on the map of the world was fading, French leaders had to reconfigure their spatial imaginations, in relation both to Europe and to Africa. Between French West Africa and Europe lay Algeria and the Sahara. Eurafrica provided a framework for thinking about this interconnected space, an alternative to other geographical imaginaries that had long been in play—the Mediterranean, Greco-Roman or Islamic worlds, "black" Africa," North Africa. Earlier, a trans-Saharan railway had entranced some French thinkers as France's equivalent of Great Britain's Cape to Cairo Railroad project. The Saharan railroad dropped out of the picture when air and sea transport offered enhanced flexibility for trade. But Eurafrica still beckoned, based on both history and geography—an extension across space that mirrored Eurasia.[84]

The significance of the Sahara was enhanced geologically in the mid-1950s with the discovery of oil. Its economic potential gave impetus to a project to create a new sort of administrative entity, the Organisation commune des régions sahariennes (OCRS, Common Organization of Saharan Regions). It was to be carved out of the southern part of Algeria and northern portions of the French Sudan, Niger, and Chad (possibly including part of Mauritania). The idea was not supposed to preclude the governance of the individual territories—their ability to act autonomously was ambiguous at this stage of the decolonization process—but to put under administrative and technocratic (in effect, French) control a region that was vast, resource-rich, and thinly populated—3.6 million square kilometers with 420,000 inhabitants.[85] Created by a French law passed in January 1957—as debates over the future of Europe were heating up—the OCRS never fully got off the ground,

---

World Interventions and the Making of Our Times (Cambridge: Cambridge University Press, 2005), 125–26.

84. Muriam Haleh Davis, "The Sahara as the 'Cornerstone' of Eurafrica: European Integration and Technical Sovereignty Seen from the Desert," *Journal of European Integration History* 23, 1 (2017): 97–112.

85. Or so it was estimated at the time. "Une 'Organisation commune des régions sahariennes' a été approuvée par le gouvernement," *Le Monde*, August 2, 1956; Davis, "The Sahara as the 'Cornerstone' of Eurafrica." The French government hoped for German investment in the Sahara, and some German industrialists were attracted to the possibility. Hansen and Jonsson, *Eurafrica*, 180–83.

constrained by the ongoing war in Algeria and the refusal of some of the sub-Saharan states to relinquish the power over Saharan lands they were beginning to acquire in that year. What the French government was able to salvage (for a time) in the peace it eventually negotiated with the Algerian FLN was rights for French companies to pump oil and for its military to use bases in southern Algeria, including for nuclear tests. With Algerian independence in 1962 the OCRS was reconstituted as the "Organisme technique de mise en valeur des richesses du sous-sol saharien" (Technical organism for the development of the riches of the Saharan subsoil).[86]

The reimaginings of a transcontinental economic space ran up against the constraints of European politics. Great Britain had been initially skeptical of European integration initiatives and was not seriously involved in the negotiations that led to the Treaty of Rome of 1957, leaving Britain's African colonies out of the debates over Eurafrica. The intense negotiations of 1956–57 involved France, Germany, the Netherlands, Belgium, Italy, and Luxembourg—known as "the Six." In the end, they—especially Germany—did not want to assume the burdens of ex-empire. Germany wanted the Common Market to succeed but perceived Africa more as a cost that had to be paid to secure France's entry into the Common Market than as a benefit to the German economy, with its substantial and expanding commercial ties around the world. Moreover, German leaders saw France's political situation in Africa—especially Algeria—as a mess in which they did not wish to get involved.[87] Italy feared that Algeria might compete in the same agricultural markets—including olive oil and wine—if it were fully inside the Six's tariff walls. Moreover, Algeria's needs for development

---

86. Thomas Deltombe, "Le Sahara, clé de voûte de l'indépendance et de la puissance de la France," in Borrel et al., *L'Empire qui ne veut pas mourir*, 215–18.

87. Guia Migani, "L'Association des TOM au Marché Commun: Histoire d'un accord européen entre cultures économiques différentes et idéaux politiques communs, 1955–1957," and Guido Thiemeyer, "West German Perceptions of Africa and the Association of the Overseas Territories with the Common Market 1956–1957," in Bitsch and Bossuat, *L'Europe Unie et l'Afrique*, 233–52, 26985. Thiemeyer (281) concludes bluntly, "Germany did not want to get involved in the problems of decolonization, and therefore refused any political responsibility for the former colonies." More generally, as Brown (*Seventh Member State*, 252) remarks, "EEC officials certainly could envision Algerian land as part of Europe; Algerian people complicated this picture."

assistance had the potential to undermine the claims of Italy's own impoverished southern provinces.[88]

Félix Houphouët-Boigny of the Côte d'Ivoire, a member of Mollet's government, went to Brussels in January 1957 to plead with France's would be partners for including Africa in the proposed common market on terms as favorable as possible. He warned that, without the advantages of Eurafrica, France's African territories would be attracted to the "Bandung group" of Asian and African states that had met in Bandung, Indonesia, in 1955 to chart a course for Afroasian cooperation against colonialism and its aftereffects (see chapter 3). As far as he was concerned, "We don't want to go to either Bandung or Cairo. It is to Paris that we turn."[89]

His mission to Brussels did not get him far. Belgium, with its African colonies of the Congo and Rwanda-Burundi, went partway in cooperating with France, but the Congo was already a free-trade zone and it had exceptional mineral wealth. Belgium had less than France to gain from a negotiated Eurafrica.[90] Italy had some interest in close relations with its former colonies of Somalia and Libya, but was more concerned with devoting resources to its own impoverished south. The other states that were actively pursuing a common market—West Germany, the Netherlands, and Luxembourg—were willing to make some compromises in providing aid and favorable trade agreements to French and Belgian territories in Africa, but were adamant that full membership, including participation in decision-making, was off the table. Although it was by then known that the Algerian desert contained large oil deposits of great interest to Europe, it was not clear that the French state and French oil companies would share their privileged access to these or other regional resources. France's partners were skeptical of Eurafrican commitments for the same reason France was eager to make them: fear that Africa could become a sinkhole for the financial resources of more affluent states.[91]

88. Brown, *Seventh Member State*, 119, 131, 136, 160.
89. Montarsolo, *L'Eurafrique*, 235. Félix Houphouët-Boigny, speech in Saint-Brieuc, France, February 1958, quoted in Borrel et al., *L'Empire qui ne veut pas mourir*, 189. On the Bandung conference, see chapter 3.
90. Migani, "L'Association des TOM au Marché Commun," 246.
91. Brown, *Seventh Member State*, 24, 122–24, 158–63, 168–69, 184.

Much as Defferre and Mollet wanted an inclusive Eurafrica that would weave together former colonies and former imperial rivals, they were not able to get it. As negotiations reached a climax in February 1957, the French government backed off its insistence that the whole French Union be included, while maintaining that Algeria, which it considered an integral part of France, should remain part of the project.[92] What French leaders did get from the planning for a European Economic Community was a special, second-level, status for their sub-Saharan ex-colonies, that of "associate" member. France's former colonies would have privileged access to European markets, and members of the Common Market would have privileged access to African markets on terms to be worked out in detail. There would be a European development fund to which West Germany would be a major contributor, although not as large a commitment as France had wanted. What was missing was what Senghor from 1948 had singled out as essential: an African voice in administering Eurafrica. Even if the Community of 1957 was strictly economic, unlike the political European Union that had been proposed in 1948, the question of who could make its rules remained vital.

When the framework for negotiations for the EEC was debated in the National Assembly in January 1957 and when the Treaty of Rome was ratified in July, African deputies worried about the details: loss of income from tariffs (the major revenue source for African governments) once duties within the Eurafrican bloc were sharply reduced, whether European markets would compensate for reduction of France's support for African export crops, whether the new European development fund would be adequate, especially for infrastructures that were not directly profitable.

In the January debate, Senghor pointedly stated that he favored "the idea of a European common market; I say precisely 'the idea'." The idea was consistent with his federalist principles. In practice, he worried that with reduced tariff revenues African governments would not be able to balance their budgets, that Europe would not

---

92. Montarsolo, *L'Eurafrique*, and Hansen and Jonnson, *Eurafrica*, provide detailed narratives of the twists and turns of the negotiations. It was clear to the top officials of the French government by the end of 1956 that the best France could do was to get associate membership for its African territories.

take enough African produce and would engage in the "dumping" of European goods at the expense of nascent African industries, that investment would be insufficient since France's partners were not eager to take up the "white man's burden." Above all, he did not like having to give a "blank check" to the French government to negotiate all these issues with its European partners. Negotiating was what the French leaders were doing—with little or no involvement of African leaders.[93]

In the parliamentary debates of July 1957, Diawadou Barry of Guinea emphasized that the legislative bodies created for African territories to run their own affairs had not been consulted and would not have any future role in regulating Africa's commerce with Europe. Reduced tariffs under the Treaty would have a "catastrophic" effect on the revenue of Overseas Territories. Regulations of imports into Europe might make exports of some African commodities less lucrative rather than more. He concluded that the treaty amounted to the "replacement of French colonization by a European neo-colonialism." He would vote against ratification.[94]

Fily Dabo Sissoko of the French Sudan, echoing earlier concerns of Senghor and others, worried that France, without the consent of elected governments in the Overseas Territories, was sacrificing the French Union to French-German reconciliation, and he concluded that "this is not the best way to constitute Europe."[95] But if Senghor had earlier worried about Africa providing the dowry for the marriage of France and Germany, some African politicians saw the result as a marriage of Africa and Europe. Maximilien Quenum-Possy-Berry, Senator from Dahomey, told a meeting of federalists, "Africa is of marriageable age. She has chosen her fiancé and it is Europe."[96]

93. Senghor, Assemblée Nationale, *Débats*, January 18, 1957, 16–67. Gabriel Lisette, a stalwart of the Rassemblement Démocratique Africain, also worried about loss of revenue and disturbances to a market in which 75 percent of the Overseas Territories' imports came from France and 71 percent of their exports went to France. But he felt that, given the options, he had to vote for the mandate for negotiations. Senghor abstained on this vote, but he came around on final ratification. Ibid., January 22, 1957, 221, 240.

94. Diawadou Barry, Assemblée Nationale, *Débats,* July 6, 1957, 3351–52.

95. Sissoko, ibid., 3362.

96. "Les fédéralistes français réclament la création d'une République fédérale française intégrée à l'Europe," *Le Monde*, October 23, 1957.

By trying to enlist Europe to provide markets and development assistance to Africa, French advocates of Eurafrica were acknowledging the limits of what France had to offer the continent. The issue for Pierre-Henri Teitgen, replying to Sissoko, was France's capacity to raise Africans' standard of living. "Is France able to furnish, by itself, in the required time frame, the necessary effort? I don't think so. . . . In consequence, we have the right to say that if Africa can and should be modernized, it will only be in the framework of European solidarity."[97] The claim to be providing European support for development carried with it an implied threat that Africa would not get what it needed if it did not accept the version of Eurafrica that was on offer.

France's Foreign Minister, Christian Pineau, tried to claim that cooperation with European partners had already produced results for what he called "the construction of Eurafrica." This must have been a much more limited Eurafrica than what both African and French leaders had been talking about since the late 1940s.[98] Senghor was well aware that the Eurafrica being voted on in July 1957 was much narrower than the one he had advocated beginning in 1948. Like other African deputies, he raised concerns about tariffs, export quotas, and the level of development funding, and he knew that the crucial details of economic relations would be negotiated by France and its partners, with little direct voice for representatives of Africa. But he concluded that he had to vote for the Treaty of Rome: "For ten years, my group [his party and parliamentary allies] has consistently supported the thesis of federalism and interdependence from the quadruple viewpoint of Black Africa, the Republic, the French Union, and Europe."[99] He was citing his long support not just for an Afro-European economic zone, but for multilayered sovereignty, in which Africans would participate in decision-making at each level. He and his colleagues knew that

---

97. Assemblée nationale, *Débats*, July 6, 195, 3364.
98. Pineau, ibid., 3371.
99. Senghor, ibid., July 4 1957, 3264. The Rassemblement Démocratique Africain, the largest West African political party, with branches in all the territories, favored the treaty despite misgivings. Jean Fremigacci, "Les parlementaires africains face à la construction européenne, 1953–1957," *Matériaux pour l'Histoire de Notre Temps* 77 (2005): 13–14.

France's European partners, on whom African claim-making had little traction, were responsible for their exclusion.

The lines of contestation were being redefined. African political parties were absorbed in struggles with the French government over the political future of the French Union, and the Eurafrica question in the European arena was now strictly economic. Senghor was not going to get political voice at the European level—as he had been insisting since 1948—but he would take what he could of Eurafrica and continue to fight for a French Union that was responsive to Africans' needs and wishes.

Some European backers of the Treaty of Rome insisted that Eurafrica had in fact been implemented. René Pleven, an influential center-right politician with a long interest in Overseas France, called the ratification of the treaty in July 1957 a "decisive step toward the European federation and the Eurafrican federation." Following up at a public meeting a few months later, Pleven promised that Africans would benefit materially from Eurafrica, especially a reduction of economic inequality, while Africans would be expected to act within the community:

> The desired union of Europe and Africa implies not only rights but also duties for Europeans as well as Africans, for the former, the duty of assistance that translates as a transfer of a larger and larger share of the national revenue for the underdeveloped countries of Africa in order to reduce progressively differences in standard of living. For the latter, active participation in this community, for in the marriage of Europe and Africa Africans know that they have to pay their share of the dowry.[100]

It was not a marriage of equals. Africa's associate status with the EEC set the framework for negotiations that would take place after most of Africa became independent, providing aid and regulating

---

100. "L'Assemblée a autorisé la ratification des traités européens, " *Le Monde*, July 11, 1957; "M. Pleven: la communauté franco-africaine, premier relais vers l'Eurafrique," *Le Monde*, December 19, 1957. The marriage metaphor also appeared in 1958 in a journal committed to Eurafrican causes, *France Outre-Mer*, which had commissioned a report and a debate on "L'Eurafrique, Mariage d'Amour ou de Raison? Un débat qui n'est pas clos." [Eurafrica, Marriage of Love or of Reason? A Debate that Is Not Over], No. 339 (1958), cited in Rice, "Reframing Imperialism," 57.

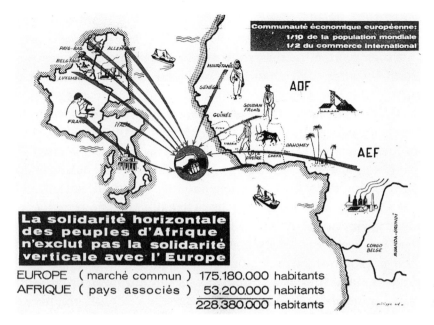

FIGURE 2.2. Eurafrica, as illustrated in a newspaper from Côte d'Ivoire, *Abidjan-Matin*, February 5, 1959. Text on map reads, "The horizontal solidarity of the people of Africa does not exclude the vertical solidarity with Europe." Other information on map: European Economic Community: 1/10 of world population, ½ of international commerce. Europe (Common market) 175,180,000 inhabitants, Africa (associated countries) 53,200,000 inhabitants, Total 228,380,000 inhabitants. AOF is the acronym of French West Africa; AEF, French Equatorial Africa.

commercial relations. But for now, France was the negotiating partner of the other members of the EEC.

Despite the disappointments of the Treaty of Rome, the newspaper *Abidjan-Matin*, the major daily in the Côte d'Ivoire, published a lengthy article on Eurafrica in February 1959, including a map showing Africa and Europe with arrows linking the two. The caption read, "The horizontal solidarity of the peoples of Africa does not exclude vertical solidarity with Europe."[101] The invocation of horizontal and vertical solidarity followed the language Senghor had used a decade earlier, and it points to the strong wish on the part of some politically engaged Africans to make good use of

---

101. *Abidjan-Matin*, February 19, 1959.

connections deriving from a colonial relationship in order to transcend that relationship.

Other political actors continued to promote and question Eurafrica after Africa had been excluded from active membership in the European Economic Community. A leading Gaullist politician, Jacques Soustelle (who would later break with de Gaulle over Algeria), was insisting in May 1959 that Eurafrica was an "obligatory reality."[102] Mollet in January 1958 still wanted to "blur" national sovereignties, bring socialist progress to Africa and Europe, and foster the "interdependence" of nations, specifically "the franco-africain community or, better still, the Eurafrican community." He criticized French settlers in Africa for trying to preserve their privileges at all costs, and warned that Algerian nationalists were not following democratic procedures, would not respect the rights of minorities of both indigenous and European origin, and would bring about the isolation of Algeria in what had become an interactive world. A year later, he insisted yet again that Eurafrica was an "urgent necessity."[103] A left-leaning economist noted for his interest in reconciling "humanism" and economics, François Perroux, argued in 1959 against the "nationalist illusion" that economic problems could be dealt with in national containers. Sovereignty could only be partial and interaction and global cooperation were necessities, not least the "association between the two continents of Europe and Africa."[104] Arguments such as these were by then underlying efforts to make "development" a global priority and a policy of the European Economic Community.[105]

Predictably, Soviet commentators described Eurafrica as a neocolonial plot. American observers were more circumspect, seeing the effort to promote mutual prosperity in Africa and Europe as

102. "M. Jacques Soustelle: l'Eurafrique est une réalité obligatoire," *Le Monde*, May 25, 1959.

103. Guy Mollet, *Bilan at perspectives socialistes* (Paris: Plon, 1958), 38–67, 45 and 47 quoted; Imlay, *Practice of Socialist Internationalism*, 446.

104. François Perroux, "Grâce à la Communauté, inventons des sociétés neuves," *Le Monde*, September 10, 1959.

105. On the EEC and development aid—including continuities in practices and personnel between the late colonial and early independence periods in Africa—see Véronique Dimier, *The Invention of a European Development Aid Bureaucracy: Recycling Empire* (Basingstock, UK: Palgrave Macmillan, 2014).

a boon to both economies and global trade in general, and also a bulwark against the expansion of communism. They worried that the close linkage of Europe and Africa might keep American corporations out but hoped that American business could benefit from African markets if the continent became more developed.[106]

At a meeting of parliamentarians from Africa and Europe in October 1959, several African participants brought up the exclusion of Africans from negotiating the treaty of Rome, insisting that "Eurafrica is only viable if the current passes in both directions." But for that to happen, Africans had to become more united. As Marcel Lihau, a Congolese jurist speaking (according to *Le Monde*) in the "name of the Belgian Congo," stated: "Eurafrica cannot be built without the unification of Africa, without a United States of Africa. . . . Otherwise, Europe, more than ever, will dominate the black continent."[107] In fact, the unification of Africa had not been part of the debates over Eurafrica, which from the beginning was limited to Belgian and French territories. Although Kwame Nkrumah called in 1958 for a "United States of Africa" (see chapter 3), he was in the late 1950s contemptuous of most of the leaders of French Africa, considering them lackeys of the French government. His relations with the leading opposition movement in white-ruled South Africa, the African National Congress, were also tense.[108]

The Treaty of Rome of 1957 had distinguished Algeria from sub-Saharan Africa, relegating the latter to a second zone while, under article 227, accepting that as a part of France Algeria was part of

106. The Soviet view is expressed in G. E. Skorov, *Komu nuzhna Evrafrika?* [Who needs Eurafrica?] (Moscow: Gospolitizdat, 1957), cited in Eric Burton, James Mark, and Steffi Marung, "Development," in James Mark and Paul Betts, eds., *Socialism Goes Global: The Soviet Union and Eastern Europe in the Age of Decolonization* (Oxford: Oxford University Press, 2022), 89–90; "Business Abroad: Eurafrica: New Deal for the Black Continent?," *Business Week*, April 20, 1957, 112–20.

107. Pierre Drouin, "Comment éviter les pièges du néo-colonialisme?" *Le Monde*, October 7, 1959. European and African parliamentarians continued for a time to meet and promote some idea of Eurafrica, now conceived of as a dialogue of North and South. Urban Vahsen, "La conférence parlementaire eurafricaine de Strasbourg (12–24 Juin 1961)," in Bitsch and Bossuat, *L'Europe unie et l'Afrique*, 375–91.

108. Jeffrey Ahlman, "Road to Ghana: Nkrumah, Southern Africa and the Eclipse of Decolonizing Africa," *Kronos* 37 (2011): 23–40; Kwame Nkrumah, *Africa Must Unite* (London: Panaf, 1963).

Europe. What this meant in practice, however, was not clear. As Megan Brown argues, the Member States of the EEC kept trying to restrict the benefits—such as social protections while working in non-French Member States—that Algerians received from their territory's status. Independence in 1962 did not suddenly alter this ambiguous situation, and it took another fourteen years to complete what Brown calls the "plodding extraction of Algeria from Europe." Algerian's new rulers were seeking a position of leadership among other newly independent states, challenging a western-dominated global order, but at the same time they continued to engage in economic relations with Europe—Algeria's major export market and major source of imports—and continued to get as much as they could from Algeria's special relationship to the EEC.[109]

The hopes and the doubts attached to the different versions of Eurafrica debated in the 1950s touched on many specific issues—tariffs and export quotas for instance—but behind them lay a broader hope on the part of African leaders for the melding of horizontal and vertical solidarity on a transcontinental scale and a vision of multiple civilizations interacting and sustaining each other. Those aspirations had run into the unwillingness of France's would-be partners to foot the bills for a full integration of impoverished ex-colonies into Europe, especially if those colonies would be in a position to make claims.

The implications of African territories' relegation to associate status in Europe hark back to the French government's "territorialization" policy of 1956: Africans' claim-making at the level of the French Union had raised the price of keeping African territories within a French polity. The thorny problem all along concerned participation in decision-making, in other words, power. As Quinn Slobodian has argued, one of the great fears of advocates of free-market liberalism was democracy. If decisions were left to a majority, that majority would allocate resources to itself at the expense of the accumulation of capital in the hands of entrepreneurs; in short,

---

109. Brown, *Seventh Member State*, 133, 136, 156, 177; Jeffrey James Byrne, *Mecca of Revolution: Algeria, Decolonization, and the Third World Order* (Oxford: Oxford University Press, 2016). Brown's title reflects the possibility that Algeria would maintain as an independent state the affiliation with Europe that it had acquired through France.

democracy would become social democracy.¹¹⁰ The French legislation of 1956 was a response to successful claim-making within a French Union that was run by partially democratic processes and in which Africans were insisting on fuller participation. The rejection of a Eurafrica in which Africans were active participants took Europe's role in promoting development and welfare out of the hands of institutions in which Africans would be in a position to make claims and left development assistance to the already developed to manage.

Toward an African Africa and a European Europe

Africans were politically out and economically half in the European Economic Community, which is all that remained of the Eurafrica project after the Treaty of Rome of 1957. The focus of political discussion and contestation between French and African leaders returned to the French Union. Foreign Minister Pineau had said as much during the debate over the Treaty of Rome: "We retain on the other hand, do I need to emphasize, exclusive competence—I am responding to Mr. Sissoko—for the decisions on which the political evolution of the overseas countries and territories depend, and we will not allow on this point our sovereignty to be contested."¹¹¹ He meant, no doubt, to assure the deputies that France was not ceding sovereignty over Africa to its European partners.

Sovereignty was very much in question, although not that way. The location of sovereignty and the institutions through which it would be exercised were the subject of claims and counterclaims in the late 1950s, both within European and African France and between the two.¹¹² Africans in the Overseas Territories had been French citizens since 1946; since 1956 they had enjoyed universal suffrage and the right to elect legislative assemblies that could appoint an executive in each territory. They also could elect a small number of representatives for the National Assembly in Paris.

---

110. Quinn Slobodian, *Globalists: The End of Empire and the Birth of Neoliberalism* (Cambridge, MA: Harvard University Press, 2018).
111. Pineau, Assemblée Nationale, *Débats*, July 6, 1957, 3371.
112. Cooper, *Citizenship from Empire to Nation*.

When a second postwar constitution was ratified in September 1958 by a referendum in all of France, African as well as European, the African territories (except for Guinea, which voted against the constitution) acquired the status of Member States of the newly created Community, successor to the French Union. They no longer sent deputies to the National Assembly, but the heads of government of each Member State participated in regular meetings with the President of the French Republic and top officials who decided affairs common to the Community, including defense and foreign affairs.

Were Member States like Senegal or Dahomey states within a state? Was European France the state? Was the Community the state? Or were European France and Member States of the Community in some other kind of relationship?[113] During the writing of the Constitution of 1958—a less transparent process than that of 1946 but one that nonetheless had African input—the battle of confederation and federation was solved by a word game. The constitution writers followed the suggestion of Philibert Tsiranana, later the first president of Madagascar, to call the new entity the Community and not explain its meaning. The term "Community" was used in most official documents without the adjective "French"—to emphasize the inclusion of diverse Member States—although the adjective will sometimes be used in this book to distinguish this Community from the European Economic Community. The government in Paris, with consultation of the heads of the Member States, was in charge of foreign affairs, defense, monetary policy, and some other designated functions, while legislatures and executives in the Member States had responsibility for their internal affairs.[114] Former associated states (Morocco, Tunisia, Vietnam,

---

113. Whether Member States were really states was specifically debated during and after the drafting of the 1958 constitution, as was the question of whether the Community was a state of which the Republic was a component or whether the Republic was the only actual state, leaving the status of Member States and the Community ambiguous. There had been an earlier, unresolved debate among jurists and political commentators over whether the French Union was a state. Cooper, *Citizenship between Empire and Nation*, 198, 299–307, 352, 355–56. What is clear is that politicians and political theorists were trying to invent new political forms that corresponded to the complexity of relationships between the component parts of what had been an empire.

114. It has been argued that the Constitution of 1958 that provided the structure for the Fifth Republic was instituted from above by Charles de Gaulle and his right-hand man,

etc.) were by then independent, and Algeria was in the midst of war, its future status undetermined. De Gaulle, Senghor, and some others hoped—in vain—that creating the Community of multiple Member States might give Algerian nationalists more of a place than its prior enclosure within the French Republic. An ambitious development plan for Algeria and the opportunities for commerce and aid from the European Economic Community might make Member State status still more attractive.[115]

Within the (French) Community, Senghor continued to push for a three-layer division of sovereign functions: those of each Overseas Territory, an African federation, and a confederation of equal states, European and African. Félix Houphouët-Boigny persisted in his call for direct participation of individual territories in a French federation. Guinea alone rejected the 1958 constitution (as was its right) and became independent that year, cutting itself off from French institutions and French development assistance.[116]

The ambiguity of locating sovereignty played out in 1959 in a shifting debate over nationality at the meetings of French and African heads of state and committees they appointed. All concerned agreed that the inhabitants of the Member States would continue to have, as they had since 1946, the rights of the French citizen (as before without the obligation to come under the Civil Code). De Gaulle initially insisted that all such people possessed French nationality, the only one recognized worldwide. But African leaders objected that France would have its own nationality while other states of the Community could not have theirs. After months of back and forth and the deliberations of committees of jurists, the heads of state agreed that each Member State could have its own nationality, write its nationality laws, and regulate who was considered a national, and that this nationality would automatically confer the "superposed nationality"

Michel Debré, but the detailed records of the writing process reveal that there was a great deal of give and take and significant accommodations to African demands, even though (unlike the case of the 1946 Constitution) most of the exchanges took place behind closed doors rather than in a legislative assembly. Cooper, *Citizenship from Empire to Nation*, chapter 6.

115. On the FLN's mitigated reaction to French development plans and Eurafrica, see Davis, *Markets of Civilization*, 92–95, 147–48.

116. On Guinea, see Schmidt, *Mobilizing the Masses*.

"of the French Republic and of the Community." A bureaucrat in Dakar could thus decide that an individual had Senegalese nationality and therefore the superposed nationality that gave that individual the possibility of exercising the rights of the citizen in European France or anywhere in the Community.[117]

Alongside the layering of state functions between Member States and the French Republic, this conception of nationality revealed the uncertainty of where sovereignty was located. Even such a state-minded leader as Charles de Gaulle had to accept this ambiguity as the price of maintaining some kind of France larger than a mid-sized state in the western part of a Eurasian landmass.

The concept of superposed nationality in the Community became irrelevant before it was fully implemented. Unable to unite among themselves and facing a French government that wanted to preserve the Community but not pay the costs of a community of equals, African leaders came to accept that relations with France had in reality become bilateral and that aspirations to participate in international institutions and relations with other states could best be served by negotiated independence. Senghor made a last effort to form an African federation—the Federation of Mali—with the one other Member State of the Community willing to join him, the Sudan. It was the Mali Federation that negotiated independence with France, achieving that status in June 1960. But torn by power plays between the leaders of Senegal (Senghor and Mamadou Dia) and Sudan (Modibo Keita), the Mali Federation broke up in acrimony in August. Senghor's Senegal became a sovereign, territorially defined state in September 1960. The other African former colonies were by then on the same path.[118]

But the boundaries of sovereignty were not fully set. Reluctant to separate the citizens of Mali from those of France as independence would seemingly imply, the separating states negotiated treaties

---

117. Cooper, *Citizenship between Empire and Nation*, 353–68.

118. Ibid., chapters 7 and 8. Some critics have argued that France wanted to sabotage the Mali Federation for fear that it would be too strong and too radical an interlocutor, but France had no qualms negotiating from late 1959 to the middle of 1960 with the Mali Federation—not Senegal or Sudan—over the terms of independence. The detailed record of negotiations in the archives suggests that France's main objective was to retain some form of the Community, even if that entailed making compromises.

that gave the citizens of each the right to enter and leave, to reside in, to possess property in, and to seek work in the other. Moreover, Malians born before the date of independence could obtain French nationality without having to go through naturalization as long as they established residence in the remaining territory of the French Republic. This blurring of the boundaries of citizenship implied that in terms of how people could move around space, there still was a Franco-African configuration. The Franco-Malian agreement became the model for the independence treaties negotiated by France and the other Member States.

These arrangements persisted until the mid-1970s, but they were defined by treaty rather than constitutional law, and treaties can be abrogated. When the French government decided in 1974 that it no longer wanted to support labor immigration, from its former colonies or elsewhere, the decision was its own to make. A road to French nationality was still available on the basis of family reconciliation to close relatives of Africans who had already acquired rights in France, but the pathways were narrowing. Fourteen years after independence, the spatial boundedness of French national sovereignty, separated from other parts of what had been the French empire, Union, and Community, were firmly established.

The project of Eurafrica—not least the efforts of African leaders to bring it about—appears inconsistent with conventional narratives of decolonization that oppose a militant African nationalism and a rigid French colonialism. African leaders were willing to acquiesce to a continued, if modified inclusion in a polity that identified itself as French and European, and French leaders were willing to dilute some of France's sovereignty to both European partners and former colonial subjects. Both sides' actions preserved a vertical relationship to each other. French advocates of Eurafrica like Schuman, Defferre, and Mollet, and Africans like Senghor and Houphouët-Boigny, saw Eurafrica as a way of turning a colonial relationship into something different. The European side wanted to preserve in some form their privileged relationship with African territories, the African side to claim resources within political structures in which they had a constitutionally mandated voice.

Neither got what they sought. Vertical relationships did not disappear with the end of colonial rule, but their nature was transformed. With decolonization, a sovereign state would be asking for aid from another sovereign state, from Europe, or from an international organization. It could negotiate treaties to redefine terms of trade or to regulate investment. At the same time, the new states of Africa could try to create horizontal relationships with other states in a similar position in the world economy, but they would be doing so *as states*, not as members of a political unit—as in the brief existence of the French Union and Community—or as a global political movement. This is a theme taken up in the next chapter.

Efforts to develop horizontal solidarity among the states of Africa and Asia—as well as Latin America—persisted, but they ran up against the realities of vertical relationships: the quotidian need of impoverished states for aid and economic relations with wealthy states, transnational corporations willing to invest within the country, and international financial institutions that could provide resources at their own will. Even Algeria, despite the bitterness of both the war and the peace, maintained a significant but uneasy relationship with France and the EEC.

While France stepped out of a political and administrative relationship with African territories it had once governed, French leaders decided they liked some of the ideas that had surfaced during the 1940s and 1950s, as applied not to its former African colonies but to its former European rivals. The European Union that came into being in the 1990s was in effect a confederal structure, ceding control of typically sovereign functions to common bodies (not coterminous with each other), including money (the euro) and border control (the Schengen system). The European Union has an elected parliament and an executive. The European Union has defined a European citizenship. This superposed citizenship, derived automatically from citizenship in a member state, recalls the agreement of 1959 on the superposed nationality of the French Republic and of the Community.[119]

---

119. Dieter Gosewinkel, *Struggles for Belonging: Citizenship in Europe, 1900-2020* (Oxford: Oxford University Press, 2021). Jan Zielonka argues that today's European Union is less like a national state than a medieval empire. The comparison is strained, but it does usefully point to a "multilevel governance system of concentric circles, fuzzy borders, and soft forms of external power projection." *Europe as Empire: The Nature of the Enlarged European Union* (Oxford: Oxford University Press, 2006), 1.

From the perspective of its African advocates, Eurafrica was an act of militant reimagining, of turning an assertion of domination into a demand for redistribution of resources and power. For French leaders, it was also an act of reimagining—of confederal relations and superposed citizenship that might have remade France's relations with its former colonial subjects and was later implemented to refashion relations with fellow Europeans.[120]

Other Eurafricas

Other Eurafricas appeared both while the one described in these pages was under discussion and later, after 1957, when it became clear that African territories would not be full participants in the European Economic Community, after France's sub-Saharan colonies became independent in 1960, and after Algeria's independence in 1962. One of these movements came to be called—by its critics—*Françafrique*. The intellectuals and activists who used this term were describing what they saw as a cynical reconfiguration of colonial relationships, in effect the opposite of the Eurafrica that Senghor had sought. The term refers to under-the-table arrangements between French officials and businesses and top African leaders in formerly French territories. It implies French support for cooperative leaders, including military help against attempts to subvert their power in their respective countries as well as corrupt arrangements for contracts with French corporations.[121] French President Emmanuel Macron could still refer in November 2020 to an "Afro-European

---

120. Brown suggests that Eurafrica was for a time a "possibility that postwar imperial reforms could have led to a fundamentally different way of organizing the world," *Seventh Member State*, 19.

121. François-Xavier Verschave, *La Françafrique: le plus long scandale de la République* (Paris: Stock, 1998); Pascal Airault and Jean-Pierre Bat, *Françafrique: opérations secrètes et affaires d'État* (Paris: Tallandier, 2016); Borrel et al., *L'Empire qui ne veut pas mourir*; Alexander Keese, "First Lessons in Neo-Colonialism: The Personalisation of Relations between African Politicians and French Officials in Sub-Saharan Africa, 1956–66," *Journal of Imperial and Commonwealth History* 35, 4 (2007): 593–613. The diplomatic side was masterminded by the advisor on African affairs to Charles de Gaulle and his successors, Jacques Foccart, who developed his formidable array of contacts during France's final attempt, from 1958 to 1960, at reconfiguring its relations to African territories. One can take with a grain of salt the coherence of Françafrique or Foccart's self-cultivated image of his Machiavellian role, but it is clear enough that France's relations with its

axis," and while he shrouded his comments in the language of "partnership," French military action in the Sahel, its selective provision of foreign aid, and its efforts to stem African migration into France suggest something other than Senghorian Eurafrica.[122] French leaders repeatedly claim that they have repudiated or are about to repudiate Françafrique in favor of a more transparent, less unequal, or perhaps less important relationship with former colonies. As the philosopher Nadia Yala Kisukidi points out, "One of the paradoxes of Françafrique is that its official existence is constantly reaffirmed by means of proclaiming its end."[123] Trying to put Franco-African relations on a new footing, President Macron has acknowledged the wrongs perpetrated by France in Algeria and its other colonial ventures. In so doing, Macron is insisting that what is problematic in France's actions is a phenomenon of the past.

One should not push the Françafrique thesis so far that it consigns African leaders to a passive role. They had their own reasons to pursue strategic connections at home and abroad. Sovereignty gave African leaders some room to choose their patrons, even if the position of their countries in the global economic order made it difficult to avoid clientalistic relations with wealthier states, corporations, and financial institutions.[124] African leaders' earlier idea

---

ex-colonies include military interventions, close relations with dubious regimes, and a lack of transparency.

122. Interview with President Macron, November 16, 2020, on the website Le Grand Continent, https://legrandcontinent.eu/fr/2020/11/16/macron/, accessed September 28, 2021. The connection was also promoted in the "Nouveau Sommet Afrique France" held in Montpellier on October 8, 2021, sponsored by the French government but without African heads of state, focused apparently on youth, entrepreneurs, artists, etc. See "Le pari du sommet Afrique-France nouvelle formule," *Le Monde*, October 7, 2021. The "Eurafrican Forum" also claims to bring the continents together and has organized meetings to do so, including in July 2022. Its website claims that "Innovators, opinion-formers, game-changers, pioneers, dreamers and mavericks who are shaping the Africa of today gather each year constituting the 'EurAfrican Community Network'." www.eurafricanforum.org, accessed September 14, 2022.

123. Nadia Yale Kisukidi, "Epilogue: Françafrique, mémoires vives," in Borrel et al., *L'Empire qui ne veut pas mourir*, 961. Todd Shepard has argued that after proclaiming for decades that Algeria was an integral part of France, French elites had to insist that it had all along been a colony in order to proclaim that it had been decolonized. *The Invention of Decolonization*.

124. French ex-colonies have to a significant extent been able to "diversify their international relations," while France has also looked beyond its ex-empire to diversify its own foreign connections. Cogneau, *Un empire bon marché*, 422–26, 422 quoted.

of Eurafrica would have given them a place in officially constituted, openly functioning decision-making institutions. The Françafrique they ended up with was in this sense quite different from the Eurafrica they had sought.[125]

Another Eurafrica emerged from initiatives taken by Africans during the period when as citizens they could enter European France, a possibility protected by the treaties granting independence to former colonies until France restricted such migration in the 1970s. Large numbers of Africans came to France for employment opportunities when the regime of "free circulation" of African migrants from former French colonies coincided with a boom in the French economy. Many settled, and many of them became French citizens. Others moved back and forth between African countries and France; migration continued even when it became legally and physically dangerous. Similar conditions brought significant populations of African origin to other European countries, particularly Great Britain, Belgium, and Italy. For many families, the relatively open possibilities until the mid-1970s for settling in Europe provided an economic opportunity that the struggling economies of states emerging from colonial rule could not offer.[126] Whether French citizens or not, many people of African descent in France faced—and continue to face—discrimination, residential segregation, and obstacles to economic advancement.

Many people from the African diaspora have called attention to the racism and deprivation that people of color face in the postcolonial situation. On the other side, a significant portion of the French political spectrum complains that Africans—from North as well as sub-Saharan Africa—are unassimilable, burdens on the

---

125. The journalist Antoine Glaser argues that Françafrique meant that African leaders were manipulating their French counterparts at least as much as the other way around. Be that as it may, Françafrique was a direct relationship among elites shielded from visibility and accountability. *AfricaFrance: Quand les dirigeants africains deviennent les maîtres du jeu* (Paris: Fayard, 2014).

126. The British Nationality Act of 1948 had a similar effect on migration from the British Empire to the British Isles as did the French citizenship law of 1946. The 1950s and early 1960s were a high point in creating a Britain that was multiracial and multicultural—and in which racial tensions and racial discrimination became political issues. Randall Hansen, *Citizenship and Immigration in Post-War Britain: The Institutional Origins of a Multicultural Nation* (Oxford: Oxford University Press, 2000).

state, or pose dangers of "communitarianism" or "radical Islam." Critics of discrimination and xenophobia in today's France sometimes interpret such arguments as a continuation of the racialized politics of colonialism, but in another sense exclusionary politics directed against Africans represents a *reversal* of the politics that emerged during the brief period after 1945, when France sought to legitimize its continued existence as a Eurafrican polity in which all inhabitants had citizenship rights and Africans insisted that such a polity be open and inclusive. When France gave up on that project, it became much more of a nation-state than it had been before—and more European than earlier. Its type of citizenship became more brittle and more exclusionary. Africans who came to France were divided into those with "papers"—as citizens or as legal immigrants—and those without. The citizenship status Africans once had was often forgotten.

Conclusion

Eurafrica, before World War II, had represented a call of Europeans to look beyond inter-empire rivalries toward a more rational, and hopefully peaceful, exploitation of African material and human resources. The project ran into rivalries it was supposed to overcome. After the disaster of war, "young Eurafrica" was born of France's two-sided desperation. Recovery from war and renewal of France's status as a great power depended more than ever on African resources, but the means of controlling African territories were much diminished. That weakness was also a source of possibility, since it applied to European states generally. Freed from the danger of one European empire dominating another, Europeans could afford to be both more national in focus and more open to cooperation.

For African leaders, Eurafrica posed the danger of an internationalization of colonialism but also the possibility of expanding the resource pool on which they could make claims and larger markets to which they could export their products. For leaders like Senghor or Houphouët-Boigny, a Eurafrica in which Africans could have political voice complemented a French Union in which they as citizens had rights. The possibilities and the dangers both grew from the fact that colonialism—a political relationship of extreme verticality—was after all a relationship. Colonialism produced connections that enabled assertions of power and claims on people in power, hence the frequent metaphors of marriage—another kind of relationship in which intimacy does not imply equality—in the debates on Eurafrica.

Some observers argued during the 1950s that France could not prosper without Africa and that Africa could not prosper without France. One-half of that proposition was more true than the other. France prospered in the same era that it was giving up its colonies: the years 1945–75 are known as the "trente glorieuses," the "glorious thirty," three decades of economic growth and social betterment. Africa—for reasons that economists and historians have been wrangling over ever since—was not in a position to overcome on its own the structural problems its historical trajectory had produced.[127] The very reason why African leaders thought Eurafrica could be useful to them was why European leaders decided it would be too much of a burden.

The relegation in the Treaty of Rome of 1957 of French African territories to the status of associate members of the European Economic Community had profound implications. Africans would be able to ask for "development assistance," but they would not be in a position to make claims as full members of a Eurafrican political community. Treaties were negotiated and renegotiated between European and African states to define terms of trade and conditions for investment in Africa, but they did not address the foundations of an unequal relationship.[128] In the end, this effort to overcome territorial fragmentation and inequality demonstrated how profound political fragmentation and social inequality were across the space of what might have been Eurafrica.

---

127. Frederick Cooper, *Africa in the World: Capitalism, Empire, Nation-State* (Cambridge, MA: Harvard University Press, 2014). For a wider approach to global inequality, see Thomas Piketty, *Capital and Ideology*, trans. Arthur Goldhammer (Cambridge, MA: Harvard University Press, 2020).

128. European elites did not dodge the fact that "political realities" had changed with independence and that their desire to maintain favorable relation with ex-colonies now had to pass through negotiations in which formal equality was maintained. Assistance had to be provided, but in the name of supporting "indigenous economies." Report prepared by Consultative Assembly of the Council of Europe, *Europe and Africa* (Strasbourg: Council of Europe, 1960), 10, 19–20.

By the 1950s, French society was benefitting from a range of social benefits, including strong legislation to protect the rights of workers, family allocations to support child-rearing, a mix of private and public medical services, and retirement programs—in short what is called in French the *État providence* and in English the welfare state. In the 1950s, the escalation of pressure for social equality coming from African politicians and trade unions posed the possibility of expanding the reach of social benefits and services and wage regulation to French Africa in the name of a citizenship that now embraced all the Overseas Territories—a welfare state on an imperial scale. The new labor code of 1952 as well as a range of programs that went under the name of development were steps in this direction. In these conditions, Eurafrica, as envisioned by Senghor, Houphouët-Boigny, and other African leaders, meant a demand for the redistribution of resources and the power to allocate resources across a transcontinental space. Eurafrica could have transformed political spaces defined by colonization into dynamic, transformative linkages between two entities that were themselves transfigured, the Franco-African Community and the European Economic Community.

French politicians and administrators came to realize that there was no logical end point to demands from African citizens short of full social and economic equality. Still hoping to hold some version of greater France together, the French government had good reason to diffuse some of its current burdens onto its would-be partners in a Eurafrican polity, even if it meant sharing in the benefits of African markets as well. Its partners in the final negotiations over the Common Market did not have the same interests. Whatever doubts African leaders had expressed about Eurafrica, what stood in the way of the project was not Africa but Europe.

For both the French government and African political movements, the rejection of Eurafrica reset the political calculus. France would have to balance its own political and economic interests in Africa against the costs resulting from a political system that had put Africans in a position to make claims. African leaders would have to weigh the realities of a bilateral relationship with France, the uncertainties of their political bases in their respective territories, and the difficulties of relationship with each other against the freedom and opportunities that full sovereignty would give them at home and in the international arena. It was in a changing context— territorial, national, imperial, regional, and international—that independence for sub-Saharan French Africa, in the form of territorial states, could be imagined and negotiated.

The end of colonial empire transformed the idea of "development" from a colonial project into one that was both national—the task of each newly sovereign government—and international, a global project, or so it was claimed, for the betterment of humankind. The relegation of French African territories to associate membership in the EEC settled the question of power. The new states of Africa were left in the position of insisting on their independence and integrity and pleading their needs for assistance.

What became of the political leaders of French Africa who had advocated a continent-crossing Franco-African community or a Eurafrican polity? Senghor became president of Senegal, a small, economically vulnerable state, albeit one connected with other parts of the world through elite contacts and labor migration. Senghor, in effect, became what he had warned against in his critique of politics confined to national containers. He was caught up in the zero-sum politics for control of the state, whose limited resources made it difficult for him to demonstrate to voters the benefits of citizenship in a complex sovereign entity. He imprisoned his most important collaborator and rival, Mamadou Dia, abolished opposing political parties, and remained in power for twenty years, although he eventually restored a multiparty regime and took an honorable retirement. Houphouët-Boigny clung to power for thirty-three years, presiding over a state whose agricultural potential and strong links to global capitalism allowed it a measure of prosperity until the market for its crops collapsed in the 1980s and 1990s, and the vacuum left by the collapse of his personalized power structure led to violent conflict. Sékou Touré, who like Senghor had advocated a federation of French African states as part of a Franco-African community before his radical break with France in 1958, remained president of Guinea for twenty-six years. He found that his efforts to link up with other radical African leaders and to gain support from the USSR and its allies did little to bring his country out of poverty. His repressive regime drove thousands of Guinean citizens into exile, many into the more open environment of Senegal. Despite their differing relations to France and to other powers, none of the three found a path to prosperity or away from dependence on international financial institutions and development assistance. Senegal did return in the 1980s to a relatively democratic political structure and relative political stability; Guinea remains both repressive and conflict ridden; Côte d'Ivoire has at least partly recovered from its civil wars of 2002–07 and 2011.[129]

It is of course impossible to know what a "Eurafrican" Africa would have looked like had it been implemented. Possibly such an entity would have come under the thrall of European institutions; possibly it would have fallen apart under pressure of divergent expectations and interests in a structure that was inherently asymmetrical; possibly it would have done what Senghor hoped and allowed African leaders to keep pressure on European institutions to provide resources for African economic development. The point to remember is that the dangers and limitations of national independence were anticipated by leading political actors in the 1940s and 1950s.

The unequal relations of Africa with other parts of the world has a long history, going back to the times of the slave trade, of colonization, and of the particular paths out of empire taken by African states. Even as the possibility for a new kind of relationship between Europe and Africa was opening and closing over the course of the 1950s, still more post-imperial projects were debated among leaders of Africa and Asia. One was for formerly colonized territories to work together, rejecting continued ties with former colonizers. Afroasia was in this sense the antithesis of Eurafrica, but it also developed in the interstices between colonial empire and the nation-state. Its advocates both profited from and were constrained by the growing number of states emerging from colonial empires. The possibilities and constraints faced by the advocates of Afroasia are the subject of the next chapter.

129. Frederick Cooper has written elsewhere at greater length on the issues discussed here. *Africa Since 1940: The Past of the Present*, 2nd ed. (Cambridge: Cambridge University Press, 2019), and *Africa in the World*.

CHAPTER THREE

Afroasia

AS COLONIAL EMPIRES collapsed in the 1960s, the story that most activists, intellectuals, and scholars wanted to tell proceeded colony by colony toward the formation of a new world of national states.[1] But much of what was going on at the time doesn't fit within national containers. Cooperation among rival empires who shared imperialist discourses and practices was one part of a different, more complex history; linkages among the movements against the imperial powers, with their own shared discourses and boundary-crossing networks, is another.[2] By following conflict in and over colonial empire step by step, scholars can try to avoid the danger of writing this history backward. Rather than assuming that the natural end point of political action in empires is their breakup into states defined by the identification of a single national body in a

---

1. Classics of American political science from the 1960s, with their focus on how particular colonies became independent states, include books by David Apter on Ghana, Aristide Zolberg on Côte d'Ivoire, James Coleman and Richard Sklar on Nigeria, Carl Rosberg and John Nottingham on Kenya, and Crawford Young on the Congo. Exceptions to the national focus from that era are studies of French West Africa by Ruth Schachter Morgenthau and William Foltz that take the federalism question seriously. A good entry point to the current state of scholarship on the ends of empires is Martin Thomas and Andrew Thompson, eds., *The Oxford Handbook of the Ends of Empire* (Oxford: Oxford University Press, 2018).

2. On connections among imperial powers, see Florian Wagner, *Colonial Internationalism and the Governmentality of Empire, 1893–1982* (Cambridge: Cambridge University Press, 2022) and Daniel Hedinger and Nadin Heé, "Transimperial History: Connectivity, Cooperation and Competition," *Journal of Modern European History* 16, 4 (2018): 429–52. A pioneering text on connections among anti-imperialist movements is Vijay Prashad, *The Darker Nations: A People's History of the Third World* (New York: New Press, 2007).

given territory with a single government, they can explore alternatives as they emerged and disappeared.

Arguments against European empire—not just against individual imperial powers—date at least to the eighteenth century, but the goals of anti-imperialist movements have been more varied and more elusive than the empire to nation-state narrative implies.[3] In the twentieth century, communist revolution was an objective that transcended territory, promising to upend the social structures of the colonizing powers as well as those of the colonies. As the previous chapters have shown, activists and intellectuals in a variety of imperial contexts were thinking about transforming imperial systems themselves, about new kinds of political formations whose size and diverse resources would make them strong players on the world scene, or about inclusive cultural formations that could counter western European claims to hegemony.

This chapter examines political imaginaries that crossed the lines of specific territories, individual empires, and continents, efforts to design a new world in which cooperation for social and economic progress among the once colonized could replace domination and exploitation by imperial powers. It also explores how these projects were constrained both by the shifting policies of the powers they were attacking and by the different trajectories out of empire that political movements were able to take.

Imperialism and Anti-Imperialism between Two Empire-Wars

In 1919, a wave of demonstrations and uprisings—in Egypt, Korea, China, and elsewhere—challenged the Japanese and European powers that had emerged seemingly unscathed from the reconfiguation of imperial order under the Versailles treaties. Following the imposition of the mandate system, violent rebellions took place in Syria, Iraq, and other territories. Some scholars link these rebellions to the influence of the Wilsonian doctrine of self-determination and the disappointments of its non-application outside of Europe. Others

---

3. Sankar Muthu, *Enlightenment against Empire* (Princeton, NJ: Princeton University Press, 2003).

see the origins of political ferment in the tensions of empire in different parts of the world more than in the possibilities or shortcomings of self-determination as defined at Versailles.[4]

Among the currents of the pre- and postwar years were "pan" movements: pan-African, pan-Asian, pan-Arab, pan-Islamic, pan-Slavic. These projects attempted to define a set of kindred people wherever they might be residing.

Pan-Africanists sought to unite people living on the African continent with the descendants of Africans throughout the world. They were thinking about political affinity across space. Pan-Africanism's antecedents predated the American civil war, when political leaders descended from slaves proclaimed their identification with the African continent and looked to it for inspiration in their quest for liberty.[5] A series of Pan-Africanist conferences began in 1900. After World War I, pan-Africanists posed a direct challenge to imperial dominance by holding their own conference in Paris, under the leadership of W.E.B. Du Bois, at the same time that the leaders of France, Britain, the United States, and other world powers were meeting nearby to remake the postwar world. In speeches and resolutions, the pan-Africanists insisted on having a voice in the postwar order, combating racial prejudice and discrimination, and countering the violence and exploitation of colonial rulers. There were differences among the pan-Africanists over focusing on the race question in the Americas or the colonial question in Africa, but one fact stands out: the great powers ignored the people of color meeting next door.[6]

---

4. Erez Manela, *The Wilsonian Moment: Self-Determination and the International Origins of Anticolonial Nationalism* (Oxford: Oxford University Press, 2007). For a critique of Manela's argument, see the review of his book by Rebecca Karl in *American Historical Review* 113, 4 (December 2008): 1474–76.

5. Hakim Adi, *Pan-Africanism: A History* (London: Bloomsbury, 2018); Reiland Rabaka, ed., *Routledge Handbook of Pan-Africanism* (London: Routledge, 2020); Brent Hayes Edwards, *The Practice of Diaspora: Literature, Translation, and the Rise of Black Internationalism* (Cambridge, MA: Harvard University Press, 2003); J. Ayodele Langley, *Pan-Africanism and Nationalism in West Africa, 1900–1945* (Oxford: Clarendon Press, 1973); Toyin Falola and Kwame Essien, eds., *Pan-Africanism, and the Politics of African Citizenship and Identity* (London: Routledge, 2014).

6. Sarah Claire Dunstan, "Conflicts of Interest: The 1919 Pan-African Congress and the Wilsonian Moment," *Callaloo* 39, 1 (Winter 2016): 133–50.

Several organizations, of varying degrees of longevity, continued to push for pan-African ideals in the 1920s and 1930s. In addition to the Pan-African Congresses held in 1921, 1923, and 1927, notable contributions came from the League for Coloured Peoples, the West African Student Union, La Ligue Universelle pour la Défense de la Race Noire (the Universal League for the Defense of the Black Race), and the International African Service Bureau.[7] The Universal Negro Improvement Association, founded during the war by Jamaican-born Marcus Garvey, spread along sea routes through the efforts of sailors and migrating workers, and pushed into the hinterland of port cities in the West Indies, the United States, and Africa in the 1920s and 1930s. Garvey advocated Black control of economic and political institutions. He popularized his views through newspapers and other means and attracted followers across the African diaspora. His movement extended well beyond the educated elites who populated other pan-Africanist endeavors.[8]

Another West Indian, George Padmore, published sharp analyses in newspapers, pamphlets, and books on issues of both race and class. Padmore passed through the Moscow-centered circuit of Black communists, and after breaking with communism in 1933 he devoted his energies to pan-Africanist political networks and writing. At the core of Padmore's thought, as his biographer puts it, was his view of "empire, racism, and economic degradation as part of a *system* that fundamentally required the application of a *strategy* to their destruction."[9] The positions and objectives of the pan-Africanist opponents of imperialism varied from pushing for rights within existing imperial structures, to demanding national

---

7. On the varieties of pan-Africanism, see Arno Sonderegger, "Ideas Matter: Framing Pan-Africanism, Its Concept and History," *Stichproben: Vienna Journal of African Studies* 38 (2020): 5–32; Philippe Dewitte, *Les mouvements nègres en France, 1919–1939* (Paris: L'Harmattan, 1985); Marc Goulding, "Vanguards of the New Africa: Black Radical Networks and Anti-imperialism in the 1930s," PhD dissertation, New York University, 2012.

8. See the monumental collection edited by Robert Hill, *The Marcus Garvey and Universal Negro Improvement Association Papers* (vols. 1–10, Berkeley: University of California Press, 1983–2006, vols. 11–13; Durham, NC: Duke University Press, 2011–2016).

9. Leslie James, *George Padmore and Decolonization from Below: Pan-Africanism, the Cold War, and the End of Empire* (Basingstoke, UK: Palgrave Macmillan, 2015), 2. For Padmore's version of the history of pan-Africanism, his attack on colonialism, and his critique of communist initiatives in the colonial world, see George Padmore, *Pan-Africanism or Communism* (Garden City, NY: Doubleday, 1972 [1955]).

independence, to creating a political entity embracing all of Africa and its diaspora. Looking at the range of writing by Black activists on both sides of the Atlantic, Musab Younis concludes that they "prioritized the scale of the world—not at the expense or exclusion of other scales, but in the face of the relentlessly provincializing discourses of colonial rule."[10]

A range of Asianisms were also in play from at least the beginning of the twentieth century.[11] That colonial power, extended across much of the world during the nineteenth century, justified itself on a racist claim to European superiority elicited responses on an equally broad scale—an inclusive vision of civilization.[12] From Russia came Trubetskoi's plea for a revolt of all humanity against Europe (chapter 1). Other proposals were based on the idea that Asia was a single space, distinct from the rest of the world. Some theories were "Sino-centric," growing out of the extensive trade connections and Chinese diaspora in Southeast and East Asia. Sun Yat-Sen, the leading architect of the Chinese republic that was formed after the collapse of the Qing dynasty, evoked a "Greater Asianism." As Wang Hui describes Sun Yat-Sen's goals, "He hoped to be able to unite the pluralism of the culture of the empire with new types of relations among nation-states so as to resist the colonialist policies of imperialism and the tendency toward the high degree of cultural homogenization found in the nation-state."[13]

Sun Yat Sen's cultural vision was one of affinity, not identity, across Asia, and his political ideas stressed connection, not unity.[14] His ideas emerged from the experience of Chinese empire across a vast and diverse space. Cultural complexes could be imagined in

10. Musab Younis, *On the Scale of the World: The Formation of Black Anticolonial Thought* (Berkeley: University of California Press, 2022), 8.

11. Cemil Aydin, *The Politics of Anti-Westernism in Asia: Visions of World Order in Pan-Islamic and Pan-Asian Thought* (New York: Columbia University Press, 2007); Sven Saaler and Christopher W. A. Szpilman, eds., *Pan-Asianism: A Documentary History*, 2 vols. (Lanham, MD: Rowman & Littlefield, 2011); Carolien Stolte and Harald Fischer-Tiné, "Imagining Asia in India: Nationalism and Internationalism (ca. 1905–1940)," *Comparative Studies in Society and History* 54, 1 (2012): 65–92.

12. Nicole CuUnjieng Aboitiz, "AHR Reflections: Race and Nationalism in Anticolonial Asia," *American Historical Review* 127, 1 (2022): 355–60.

13. Wang Hui, *The Politics of Imagining Asia* (Cambridge, MA: Harvard University Press, 2011), 32.

14. Ibid., 60–61.

other forms. A shared sense of a Malay culture linking Malaya, Indonesia, and the Philippines influenced some intellectuals and politicians. The development of politics in turn-of-the-century Asia, Nicole CuUnjieng Aboitiz argues, included combinations of claims to the particularity of place and culture, connections across Asia, universalistic moral visions, and critique of western pretensions and power.[15]

Both the possibilities and the difficulties of spatial connections were evident in the volatile relationship between the two giants of Asia—India and China. Both had extended economic, cultural, and political influence well beyond their borders. In the 1920s, as Tansen Sen remarks, "unity between India and China had become an integral part of this discourse on Asianism." Intellectuals from both sides of the Himalayas promoted this linkage, including as illustrious an intellectual as Rabindranath Tagore, who pointed out the time depth of Buddhist connections.[16] Tagore's culturalist vision of Asia led him to criticize nationalism, challenging the dominant view in the Indian National Congress (INC).

Other Asianists pushed a "Greater India" perspective, insisting that India was the cradle of the cultural complex that defined Asian commonality (sometimes assimilating Buddhist and Hindu religions to each other). Still others, including Jawaharlal Nehru of the INC, insisted that whatever the cultural commonalities, the fundamental issue was political—the struggle against European imperialism. The leading political parties of India and China in the 1920s, the INC and the Guomindang (GMD), developed, for a while, cooperative relations. Meanwhile the world-spanning Indian diaspora provided a basis for organizations with extensive linkages, such as the radical Ghadar movement founded in San Francisco

15. Nicole CuUnjieng Aboitiz, *Asian Place, Filipino Nation: A Global Intellectual History of the Philippine Revolution, 1887–1912* (New York: Columbia University Press, 2020). Alongside her focus on connections, Aboitiz makes clear that "for the colonized, no strategy could afford to be purely transnational" (13). Whereas China was a source of both cultural and political inspiration in early twentieth-century Southeast Asia, Rebecca Karl points out that political movements throughout Asia had a strong influence on Chinese nationalists. *Staging the World: Chinese Nationalism at the Turn of the Twentieth Century* (Durham, NC: Duke University Press, 2002).

16. Tansen Sen, *India, China, and the World: A Connected History* (Lanham, MD: Rowman & Littlefield, 2017), 294.

just before World War I. These far-flung networks expressed a mix of ideologies—anarchism, socialism, nationalism, and revolutionary romanticism.[17]

Japan provided an inspiration to Asianists both through its selective adaptations of western technology and statecraft and its defiant assertion of its power as an autonomous state on the world scene. This reputation was enhanced by the Japanese defeat of Russia in the war of 1905. But Japan's intensifying subordination of Korea, especially after 1910, put the country in an ambiguous position in relation to other Asian peoples. Japan was an opponent of European imperialism but was imperialist itself. Japanese claims to be an Asian "big brother" to its neighbors were not generally convincing, and after Japan's military intervention into China in 1931, Indian and Chinese leaders increasingly defined themselves against Japanese as well as European imperialism.[18]

Attempts to forge an Asiatic Labour Congress, instigated by Indian trade unionists in the late 1920s, also reflected a pan-Asianist and internationalist approach to social questions, but these efforts were bedeviled by splits between communists and reformists, the Sino-Japanese conflict, and other tensions. Indian women's groups, some associated with the INC, made international connections of their own, developing perspectives on political mobilization that were simultaneously nationalist and cosmopolitan.[19] Activists in Southeast Asia—divided by geography and the multiplicity of historical trajectories in the region, including colonization by different European powers—joined meetings and networks trying to develop Asian solidarity, but they were anxious about the dangers of Indian or Chinese dominance and sensitive to the mixed loyalties of the

17. Maia Ramnath, *Hajj to Utopia: How the Ghadar Movement Charted Global Radicalism and Attempted to Overthrow the British Empire* (Berkeley: University of California Press, 2011).

18. Tim Harper, *Underground Asia: Global Revolutionaries and the Assault on Empire* (Cambridge, MA: Harvard University Press, 2020), 33. The Japanese anti-western model and Japanese connections were particularly influential among nationalists in the Philippines, from the fight against Spanish and American imperialism at the end of the nineteenth century until the experience of Japanese imperialism in the 1940s. Aboitiz, *Asian Place, Filipino Nation*.

19. Rosalind Parr, *Citizens of Everywhere: Indian Women, Nationalism and Cosmopolitanism, 1920-1952* (Cambridge: Cambridge University Press, 2021).

extensive Indian and Chinese diasporas in many countries of the region.[20]

A variety of political ideas inspired and sometimes brought together opponents of imperialism in South and Southeast Asia both before and after World War I. Anarchists—influenced by the Russian Peter Kropotkin, among others—formed small cells that communicated with each other and sometimes engaged in demonstrative acts of violence. Long-term organization was not their strong point. Christian missions and educational efforts, on the other hand, spawned hubs of activists who made clear how much colonial regimes violated their stated principles. Muslim and Buddhist networks, whether or not they confronted colonial regimes directly, offered alternative moral visions of society.[21]

In 1917, Bolshevik Russia inaugurated its global project. The Communist International (Comintern), founded in 1919, provided material and ideological support to activists from India, Vietnam, Indonesia, the Middle East, and elsewhere. The next year, the Comintern organized the conference of "Peoples of the East" in Baku, attended by nearly two thousand delegates from thirty-seven countries.[22] Support of the Comintern helped leftist activists like M. N. Roy and Nguyen Ai Quoc (later Ho Chi Minh) travel around the world in attempts to launch a worldwide movement against western imperialism.

20. Stolte and Fischer-Tiné, "Imagining Asia in India." On the labor front, see Carolien Stolte, "Bringing Asia to the World: Indian Trade Unionism and the Long Road toward the Asiatic Labour Congress, 1919–37," *Journal of Global History* 7, 2 (2012): 257–78.

21. Harper, *Underground Asia*; Aydin, *The Politics of Anti-westernism in Asia*. For the complex politics of Japanese anarchists, see Tatiana Linkhoeva, *Revolution Goes East: Imperial Japan and Soviet Communism* (Ithaca, NY: Cornell University Press, 2020), 127–58. On Kropotkin, see Jane Burbank, *Intelligentsia and Revolution: Russian Views of Bolshevism, 1917–1922* (New York: Oxford University Press, 1986), 99–105. Anarchism in Russia was destroyed by the Bolshevik government.

22. On the Bolsheviks' initial outreach efforts and the Baku conference, see, among others, Masha Kirasirova, "The Eastern International: The 'Domestic East' and the 'Foreign East' in Soviet-Arab Relations, 1917–68," PhD dissertation, New York University, 2014. More generally see Silvio Pons, *The Global Revolution: A History of International Communism, 1917–1991* (Oxford: Oxford University Press, 2014); *Cambridge History of Communism*, 3 vol. (Cambridge: Cambridge University Press, 2017); and Holger Weiss, ed., *International Communism and Transnational Solidarity: Radical Networks, Mass Movements, and Global Politics, 1919–1939* (Leiden: Brill, 2017).

Manu Goswami has underlined the variety of internationalist perspectives in Asia, insisting that they were "crafted from heterogeneous worlds" and were "neither reducible nor opposed to nationalism."[23] These efforts worked best when linked to local organizers, including trade unions that were able to foment large-scale strikes. Over the 1920s and 1930s, communist anti-imperialists set up organizations in imperial capitals as well as colonial cities. Activists, however, were obliged to adjust to changing strategies dictated by Soviet leaders—including whether or not to work alongside non-communist movements against colonial rulers—often to the frustration of the ablest organizers. Followed by the secret services of the colonial powers, often struggling to link their cosmopolitan theories and ways of being to the lives of workers and peasants, communist anti-imperialists in the interwar years could not bring about the world revolution that was their ultimate goal. They nonetheless contributed to the ferment that would lead to other kinds of anti-imperial actions.[24]

Communists were not the only opponents of colonial rule to make connections across space. In the late 1920s, the leaders of two of the strongest nationalist parties in Asia, the Indian National Congress and the Guomindang, were not only talking to each other but reaching out beyond the continent. The INC and the GMD took part in the creation of the League against Imperialism in Brussels in 1927. A German communist, Willi Münzenberg, was instrumental in founding the League, and in its early years, the League brought together a broad spectrum of anticolonial movements. Its executive committee had members from China, Mexico, India, Philippines, North Africa, South Africa, Egypt, Persia, Japan, Puerto Rico, and Korea, as well as all major European states. The League's initial conference produced resolutions condemning "all forms of oppression against colonial peoples" and pledges to work together against imperialism in its various forms. It identified imperialism and capitalism as global problems that could only be overcome with the mobilization of all their victims. The 1927 meeting left its

---

23. Manu Goswami, "Imaginary Futures and Colonial Internationalisms," *American Historical Review* 117, 5 (2012): 1461–62, 1474.
24. Harper, *Underground Asia*.

delegates with a sense of participation in a common struggle and led to contacts among anticolonial activists from different continents. It had a durable influence on individual careers in politics, on the course of struggles for independence through the formation of League branches in different territories, and on future efforts at collaboration and solidarity across the colonial empires.[25]

Indian and Chinese delegates to the 1927 Brussels conference affirmed that a long history of cultural connection brought them together and helped them make common cause against imperialism. But soon after the League's founding, the GMD broke with the Chinese Communist Party and initiated a massacre of communists in China, to the consternation of many members of the League. Communist-socialist splits in Europe also contributed to these divisions, and by 1931, the League drifted toward becoming an organization of those who were willing to follow the shifting lines of the Comintern. The League lasted until 1937; some of its leading lights went on to form other inter-empire movements engaged in the fight against colonialism.[26]

The interplay of nationalism and internationalism was particularly vivid in the ideas of Jawaharlal Nehru. Joining the International League against Imperialism at its inception in 1927, he contended that national sovereignty was "only halfway" to achieving anti-imperialist goals. Nehru put the Indian National Congress's conflict with Great Britain into a wider trans-imperial context. If internationalism for some members meant a single global project uniting the oppressed people of the world, for Nehru and others at the end of the 1920s and through the 1930s it entailed a relationship among existing or would-be states, each of which asserted its distinctiveness as well as its participation in a common cause against capitalist imperialism.[27]

---

25. Michele Louro, Carolien Stolte, Heather Streets-Salter, and Sana Tannoury-Karam, "Introduction," to Louro, Stolte, Streets-Salter, and Tannoury-Karam, eds., *The League Against Imperialism: Lives and Afterlives* (Leiden: Leiden University Press, 2020), 18 quoted; Disha Karnad Jani, "The League against Imperialism, National Liberation, and the Economic Question," *Journal of Global History* 17, 2 (2022): 210–32.

26. Louro et al., *The League Against Imperialism*.

27. Michele Louro, *Comrades against Imperialism: Nehru, India, and Interwar Internationalism* (Cambridge: Cambridge University Press, 2018). See also Carolien Stolte,

The overlapping networks and discourses of activists came together in, among other places, imperial capitals. Paris and London were prominent as hubs of networks of intellectuals and political activists critical of the regimes directed from those capitals. Émigrés from communist Russia also congregated in European cities, grouped by political and other allegiances, and unlikely to have contact with anti-imperialists coming from Africa and Asia. Moscow, however, was a necessary stop on the circuits of communist-inspired activists from different continents. Hamburg and Berlin emerged as centers for activists who needed to get beyond the repressive reach of French or British empires, and some Nazi leaders thought that opposition to enemy imperialisms was worth cultivating.[28]

The sites of connection-making were not limited to the imperial capitals of Europe. Bombay, Calcutta, Colombo, Rangoon, Singapore, Batavia, Surabaya, Saigon, Manila, Hong Kong, Canton, Amoy, and Shanghai were all, writes John Sidel, "increasingly vibrant, densely populated, and ethnically diverse cosmopolitan entrepôts." In these cities, coffee shops, lodging houses, and local printing shops became meeting points for activists from different parts of Asia, facilitating the activities of Muslim, Christian, communist, and other boundary-crossing communities.[29]

The immediate objectives of internationalist activists were varied, and in the interwar years did not necessarily converge on national independence. Anticolonial, anticapitalist activists such

---

"Towards Afro-Asia? Continuities and Change in Indian Anti-imperialist Regionalism, 1927–1957," in Louro et al., *The League against Imperialism*, 347–69.

28. Michael Goebel, *Anti-Imperial Metropolis: Interwar Paris and the Seeds of Third World Nationalism* (Cambridge: Cambridge University Press, 2015); Jennifer Anne Boittin, *Colonial Metropolis: The Urban Grounds of Anti-Imperialism and Feminism in Interwar Paris* (Lincoln: University of Nebraska Press, 2010); Marc Matera, *Black London: The Imperial Metropolis and Decolonization in the Twentieth Century* (Berkeley: University of California Press, 2015); David Motadel, "The Global Authoritarian Movement and the Revolt against Empire," *American Historical Review* 124, 3 (2019): 843–77. On Bolshevik and anti-Bolshevik networks coming out of Russia, see Marc Raeff, *Russia Abroad: A Cultural History of the Russian Emigration, 1919–39* (New York: Oxford University Press, 1990), and Masha Kirasirova, "The 'East' as a Category of Bolshevik Ideology and Comintern Administration: The Arab Section of the Communist University of the Toilers of the East," *Kritika: Explorations in Russian and Eurasian History* 18, 1 (2017): 7–34.

29. John Sidel, *Republicanism, Communism, Islam: Cosmopolitan Origins of Revolution in Southeast Asia* (Ithaca, NY: Cornell University Press, 2021), 9 quoted.

as Nguyen Ai Quoc of Vietnam, Tan Malaka from the Dutch East Indies, and M. N. Roy of India had frequent encounters with people who shared their views, and their actions gave rise to networks that crossed both national and imperial boundaries. As Tim Harper puts it, "many of these men and women believed that the solidarities they made—born from a shared history of oppression and exploitation, and of negotiation of borders and exclusion—would prevail over the narrowness of nations and usher in a common utopian destiny."[30] Some activists in these circuits wanted an imperial citizenship that would actually convey rights,[31] others rejected any association with a colonizing power, and still others promoted global communist revolution or else looked toward connections among Muslims or Christians to transform values and promote family life around the world. In these same years some intellectuals and political leaders—in the spirit of Coudenhove-Kalergi (chapter 2)—advocated diplomatic initiatives to turn rival empires into peacefully coexisting federations.

Benedict Anderson used the concept of circuits to analyze the transformation from the late eighteenth century onward of ideas expressed in imperial capitals and in imperial languages into nationalist discourses in vernacular languages.[32] Rather than looking for a transition from one kind of circuit to another and for a spread outward from established capitals, we begin our exploration of Afroasia's formation with political activists moving, simultaneously or otherwise, among multiple circuits and then explore how their different possibilities expanded or contracted over time.

There were obstacles to worldwide political projects aimed at countering the broad reach of imperial powers in the interwar years. Educated elites from different colonial terrains might meet in Paris, London, or Moscow, but the weaknesses of communication and the often extreme differences between a literate, urban-based elite and rural-based people made it difficult to turn those

30. Harper, *Underground Asia*, 19.

31. On demands for citizenship rights within empire, see among other sources Sukanya Banerjee, *Becoming Imperial Citizens: Indians in the Late-Victorian Empire* (Durham, NC: Duke University Press, 2010).

32. Benedict Anderson, *Imagined Communities: Reflections on the Origin and Spread of Nationalism* (London: Verso, 1983).

connections into mass movements in the colonies.[33] Moreover, the structure of empire fragmented networks even as it shaped their long-distance character. Opponents of empire made their cases in English, French, Dutch, Portuguese, Japanese, and other imperial languages, drawing on different traditions to expose the hypocrisies of colonial rule and to propose alternatives. Pan-African organizations between 1900 and 1945 were largely anglophone and the négritude movement largely francophone, even though the conception of empire-wide unity of people of African descent was similar in the two instances.

Anti-empire connections were not always integrative. Tensions over the autonomy of Tibet between Indian and Chinese elites were already present in the 1930s, and would push relations to a breaking point later on.[34] Movements developed in local and regional contexts, and histories, cultures, and economic conditions differed even within a single colonial territory, let alone among them. The process of making demands on imperial powers or petitioning the Permanent Mandates Commission of the League of Nations could push activists into claim-making for individual territories. Michael Barnett suggests that the procedures of claiming and petitioning—rather than intrinsic national sentiment—created "path-dependence" in the Middle East, redirecting the pan-Arabism of intellectuals and political activists toward a politics more focused on each territory.[35]

For all the efforts of activists to stress the common experience of subordination to imperial rule, the world of empires was itself the most important source of fragmentation. People across Africa and Asia experienced imperial subordination, but not in the same way. Even the intercontinental experience of Mohandas Gandhi—an iconic moment in accounts of his political formation—underscores different positionings as much as commonality. Gandhi was drawn

---

33. Louro et al. point out that "the spaces most conducive to the growth of international antiocolonial movements tended to be in European or American cities," not least because of the repression within the colonies (*The League Against Imperialism*, 34).

34. Sen, *India, China, and the World*, chapter 4.

35. Michael Barnett, "Sovereignty, Nationalism, and Regional Order in the Arab States System," in Thomas Biersteker and Cynthia Weber, eds., *State Sovereignty as Social Construct* (Cambridge: Cambridge University Press, 1996), 148–89.

into politics at the beginning of the twentieth century by his revulsion at the discriminatory treatment of Indians living in South Africa at the hands of a racially repressive regime. At the time, he sought an alternative not in Afroasian solidarity, but in imperial citizenship. In 1906, he backed the British government's suppression of a rebellion by Africans; he supported the British cause during the World War of 1914–1918.[36] It was both the failure of the British government to make good on its promise of conceding representative government to Indians in return for their contribution to the war effort and the refusal of the dominions—especially Canada and Australia—to allow Indians to enter and reside in their territories that drove the Indian National Congress, by the end of the 1920s, away from its demand for full citizenship rights within the British Empire and toward seeking full independence.[37]

Colonization, much as it was linked to premises of white superiority, fostered differentiation among the people it subordinated, both as a conscious strategy and as a consequence of exploiting people in particular ways in particular places. Colonial regimes allowed limited pathways to economic advantage to certain people and not to others. Afroasian solidarity did not follow directly from the experience of colonization; it required work.

Tension between Indians and Africans emerged in East Africa, where substantial Indian immigration had taken place. Some people of South Asian origin took an active role in trade union and other movements that challenged colonial rule in Africa, but a significant fraction of Asian migrants were more concerned with building their own communities and achieving success in commerce than with political action.[38] Imperial governments were able to play on and exacerbate distinction to avoid broad mobilization against their authority. In Kenya during the 1920s, for example,

---

36. Ashwin Desai and Goolam Vahed, *The South African Gandhi: Stretcher-Bearer of Empire* (Stanford, CA: Stanford University Press, 2016).

37. Mrinalini Sinha, "Whatever Happened to the Third British Empire? Empire, Nation Redux," in Andrew Thompson, ed., *Writing Imperial Histories* (Manchester: Manchester University Press, 2013), 168–187; Radhika Mongia, *Indian Migration and Empire: A Colonial Genealogy of the Modern State* (Durham, NC: Duke University Press, 2018).

38. On efforts at both cultural and political cooperation between Indians and Africans, see Shobana Shankar, *An Uneasy Embrace: Africa, India and the Spectre of Race* (London: Hurst, 2021).

the colonial government was so worried over African-Asian cooperation that it declared its policy to be "African paramountcy"—a thinly veiled attempt to play Africans off against Kenyan Asians, although the government was for the most part acting in support of white settlers.[39]

Taken together, studies of the different regional and global movements against imperialism reveal the complexity of politics in the interwar period, when activists faced multiple possibilities and myriad constraints. The air of inevitability or normality attached to the concept of empire—with its millennia-long history—was being questioned in many places at the same time. Nonetheless, as Ali Raza, Franziska Roy, and Benjamin Zachariah point out, the internationalist movement of the interwar years "contained within it the seeds of its own destruction."[40] To the extent that mobilization made an imperial power nervous enough to modify its behavior, it encouraged political action within each imperial framework. Anti-imperialists' efforts to reconcile national and international aspirations, as Nehru had hoped, faced the problem that the second objective—the radical restructuring of global politics—was the more difficult to attain.

The interwar years were in some ways the high point of trans-imperial, transcontinental efforts to organize an anti-imperialist, anti-racist front. Racialized imperialism from the early twentieth century through the 1930s constituted a global target for its enemies to attack.[41] World War II would drastically alter the politics of anti-imperialism.

---

39. Sana Aiyar, *Indians in Kenya: The Politics of Diaspora* (Cambridge, MA: Harvard University Press, 2015); Robert Gregory, *India and East Africa: a History of Race Relations Within the British Empire, 1890–1939* (Oxford: Oxford University Press, 1971); Jagjit Singh Mangat, *A History of the Asians in East Africa, c.1886 to 1945* (Oxford: Oxford University Press, 1969).

40. Ali Raza, Franziska Roy, and Benjamin Zachariah, "Introduction: The Internationalism of the Moment—South Asia and the Contours of the Interwar World," in *The Internationalist Moment: South Asia, Worlds, and World Views 1917–39* (Los Angeles: Sage, 2015), xxxii.

41. Marilyn Lake and Henry Reynolds point out that racialization came not only from imperial centers but from settler colonies. *Drawing the Global Colour Line: White Men's Countries and the International Challenge of Racial Equality* (Cambridge: Cambridge University Press, 2008).

Empire and Its Enemies from World War II to Bandung

At first glance, the work of anti-imperialist networks and anti-colonial internationalism should have been given a boost by the extreme damage that World War II inflicted on France, Great Britain, the Netherlands, and other imperial powers. The war did change the configuration of power, but not in the way anti-imperialists had envisioned.

Pan-Africanists tried to seize the moment at their conference held in Manchester, England, in October 1945, animated by established leaders such as Du Bois and Padmore and joined by future leaders Kwame Nkrumah and Jomo Kenyatta. The conference issued a searing condemnation of colonialism and offered a vision of the future in which people of African descent on the African continent and in the diaspora would govern themselves. The resolutions did not, however, provide a clear explanation of what kind of institutions pan-African governance would entail or how one could get from the colonial present to a liberated future.[42]

The Asian Relations Conference was organized in March 1947 by the Indian Council of World Affairs (with Nehru playing a major role) and attended by representatives from twenty-eight countries. Held in Delhi just before India became independent, the conference was boycotted by the Muslim League that was about to lead Pakistan to its separate nationhood. Nehru wanted to continue the anti-imperial campaign begun before the war and establish a basis for cooperation among emerging Asian states without forming a "bloc" opposed to the United States and the Soviet Union. The meeting was characterized by intense debates, revealing multiple visions of how diverse territories could work together. The speeches made a case for historical and cultural connections and highlighted the shared goal of fighting imperialism and colonial capitalism. But the conference also exposed fissures: between Muslims and Hindus in South Asia, Chinese and Indians over Tibet, between China and India on the one hand and smaller states fearful of the power of the

---

42. Hakim Adi and Marika Sherwood, *The 1945 Manchester Pan-African Congress Revisited* (London: New Beacon Books, 1995).

large ones on the other.⁴³ In conferees' speeches about expanding the anti-imperialist network, a tone of paternalism toward Africa could be heard, as in Nehru's assertion that the people of Asia "have a special responsibility to the people of Africa."⁴⁴

The conference addressed the tension between an Asia-wide confrontation with imperialism and the aspirations of each territory for sovereignty. With India on the verge of independence, its position was particularly sensitive. India had long made the cause of Indians outside the country—labor migrants, business people, and others—part of its political stance, but with independence approaching and countries with large numbers of Indian immigrants worried about migrants' loyalty to emerging states, positions shifted. The conference ended up supporting the position that Indians abroad could no longer claim protection by the Indian state and that each state would define its own citizenry and be entitled to treat others, Asians included, as aliens. The conference thus took a significant step toward seeing the future as an Asia of self-governing states.⁴⁵

Similarly, the Congress of the Peoples of Europe, Asia, and Africa, put together by socialist organizations in Europe and India and held in France in June 1948, assembled three hundred delegates from thirty-seven countries. The meeting revealed both widely shared criticism of colonial regimes and many differences over the question of independence for colonies, the participation of socialists in governments (including France and Britain) that were holding on to colonies, and opposition to Stalin's Russia. Some European socialists expressed condescending views toward Africans. Attempts to follow up came to naught.⁴⁶

---

43. Stolte, "Towards Afro-Asia?"
44. Nehru, quoted in ibid., 360.
45. Carolien Stolte, "'The Asiatic Hour': New Perspectives on the Asian Relations Conference, New Delhi, 1947," in Natasa Miskovic, Harald Fischer-Tiné, and Nada Boskovska, eds., *The Non-Aligned Movement and the Cold War: Delhi-Bandung-Belgrade* (London: Routledge, 2014). 57–75; Vineet Thakur, "An Asian Drama: The Asian Relations Conference, 1947," *International History Review* 41, 3 (2019): 673–95; Itty Abraham, *How India Became Territorial: Foreign Policy, Diaspora, Geopolitics* (Stanford, CA: Stanford University Press, 2014), 68–70.
46. Anne-Isabelle Richard, "The Limits of Solidarity: Europeanism, Anti-colonialism and Socialism at the Congress of the Peoples of Europe, Asia and Africa in Puteaux, 1948," *European Review of History (Revue européenne d'histoire)* 21, 4 (2014): 519–37.

After 1945, the prospects for coordinated African, Asian, or Afroasian action were confronting a new problem in addition to older impediments to common action: their target was a moving one. By the fall of 1946, subjects of the French empire, from Indochina to Africa, had acquired—in large part through the ability of a small number of politicians from the colonies to play on the anxieties of French leaders—French citizenship. Activists in that empire were beginning a long struggle to make good on their claims for political, economic, and social rights based on that citizenship. It was in this context that Eurafrica emerged as a framework for Africans to call for political voice and economic resources (chapter 2). Britain was also making concessions to its increasingly militant African subjects in the form of new constitutions for Ghana, Nigeria, and other colonies as well as economic development programs, and it was preparing to concede power in India. In 1948, the British Nationality Act conferred something like an empire-wide citizenship on colonies as well as dominions, including the right of people throughout the empire to enter and work in the United Kingdom itself.[47]

Imperial regimes were well aware of the dangers they faced if they did not make concessions. Armed struggle in the Dutch East Indies, British Malaya, and French Indochina in the immediate aftermath of World War II, later in Cameroon, Kenya, Algeria, and elsewhere, gave the British and French governments strong reason to try to bring about change in other territories at a pace they thought they could control. However compromised, imperial reform turned into an opening wedge for continuing calls for more far-reaching change, while the independence of India (1947) and Indonesia (1949) provided models of national independence.

That alternative possibilities were emerging encouraged some political movements to focus on what seemed attainable—in their own locations. In the United States, political organizations

47. Randall Hansen, "The Politics of Citizenship in 1940s Britain: The British Nationality Act," *Twentieth Century British History* 10, 1 (1999): 67–95. More generally, see John Darwin, *The Empire Project: The Rise and Fall of the British World System 1830–1970* (Cambridge: Cambridge University Press, 2009). One of the first groups to take advantage of the Nationality Act were West Indians who came to Britain in 1948 on a ship that gave its name to an entire generation of migrants: the *Windrush* generation. Their arrival led to racialized anxiety among many Britons that has persisted for decades, although the new arrivals were fully within their legal rights to settle in Great Britain.

of African Americans were making claims in terms of the rights spelled out—but in practice denied—in the post–Civil War constitutional structure. Leaders evoked the wartime service of Black Americans and hoped that the ideology of white supremacy was losing public support. Prominent figures in the National Association for the Advancement of Colored People and other elite organizations focused the struggle on civil rights within the United States. While some activists—including Du Bois—maintained that the claim for rights in the United States was part of the global struggle against racialized imperialism, others feared that too close association with anti-imperialist struggles elsewhere, especially in the context of heightened fears of communist revolution, would compromise a cause that now seemed to offer real possibilities for reform.[48] Some battles appeared to be winnable, others much less so.

Bandung

The last point underscores both the breakthrough and the limitations of the iconic event in the history of Afroasian solidarity, the Bandung Conference of 1955. The initiative that gave the immediate impetus to Bandung was a conference in Colombo, Ceylon (now Sri Lanka) that brought together the leaders of Ceylon, India, Indonesia, Burma, and Pakistan in 1954. This group of newly independent states, which became known as the Colombo Powers, became the hosts at Bandung. Cindy Ewing argues that these five states "were not interested in revolution or liberation struggles of the kind they themselves had waged to gain independence. Rather, the Colombo Powers sought to bring onto the international stage a new coalition of Asian sovereigns that stood independently of bloc politics and yet were actively engaged in international relations."[49]

---

48. Penny von Eschen brings out the national framework of leading American civil rights activists in the 1950s in *Race Against Empire: Black Americans and Anticolonialism, 1937–1957* (Ithaca, NY: Cornell University Press, 1997). John Munro argues that a current of thought and action among African American activists continued to think in terms of an anticolonial struggle that included the United States as well as the formal empires of European powers. *The Anticolonial Front: The African American Freedom Struggle and Global Decolonisation, 1945–1960* (Cambridge: Cambridge University Press, 2017).

49. Cindy Ewing, "The Colombo Powers: Crafting Diplomacy in the Third World and Launching Afro-Asia at Bandung," *Cold War History* 19 (2019): 1–19. 2 quoted.

The Colombo Powers did not wish to dissolve their sovereignty in a larger Asian entity. They were instead asserting both their sovereignty and their interest in shaping through diplomatic channels the politics of Asia. Recognizing that Africa was also the site of states gaining sovereignty, they sought to include those states in what was taking shape as an Afroasian conference.[50]

Much myth-making surrounds Bandung, but the event nonetheless serves as a dramatic indicator of how the colonial question was changing during the 1950s. The conference was not a meeting of Afroasian people as such, but of heads of state and their closest collaborators. Of the leading lights of the conference, Sukarno of Indonesia (the host) and Nehru of India led countries that had become independent in the late 1940s; Gamal Abdel Nasser of Egypt, who had come to power via military coup in 1952, headed a country that had been nominally independent for decades but whose previous government had had clientelistic relations with Great Britain that Nasser was now seeking to transform. Africa was only partially represented, for most countries there were not yet independent states. African participants or observers came from Egypt, Ethiopia, Liberia, Libya, Sudan, and self-governing but not yet independent Gold Coast (later Ghana). Some later commentators placed Kwame Nkrumah at the conference, but he wasn't there.[51]

The delegates to Bandung condemned the "evil" of colonialism and put forth their goal of cooperation in pursuit of economic development.[52] The strongest tie among the participants was that

---

50. There was also an Arab-Asian group at the UN, formed by some of the first former colonies to gain admission to that world body. Beginning in the 1949–50 General Assembly session, this group put criticism of colonialism on the agenda. Cindy Ewing, "'With a Minimum of Bitterness': Decolonization, the Right to Self-determination, and the Arab-Asian Group," *Journal of Global History* 17, 1 (2022): 254–71.

51. Robert Vitalis, "The Midnight Ride of Kwame Nkrumah and Other Fables of Bandung (Ban-doong)," *Humanity: An International Journal of Human Rights* 4, 2 (2013): 261–88. Among the now numerous books on Bandung are Christopher Lee, ed., *Making a World after Empire: The Bandung Moment and Its Political Afterlives* (Athens: Ohio University Press, 2010); J.A.C. Mackie, *Bandung 1955: Non-Alignment and Afro-Asian Solidarity* (Singapore: Editions Didier Millet, 2005); George McTurnan Kahin, *The Asian-African Conference, Bandung, Indonesia, April 1955* (Ithaca, NY: Cornell University Press, 1956). See also Sunil Amrith, "Asian Internationalism: Bandung's Echo in a Colonial Metropolis," *Inter-Asian Cultural Studies* 6, 4 (2005): 557–69.

52. The final communiqué to which the conference members agreed is available on a number of websites, such as https://www.cvce.eu/en/obj/final_communique_of_the

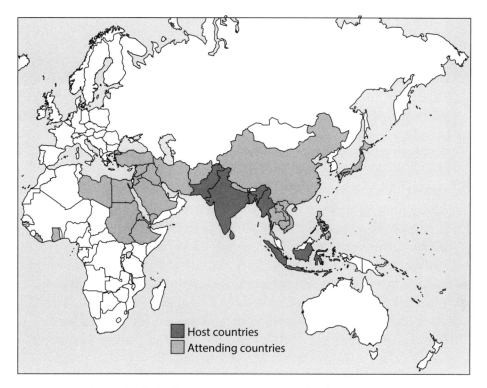

MAP 3.1. Countries (including some not yet independent) participating in the Afro-Asian Conference at Bandung, 1955

they shared, in the words spoken there by the distinguished Philippine diplomat Carlos Romulo, "a common historical experience. We belong to the community of hurt, heartbreak, and deferred hopes."[53] They endorsed the principle of self-determination and called for "respect of the sovereignty and territorial integrity of all nations." They insisted upon "recognition of the equality of all races and of the equality of nations large and small." They warned of the dangers of nuclear war and the machinations of great powers and argued for cooperation to maintain international peace. The participants

---

_asian_african_conference_of_bandung_24_april_1955-en-676237bd-72f7-471f-949a-88b6ae513585.html, accessed March 15, 2022.

53. Indonesia, Ministry of Foreign Affairs, *Asia-Africa Speaks from Bandung* (Jakarta, 1955), 202, cited in Margaret Macmillan and Patrick Quinton-Brown, "The Uses of History in International Society: From the Paris Peace Conference to the Present," *International Affairs* 95 (2019): 191. Carlos Romulo, *The Meaning of Bandung* (Chapel Hill: University of North Carolina Press, 1956), 2.

denounced the racist policies of South Africa, but gave explicit support to anticolonial movements only in Algeria, Tunisia, and Morocco. Many criticized the United States as a supporter, and more and more the key instigator, of an imperialist order. They advocated future cooperation and set the precedent for a series of meetings, but they did not establish institutions for collective action.

There were tensions: between the aspirations of its leading figures to be at the forefront of whatever movement emerged, between states that were accepting aid from the United States (Iran, Turkey, Philippines, and others) and the People's Republic of China whose high-placed representative Zhou Enlai defended communism.[54] Africans worried that some of the Asian leaders, including Nehru, had a paternalistic attitude toward them, although this awareness did not stop many of them from later making use of the personal connections they established with Asian activists or from appreciating the spirit of cooperation in struggles that ensued from Bandung and other meetings.[55] Although sometimes seen as the founding moment of the Non-Aligned Movement or "Third World" politics, the final resolutions, given the diversity of viewpoints represented, finessed Cold War questions.[56]

The conference revealed dilemmas faced by postcolonial states that have been the focus of concern and debate ever since. Carlos Romulo pointedly asked, "Do we fight to regain our manhood from Western colonial rulers only to surrender it to rulers among ourselves who seize the power to keep us enslaved?" He was strongly critical of western racism, but also warned against any "counterracism" of Black against white. Most revealing were his reservations about nationalism despite his strong belief in the self-determination of peoples: "But let us not have too many illusions

---

54. Romulo, *The Meaning of Bandung* (16–22) explains the sharp disagreements between opponents and proponents of communism at the conference.

55. Gerard McCann, "Where Was the *Afro* in Afro-Asian Solidarity? Africa's 'Bandung Moment' in 1950s Asia," *Journal of World History* 30, 1–2 (2019): 89–123.

56. Ewing ("The Colombo Powers," 15) points out that Sukarno had kept his revolutionary fervor and emphasized at the conference the ongoing struggle against colonialism, while the leaders of the Five Colombo Powers were more concerned with "preserving sovereignty." She concludes that the Bandung Conference revealed "how differently the sponsoring nations viewed the future of the region." Ibid., 16.

FIGURE 3.1. Afro-Asian Conference, 1955. Prime Minister Zhou Enlai of People's Republic of China listening to debates while Premier Gamal Abdel Nasser of Egypt talks to another delegate. *Source:* Bettman/Getty Images.

about national independence . . . We have to strive to become nations in a time when history has already passed from the nation to larger units of economic and social coherence: the region, the continent, the world." The lesson he derived from the history of the western world was that "the nation, as such, has outlived its usefulness as an instrument of progress." He was particularly concerned that "the independence of the small or weak nation is at best a precarious and fragile thing."[57]

Indeed, the Bandung agenda aimed at building on the sovereignty that Afroasian states had recently acquired to create something more inclusive and stronger. The final resolutions of the Conference emphasized both national independence and cooperation among the new nations. It demanded "respect for fundamental human rights and for the purposes and principles of the Charter of the

---

57. Carlos Romulo, Statement to Bandung Conference, reprinted in his *Meaning of Bandung*, 68, 70, 72, 76.

United Nations"—leaving the door open to the enunciation of principles that transcended national sovereignty.[58]

The distinguished philosopher Souleymane Bachir Diagne sees in the Afro-Asian Conference at Bandung "the advent of a postcolonial world."[59] Unlike the other cross-continental concepts considered in this book, the Afro-Asian Conference dispensed with the "Eur"—with Europe. For Diagne, the break was not just a matter of setting up international alliances but an epistemic transformation, imagining a world in which political relationships and conceptual schemes did not have to pass through Europe.

The conceptual breakthrough might be seen as both wider and narrower—wider in that Bandung was one of many individual and collective initiatives to rethink international order and European claims to civilizational superiority and to shape a world in which political relationships were less vertical and more horizontal.[60] Narrower in that it would take the United Nations another five years to pass a resolution that definitively rejected the legitimacy of colonial rule, and in that the Bandung meeting itself was based on the presumption that the basic units of the world politics of the future would be territorial states, a model that European states had already claimed for themselves.[61] Even as participants in Bandung looked beyond what Romulo called "narrow nationalism" toward

---

58. Final communiqué as cited above (also reprinted in ibid., 101 quoted). As discussed in the introduction, the question of whether self-determination and human rights are complementary or contradictory frames is controversial among historians. The record at Bandung suggests that at least some Afroasian political leaders were trying to work in both frames.

59. Souleymane Bachir Diagne, "On the Universal and Universalism," in Diagne and Jean-Loup Amselle, *In Search of Africa(s): Universalism and Decolonial Thought*, trans. Andrew Brown (Cambridge: Polity Press, 2020), 166 n7.

60. Among the most direct challenges to European claims to epistemological dominance from the 1950s were Aimé Césaire, *Discours sur le colonialisme* (Paris: Présence Africaine, 1955), and Frantz Fanon, *Peau noir, masques blancs* (Paris: Seuil, 1952). The challenges date back much earlier and came from actors on different continents, Gandhi and Du Bois among the most influential. See chapter 1 on N. S. Trubetskoi's earlier critique of Eurocentrism.

61. Partha Chatterjee later referred to nationalism—at least in the form of claims to the nation-state—as a "derivative discourse," although he (and others) later presented more nuanced views of ways in which postcolonial conceptions of state and society both conformed to and broke away from European models. Partha Chatterjee, *Nationalist Thought and the Colonial World: A Derivative Discourse* (London: Zed Books, 1986); Partha

interconnections among the new states of Africa and Asia, those connections were to be among states.[62] Still, Bandung signaled that colonialism was no longer an ordinary condition, provided further impetus toward the demise of imperial power, and promoted thinking about alternative forms of international politics.

Looking back at Bandung a few years later, Léopold Sédar Senghor called the conference a "moral victory for the coloured peoples of the world," but insisted "that in the twentieth century absolute independence can only be theoretical, and that it must actually fit in with *interdependence*," including the cooperation of African nations with Europe, conditioned on "the end of colonialism."[63] In the ensuing years, the nation-state form would prove to be a platform for attacking global hierarchy but also a limitation on collective action. The national polities that were emerging from the colonial yoke in the 1950s and 1960s were each confronted with the continued constraints of vertical relations with the rich and powerful states of the world, with transnational corporations, and with international financial institutions, even as they sought to establish horizontal relations with each other.

For these reasons, the historian Michele Louro sees Bandung occupying a quite different place in an historical sequence than does Diagne: "Instead of inaugurating the third world project rooted in the ideas of the interwar period, the Bandung Conference must be seen as a closure."[64] For Louro, the salient feature of

---

Chatterjee, *The Nation and Its Fragments: Colonial and Postcolonial Histories* (Princeton, NJ: Princeton University Press, 1993).

62. Romulo, *Meaning of Bandung*, 26. The phrase "narrow nationalism" had also been used by Senghor's political group in the French National Assembly in 1948, cited in Cooper, *Citizenship between Empire and Nation*, 190.

63. Senghor, translated extract from "Les nationalismes d'outre-mer et l'avenir des peuples de couleur," *Encyclopédie française* 20 (1959), part 2, section C, chapter 11, in Philippe Braillard and Mohammad-Reza Djalili, *The Third World and International Relations* (London: Pinter, 1986), 58–59.

64. Louro, *Comrades against Imperialism*, 16. Luis Eslava, Michael Fakhri, and Vasuki Nesiah suggest that "it might make more sense to describe our contemporary international order as *Bandungian* rather than as *Westphalian*." It does make more sense to date the principle of a world of states autonomous of and juridically equivalent to each other to 1955 rather than 1648. As these authors point out, the idea of the Westphalian state is pure myth, and Bandung has produced its share of myths as well. "The Spirit of Bandung," in Luis Eslava, Michael Fakhri, and Vasuki Nesiah, eds., *Bandung, Global History, and*

the conference was that its participants came as representatives of states rather than a conference, like those of the interwar era, of political movements or men and women who considered themselves to be representing peoples struggling against imperialism on a global scale. As more and more states became independent after 1955, the question of how and how much they could make common cause *as states* became increasingly critical. Independence now entailed membership in the United Nations and other international bodies—fora where Afroasian states could interact with each other, make demands on richer states, and influence opinions around the world. They were inserting themselves in inter*national* politics.

The conference's significance lies above all in what people made of it afterward, in myths and reality. The very act of bringing together the leaders of states most of which had emerged from colonial empires signaled, to both those who attended and those who did not, that there were possibilities for cooperation and alliances outside of the imperial frameworks that up to then had structured world politics. As the Nassers, Nehrus, Sukarnos, and others jockeyed for influence, they both reinforced their territorial bases through their international visibility and addressed a wider audience.[65]

After Bandung: Afroasian Solidarity and the Great Powers

Among the observers keeping an eye on what was said at Bandung were officials of the United States. As plans for the conference became known, State Department officials expressed a mix of anxiety that it would take an anti-American turn and hope that it would at least chart a path away from the communist bloc. For these observers, the conference produced more relief than concern, for

---

International Law: Critical Pasts and Pending Futures (Cambridge: Cambridge University Press, 2017), 16–17.

65. As Sunil Amrith puts it, "The fundamental consensus of Bandung was an emphasis on the absolute sovereignty of the post-colonial state." "Asian Internationalism," 560. Christopher Lee makes much the same point. "Introduction: Between a Moment and an Era: The Origins and Afterlives of Bandung," in Lee, ed., *Making a World after Empire: The Bandung Moment and Its Political Afterlives* (Athens: Ohio University Press, 2010), 15–19.

the pronouncements of the most influential delegates seemed to be claiming a place in a state-centered order rather than trying to turn that order upside down. The anxieties the conference generated nonetheless pushed the American government further along its path away from supporting the continued colonial ventures of some of its allies.[66] A year after Bandung, the United States deployed economic threats to force Great Britain, France, and Israel to pull back after they invaded Egypt in response to Nasser's nationalization of the Suez Canal.

The American position on colonialism had been and remained ambiguous. During the war, the Roosevelt administration had given some indication that it, unlike Churchill, believed that the Atlantic Charter's denunciation of the conquest of one people by another applied generally, not just to Europe. The United States avoided acting on the basis of this interpretation in order to prioritize the struggle against the Nazis and Japan and then against the Soviet Union. Out of a combination of anti-communism and racism, American leaders feared what could happen if Africans or Asians governed themselves, but they tentatively tried to integrate decolonizing states into market economies and international institutions, while avoiding too explicit recognition of sovereign states' rights to control their own economic resources.

Early on, the United States had shown an ability to distinguish between reformers and nationalists who could be tolerated (like Sukarno in Indonesia) from communists who had to be combated (Ho Chi Minh in Vietnam), but American leaders proved capable of conflating the two. The United States orchestrated coups against what it perceived to be leftist governments in Iran in 1953 and Guatemala in 1954 and was part of the intrigue that led to the murder of Patrice Lumumba in the Congo in 1960. The United States abstained from the UN resolution of 1960 condemning colonialism, failed to budge Portugal from its violent defense of colonial empire

---

66. Jason Parker, "Cold War II: The Eisenhower Administration, the Bandung Conference, and the Reperiodization of the Postwar Era," *Diplomatic History* 30, 5 (2006): 867–92. Samuel Moyn asserts that the great powers were relieved that "the decolonization agenda was so traditional." "The High Tide of Anticolonial Legalism," *Journal of the History of International Law* 23, 1 (2021): [5–31], 14.

into the mid-1970s, and gave tacit support to South Africa while claiming to oppose apartheid.[67]

The US government was learning to adapt to a world-historic transformation, using its wealth and power to shape a system of independent, territorially defined states in line with its interests and vision of how an orderly, modern world could be constituted. That the new states might work more closely with each other than with the United States or its allies was a potential problem, but not necessarily an unsolvable one. The United States could provide both incentives and punishments to states that had torn themselves loose from colonial overrule. By sorting out sovereign states in relation to its Cold War priorities, the United States could sometimes get its way, but it also risked promoting what it sought to avoid. As Odd Arne Westad concludes, "By around 1970 the United States had done much to create the Third World as an entity both in a positive and negative sense." Above all, he notes, the economic system of which the United States was such a powerful part helped to perpetuate the conditions that made the Third World what it was and left the problems of poverty and inequality unsolved.[68] Bandung had at least raised the possibility that concerted action by formerly colonized territories could do what the richer and more powerful states of the world were not willing to even try.[69]

---

67. There is a substantial literature on the attitudes and policies of the United States toward colonialism and the emergence of the "third world," recently inflected by scholarship that focuses on the United States as itself an imperial power. See for example Daniel Immerwahr, *How to Hide an Empire: A History of the Greater United States* (New York: Farrar, Straus and Giroux 2019); and more generally Jason Parker, *Hearts, Minds, Voices: US Cold War Public Diplomacy and the Formation of the Third World* (Oxford: Oxford University Press, 2016). American and European thinking and policy toward South Africa revealed the difficulties of dealing with normative changes in international relations. See Ryan Irwin, *Gordian Knot: Apartheid and the Unmaking of the Liberal World Order* (Oxford: Oxford University Press, 2012).

68. Odd Arne Westad, *The Global Cold War: Third World Interventions and the Making of Our Times* (Cambridge: Cambridge University Press, 2005), 157. Wm. Roger Louis and Ronald Robinson argue that a world order in which the British Empire had played a key part was transformed to one in which "integrating countries into the international capitalist economy" was the main objective, with the United States now taking the lead. "The Imperialism of Decolonization," *Journal of Imperial and Commonwealth History* 22, 3 (1994): 462–511, 495 quoted.

69. Frank Gerits suggests that "first world" states perceived Bandung as a demand for development assistance. Such a reading is consistent with Senghor's ideas of conjugating

Stalin had been skeptical of the revolutionary possibilities in the colonial world, but the year after Bandung, Nikita Khrushchev, in his famous speech to the congress of the Communist Party, noted the possibilities that the collapse of colonial empires offered. The USSR began to provide military and economic aid to India, Indonesia, Egypt, and other countries. Most states in Africa and Asia receiving Soviet aid—like those getting it from the United States—guarded their autonomy, sometimes played one side against the other, and often selected aspects of communist and capitalist models to follow. The model of economic planning given prominence by the Soviet Union was not incompatible with a country's seeking wealth in export markets or an elite connected to the state seeking wealth for itself.[70] One of Lenin's most dubious ideas—the single-party state—was one of the most popular among third world elites.

The USSR's renewed efforts to appeal to a rising generation of citizens in Asia and Africa made a lasting impact through its educational and vocational outreach. Students were brought not just to Russia but to East Germany, Czechoslovakia, and other countries in the Soviet sphere for training in multiple fields. They came from a wide range of places, not just from countries that were Moscow's political allies.[71] Workers from Africa went to Eastern Europe,

---

horizontal and vertical connections, that is, an assertion of ex-colonies' horizontal affinity in order to pose a collective demand for a politics of verticality, for the rich to redistribute some of their resources to the poor. "Bandung as the Call for a Better Development Project: US, British, French, and Gold Coast Perceptions of the Afro-Asian Conference (1955)," *Cold War History* 16, 3 (2016): 255–72.

70. Mark Philip Bradley, "Decolonization, the Global South, and the Cold War, 1919–1962," in Melvyn Leffler and Odd Arne Westad, eds., *The Cambridge History of the Cold War, Vol. 1: Origins* (Cambridge: Cambridge University Press, 2010), 475–77; Alessandro Iandolo, *Arrested Development: The Soviet Union in Ghana, Guinea, and Mali, 1955–1968* (Ithaca, NY: Cornell University Press, 2022).

71. James Mark, Artemy M. Kalinovsky, and Steffi Marung, eds., *Alternative Globalizations: Eastern Europe and the Postcolonial World* (Bloomington: Indiana University Press, 2020); Elizabeth Banks, Robyn d'Avignon, and Asif Siddiqi, eds., "The African-Soviet Modern," special section of *Comparative Studies of South Asia, Africa and the Middle East* 41, 1 (2021); special dossier, "L'Est socialiste et le Sud: Coopération éducative et formation des élites," *Cahiers du Monde Russe* 63, 3 (2022). Some of the countries in the Soviet sphere of eastern Europe acted somewhat on their own in developing relations with African and Asian countries, in part hoping that helping ex-colonial countries solidify their sovereignty would support their own. By the 1970s, they were increasingly interested in market relations with African and Asian countries, not just in promoting the communist cause on a

seeking apprenticeship in industrial occupations but also providing cheap labor.[72] While North Vietnam after 1954 and all of Vietnam from 1974 was a wholehearted participant in the communist project until its collapse, countries like Mozambique established close connections without losing their autonomy, eventually abandoning socialist policies.[73]

Others kept an even greater distance. What the Soviet Union could not offer was the level of resources that western European and North American states could bring to bear if they so chose and, most important, the advantages to ruling elites of relations with transnational corporations and financial institutions.[74] When the worldwide economic crises of the late 1970s and 1980s and the austerity creed preached in the west created what could have been an opportunity for an anticapitalist approach in Africa and Asia, the USSR was not in a position to take advantage of it.[75] During the 1980s and after the fall of the Soviet Union, the geopolitical imagination of Russian intellectuals began to cultivate a revival of Eurasianism that was more geographically and politically bounded than the USSR's initiatives of the previous decades in the Afroasian world (chapter 4).

Unlike the USSR, China was represented at Bandung; its model of peasant-centered revolution seemed to many in the ex-colonial world to be more relevant than the state-controlled industrialization associated with the Soviet Union. China tried

---

global level. James Mark and Paul Betts, "Introduction," in Mark and Betts, eds., *Socialism Goes Global: The Soviet Union and Eastern Europe in the Age of Decolonization* (Oxford: Oxford University Press, 2022), 1–24; Eric Burton, James Mark, and Steffi Marung, "Development," *Alternative Globalizations*, 75–114.

72. Marcia Schenk, *Remembering African Labor Migration to the Second World: Socialist Mobilities between Angola, Mozambique, and East Germany* (London: Palgrave Macmillan, 2022).

73. Elizabeth Banks, "Sewing Machines for Socialism? Gifts of Development and Disagreement between the Soviet and Mozambican Women's Committees 1963–87," *Comparative Studies of South Asia, Africa and the Middle East* 41, 1 (2021): 27–40.

74. The vast inequality in resources brought to the Cold War by the United States and the USSR is emphasized by Odd Arne Westad, "The Cold War and the International History of the Twentieth Century," in Leffler and Westad, *The Cambridge History of the Cold War, Vol. 1: Origins*, 10–11. Iandolo (*Arrested Development*, 222) concludes that "the complexity of development in West Africa was too much for the Soviet Union."

75. Mark and Betts, "Introduction," *Socialism Goes Global*, 23.

to push for a second Bandung conference, but not all of the participants in the first one or states that had become independent since 1955 were enthusiastic. The effort ran into rival projects in the early 1960s, notably the rise of the Non-Aligned Movement, and the ideological clash that separated China and Yugoslavia from the USSR, leaving elites in Africa and Asia having to choose among different communist powers in a quest for connections.[76] China made a few highly touted interventions in the ex-colonial world, such as constructing in the early 1970s the railroad connecting the Tanzanian port of Dar es Salaam with the landlocked mining enclave of Zambia.[77] The Cultural Revolution between 1966 and 1976 severely limited the Chinese government's will and capacity to lead a Maoist version of an Afroasian movement. China's much more extensive involvement in Africa beginning in the 1980s and 1990s would have a different ideological and practical valence.

Given the limits on what the second world could do for the third, the most important question for newly independent states was what political movements and sovereign governments could do with the autonomy they had won.[78] If Bandung marked the transition from an anti-imperialism of movements to an anti-imperialism of states, sovereignty generated possibilities. The Non-Aligned Movement (NAM) was prominent among them. Founded at a convocation in Belgrade, Yugoslavia, in 1961, it was another association based on states—25 of them at its inception, 47 by 1964, 75 in 1973, 99 in 1983. Its name posited a positioning between superpowers, but its ambitions were aligned at least as much on a North-South axis as an

---

76. Jeffrey James Byrne, "Beyond Continents, Colours, and the Cold War: Yugoslavia, Algeria, and the Struggle for Non-Alignment," *International History Review* 37, 5 (2015): 912–32. For more on China in the context of the Cold War, see Chen Jian, *Mao's China and the Cold War* (Chapel Hill: University of North Carolina Press, 2001); Odd Arne Westad, *Brothers in Arms: The Rise and Fall of the Sino-Soviet Alliance, 1945–1963* (Stanford, CA: Stanford University Press, 1998).

77. Jamie Monson, *Africa's Freedom Railway: How a Chinese Development Project Changed Lives and Livelihoods in Tanzania* (Bloomington: Indiana University Press, 2009).

78. On the importance of looking at the relationship of decolonization and the Cold War without prioritizing the latter, see Matthew Connelly, *A Diplomatic Revolution: Algeria's Fight for Independence and the Origins of the Post–Cold War Era* (Oxford: Oxford University Press, 2002).

East-West one. Its membership was as heterogeneous, in terms of the domestic politics and international networking of its members, as that of the Bandung Conference.[79]

Jeffrey James Byrne argues that the NAM was more radical than the Afroasianism emerging from Bandung; NAM went beyond ending colonialism toward remaking world order through what he calls "insurgent neutralism." With Josip Broz Tito of Yugoslavia and Gamal Abdel Nasser of Egypt taking the lead in the formation of the NAM, the new movement emphasized that its basis was a political project. NAM avoided defining itself as a movement of nonwhites against European imperialism as China had been advocating since Bandung without gaining much traction.[80]

African nationalists saw the NAM both as an expression of what Frank Gerits called a "liberationist imagination" and as a means to gain leverage in the context of fading colonialism and Cold War rivalry.[81] The "Declaration" of 1961 supported "the immediate, unconditional, total and final abolition of colonialism" and demanded that "an immediate stop be put to armed action and repressive measures of any kind directed against dependent peoples." It drew particular attention to the continued struggles of the people of Algeria, Angola, South Africa, and Palestine. It affirmed the rights of all states to dispose of their natural resources and called for a UN fund to promote development. The non-aligned nations advocated disarmament of all countries and were especially concerned with nuclear weapons and with the dangers to the entire world of conflict between the two great powers. They wanted reform of the UN to give them more influence, and within the organization gave voice to smaller states and not just the giants like India. For all their affirmation of their distinct position and point of view, the non-aligned countries' Declaration stated that they "do not wish to form a new bloc," but instead proposed to "co-operate with any Government which seeks to contribute to the

---

79. Jürgen Dinkel, *The Non-Aligned Movement: Genesis, Organization and Politics (1927–1992)* (Leiden: Brill, 2019), 5–13.

80. Byrne, "Beyond Continents."

81. Frank Gerits, *The Ideological Scramble for Africa: How the Pursuit of Anticolonial Modernity Shaped a Postcolonial Order, 1945–1966* (Ithaca NY: Cornell University Press, 2023), 10 quoted.

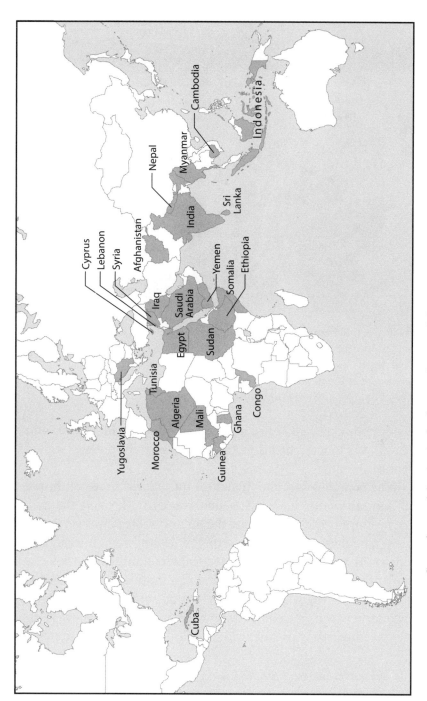

MAP 3.2. Countries participating in the first conference of the Non-Aligned Movement, Belgrade, 1961

FIGURE 3.2. Conference of the Non-Aligned Movement, Belgrade, 1961. From left to right: President of Yugoslavia Josip Broz Tito, Egyptian President Gamal Abdel Nasser, President Youssef Ben Khedda of the Provisional Government of the Republic of Algeria, and Malian President Modibo Keita. *Source:* Photo by -/AFP via Getty Images.

strengthening of confidence and peace in the world." To be "non-aligned" was to work together, to act interactively, not as a walled-in political unit.[82]

Byrne nonetheless argues that after the failure in 1965 of the second Bandung conference (see below), the NAM became the main force for third world politics, and the organization continued to hold regular meetings and put pressure on the UN and other international agencies. It was constrained by the same conditions that affected other threads of third world politics: the mutual hostility of Russia, China, and Yugoslavia, the different patronage and ideological networks in which ex-colonial states were involved, and above all the different interests, constituencies, political affinities, and strategies

---

82. Declaration from the First Conference of Heads of State or Government of Non-Aligned Countries, Belgrade, September 1961, reprinted in Braillard and Djalili, *Third World and International Relations*, 109–14.

of third world states within a nation-state system. The NAM sponsored a new round of meetings in the 1970s and 1980s—extending into the twenty-first century—and it was an influence on the politics of the New International Economic Order (see below).[83]

The specifically Afroasian focus of Bandung was extended in the Afro-Asian Peoples Solidarity Organization (AAPSO) founded in Cairo in 1957, a location chosen to highlight the importance of Egypt's successful takeover of the Suez Canal in the face of a British, French, and Israeli invasion. Evoking the "spirit of Bandung," the AAPSO Conference of 1957 as well as those of 1958, 1960, 1963, and 1965, focused on the continuing anticolonial struggles and on combating the machinations of western powers in Africa. AAPSO had a permanent secretariat in Cairo and still claims to have national committees in ninety countries.[84] Lawyers from Africa and Asia got together to try to eliminate the imprint of imperialism on international law, forming the Asian-African Legal Consultative Committee in 1957 and taking on issues of property and trade regulation that would in the 1970s influence the quest for the NIEO.[85] Taken together these initiatives helped to change international discourse, expunging the remnant verbiage of colonial rule and opening discussion of organizing a world without colonial empires.

Whatever the limitations of the political projects of the conferences and networks, they had a cultural impact beyond the actions of states, through associations of writers and artists that intersected artistic movements in different localities. A 1958 conference in Tashkent, for example, put together plans for an Afro-Asian Writers Bureau that met periodically in the 1960s and 1970s. The writers attending the Tashkent conference made clear their Afroasian cultural affinity, but their meeting in a modern Soviet

---

83. Byrne, "Beyond Continents."

84. Katharine McGregor and Vannessa Hearman, "Challenging the Lifeline of Imperialism: Reassessing Afro-Asian Solidarity and Related Activism in the Decade 1955–1965," in Luis Eslava, Michael Fakhri, and Vasuki Nesiah, eds., *Bandung, Global History, and International Law: Critical Pasts and Pending Futures* (Cambridge: Cambridge University Press, 2017), 165–73. On AAPSO today, see its wesite, www.aapsorg.org, accessed November 17, 2022.

85. Idriss Paul-Armand Fofana, "Afro-Asian Jurists and the Quest to Modernise the International Protection of Foreign-Owned Property, 1955–1975," *Journal of the History of International Law* 23, 1 (2021): 80–112.

city also induced ambivalence about the relationship of their projects to the Soviet ones. The modernization of Central Asia was both inspiring and revealing of the subordinated status of Asians within the USSR.[86]

The post-Bandung spirit was also echoed in an Afro-Asian Students Conference, a Conference of Afro-Asian Journalists, and an Afro-Asian Conference on Women that met in the late 1950s. Literary, musical, and artistic festivals and networks were trying to counter long-standing European claims to be setting the standards of cultural expression.[87] At the Congress of Black Writers and Artists in 1956, Jacques Rabemananjara, poet and politician from Madagascar, claimed that the "striking of the gong of Bandung had sounded the spectacular end of the [European] monologue that had lasted many centuries."[88] African and Asian social scientists and historians also met over the post-Bandung years, developed their critiques of imperialism and global capitalism, and taught students to think in such terms.[89] The influence of intellectual and artistic production among anticolonial activists remains strong to this day—in Africa, Asia, and beyond.

---

86. Marek Eby, "Global Tashkent: Transnational Visions of a Soviet City in the Postcolonial World, 1953-1966," *Ab Imperio* 2021, 4: 238-64; Artemy M. Kalinovsky, "Writing the Soviet South into the History of the Cold War and Decolonization," in Steffi Marung, Artemy M. Kalinovsky, and James Mark, eds., *Alternative Globalizations: Eastern Europe and the Postcolonial World* (Bloomington: Indiana University Press, 2020), 189-208.

87. Amrith, "Asian Internationalism," 561-63; Su Lin Lewis and Carolien Stolte, "Other Bandungs: Afro-Asian Internationalisms in the Early Cold War," *Journal of World History* 30 (2019): 1-19; Luis Eslava, Michael Fakhri, and Vasuki Nesiah, eds., *Bandung, Global History and International Law: Critical Pasts and Pending Futures* (Cambridge: Cambridge University Press, 2017); Afro-Asian Networks Research Collective, "Manifesto: Networks of Decolonization in Asia and Africa," *Radical History Review* 131 (2018): 176-82.

88. Quoted in Sarah Dunstan, *Race, Rights and Reform: Black Activism in the French Empire and the United States from World War I to the Cold War* (Cambridge: Cambridge University Press, 2021), 249.

89. For African examples, one can note the work of Samir Amin, Claude Ake, and Isa Shivji from the 1970s as well as of the historian of Guyanese origin Walter Rodney who taught for many years in Tanzania and helped to found what became known as the Dar es Salaam school of history. See his book *How Europe Underdeveloped Africa* (London: Bogle-L'Ouverture, 1972) and for a retrospective, Gregory Maddox, "The Dar es Salaam School of African History," *Oxford Research Encyclopedia of African History*, 2018, https://doi.org/10.1093/acrefore/9780190277734.013.314.

These meetings, festivals, and networks suggest that in the 1960s and 1970s, there was still an Afroasianism of people and of movements, not just an Afroasianism of states.[90] The inspiration came both from the example of Bandung and from gatherings of militants in different locations in both continents. Ismay Milford, for example, traces the actions and writings of a cohort of young Africans from different British territories in East and Central Africa, some of whom met at Makerere University in Uganda in the mid-1950s, published journals like *Resurgent Africa* and *Uganda Renaissance*, participated in meetings of AAPSO, founded their own organizations, traveled to India and Great Britain, and tried to influence international socialist organizations to make anticolonial agitation a priority. They were generally opposed to the communist strand of internationalism, were alienated at times by the paternalism of Indian comrades, and saw their role as influencing global discourse rather than bringing about violent revolution. They opened offices and held meetings in hubs of anticolonial agitation—Cairo, then Accra and Dar es Salaam. Milford emphasizes the dialectic of connection and situation; African activists looked beyond their region and beyond their continent while engaging in the political struggles of Kenya, Uganda, Tanganyika, Northern and Southern Rhodesia, and Nyasaland. They were sometimes imprisoned by colonial authorities.[91]

Both movement activists and state leaders were well aware of the importance of extending the reach of their ideas. The two sides of the Cold War made use of radio and other media as well as development assistance to reach a broad populace. After Nasser assumed power in Egypt, Radio Cairo became part of the effort to make Egypt into a center for the diffusion of ideas. The station broadcasted on short-wave frequencies in Swahili, Somali, and

90. There were festivals within an African diaspora framework, for example the First World Festival of Negro Arts, held in Dakar in 1966, and the Second World Black and African Festival of Arts and Culture, in Lagos in 1977.

91. Ismay Milford, *African Activists in a Decolonising World: The Making of an Anticolonial Culture, 1952–1966* (Cambridge: Cambridge University Press, 2023); Eric Burton, "Hubs of Decolonization. African Liberation Movements and 'Eastern' Connections in Cairo, Accra, and Dar es Salaam," in Lena Dallywater, Chris Saunders, and Helder Adegar Fonseca, eds., *Southern African Liberation Movements and the Global Cold War 'East': Transnational Activism 1960–1990* (Berlin: De Gruyter, 2019), 25–56.

Amharic to East Africa, Asante in West Africa, and Arabic in North Africa and throughout the Middle East. During the 1950s, Radio Cairo's virulent attacks on European colonialism and repeated calls for anticolonial mobilization were sufficient to frighten British officials into expanding their own use of radio and other media.[92] Toward the end of the decade, however, Radio Cairo's emphasis became more pan-Arab than pan-African, while the Ghana Broadcasting System and the Tanganyika Broadcasting System took up the mantle of bringing the critique of colonialism to parts of the African continent that had not yet been liberated.[93]

The difficult question that such activists faced was translating their penetrating anticolonial rhetoric and the transcontinental networks and organizations they joined or constructed into political institutions. As political parties clawed away at colonial rule and consolidated their power within the emerging states, ideas for remaking colonial societies were not necessarily what the leaders of new and fragile political regimes wanted to hear. The regional and cross-continental perspectives that had emerged during the 1950s were facing the challenge of top-down state-building. The desire of newly sovereign states to find a third way toward progress was compromised by elites' need to gain material support from one side or the other.[94] Milford says of east and central Africa, "As independence approached in the region, this anticolonial culture turned inward." She cites a Tanzanian observer from 1967: "The spirit of Bandung no longer exists because the objective conditions which obtained at Bandung no longer exist."[95] Indeed, Bandung's emphasis on national sovereignty could be interpreted by elites to mean "that state authorities could govern their territories as they saw fit,"

---

92. James Brennan, "Radio Cairo and the Decolonization of East Africa, 1953–64," in Christopher Lee, ed., *Making a World After Empire: The Bandung Moment and Its Political Afterlives* (Athens: Ohio University Press, 2010), 173–95.

93. Milford, *African Activists*, 237–38.

94. Gerits, *Ideological Struggle for Africa*, 160.

95. Milford, *African Activists*, 242. One of the more ambitious efforts to coordinate political movements across East and Central Africa with the goal of completing the process of decolonization was PAFMECA, The Pan-African Freedom Movement of East and Central Africa, founded at Makerere University in 1958, reaching its peak of influence in 1962, and dissolved in 1964. Milford, *African Activists*, 125–33.

in some cases acting directly contrary to the "Bandung principles of equality and justice."[96]

Racial Solidarity and Anticolonial Internationalism

Antoinette Burton points to "the jagged and underexamined hyphen between Afro and Asia."[97] The issue of race in decolonizing situations deserves—and is getting—extensive examination; our concern in this book is what the category of "Afroasian" meant in racial terms. W.E.B. Du Bois had a half-century before Bandung called race "the problem of the Twentieth Century," and as the challenges mounted to colonial empires, the racial categories that sustained and were sustained by colonial regimes came under fire. The question of whether the goal of the struggle against colonial racism was to create a race-blind society or for Africans or Asians to take for themselves the power from which they had been excluded came to be the focus of soul-searching and debate. The answers were not simple. The discourse at the Bandung conference was primarily about colonialism and about new states taking a claim to a seat in the halls of international power. But, as Burton argues, the relationship or lack thereof of race to the afterlives of Bandung is by no means "self-evident."

The question played out in opposed directions. One was the attempt by some movements to proclaim the unity of what Vijay Prashad later called the "darker nations" in their struggle against the aftereffects of colonialism.[98] Could racial solidarity be a force in the struggle? Although Chinese leaders after Bandung argued for situating the struggle against imperialism in racial terms, most of the leaders emerging from the Bandung process were skeptical about defining the effort that way.[99] But it was hard to separate

96. Eslava, Fakhri, and Nesiah, "Spirit of Bandung," 26.
97. Antoinette Burton, "Epilogue: The Sodalities of Bandung: Toward a Critical 21st Century History," in Lee, *Making a World after Empire?*, 354.
98. Prashad, *The Darker Nations*. Prashad details numerous instances in which connections and common projects were formulated among Asians and Africans in attacking colonial racism. To go from there to Afroasian solidarity, however, requires a leap.
99. Zhou Enlai's tour of Africa in 1964 ran into African leaders' focus on their national projects rather than a common front of non-Europeans. W.A.C. Adie, "Chou En-Lai on Safari," *China Quarterly* 18 (1964): 174–94.

anti-imperialism from anti-racism when imperialism had done so much to foster racism. Julius Nyerere put it this way in 1974: "Let us make it clear. We oppose racial thinking. But as long as black people anywhere continue to be oppressed on the grounds of their colour, black people everywhere will stand together in opposition to that oppression, in the future as in the past."[100] In the United States, some African American activists looked to a "World Black Revolution," while others held to the more national focus of established organizations like the NAACP.[101]

Whereas Du Bois had called attention to the global nature of racialized imperialism at the beginning of the twentieth century, in the second half of the century anti-imperialist movements across the continents continued to underscore the systemic nature of the problem. As more former colonies became independent in the 1960s, their capitals became loci where movements in the remaining colonies could set up headquarters in exile and where activists passing through encountered each other and colleagues who had established a home away from home.

Dar es Salaam in Tanzania, independent since 1961, attracted militants who put the emphasis on different combinations of racial and political solidarity. An impressive array of activists from different continents came through Dar es Salaam, some in passing, some staying on for years: Che Guevara, Malcolm X, C.L.R. James, Walter Rodney, Angela Davis. Radical African Americans came to Dar—as they did to Algiers and Accra—making clear that the quest for racial justice in different contexts was part and parcel of the struggle against colonialism and its aftermaths. Leaders

100. Quoted in Monique Bedasse, *Jah Kingdom: Rastafarians, Tanzania, and Pan-Africanism in the Age of Decolonization* (Chapel Hill: University of North Carolina Press, 2017), 127. Bedasse's book shows that Rastafarians from Jamaica were welcomed as a gesture of racial solidarity to establish a small community in Tanzania, but not without ambivalence on the part of some Tanzanians who defended a specifically national project.

101. Michael Fischbach, "Transnational Peoples of Color: Black Power in America and the Middle East," *International Journal of Middle East Studies* 52, 1 (2020): 167–72. On the unrealized quest for a "World Black Revolution," see Robin D. G. Kelley and Betsy Esch, "Black Like Mao: Red China and Black Revolution," in Fred Ho and Bill Mullen, eds., *Afro Asia: Revolutionary Political and Cultural Connections between African Americans and Asian Americans* (Durham, NC: Duke University Press, 2008), 97–154. See also the "AHR Conversation: Black Internationalism," in *American Historical Review* 125, 5 (2020): 1699–1739.

and some of the rank and file of the African National Congress of South Africa, and FRELIMO, the most important anticolonial party in Mozambique, established exile headquarters in Dar. They influenced each other's thinking, encouraged self-confidence in the anti-imperialist cause, and promoted networks to assist the liberation movements exiled there. They overlapped in Dar with some of the most innovative and influential scholars (white as well as Black) studying Africa in the 1960s and 1970s—Walter Rodney, Terrence Ranger, Immanuel Wallerstein, as well as leftist Tanzanian scholars like Isa Shivji. Dar—like Algiers—contributed to a development of critical scholarship about African history, colonialism, and politics.[102]

A rich body of thought and writing that remains powerful to this day has followed from the work of people, from Du Bois beginning in the early 1900s through George Padmore, Frantz Fanon, and Walter Rodney, who were movement activists as well as acute observers and analysts of the systemic nature of racialized imperialism.[103] Their writings have contributed to emerging fields of scholarship, including post-colonial studies, Subaltern Studies, and diaspora studies, provoking a generous dose of controversy in the press and scholarly circles.

Translating anti-imperialist thinking and strategizing into action in the second half of the twentieth century ran up against the power not only of the wealthy countries and economic institutions

---

102. Andrew Ivaska's forthcoming book, *Liberation Itineraries: Dar es Salaam, Political Exile, and the Making of the 1960s*, will shed light on the successes of the activists who came through Dar in shaping political discourse across continents, while making clear the obstacles they faced in effecting socioeconomic change. See also Seth Markle, *A Motorcycle on Hell's Run: Tanzania, Black Power, and the Uncertain Future of Pan-Africanis, 1964–1974* (East Lansing: Michigan State University Press, 2017), George Roberts, *Revolutionary State-Making in Dar es Salaam: African Liberation and the Global Cold War, 1961–1974* (Cambridge: Cambridge University Press, 2022), and on Algiers, Jeffrey James Byrne, *Mecca of Revolution: Algeria, Decolonization and the Third World Order* (Oxford: Oxford University Press, 2016). On Accra, see Matteo Grilli, *Nkrumaism and African Nationalism: Ghana's Pan-African Foreign Policy in the Age of Decolonization* (Cham, Switzerland: Palgrave Macmillan 2018), and Kevin Gaines, *African Americans in Ghana: Black Expatriates and the Civil Rights Era* (Chapel Hill: University of North Carolina Press, 2006).

103. Cedric Robinson, *Black Marxism: The Making of the Black Radical Tradition* (London: Zed, 1983).

but also that of rulers of many ex-colonial states, who were well aware that international radicalism might prove a challenge to them. Even in Tanzania, where Black militants from around the world had found a welcome, their cosmopolitan versions of racial solidarity could clash with Tanzanians' ideas of national culture.[104] Communication within the cosmopolitan elite could be closer than that between its members and the majority of peasants and workers in their respective societies; hierarchy and solidarity were in tension with one another, within and across national boundaries.

The spirit of Afroasian collective struggle ran into tensions intrinsic to the social complexities of an interconnected and unequal world. Where people of one origin had settled in what others regarded as their own territory, conflicts often arose. In East Africa, uneasy relationships in earlier periods between people of South Asian and African origin manifested themselves during decolonization. Some South Asians joined the African majority in their anticolonial efforts, and in cities like Durban in South Africa, with its well-established population of South Asian origin, there were diverse forms of social interaction and two-way cultural influence.[105] But many Africans saw South Asians as aliens who had obtained a relatively privileged position under colonial rule. Arabs and South Asians living in Zanzibar and Pemba—some rich, some poor—were the targets of revolutionary violence in 1964; a massive expulsion of people of Asian origin from Uganda took place in the early 1970s.[106]

In different parts of the Afroasian world, the boundaries of nation and the boundaries of "a people" were often in tension.

---

104. Andrew Ivaska, *Cultured States: Youth, Gender, and Modern Style in 1960s Dar Es Salaam* (Durham, NC: Duke University Press, 2011).

105. Sharad Chari's forthcoming book on Durban will illuminate this urban aspect of "Afroasian" interaction.

106. Ronald Aminzade, *Race, Nation, and Citizenship in Postcolonial Africa: The Case of Tanzania* (New York: Cambridge University Press, 2013); Jonathon Glassman, *War of Words, War of Stones: Racial Thought and Violence in Colonial Zanzibar* (Bloomington: Indiana University Press, 2011); James Brennan, *Taifa: Making Nation and Race in Urban Tanzania* (Athens: Ohio University Press, 2012); Richard Reid, *A History of Modern Uganda* (Cambridge: Cambridge University Press, 2017). There were also tensions and resentments about Indians living in various Southeast Asian countries. Stolte and Fischer-Tiné, "Imagining Asia in India," 87.

This could lead to violent conflict, sometimes expressed in racial terms (the successful secession of "African" South Sudan from "Arab" Sudan in 2011, "Africans" versus "Arabs" and "Indians" in the Zanzibar Revolution of 1964), more often in ethnicized terms (Biafra-Nigeria, Ethiopia-Eritrea-Tigray, Katanga-Congo, Nagaland-India, Kurdistan-Turkey).[107] Defining race, defining nation, defining "people," and recognizing or rejecting claims to autonomy or independence in multiethnic polities posed serious challenges to assertions that Afroasian identification or the shared experience of imperialism should themselves imply a singular political affinity. As Shobana Shankar argues, "the political rhetoric of Afro-Asian solidarity" could mask both the tensions and the "grassroots negotiations" between people who were experiencing decolonization but not necessarily the same way.[108]

Whatever the limitations of racial solidarity in Afroasian movements, mobilization and debate from the 1930s to the 1960s made one position in regard to colonialism more difficult to maintain in global discourse—complacency. The sense, once widespread in Europe and North America, that racial distinction was an ordinary and legitimate part of political life, became increasingly difficult to sustain in international institutions or in public discourse in much of the world. Mobilizations against colonial rule or racial discrimination did not coalesce into a single global movement, but they did provide and disseminate ideological and organizational tools to combat racism and xenophobia in its different contexts. Such efforts have met, up to today, with countercurrents of exclusionary and denigrating arguments and policies in countries as varied as the United States, South Africa, France, and China. The tools and the connections developed in combating colonialism are part of ongoing political struggles.

---

107. For a clear analysis of the basic problem, see Lydia Walker, "Minority Nationalisms in Postwar Decolonization," *American Historical Review* 127, 1 (2022): 351–54, as well as her forthcoming book on the Nagaland-India conflict. See also Awet Tewelde Weldemichael, *Third World Colonialism and Strategies of Liberation: Eritrea and East Timor Compared* (Cambridge: Cambridge University Press, 2016), and Cindy Ewing, "The 'Fate of Minorities' in the Early Afro-Asian Struggle for Decolonization," *Comparative Studies of South Asia, Africa, and the Middle East* 41, 3 (2021): 340–46.

108. Shankar, *Uneasy Embrace*, 55.

Unity and Disunity in a Post-Colonial World

The quest for Afroasian solidarity and the debates activists provoked over the politics of difference, discrimination, and inequality took place at a particular historical conjuncture; activists were enmeshed in both the construction of new states and globe-spanning endeavors. But an attempt to revivify the Afroasian movement with a new conference, sometimes referred to as Bandung 2, encountered the problems of a post-colonial state. Following the victory of the FLN in Algeria, the country's new leaders proposed to host the new conference in 1965. For Algerian President Ahmed Ben Bella, the conference would mark the claim that their victory was more than that of an Algerian nation against France; it was an assertion of worldwide leadership against the dominant powers in the west. Algeria, however, had an ambivalent relationship to global power structures as they were then arranged. Its new leaders were trying to facilitate favorable trade and aid relations with the European Economic Community, hoping for some aid from the United States, and playing off communist China and the Soviet Union whose split was increasingly problematic for advocates of worldwide socialist revolution.[109]

The Algiers meeting never took place. Planning was bedeviled by disputes between Afroasian states that followed Moscow's lead and that followed Beijing's. The invitation list was disputed. After constructing an impressive new conference venue, the Algerian government was overthrown in a military coup, whose timing reflected the plotting officers' wish to avoid too much credit going from the conference to the regime they wished to overthrow. The movement never fully recovered.

As Jeffrey James Byrne argues, Algeria's effort at positioning itself as a "Mecca of revolution" ran into Algeria's own quest to consolidate itself as a state, defined by territory, nationhood, and sovereignty, in the face of internal tensions and conflicting objectives, individual and collective. Having obtained international

---

109. Muriam Haleh Davis, *Markets of Civilization: Islam and Racial Capitalism in Algeria* (Durham, NC: Duke University Press, 2022); Megan Brown, *The Seventh Member State: Algeria, France, and the European Community* (Cambridge, MA: Harvard University Press, 2022).

recognition of its independence, Algeria was trying to make something of its sovereignty. Becoming a vanguard of third world revolution was a goal of the Algerian leadership, but its first priority was political survival amidst internal conflict and a global power structure hostile to revolutionary change.[110] Algeria's revolutionaries, during their conflict with France, had drawn on Marxist, Islamist, pan-Arab, pan-African, and nationalist rhetorics. Once that struggle was won, the advocates of different tendencies lost their singular focus and came into conflict with one another, at times violently.[111]

The fiasco in Algiers in 1965 was more than a blown chance at a meeting. Like Ben Bella in Algeria, other leaders who had pushed for a radically different post-imperial world order fell victim to coups, including both Sukarno and Nkrumah in 1966. Other outstanding members of the anticolonialist generation died of natural causes: Nehru in 1964, Nasser in 1970. In some places in the late 1960s, a younger generation challenged the post-colonial leadership within their own countries.[112] Whatever the strategies of national economic development, few countries had been able to distance themselves from the vagaries of the world market, and they remained dependent on investment and assistance from the former colonial powers, the United States, or on the lesser resources of the other side in the Cold War. As Gerard McCann writes, "The Bandung era crumbled into the 1960s-1970s under the pressures of Cold War, geo-economic shock and insurmountable differences of nationalist orientation across the 'third world.'" Still, the moment when Third World solidarity had fostered shared aspirations and

110. Byrne, *Mecca of Revolution*; Mark Berger, "After the Third World? History, Destiny and the Fate of Third Worldism," *Third World Quarterly* 25, 1 (2004): 9–39; Eric Gettig, "'Trouble Ahead for Afro-Asia': The United States, the Second Bandung Conference, and the Struggle for the Third World," *Diplomatic History* 39, 1 (2015): 126–56.

111. Davis, *Markets of Civilization*, 130–35, 141–43; Benjamin Stora, *La gangrène et l'oubli: La mémoire de la guerre d'Algérie* (Paris: La Découverte, 1998).

112. For examples of the challenge to African leaders, see Omar Guèye, *Mai 1968 au Sénégal: Senghor face aux étudiants et au mouvement syndical* (Paris: Karthala, 2017), and Pedro Monaville, *Students of the World: Global 1968 and the Decolonization of the Congo* (Durham, NC: Duke University Press, 2022). More generally, see Chen Jian, Martin Klimke, Masha Kirasirova, Mary Nolan, Marilyn Young, and Joanna Waley-Cohen, eds., *The Routledge Handbook of the Global Sixties: Between Protest and Nation-Building* (New York: Routledge, 2018).

possibilities should not be forgotten or minimized—and its aftereffects did not readily dissipate.[113]

Even on the scale of one continent, unity was difficult to achieve. The end of British rule in South Asia in 1947 was a victory following decades of anticolonial mobilization, but its triumph was undercut by the partition of the former Raj into two states, India and Pakistan, murderous assaults on Muslims and Hindus who found themselves on the wrong side of the partition line, and a conflict over disputed territory that persists to this day.[114] India and the People's Republic of China both attended the Bandung Conference, but their relationship became increasingly tense and in 1962 degenerated into military conflict over border disputes.

Communist revolution in China and Vietnam and communist insurrection in Malaya created a sharp division between states belonging to the communist world or western powers and those that tried to remain neutral. The formation of the Association of Southeast Asian Nations in 1967 constituted a limited start at enhancing regional cooperation among a subset of the continent.[115] Later in the twentieth century, talk about "Asia rising" and attempts to distinguish "Asian values" from European claims to universality did not amount to a coherent project.[116] China's assertive relations with its neighbors raised the question of whether it was interested in being a hegemon or a partner of other Asian states. In the 1990s, the Eurasian strategies of the Russian Federation seemed to pull the new states of Central Asia toward Moscow, but Russia's invasion of Ukraine in 2022 made many leaders leery of an affiliation with the former imperial center (chapter 4).

In the Middle East, a version of anti-imperialist socialism, led by Nasser in Egypt and Baathists in Syria and Iraq, emerged in

113. McCann, "Where Was the *Afro* in Afro-Asian Solidarity?," 123.
114. On the way in which the partition of British India into Pakistan and India conditioned politics within India, see Joya Chatterji, *The Spoils of Partition: Bengal and India, 1947–1967* (Cambridge: Cambridge University Press, 2007).
115. Marc Frey and Nicola Spakowski, "Introduction," in Frey and Spakowski, eds., *Asianisms: Regionalist Interactions and Asian Integration* (Singapore: NUS Press, 2016), 1–18.
116. Wang Hui, stressing the diversity of the continent and the tenacity of elites' attachment to the states in which they exercised power, concludes that Asia "lacks the conditions for creating a European Union-style superstate." *Politics of Imagining Asia*, 61.

the 1950s and 1960s, and confronted both conservative monarchical regimes (Jordan, Morocco) and revolutionary movements in Palestine and elsewhere. The radical movements in one region were sometimes linked up with similar organizations in others. But space-crossing rebels ran into increasingly authoritarian elites entrenched in territorial states. The bifurcation between authoritarian states and armed, revolutionary groups was a major obstacle to solidarity within the Middle East, let alone a wider Afroasia.[117]

African unity after independence from European empires was a strongly promoted but elusive goal. A series of conferences between 1958 and 1963 kept ideas of unity in play, but also revealed tensions between national and cross-national projects, advocates of including the African diaspora versus a focus on the states of the continent, desire to include North Africa versus fear that its people's loyalties were more "Arab" than African, and conflict between radical and more conservative regimes in the emerging states.[118] The most far-reaching initiative emerged in 1958 at the All-African Peoples Conference in Accra, Ghana, one year after that country became independent. The host, Kwame Nkrumah, proposed to give up some of his country's hard-won sovereignty to create a United States of Africa. He had in mind a federal or confederal structure, a layered sovereignty that would allow for internal self-government in each constituent unit but enable Africa to act as a singular and powerful player in world politics. He, as Adom Getachew explains, "explicitly positioned his project against models of Françafrique and Eurafrica, arguing that integration with European states would

---

117. Yoav Di-Capua,"The Slow Revolution: May 1968 in the Arab World," *American Historical Review* 123, 3 (2018): 733–738. See also Fawaz A. Gerges, *Making the Arab World: Nasser, Qutb, and the Clash that Shaped the Middle East* (Princeton, NJ: Princeton University Press, 2018) and Ussama Makdisi, *Age of Coexistence: The Ecumenical Frame and the Making of the Modern Arab World* (Berkeley: University of California Press, 2019).

118. G. N. Uzoigwe, "Pan-Africanism in World Politics: The Geopolitics of the Pan-African Movement, 1900–2000," in Toyin Falola and Kwame Essien, eds., *Pan-Africanism and the Politics of African Citizenship and Identity* (New York: Routledge, 2014), 218–21. At the Congress of Black Writers and Artists in 1956, tensions emerged between leading political activists and cultural figures like Senghor and Césaire and African American writers and activists like Mercer Cook, Richard Wright, and John Davis. The African Americans present were focused on reforming the United States, not seceding from it, and—as Senghor and Césaire insisted—misinterpreted the racial militancy of French African activists as a desire to separate Africa from Europe. Dunstan, *Race, Rights and Reform*, 251–58.

preserve and deepen economic dependence."[119] Despite having "All-African" in its name, the conference had an anglophone bent; the main political leaders from French Africa were notably absent.[120]

Nkrumah's fellow heads of state were more concerned with maintaining their territorial power bases than in uniting Africa. On the other side of the continent, Julius Nyerere also questioned the sufficiency of national liberation to enable Africans to find their place in a competitive and hostile world. His hopes for an East African federation foundered on the focus of his fellow leaders on their territorial bases and national projects and on the unequal distribution of resources among the territories.[121] Nkrumah—who had thought Nyerere's regional version of federalism insufficiently ambitious—ended up with smaller scale alliances, with Guinea and Mali most notably.[122] Even these alliances made clear the divisions among African states, loosely between a radical bloc known as the Casablanca group that included Ghana, and a more conservative bloc, the Monrovia group, including Côte d'Ivoire, Senegal, and Nigeria, that put more weight on relationships of trade and aid with former colonial powers or the United States. States exercised their

---

119. Adom Getachew, *Worldmaking after Empire: The Rise and Fall of Self-Determination* (Princeton, NJ: Princeton University Press, 2019), 117. There was tension as well between Nkrumah's pan-Africanist and internationalist ambitions and the domestic political situation. He was overthrown in a coup in 1966, while he was on a visit to North Vietnam. Jeffrey Ahlman, *Living with Nkrumahism: Nation, State, and Pan-Africanism in Ghana* (Athens: Ohio University Press, 2017); Grilli, *Nkrumaism and African Nationalism*. For a long-time pan-Africanist like George Padmore, who spent much of his final years in Ghana, the national focus of politics in the late 1950s was, as Leslie James puts it, "a challenge." He tried to meet it, but he ran into opposition among influential Ghanaians. *George Padmore and Decolonization from Below*, 13.

120. Dunstan, *Race, Rights, and Reform*, 271–72.

121. Michael Collins makes the point that Nyerere's critique of the nation-state—including his argument that for independence to come in the form of national states would make it difficult to create a federation later—complicates Getachew's view of nationalism and worldmaking as complementary possibilities. "Imagining Worlds beyond the Nation-State," *Comparative Studies of South Asia, Africa, and the Middle East* 40 (2020): 603–4. On the abortive East African federation, see Kevin Donovan, "Uhuru Sasa! Federal Futures & Liminal Sovereignty in Decolonizing East Africa," *Comparative Studies in Society & History*, doi: 10.1017/S0010417522000500, 2023.

122. Gerits, *Ideological Struggle for Africa*, 66, 166. Gerits (73–74, 121, 133) also makes clear the differences among African leaders over important questions starting with debates over non-violence politics versus violent revolution at the 1958 conference and over the Congo Crisis of 1960.

capacity to choose their patrons even if their economic situation made independence a relative notion.[123]

A crucial limitation to African unity emerged in 1963 within the institution that was created to express it—the Organization of African Unity. It had little power and less institutional capacity, and it is only slightly too cynical to refer to it, particularly in its early years, as a mutual protection society of African heads of state.[124] Its record at disciplining the more egregious examples of leadership malfeasance in Africa—the Idi Amins or Mobutus—was minimal. One of its first statements of principle, issued in 1963, was that the borders of existing states should not be called into question, regardless of their colonial roots and the barriers they created to connections among African people, even in the many cases of people speaking the same language whose ancestral lands were divided by borders.[125]

The 1963 resolution cut two ways. On the one hand, it was a defense of hard-won sovereignty for each state and a basis for peaceful relations among them. The continued relevance—within and beyond Africa—of the principle of maintaining borders, however compromised their origins, was affirmed in February 2022 by Kenya's ambassador to the United Nations in his condemnation

---

123. For a revealing study of how Côte d'Ivoire—often seen as a client state of France—was able to play off the United States against France in its quest for investment and aid, see Abou Bamba, *African Miracle, African Mirage: Transnational Politics and the Paradox of Modernization in Ivory Coast* (Athens: Ohio University Press, 2016).

124. Less cynical but nonetheless making clear the gap between the goals of the OAU and its ability to provide leadership on an Africa-wide scale is Klaas van Walraven, *Dreams of Power: The Role of the Organization of African Unity in the Politics of Africa, 1963-1993* (Aldershot, UK: Ashgate, 1999). See also Adekeye Adebajo, "Paradise Lost and Found: The African Union and the European Union," in Adekeye Adebajo and Kaye Whiteman, eds., *The EU and Africa: From Eurafrique to Afro-Europa* (New York: Columbia University Press, 2012), 45-79, Michael Amoah, *The New Pan-Africanism: Globalism and the Nation State in Africa* (London: I. B. Tauris & Co. Ltd, 2019), and Ulf Engel, "The Organisation of Africa Unity in the 1960s: From Euphoria to Disenchantment," *Comparativ* 29, 4 (2019): 48-67.

125. As sympathetic an observer of pan-Africanism as Horace Campbell concludes, "the OAU abandoned this global outlook and sought to domesticate Pan-Africanism as a vehicle for solidifying the power of a small clique." Pan-African ideas, he argues, flourished more than pan-African politics. "The Pan-African Experience: From the Organization of African Unity to the African Union," in Martin Shanguhyia and Toyin Falola, eds., *The Palgrave Handbook of African Colonial and Postcolonial History* (London: Palgrave Macmillan, 2018), 1036-37.

of Russia's assault on Ukraine (see introduction).[126] On the other hand, the OAU's resolution undercut efforts to construct an institutional basis for African unification, and ever since African states have taken their sovereignties in a variety of directions. Some African countries, including Nigeria and Ghana, have expelled "alien" Africans from their national territories; African immigrants to South Africa have been targets of violence.

Persuading elites to give up some of their power base for the uncertainties of unity had been difficult enough before independence, as Senghor found in his attempt to put together an African federation in the 1950s. The task became even more daunting once African elites became rulers of states.[127] Presiding over economically fragile states, African leaders had compelling reasons to cultivate vertical relations with affluent states and economic institutions rather than horizontal relations with states in the same situation as they were. Clientalistic maneuvers drew them into relations of dependency and Cold War rivalries, as well as exacerbating their own ideological differences. In the harsh assessment of Godfrey Uzoigwe, radical pan-Africanism was something that African states "could not immediately afford":

> Handcuffed by their neocolonial relationships with the West, especially in economic and military matters, torn apart by conflicting ideologies, drawn helplessly by outside forces into the Cold War, and unable to maintain a consistent line regarding the nonalignment doctrine proclaimed at Bandung and restated time and time again, African states found themselves mired in the morass of foreign policy inconsistency and confusion.[128]

---

126. In a later vote of the UN General Assembly a year after the invasion, calling for peace in Ukraine and demanding the withdrawal of Russian troops, 28 African countries voted in favor (including Kenya), 15 abstained, six didn't take part, and two voted against (Eritrea and Mali). UN Digital Library, vote on Resolution A/RES/ES-11/6, February 23, 2023, https://digitallibrary.un.org/record/4003921, accessed February 25, 2023. In some, but hardly all, cases, decisions followed historic lines of vertical connection to east or west. African spokesmen have also pointed to western powers' own abuse of power or insisted that it was not the business of African states to take sides in a European conflict.

127. Cooper, *Citizenship between Empire and Nation*.

128. Uzoigwe, "Pan-Africanism in World Politics," 215–45, 229, 233 quoted.

Beyond Afroasia, toward a New International Economic Order

Although Afroasian unity was proving elusive even as the post–World War II colonial order collapsed, other connections and strategies emerged. Many state leaders were finding that political sovereignty did not necessarily lead to economic and social progress. These frustrations in the decades after decolonization converged with a political initiative of longer standing coming out of Latin America, where the experience of repudiating colonial domination dated to the 1810s and 1820s.

Politics in many of the former Spanish colonies as well as the former Portuguese territory of Brazil had long entailed a double tension. The first was between political leaders who defended the wealth and privileges of a landed elite and popular movements of peasant and working classes, a divide complicated by distinctions among Euro-Americans, indigenous peoples, and the descendants of slaves, often concealed behind myths of racial mixing. The second tension was between Latin American states and wealthy countries, particularly the United States, whose citizens and corporations exercised a degree of economic power that undercut the pride in sovereignty felt by many people, rich as well as poor, in Latin American countries.[129]

What emerged in the 1960s was recognition on the part of visionaries from both the long-independent states of Latin America and the newly independent states of Africa and Asia of a global problem: formal sovereignty had not resolved the inequities of the world economy. On the Latin American side, critiques of global inequality had acquired a solid institutional basis in the late 1940s in the Economic Commission for Latin America and a theoretical underpinning in the ideas of the Argentinian economist Raúl Prebisch.

---

129. On the parallels and divergences between the decolonizations of the 1810s–1820s and those of the 1950s–1960s, see Frederick Cooper, "Decolonizations, Colonizations, and More Decolonizations: The End of Empire in Time and Space," *Journal of World History* 33 (2022): 491–526. Among a large literature on social and political history of Latin America, see Hilda Sabato, *Republics of the New World: The Revolutionary Political Experiment in Nineteenth-century Latin America* (Princeton, NJ: Princeton University Press, 2018).

Development economics emerged as a subdiscipline in the late 1940s and 1950s, over the opposition of older (and in some cases younger) economists who thought there were such things as good economics and bad economics but not development economics.[130] The premise of the new subfield—also the reason why conservative economists opposed it—was that special action had to be taken to get poor economies into the mainstream and that such an operation would in time allow for an orthodox path of growth. Prebisch and his colleagues took issue with both the old orthodoxy and the new orientation, arguing that economic interactions between states with different potentials had led in the past and would continue to lead to the terms of trade between primary and manufactured products diverging in favor of the latter. The producers of raw materials were doomed, unless they could themselves industrialize. The problem was not colonialism per se, but capitalism.

Latin American states that had decolonized themselves over a century before had not overcome the structural problem of their place in the global division of labor.[131] This observation led some theorists and activists to postulate that only a world revolution would set currently impoverished countries or regions on a road to prosperity, while others—including Prebisch himself—sought remedies focused on aiding poorer states to industrialize and modifying the rules of global commerce, via such measures as protective tariffs for infant industries and treaties guaranteeing more favorable treatment for raw materials exported to rich countries. The norms of market economics, in this argument, had to be suspended

---

130. Edgar Dosman, *The Life and Times of Raúl Prebisch, 1901–1986* (Montreal: McGill-Queens University Press, 2008). An intriguing discussion of the conflicts over the origins of development economics may be found in the biography of W. Arthur Lewis, who decades later won the Nobel Prize for his contributions to this field. Robert Tignor, *W. Arthur Lewis and the Birth of Development Economics* (Princeton, NJ: Princeton University Press, 2006).

131. For a subtle analysis of the politics of development in Latin America—and its relationship to the United States—see Amy Offner, *Sorting Out the Mixed Economy: The Rise and Fall of Welfare and Developmental States in the Americas* (Princeton, NJ: Princeton University Press, 2019). She points out (3) that the arguments of the economists of the Economic Commission for Latin America and their willingness to cooperate with counterparts in Cuba, Algeria, Eastern Europe, and China, as well as the industrializing states of southeast Asia "disrupt the binary logic of the Cold War," as well as a stark dichotomy between state-centered and market-centered development strategies.

at least for long enough to bring about a transformation of the global division of labor. These arguments also fed various currents of academic thought, including dependency theory, world systems theory, and Marxist theorizations of "combined and uneven development."[132]

Initiatives in rethinking global political economy provided a basis for intercontinental configurations broader than Afroasia.[133] Bandung and the limitations of its state-centered perspective had both influenced the Non-Aligned Movement and encouraged more radical leaders to push further. In the early 1960s, the success of revolutionary nationalism in Algeria and communist revolution in Cuba, as well as ongoing revolutionary movements in Vietnam and Palestine and the beginning of armed struggle against Portuguese colonialism in western and southern Africa, inspired transcontinental solidarity among radicals. The wave of activism culminated in the Tricontinental Conference of Solidarity of the Peoples of Africa, Asia, and Latin America held in Havana, Cuba, in 1966.[134] This gathering of more than six hundred delegates from eighty-two countries was explicit in its call for anti-imperialist solidarity, its denunciation of the United States, its advocacy of socialism on a global scale, and its support for the ongoing armed struggles. Out of it came a new organization, the Organization of Solidarity with the Peoples of Africa, Asia and Latin America (OSPAAL)

---

132. On the relevance of some of these theoretical orientations to the study of African and Latin American history, see Frederick Cooper, Allen Isaacman, Florencia Mallon, William Roseberry, and Steve Stern, *Confronting Historical Paradigms: Peasants, Labor, and the Capitalist World System in Africa and Latin America* (Madison: University of Wisconsin Press, 1993).

133. Jason Parker, "'An Assembly of Peoples in Struggle': How the Cold War Made Latin America Part of the 'Third World,'" in Miguel Bandeira Jerónimo and José Pedro Monteiro, eds., *Internationalism, Imperialism and the Formation of the Contemporary World: The Pasts of the Present* (Cham, Switzerland: Palgrave Macmillan, 2018), 307–26.

134. Mark Atwood Lawrence argues that the conference of 1966 emerged less from the successes of revolutionary anti-imperialism than from the setbacks such movements had faced, including coups against leftist governments in Algeria (1965) and Ghana (1966), the installation of right-wing military rule in Brazil (1964) and Indonesia (1965), the difficulties of communist regimes, and the continued strength of western ones. "Afterword: Patterns and Puzzles," in R. Joseph Parrot and Mark Atwood Lawrence, eds., *The Tricontinental Revolution: Third World Radicalism and the Cold War* (Cambridge: Cambridge University Press, 2022), 335–37.

FIGURE 3.3. Poster for the Tricontinental Conference, Havana, 1966. Statement on billboard reads, "This great mass of humanity has said, 'Enough!' and has begun to march." *Source:* Photo12/Universal Images Group via Getty Images.

and a monthly newsletter in multiple languages, *The Tricontinental Bulletin*, as well as other publications. These activities spread the ideas of leading figures in the anti-imperialist movement like Frantz Fanon, Che Guevara, Kwame Nkrumah, and Amilcar Cabral across and beyond the three continents. The Tricontinental Conference may have contributed to the widespread participation of student and labor movements in the demonstrations that broke out in many parts of the world in May 1968.[135]

What OSPAAL could not accomplish was bringing about solidarity across the three continents. The consistency and radicalism of its socialist and revolutionary ideology did not appeal to the leaders of many ex-colonial states whose economic strategies, alliances with either the first or the second world, and above

---

135. Robert J. C. Young, "Disseminating the Tricontinental," in Chen Jian, Martin Klimke, Masha Kirasirova, Mary Nolan, Marilyn Young, and Joanna Waley-Cohen, eds., *The Routledge Handbook of the Global Sixties: Between Protest and Nation-Building* (New York: Routledge, 2018), 517–47; Anne Garland Mahler, *From the Tricontinental to the Global South: Race, Radicalism, and Transnational Solidarity* (Durham, NC: Duke University Press, 2018). On connections between third world and European radical movements, see Quinn Slobodian, *Foreign Front Third World Politics in Sixties West Germany* (Durham, NC: Duke University Press, 2012).

all concerns to secure their own power within national institutions were crucial. The revolutionary fervor of the Tricontinental Conference—including criticism of some ex-colonial states for not being revolutionary enough—"made many Third World elites nervous."[136] Martin Klimke and Mary Nolan, looking at ensuing cross-continental conferences, point to the "inability of activists to produce a cohesive and integrative global platform on which they could unite."[137]

But there was another way in which the move beyond Afroasia seemed for a time to raise the possibility of change in the institutions governing world order—as a state-led initiative. This approach was opened up by participation in the United Nations, specifically its General Assembly, in which each state had equal representation and which had been transformed by the creation of new states out of the debris of empire. By the 1960s, the Latin American, Asian, and African members of the UN constituted a large and growing voting bloc, enough to force at least consideration of key propositions. Cooperation across this entire bloc produced the UN's historic condemnation of colonial rule in December 1960. A year later the UN declared the start of "the development decade." Cold War rivalries were such that the United States and the USSR worried about recruiting new states to their side, giving young governments a chance to play one patron against another and to push the rival big powers to go along with UN initiatives, while some

---

136. Jeffrey James Byrne, "The Romance of Revolutionary Transatlanticism: Cuban-Algerian Relations and the Diverging Trends within Third World Internationalism," in Parrott and Lawrence, *Tricontinental Revolution*, 163–190, 167 quoted. Byrne claims (189) that the Tricontinental approach was only occupying a "radical niche" by the late 1960s, whereas the initiatives of the Group of 77 described below proved more long-lasting. According to Byrne (190), the linkage of the tricontinentalists to political movements in Portuguese Africa may well have encouraged closer connection to communist ideas and alliances—including the deployment of Cuban troops to Angola during its bloody war of liberation, followed by its bloody civil war.

137. Martin Klimke and Mary Nolan, "Introduction: The Globalization of the Sixties," in Chen et al., *Routledge Handbook of the Global Sixties*, 3. There was a two-way influence between "third world" radicals and those in Europe, as well as a connection with African American radicalism, particularly between Algeria and the Black Panthers. R. Joseph Parrott, "Introduction: Tricontinentalism and the Anti-Imperial Project," in Parrot and Lawrence, *The Tricontinental Revolution*, 21, and Slobodian, *Foreign Front*.

international organizations tried to transcend these rivalries in order to promote third world development.

The disappointments of the development decade are well known: the refusal of the wealthy states to redistribute more than a tiny portion of their accumulating wealth, the mistakes of arrogant experts who did not consult with the people who were supposed to be helped, the ability of ruling cliques to divert resources intended for their citizens to themselves.[138] It is nonetheless the case that many people around the world acquired better health services and more access to education than they had during decades of colonization, as independent states put their own resources as well as foreign aid toward the goal of social development.[139] The effectiveness of development efforts is not what concerns us here; rather it is the sense of possibility of concerted action, the idea that the less wealthy states could put pressure on those with the means to change the rules of world trade and provide capital and technical assistance to "developing" countries. Development initiatives, even if far more limited in enactment than imagination, gave substance to the idea of all states taking an honorable and sustainable place in the world.

The UN became the focus for cooperation among states with a wide range of positions in global politics. With the addition of seventeen new states from Africa after 1960 to the Asian, Latin American, and already established African states, a majority of UN General Assembly members were in a position to push for a conference and the formation of a body to coordinate development efforts. By 1963, well over half of the UN members had come together as the Group of 77. Their number would swell to more than 120 states, but

---

138. The history of development as policy and practice and the history of thinking about development have in recent years become burgeoning fields. For a retrospective, see Iris Borowy, Nicholas Ferns, Jack Loveridge, and Corinna Unger, eds., *Perspectives on the History of Global Development* (Berlin: De Gruyter, 2022). Samuel Moyn points to the tensions between defining the problem of development in terms of reducing global inequality versus combating extreme poverty or meeting basic needs. The former entailed a more radical engagement than the latter with the structure of the world economy. *Not Enough: Human Rights in an Unequal World* (Cambridge, MA: Harvard University Press, 2018).

139. See the statistics on improved educational attainment and life span in postcolonial Africa in Frederick Cooper, *Africa since 1940: The Past of the Present*, 2nd ed. (Cambridge: Cambridge University Press, 2019), chapter 5.

they kept the name. Against the opposition of most of the wealthy states, their efforts culminated in the creation of the United Nations Conference on Trade and Development (UNCTAD), which held its first conference in 1964. It was headed by none other than Raúl Prebisch.[140] Its professional staff prepared studies to demonstrate the thesis of declining terms of trade for raw materials producers and to propose interventions to improve those terms and promote industrialization. UNCTAD was a distinctly "third world" project; it did not generate much enthusiasm from the Soviet bloc.[141] UNCTAD achieved some of its goals at the level of information and discourse, less in practical terms. It was not, in any case alone, for other well-established international institutions, such as the International Labour Office, the World Health Organization, and the World Bank, took a strong interest in development, generating different approaches and funding projects in a range of countries.[142]

The Group of 77's larger ambition of restructuring the world economy ran up against what Giuliano Garavini calls the "myopia of the European Community," concerned about its own experiment in collective economic action and improvement in mass consumption and welfare provisions for citizens of western European states. The European Economic Community made some adjustments in the treaties that had been the disappointing legacy of the Eurafrican project without addressing the basic issues of development and global inequality.[143] After a number of conferences and publications, the Group of 77 began in the early 1970s to articulate proposals for what became known as the New International Economic Order.

The success of oil-producing states, who had grouped themselves as the Organization of Petroleum Exporting Countries (OPEC), in driving up prices and putting pressure on wealthy states encouraged the Group of 77 to believe that it too could pose demands to

---

140. On the trajectory from UNCTAD to the NIEO, see Johanna Bockman, "Socialist Globalization against Capitalist Neocolonialism: The Economic Ideas behind the New International Economic Order," *Humanity* 6, 1 (2015): 109–28. See also Giuliano Garavini, *After Empires: European Integration, Decolonization, and the Challenge from the Global South 1957–1986* (New York: Oxford University Press, 2012), 35–44.

141. Burton et al., "Development," 95–96.

142. Sandrine Kott, *Organiser le Monde : Une autre histoire de la guerre froide* (Paris: Seuil, 2021), 145–78.

143. Garavini, *After Empires*, 45–89, 45 quoted.

the stronger powers.[144] What Christopher Dietrich calls an "anticolonial elite" brought together a subset of well-placed and cosmopolitan officials from Middle Eastern countries with economists and activists, especially from Latin America, who had developed a powerful critique of the structures of the world economy. OPEC and the Group of 77 both set out arguments for "economic sovereignty," for taking control of mineral and other resources in largely ex-colonial countries away from multinational—and especially European and North American—corporations. Behind moves toward nationalization of mineral exporting firms and cooperation among third world exporters was rejection of the sanctity of contracts made between unequal parties, especially in the context or aftermath of colonial rule, and insistence that the regulation of property rights and international commerce had to take into account the interest of the people of the poorer countries.[145]

The Group presented its demands as an extension of the right to independence: each country should control its own economic resources and benefit from more favorable rules for participation in world markets.[146] The Group's initiatives consolidated earlier UN declarations on rights to resources, notably the 1962 resolution that delineated the "rights of peoples and nations to permanent sovereignty over their natural wealth and resources" to be used "in the national interest of their economic development and of the well-being of the people of the state concerned." Foreign capital would be subject to both international and domestic law, including

---

144. Giuliano Garavini emphasizes the importance of Algeria, and especially its President Houari Boumediene, in pushing the G-77 beyond the OPEC focus on oil toward a broader address to global economic inequality and the NIEO. "From Boumedienomics to Reaganomics: Algeria, OPEC, and the International Struggle for Economic Equality," *Humanity* 6, 1 (2015): 79–92.

145. Christopher R. W. Dietrich, *Oil Revolution: Anticolonial Elites, Sovereign Rights, and the Economic Culture of Decolonization* (Cambridge: Cambridge University Press, 2017).

146. On the NIEO as an extension of the right to independence, see Getachew, *Worldmaking after Empire*, 144–71, and Vanessa Ogle, "State Rights against Private Capital: The 'New International Economic Order' and the Struggle over Aid, Trade, and Foreign Investment, 1962–1981," *Humanity* 5, 2 (2014): 217–18. On the rights framework more generally, see A. Dirk Moses, Marco Duranti, and Roland Burke, eds., *Decolonization, Self-Determination, and the Rise of Global Human Rights Politics* (Cambridge: Cambridge University Press, 2020).

a state's right to expropriate an enterprise with "appropriate" compensation. The notion of "permanent sovereignty" put the resource question in legal terms; it amounted to a demand for reformulating international law to favor states and people over property.

In 1974, the General Assembly formally approved the New International Economic Order in its resolution 3201, affirming national sovereignty over resources and specifying the rights of countries to expropriate foreign investments and to intervene in regard to commodity prices, technology transfer, and other commercial and financial interactions.[147] National courts would be empowered to adjudicate disputes. The resolution called for foreign aid, debt relief, and a voice for the least developed countries in the decision-making bodies of international organizations.[148] Here was Senghor's formulation put into effect: the horizontal solidarity of poorer countries mobilized to turn vertical connections between rich and poor states into programs to make it possible for poorer countries to improve their economic position.

The campaign for the NIEO is all the more remarkable because the Asian, African, and Latin American group included democracies (Senegal, Mexico, India), dictatorships of the right (Argentina, Brazil, Chile) and of the left (Cuba, North Korea), states that cooperated diplomatically with the United States and those linked to the USSR or China, states dominated by small, wealthy elites and others that at least made gestures to social democracy or populism. Consensus could be attained because its central premise was national

147. United Nations, General Assembly—Sixth Special Session, 3201 (S-VI), "Declaration on the Establishment of a New Economic Order," followed by 3202 (S-VI), "Programme of Action on the Establishment of a New International Economic Order," https://digitallibrary.un.org/record/218450?ln=en, and https://digitallibrary.un.org/record/218451?ln=en (accessed February 21, 2023). See also Sundhya Pahuja, *Decolonising International Law: Development, Economic Growth and the Politics of Universality* (Cambridge: Cambridge University Press, 2011), and Glenda Sluga, "The International History of (International) Sovereignty," in Steffi Marung and Matthias Middell, eds., *Spatial Formats under the Global Conditions* (Berlin: De Gruyter, 2019), 257–74.

148. Ogle, "State Rights against Private Capital," 211–34. There is substantial writing from the time by economists and other social scientists, for example, Jadish Bhagwati, ed., *The New International Economic Order: The North South Debate* (Cambridge, MA: MIT Press, 1977) and Karl Sauvant and Hajo Hasenpflug, *The New International Economic Order: Confrontation or Cooperation between North and South?* (Boulder, CO: Westview Press, 1977).

sovereignty—giving states more control over their natural resources and reinforcing their claims to obtain and redistribute more global resources. In its focus on states and in stopping short of calling for a radical restructuring of the capitalist world economy, the NIEO's premises were successors to those of the Bandung Conference.[149] The Group of 77 shared common interests in linking sovereignty and development—and their demands would have benefitted many of their citizens. The advocates of the NIEO, however, did not address the thorny question of the distribution of wealth resources *within* the states of the group.[150]

These reforms were only one set of priorities for the leaders of the states involved; they had other possibilities and fears on their minds. The unity of the movement depended on efforts to help ex-colonial states make something of their decolonization, whether dating to the nineteenth century or the twentieth. This was also the movement's weakness, for exercising sovereignty was more compelling than the abstract principle of sovereign right. The OPEC states and the Group of 77 included states whose elites were not necessarily devoted to the interests of "their" people. Nor were the states involved in equivalent positions in the world economy. OPEC may have been an inspiration and a source of initial support for the NIEO, but the interests of oil-producing and oil-consuming states in the ex-colonial world diverged.

In the international arena, opposition to the NIEO was formidable. The Group of 77 found "first world" allies for some of its third-worldist arguments, but not much support from the "second world." Much of the socialist left in Europe, including labor unions, were fickle allies of the third world reformers, focused as they were on social politics in Europe itself. The Independent

149. Priya Lal argues that Tanzania's strong advocacy of the NIEO stemmed from the impossibility of bringing about development by itself, including failure to reach agreement with Kenya and Uganda for an East African Federation. President Nyerere proposed what he called a "trade union for the poor," a collective movement of states to claim economic rights, as opposed to the "atomizing, depoliticizing movement for individual human rights." "African Socialism and the Limits of Global Familyhood: Tanzania and the New International Economic Order in Sub-Saharan Africa," *Humanity* 6, 1 (2015): 17–31, 22 quoted.

150. Getachew, *Worldmaking*, 168; Bret Benjamin, "Bookend to Bandung: The New International Economic Order and the Antinomies of the Bandung Era," *Humanity* 6, 1 (2015): 33–46.

Commission for International Development Issues, established in 1977 and later headed by former German Chancellor Willi Brandt, conducted studies of poverty and inequality of resources; its report was a strongly worded call to action against global poverty and inequality.[151]

But the NIEO's position on redistribution and restructuring was perceived by multinational corporations, the United States, and other wealthy countries as a serious threat to their economic activities in "underdeveloped" countries. The rich states had a long-standing architecture of bilateral treaties and international organizations to protect the interests of foreign corporations and commercial linkages in developing states; corporations knew how to both exercise direct economic power and lobby international organizations.

The pushback went well beyond rejection of the specific demands of the NIEO. The ideological basis of the rebuttal had been worked out well before—in the theories of political economists like Friedrich von Hayek, going back to the 1930s, and the attack on development economics by Peter Bauer from the 1950s. As Quinn Slobodian has pointed out, this theoretical current, which became known as neoliberalism, was more complex than a defense of the market against government intrusion. It relied on a theory of governance, of the market constrained by international law and administrative agencies rather than by political processes. Neoliberalism provided a rationale to protect capitalists from too much democracy, especially from the danger that capital might be restrained in the interest of a collective good.[152]

When Margaret Thatcher became Prime Minister of Great Britain in 1979 and Ronald Reagan became President of the United States in 1981, the attack on redistributive economics and protective social policy gained backers in high places. At a summit

---

151. Kott, *Organiser le monde*, 164–65; Burton et al., "Development," 100; Nils Gilman, "The New International Economic Order: A Reintroduction," *Humanity* 6, 1 (2015): [1–16] 6–8. Giuliana Chamedes's forthcoming book, *Failed Globalists: European Socialists, Distributive Justice, and the Challenge of the Global South, 1919–2019*, will illuminate the position of socialist parties, labor unions, and left politicians in Europe toward the NIEO and other third-worldist reform initiatives.

152. Quinn Slobodian, *The Globalists: The End of Empire and the Birth of Neoliberalism* (Cambridge, MA: Harvard University Press, 2018).

meeting in Cancún, Mexico, where world leaders gathered to discuss development, responding to international investigations into global poverty, Reagan not only rejected the demands for a NIEO, but lectured the conferees on his alternative, which he called "freedom."[153] Improving the climate for investors was, he argued seconded by Thatcher, a better way than government actions to ameliorate the lives of people in the poorer parts of the world. As Vanessa Ogle puts it, the "neoliberal revolution... closed the door on both Western-funded state-led development programs and developing countries' claims to bolster the rights of states against the onslaughts of free-market capitalism."[154]

The wealthy states thus waged ideological warfare against the Group of 77's underlying premises.[155] They insisted that the poor states had no legitimate basis for making claims against the rich—not the sins of the colonizers, not present-day poverty. Those states should get their own economic houses in order, eliminate impediments to the free circulation of capital and profits, control budgets even if that meant the reduction of social services, and avoid subsidies, currency manipulations, or other mechanisms intended to shore up the buying power of workers. The captains of capital were pulling back from previous decades in which development was the watchword of policy (even if never funded as promised) in favor of the contention that the market was the universal arbiter of economic justice. They were rejecting a horizontal politics—the common position of the Group of 77—whose goal was to reshape vertical economic relations. Instead of vertical solidarity, those on top would leave those on the bottom to play by the supposed rules of market economics—for better or worse.

Reagan's rejection of third world demands in 1981 suggests that a circle had closed: events of the mid-1950s, including Bandung, had made Washington nervous enough to try to win the hearts and minds of elites in the ex-colonies. Twenty-five years later, the

153. Ogle, "States Rights against Private Capital," 224.
154. Ibid., 225.
155. Jennifer Bair, "Taking Aim at the New International Economic Order," in Philip Mirowski and Dieter Plehwe, eds., *The Road from Mont Pelerin: The Making of the Neoliberal Thought Collective* (Cambridge, MA: Harvard University Press, 2009), 347–85; Slobodian, *Globalists*, 219–24.

United States didn't think it had to bother. It was still willing to wield its sticks—subverting leftist regimes in Central America for example—but it no longer felt the need to undertake a broad initiative to ensure that the states of Asia and Africa would attain a secure and stable place in a global order. In a larger sense, the great powers were—for the time being at least—closing down the broad questions that the mobilization against colonialism had opened up, even as the nation-state was now recognized as the basic unit of world politics. With social and economic rights marginalized in international discourse, the claim to rights that were most likely to be heard were those of individuals against states, what came to be known as human rights. That included property rights, corporate as well as individual. As Roland Burke, Marco Duranti, and A. Dirk Moses conclude, "This refashioning of human rights in the 1970s cast aside much of the most vital content and appeal of human rights for postcolonial peoples."[156]

The crisis of the world economy in the 1970s, instead of leading to systemic change, caused lasting damage to the weaker economies, particularly those in Africa. The oil price increases of 1973 and after led to a worldwide recession, lower prices for tropical exports, and defensive actions including higher interest rates by the wealthy industrial states. Whereas OPEC had been an inspiration for the Group of 77, the price rises won by the oil producers helped to drive many of the Group of 77's members into the arms of the International Monetary Fund, symbol and substance of what the group was trying to combat.

Faced with foreign currency shortages and increasing levels of debt, most African countries had to accept loans from the IMF and other international financial institutions under the "conditions" set by outside economists and regulators. "Structural adjustment agreements" as the new policies were called, were negotiated country by country. Many countries were in such desperate need that they could only go along with the conditions, including reduction of expenditures on social services and deregulation of foreign

---

156. Roland Burke, Marco Duranti, and A. Dirk Moses, "Introduction: Human Rights, Empire, and After," in Moses, Duranti, and Burke, eds., *Decolonization, Self-determination, and The Rise of Global Human Rights Politics* (Cambridge: Cambridge University Press, 2020), 20; Moyn, *Not Enough.*

investment. Their vulnerability extended beyond the acceptance of imposed conditions to acquiescence to the free-market narrative. The horizontal solidarity developed by the Group of 77 had proved unable to redirect the vertical structures of the world economy.[157]

The sovereignty regime that had put more than seventy-seven countries in a position to make demands also made it possible for the United States, Britain, and other wealthy countries, as well as the international financial institutions, to reject those demands and their underlying logic.[158] The post-imperial sovereignty regime had in the early years of decolonization posed challenges to the wealthy countries of Europe and North America, but these states and international capital had both material and ideological resources to confront the claims of people in need that were funneled through their various states.

It was not a threat to the wealthy states that a number of ex-colonies could become important economic actors on the world scene. Some Asian countries—South Korea, Singapore, Taiwan, and Malaysia among them—emerged as "success stories" during the 1980s and 1990s, while other countries in Africa and Asia—Tanzania, Bangladesh—were treated as "failures."

These varied trajectories made Afroasian solidarity an even more elusive goal. Economic and political progress in late twentieth-century Ghana; catastrophic conflict and impoverishment in the Central African Republic or Somalia; a combination in South Africa after the end of white rule in 1994 of newly affluent and professional Black Africans with ongoing poverty and social dislocation of an African underclass; high levels of education, industrialization, and wealth production in South Korea; poverty in North Korea; an exploited labor force in Bangladesh; a mix of high technology and rural poverty in India—these vastly variable conditions undermined commonalities. Some state leaders who criticized the

---

157. Giuliano Garavini traces the effort of state leaders from the "Global South" to refashion their relation to Europe, of which the NIEO was a high point. He makes clear the importance of ideological differences among the Group of 77 and even more important the divergent economic positions they found themselves in (particular between oil exporting and oil importing states) in the late 1970s and 1980s. *After Empires*, esp. 222–23, 242–49.

158. For different analyses of the relationship of decolonization, the Cold War, and international order, see Odd Arne Westad, *The Cold War: A World History* (New York: Basic Books, 2017), and Garavini, *After Empires*.

actions of western states and foreign capital acted at home to suppress democratic political movements, trade unions, and efforts to promote personal liberty or gender and ethnic equality. The postcolonial world was not binary—not divided neatly between ex-colonizers and ex-colonized—but it was not a world of equivalence or symmetry.

Although some scholars regard the end of the "third world" as a viable political project as coterminous with the demise of the "second world" in 1989–91, leaving capitalism, in liberal or other variants, dominant worldwide, the undermining of a global anti-imperial project was both earlier and more gradual. The process was also never complete, for extremes of inequality and fragmentation produce tensions that refuse to go away.[159]

Worldmaking in Question

Adom Getachew considers the rejection of the NIEO to be the last gasp of an effort by political leaders from Africa, Asia, and later Latin America at "worldmaking," claiming not only sovereignty but new global structures that would enable former colonial states to make something of their independence.[160] The idea of worldmaking should be seen as part of the long sequence of claim-making and mobilization against colonial empire going back to the early twentieth century, to the time of the early pan-Africanists, to Trubetskoi's demand for an uprising of "humanity" against European oppression and the Soviet project (chapter 1), passing through the anti-imperial movements in each empire and in each colonial territory, the radical promises of international communism, the League against Imperialism, the Bandung conference and other attempts at coordinated action by the leaders of ex-colonial states as well as the mobilizations of a wide range of social movements across borders

159. The argument for a simultaneous collapse of the second and third worlds third is made in Odd Arne Westad, "The Third World Revolutions," in David Motadel, ed., *Revolutionary World: Global Upheaval in the Modern Age* (Cambridge: Cambridge University Press, 2021), 189. Dinkel (*Non-Aligned Movement*, 270) concludes that by the 1990s the initiative had passed from the UN and UNCTAD to the World Bank and the International Monetary Fund, "along with the neoliberal economic theories championed by these institutions, that now dominated global economic debates."

160. Getachew, *Worldmaking after Empire*, 171–81.

throughout the twentieth century. By the 1940s, these movements of thought and mobilization forced colonial regimes in western Europe to take seriously and devote resources to economic development on an imperial scale, something to which they had for the most part only paid lip service. They helped to push some colonial governments—Britain and France most notably—to allow colonized people a measure of political voice, and they brought before an ever-wider public opinion evidence of the extremes of exploitation, denial of justice, and violation of human rights in colonial regimes.

Reformist initiatives after World War II did not have the intended effect of providing renewed legitimacy to the colonial endeavor. Instead, they raised the stakes in conflict over power as anticolonial movements insisted that only they could ensure that investment and modernization would be in the interest of once colonized people. Demands for justice and resources eventually transformed discourse in the international arena: "development" came to be recognized first as an imperial project and then as a national project of decolonizing states. Wealthy and powerful states, for a time at least, gave an international dimension to development, as they considered what it would take to reconfigure a world of empires into an orderly world of nation-states in which the cleavages of rich and poor could be managed. Afroasian initiatives from Bandung to the Group of 77 signaled that the industrialized states and international financial institutions would not be allowed to go unchallenged in their efforts to redesign global economic order as they saw fit.

In rejecting the NIEO, the "first world" distanced itself from responsibility for reforming the unequal order it had helped to produce, but it did not silence debate on questions of poverty and inequality. Development aid did not cease to flow in the 1980 and 1990s, and those years were never fully dominated by what its boosters smugly called the "Washington Consensus." A lot of dissensus remained. By 2000, development initiatives were again gaining support from international institutions like the World Bank and from some of the economists who had earlier pushed market reforms.[161] Ending poverty by 2015 became a stated objective

---

161. Jeffrey Sachs, *The End of Poverty: Economic Possibilities for Our Time* (New York: Penguin, 2005).

of international organizations, like previous ones never fulfilled but nonetheless defining an objective that could attract commitment from individuals, institutions, and governments, in both richer and poorer countries. Nor have arguments about the deleterious long-term effects of colonial rule on the welfare of colonized people dissipated; talk of reparations surfaces in some quarters, although the kind of coalition that had pushed for the NIEO in the 1970s is not now in evidence.[162]

Continued movement activism and efforts of scholars and intellectuals in Africa, Asia, Europe, Australia, and the Americas have kept alive debate over global poverty and inequality. Translating critique into action has been difficult, not least because its target was not fixed but moving, and different parts of the formerly colonized world have followed their own trajectories. Bandung in 1955 was already a meeting of state leaders, not of peoples or movements. The interests and worldviews coming out of oil-producing and oil-consuming states, industrializing economies and agricultural exporters, states hampered by unresolved conflict and civil war and those that have managed orderly economic growth have given rise to a world that is more fragmented than a dichotomy of rich and poor, of former colonizers and former colonies.

Former colonies in Asia and Africa are home to elites who enjoy a luxurious and cosmopolitan life as well as larger numbers of citizens living in poverty and desperate, angry youth willing to engage in radical action against their own governments. Migrants from African and Asian countries—from educated elites to unskilled workers to vulnerable refugees—are a presence in Europe and North America; some are well integrated (a woman of African and Asian descent is at this time Vice President of the United States, a descendant of immigrants from India is Prime Minister of Great Britain); others are the objects of discrimination and exploitation. Some

---

162. There have been counterattacks too, such as a law passed by the French National Assembly in 2005 but never implemented that would have required schools to teach the "positive" aspects of France's colonial past. In Britain, arguments for a positive view of the colonial past are linked to promotion of the free market against state intervention at home and abroad. On the other side, arguments that "decolonization" remains an incomplete project have considerable academic currency and unclear effect on public policies.

migrants are militant critics of the social order in their countries of origin as well as in the countries where they now live.

That an effort as serious—and as threatening to the interests of first world institutions—as the drive for the NIEO could be mounted nearly twenty years after Bandung is testament to the possibilities as well as the limitations of interstate cooperation. Some of the language used in attacks on colonial regimes in the 1950s and in calls for economic decolonization in the 1970s have been turned into critiques of regimes that won independence and continue to hold power. Young Africans called for a "second liberation"; the mass movements of the "Arab Spring" in 2011 sought an end to authoritarian regimes; an Algerian movement known as "hirak" criticized a repressive and sclerotic regime that has continuously evoked its anticolonial heritage to justify its retention of power.[163]

The past of Afroasia leaves us with a question about the present and the future. Was Afroasian solidarity as much a phenomenon restricted to a singular moment in history as was Eurafrica, or does it represent a set of needs and aspirations that today remain to be addressed, in one way or another?[164]

163. Davis, *Markets of Civilization*, 172–75.
164. In a reflection on the significance of past quests for African unity on the present, Toyin Falola writes, "Divided, Africa is made up of weak economies that have little power in the face of globalization. To rise above a peripheral status, it is vital for all African states to give up their individual sovereignty, joining together as one union with a common economic policy, rather than remaining weak and retaining the competing economic systems of individual states." "How Africa Can Unite," in Matteo Grilli and Frank Gerits, eds., *Visions of African Unity: New Perspectives on the History of Pan-Africanism and African Unification Projects* (Cham, Switzerland: Palgrave-Macmillan, 2020), 378–79.

CHAPTER FOUR

Eurasia Redux

WHEN EASTERN EUROPEAN polities that had been subordinated by the Soviet Union asserted their sovereignty in 1989 and later when the Soviet Union dissolved into fifteen states, it seemed that a second wave of nation-state formation was taking place in another post-imperial space. Pundits in the United States and western Europe asserted that the "end of history" had arrived. The world was made up of territorialized states each claiming to represent a nation; capitalist relations of production predominated; and alternative conceptions of economic and political organization had failed or been marginalized.[1]

Theories of global convergence were problematic from the start and their triumphalist aura was clouded over during the 1990s by the wars in Yugoslavia, conflict in the Middle East, and fears of "radical Islam" in Europe and North America, as well as by seemingly intractable poverty and civil strife in much of the formerly colonized world. In Russia, where capitalism and liberal democracy were thought to be welcome, ideological challenges to the "west" and its ways captured the imagination of many in the resentful, disheartened elite. Eurasianism reemerged on Soviet and post-Soviet terrain in the 1990s and became increasingly influential in the 2000s.

The central tenets of the doctrine had been articulated in the 1920s by intellectuals who repudiated European imperialism and

---

1. Francis Fukuyama, *The End of History and the Last Man* (New York: Free Press, 1992).

European claims to civilizational superiority (chapter 1). Although Trubetskoi and other original Eurasianist émigrés opposed the Bolshevik revolution of 1917, some of their ideas were consistent with the reconfiguration of the Russian state by the leaders of the Communist Party in the 1920s. The formation of the Union of Soviet Socialist Republics as a composite of republics, each based on a nationality, was a Soviet version of Trubetskoi's "unity in diversity."

The USSR was officially a federation that, after reconquests of imperial terrain, incorporated into its political structure the "east" so critical to Eurasian thought. The Communist party created unity by channeling cadres of the appropriate ethnicity into commanding positions in each of the parts of the multiplex state. These intermediaries provided what Trubetskoi might have imagined as the links between the top and bottom stories of culture and power. Communist policy promoted study of "native" languages and preservation of the distinctive cultures of myriad peoples—far more numerous than the number of republics—under Soviet rule. Despite the apparent correspondence of communist structures to Eurasianist ideas, Eurasianism and Eurasianists were not welcome in the USSR and instead were persecuted for decades by the Soviet state.

But some ideas have long lives. As a Moscow-based sociologist wrote in 1998, "the Eurasian idea revives in critical epochs, times of rupture for the country."[2] In the Russian Federation, in other formerly Soviet states, and beyond,[3] Eurasia appealed to some as an alternative foundation on which to challenge western power and civilizational hubris.

The Russian Federation, configured in 1991 as the successor to the former Russian Soviet Federal Socialist Republic (RSFSR) of the USSR, needed a founding principle, many thought. To discontented elites, Eurasianism offered a foundation for the revival of the former multinational state, an explanation for Russia's reduced stature in

2. I. B. Orlova, *Evraziiskaia tsivilizatsiia. Sotsial'no-istoricheskaia retrospektiva i perspektiva* (Moscow: Norma, 1998), 121.

3. On Eurasianist contacts and influences in Europe, see Marlène Laruelle, ed., *Eurasianism and the European Far Right Reshaping the Europe–Russia Relationship* (Lanham, MD: Lexington Books, 2015). On Turkey's Eurasianists, see Vügar İmanbeyli, "'Failed Exodus': Dugin's Networks in Turkey," ibid., 145–74, and Suat Kınıklıoğlu, "Eurasianism in Turkey," SWP Research Paper 2022/RP 07, 22.03.2022, doi:10.18449/2022RP07; https://www.swp-berlin.org/en/publication/eurasianism-in-turkey, accessed December 7, 2022.

global affairs, and a recipe for revitalization of Russian power. By weaving a Eurasian theory of civilization into a politics of Eurasian sovereignty, ideologues managed to turn upside down the assertions of the 1990s about the inevitability of liberal democracy, the universality of human rights, and the virtues of self-regulating markets.

In several of the newly independent states, leaders could see Eurasianism as a way to combine nationalist enthusiasm with trans-state connections to Russia, thereby bulking up their hold on power. Some post-Soviet states joined an economic alliance in 2015. The Eurasian Economic Union emerged from negotiations among heads of the new states, most with long years of experience in the ranks of the Soviet system. The institution seemed to mirror the European Union, but its powers were not based on elections, civil rights, and individual freedom.

Efforts to counter the purported hegemony of "the West" are not unique to the ex-USSR in the twenty-first century. China invokes "Asian values" to reject American and European assertions that it violates the rule of law or tramples on the rights of ethnic minorities. Within the European Union, Hungary's officials posit that their "illiberal democracy" is a preferable alternative to the allegedly universal standards espoused by France and Germany. Claims from western powers and social scientists in the 1960s that the repudiation of racism and colonialism had opened a path to global "modernization" have given rise to counter-claims that the west's kind of modernization was a new version of colonial hegemony. Some scholars and theorists, like the early Eurasianists, attack the arrogance of western efforts to impose "universal" values on others. Both defenses of cultural authenticity and assertions of a clash of civilizations have undermined expectations of post-imperial harmony. Mindful of the multiple conflicts over what a world after empire had or could become, we turn to the revival of Eurasianism on the terrain of collapsed communist Russia.

Lev Gumilev and the Life Course of Ethnic Diversity

The Eurasianist movement seemed to have died out in the 1930s, but in Russia intellectual concern with the population's diversity was perennial and had unanticipated results. The multiplicity of ethnic groups inside the polity proved to be a field ripe for both power politics and academic research.[4] Even after purges of nationalist activists who had assisted the Bolsheviks in the civil war and the genocidal famines of the 1930s,[5] study of the peoples of the USSR was encouraged in Soviet academic and research institutions. Ethnography, a discipline inherited from imperial Russia,[6] continued to attract, although sometimes endanger, Soviet researchers. Scholars could find themselves pressured to produce politically correct results, such as finding ancestors of the appropriate ethnicity in particular regions.[7] In 1939, the Academy of Sciences formed a committee to study *etnogenez*—"ethnogenesis."[8] The goal was to uncover the ancient roots of each ethnic group.

In the Soviet cauldron of intellect and persecution, Lev Nikolaevich Gumilev developed what became the most influential foundation for ideological reconstruction in Russia in the 1990s and the early twenty-first century. His writings set forth propositions about ethnic development, state formation, and world history that inspired Eurasianists, Russian and other nationalists, environmentalists, critics and preservationists of Soviet power, theorists of Russian governance, makers of Russia's foreign policy, and eventually the second president of the Russian Federation, Vladimir Putin. Gumilev produced a totalizing theory of how ethnicities formed, transformed,

---

4. Francine Hirsch, *Empire of Nations: Ethnographic Knowledge and the Making of the Soviet Union* (Ithaca, NY: Cornell University Press, 2005); Krista A. Goff, *Nested Nationalism: Making & Unmaking Nations in the Soviet Caucasus* (Ithaca, NY: Cornell University Press, 2020).

5. On the purges of nationalist cadres in the Communist Party, see Borys Levytsky, *The Stalinist Terror in the Thirties: Documentation from the Soviet Press* (Stanford, CA: Hoover Institution Press, 1974), 327–88. On the famine in Ukraine, see from an enormous literature, Robert Conquest's classic study, *The Harvest of Sorrow: Soviet Collectivization and the Terror-Famine* (New York: Oxford University Press, 1986) and Serhii Plokhy's judicious account, *The Gates of Europe: A History of Ukraine*, rev. ed. (New York: Basic Books, 2021), 249–54. On the famine in Kazakhstan, see Sarah Cameron, *The Hungry Steppe: Famine, Violence, and the Making of Soviet Kazakhstan* (Ithaca, NY: Cornell University Press, 2018).

6. Marina Mogilner, *Homo Imperii: A History of Physical Anthropology in Russia* (Lincoln: University of Nebraska Press, 2013).

7. On the politics of ethnographic research, see Marlène Laruelle, "The Concept of Ethnogenesis in Central Asia: Political Context and Institutional Mediators (1940–50)," *Kritika: Explorations in Russian and Eurasian History* 9, 1 (Winter 2008): 169–88.

8. Mark Bassin, *The Gumilev Mystique: Biopolitics, Eurasianism, and the Construction of Community in Modern Russia* (Ithaca, NY: Cornell University Press, 2016), 151.

and, in the case of great powers, provided the basis for cultural coherence. For Gumilev, diversity was both a fact and a process.[9]

Gumilev was the child of superstars of Russian Silver Age poetry. His father, Nikolai Gumilev, was accused of participation in a monarchist conspiracy and executed by the Bolsheviks in 1921.[10] His mother was the famous poet Anna Akhmatova, who survived Stalin's purges. Lev Gumilev was arrested three times, twice in the 1930s and after his return from military service in World War II; he spent thirteen years in the gulag. Educated in Leningrad as best as he could manage with this compromising parentage, he eventually received doctoral degrees in history and geography. His academic research focused on steppe peoples—the Xiongnu, Khazars, Mongols, and Turkic khanates. Assisted by supportive academics, he held research positions, but never received an appointment as a professor. He lived to see the end of the Soviet Union, an event he did not celebrate, and died in June 1992.[11]

In 1956, after Khrushchev's world-shaking speech at the 20th Communist Party Congress, Gumilev was released from prison camp and officially rehabilitated. He returned to Moscow, later settled in Leningrad, and began, with difficulty, to publish his ideas. His ethnographic articles appeared in scientific journals from 1959; in the 1960s his radical ideas on ethnicity, climate, and the significance of steppe peoples circulated both in print and via informal circles of scholars and other intellectuals.[12] By the 1970s,

---

9. On Gumilev's life and works, see Bassin, *Gumilev Mystique*. This study provides an extensive survey of Gumilev's works and a convincing analysis of their place in Soviet and post-Soviet Russian politics. Among other sources, see Marlène Laruelle, "Lev Nikolaevič Gumilev (1912–1992): Biologisme et Eurasisme dans la Pensée Russe," *Revue des études slaves* 72, 1/2 (2000): 163–89; Marlène Laruelle, *Russian Eurasianism: An Ideology of Empire* (Washington, DC and Baltimore, MD: Woodrow Wilson Center Press and Johns Hopkins University Press, 2008), 50–82.

10. For a sympathetic sketch by a contemporary of Nikolai Gumilev's life, poetry, and fate, see Nikolai Otsup, "N. S. Gumilev," in N. Gumilev, *Izbrannoe*, ed. N. Otsup (n.p.: Orfei, 1982), 7–19.

11. See Gumilev's moving account of his hard life: "Lev Gumilev o sebe" in Lev Gumilev, *Entsiklopediia* (Moscow: Khudozhestvennaia literatura, 2013), 680–96; Bassin, *Gumilev Mystique*, 6–19; Laruelle, *Russian Eurasianism*, 51–55.

12. "Lev Gumilev o sebe," 689–93. For his publications, see the list in L. N. Gumilev, *V poiskakh vymyshlennogo tsartva* (St. Petersburg: Abris, 1994), 370–71. In 1964, Gumilev's article, "Khazaria and Caspian," which explored the links between Eurasian nomadism

he was famous, the object of support, resentment, and surveillance on the part of academic and political supervisors. In the late 1980s, Gumilev's ideas became accessible on Soviet television and in the press; in 1989, the authorities allowed the publication of his major work.[13] After Gumilev's death, his star shone only brighter. Gumilev's success as what Russians like to call a "ruler of thoughts"[14] testifies to the power of informal networks, personalized connections, and individual mystique in Russian society, but also to the wide appeal of his theories.[15]

One of Gumilev's personal connections was to the early Eurasianists. While in the gulag, Gumilev had learned from another condemned scholar about Petr Savitskii's ideas and existence. The two men began an intense correspondence in 1956, when Savitskii was also released from the camps. In their letters, Gumilev and Savitskii shared passionate interests in steppe peoples, climate, and landscape; hostility to Europe; enthusiasm for theoretical creativity; and love of poetry. Gumilev's archives contain around one hundred letters from Savitskii, expressing deep affection and admiration along with detailed commentary on texts and ideas.[16] "The task of our epoch," wrote Savitskii in 1959, on the "day of the second Russian rocket into the cosmos," is to "destroy western pride at its very root." The way forward was to study and learn from the steppe peoples:

---

and environmental change, was published in both Russian and English. On this article and its impact, see Konstantin Kaminskij, "Climate Change and Cultures of Environmental Migration in Eastern Eurasia: From Gumilev to Nazarbaev," in Nina Friess and Konstantin Kaminskij, eds., *Resignification of Borders: Eurasianism and the Russian World* (Berlin: Frank & Timme, 2019), 188–93.

13. On his publication travails and reputation, see Laruelle, *Russian Eurasianism*, 52–55.

14. *Vlastitel' dum*: an influential personage, hilariously translated by Google as "master of doom"!

15. On Gumilev's status and reception, see Bassin, *Gumilev Mystique*, 15–19, 135–45, 177–78, 189–205, 209–22, 273–306. Bassin argues that Gumilev's ideas were "malleable," and that advocates for various, sometimes conflicting, causes could extract or emphasize useful elements from his works or his imagined positions and exploit his fame to enhance their own (306).

16. Excerpts from the letters are published in L. N. Gumilev, *Ritmy Evrazii: Epokhi i tsvilizatsii* (Moscow: Ekopros, 1993), 205–34. On Gumilev's acquaintance with Savitskii, see S. B. Lavrov, "Lev Gumilev i evraziistvo": Gumilev, *Ritmy Evrazii*, 11–14.

Characteristic of the history of the nomads is a great scale that doesn't exist in western history: a political-geographical scale—in the 13th and 14th centuries the entire Old World was a genuine Mongolsphere—and a spiritual scale—the great spirit of Chinggis's tolerance."[17]

In his letters to Gumilev, Savitskii enthusiastically referred to the works of the early Eurasianists, delicately pointing out similarities between Gumilev's ideas on Russian and Tatar relations in the thirteenth and fourteenth centuries and those of Trubetskoi.[18] Describing his own ardent efforts to call attention to the multiple contributions of the Mongols to Russia's formation, Savitskii enjoined Gumilev to try to locate Trubetskoi's *The Legacy of Chinggis Khan* in the Leningrad library.[19]

The impact of Savitskii's communications about Eurasianism is visible in Gumilev's later works. The term place-development so central to Savitskii's environmental theory figures in Gumilev's account of the influence of the landscape on the inhabitants of Eurasia.[20] An extensive essay entitled "Remarks of the last Eurasianist (Foreword to the collected works of Prince N. S. Trubetskoi)" was one of several unpublished manuscripts in Gumilev's archive.[21]

In interviews and publications that appeared during *perestroika*, Gumilev recognized the scholarly achievements of the earlier Eurasianists and the uphill battle they had fought in the 1920s. Questioned about his association with Eurasianism, Gumilev answered that he had studied this "powerful historical school." He mentioned that he had met Savitskii in person in Prague, and had corresponded with the Russian, later American, Eurasianist historian

---

17. Gumilev, *Ritmy Evrazi*, 228. The day the letter was written was probably September 12, when the Soviet space ship, *Luna 2*, was successfully launched. It made the first moon landing two days later.

18. Lev Gumilev, *Chernaia Legenda: Druzia i nedrugi velikoi stepi* (Moscow: Airis Press, 2004), 475.

19. See Savitskii's description of the controversy among émigré intellectuals in the 1920s over the role of the Mongols in his letter from November 29, 1965. Ibid., 480–82.

20. "Ritmy evrazii," in *Retmy Evrazii*, 190. The article was first published in *Nash sovremennik*, 1992, no. 10: 3–7.

21. "Zametki poslednego evraziitsa (Predislovie k sochineniam kn. N. S. Trubetskogo)." This text was published in 1993 in a posthumous collection of Gumilev's works: Gumilev, *Ritmy evrazii*, 33–66.

George Vernadsky.²² Gumilev described himself as fully in accord with the Eurasianists' message of Eurasian unity but observed that their work was limited to the science of their times. Writing about Trubetskoi and in a tone worthy of his predecessor's positivist standards, Gumilev averred that now it was possible to "make corrections and to check the strength of N. S. Trubetskoi's conception, using materials unknown to the author. If his conception is on the whole true, then conclusions must be drawn."²³

Seemingly taking up where Trubetskoi left off, Gumilev focused on the question of where ethnic groups came from in the first place, before they could be grouped into the cultural formations that had interested Eurasianists. Gumilev defined the basic unit of human society as the *etnos*, a group based on shared behaviors and habits. An etnos was not determined by race or genetics; it emerged in a particular geographical environment that nurtured its "stereotypical" behaviors. (Savitskii's theory of place-development is recognizable here.) These behaviors were then passed on from generation to generation; the transmission and sustenance of ethnicity was cultural, not biological. But what triggered the formation of such a group?

Gumilev took off from here into what may seem fantasy, although he insisted that his theory was grounded in science. His 1989 magnum opus, based on a lifetime of work, was entitled *Ethnogenesis and the Biosphere of the Earth*.²⁴ According to his theory, all ethnic groups were the result of cosmic energy. Rays from the biosphere intermittently stimulated a dynamic individual who would subsequently inspire the formation and development of an ethnic group. Gumilev called this energy *"passionarnost',"* a neologism that

---

22. "Menia nazyvaiut evraziitsem (Interv'iu Andreia Pisareva s L. N. Gumilevym," in Gumilev, *Chernaia Legenda*, 290. This article first appeared in *Nash sovremennik*, 1991, no. 1: 62–70. Gumilev at last met Savitskii at an archeological congress in Prague in 1966: P.N. Savitskii, *Nauchnye zadachi evraziistva: Stat'i i pis'ma* (Moscow: Dom russkogo zarubezh'ia im. A. Solzhenitsyna Vikmo-M, 2018), 657, note 490. George Vernadsky's histories of Russia inflected with his Eurasianist views were widely read in the United States.

23. "Zametki poslednego evraziitsa," 55.

24. According to Bassin, the great Soviet scientist V. I. Vernadskii had popularized the notion of the "biosphere" in the 1920s: *Gumilev Mystique*, 46–49. Gumilev references Vernadskii's work in his discussion of the biosphere: L. N. Gumilev, *Etnogenez i biosfera zemli* (Leningrad: Gidrometeoizdat, 1990), 316–18.

caught the imagination of many a disciple. Alexander the Great had passionarnost', Chinggis Khan had it, Mohammad had it, and so on. Ethnic groups were the product not of race, but of radiation.[25]

This was not the end of the story: ethnic groups had life stages. After the initial mutation provoked the formation of an etnos in a particular environment, this group would follow a cycle of incubation, growth, intensive activity, entrance into world history, well-being, breakdown, stasis, and finally, disappearance.[26] The time frame for an ethnic group's passage into each stage was not fixed: bursts of passionarnost', interactions with other groups, invasive destruction by a parasitical etnos—all this could speed up or slow down the life course of an ethnic unit. These units could subdivide or unite, in the latter case into a "super-etnos" of several ethnic groups formed in the same geographical region. These large units exist in antagonistic relationships with other super-etnos formations.[27]

The interactions of ethnic groups could destroy or enhance the energies of each. In Gumilev's worst case, a dislocated and degenerate ethnic group could invade and subvert a super-etnos. The energy of the attacking etnos, which had lost its original geographical homeland, is negative; it is hostile to the cultural transmission ongoing in its host etnos and produces an "anti-system" effect. This concept of an invading deterritorialized "chimera" caught on with anti-Semitic nationalists; they considered Jews to be outsiders endangering the Russian etnos.[28]

Gumilev put ethnic diversity and the dynamism of ethnically inspired conflict at the center of not just Russian, not just world, but cosmic history. In the long run—and Gumilev's perspective was eternal, it seems—the energy of the cosmos and the responses of natural life on earth would keep our human ethnic creativity in motion. In the concluding pages of his masterwork, he cited an American scientist's observation of sunspot activity over five thousand years; the data showed that outbursts of passionarnost' and

25. On passionarnost', see Gumilev, *Etnogenez*, 258–98.
26. Ibid., 351–451; table of the "phases of ethnogenesis" on 400.
27. Ibid., 112–19.
28. On chimeras and the effects of ethnic collisions, see ibid., 312–16, 471–72.

ethnic mutations coincided with the penetration of cosmic rays.[29] This mix of scientific claim with unconventional social theory put Gumilev beyond the pale of what many considered responsible scholarship,[30] but his narratives, abundant in imaginative formulations and creative terminology (much of it with "western" echos),[31] proved enormously influential in Russia and lit the fire of revived and revised Eurasianism.

Eurasianism in Post-Soviet Space

In the 1990s, after the dissolution of the Soviet Union, Gumilev's theories of ethnicity, historical process, and cosmic connection appealed to people who were making their ways through times of uncertainty and fearful state reconstruction. As if fulfilling Gumilev's wish to live on "in others' words,"[32] disciples consolidated his writings into anthologies and monographs, published under his best-selling name. *Rhythms of Eurasia: Epochs and Civilization* (1993) offered a selection of Gumilev's writings and tied him tightly to the Eurasianist revival.[33] The enticing volume *In Search of the Imagined Tsardom* appeared a year later; Gumilev dedicated this project to "the brotherly Mongol people."[34]

Some figures in the communist elite turned into Eurasian enthusiasts, hoping to transform the Soviet "friendship of peoples" into a

---

29. Ibid., 484–85.

30. Gumilev's work, while it attracted interest from scholars, has been rejected by professional historians, both Russian and foreign. See Ronald Grigor Suny's "Foreword" to Bassin, *Gumilev Mystique*, ix–xi, and Marlène Laruelle's harsh assessment—"Gumilev was not a brilliant Oriental scholar, but an ideologist: . . . full of contempt for the historical and archeological sources at his disposal." Laruelle, *Russian Eurasianism*, 82. In the Soviet Union, Gumilev was harshly criticized many times; the most dramatic dust-up was between him and the prominent anthropologist Iu.V. Bromlei. For a short summary, see "Bromlei, Iuliian Vladimirovich," in Gumilev, *Entsiklopediia*, 114.

31. *Etnogenez* (495–500) included a five-page dictionary of terms, drawn up by Gumilev's editor.

32. See his moving poem, handwritten in 1936 when his life hung on a string, in the appropriately titled anthology, "So that the candle is not put out": Lev Gumilev, *Chtoby svecha ne pogasla: Sbornik esse, interv'iu, stikhotvorenii, perevodov* (Moscow: Airis Press, 2003), 6.

33. Gumilev, *Ritmy Evrazii*.

34. L. N. Gumilev, *V poiskakh vymyshlennogo tsarstva* (St. Petersburg: Abris, 1994).

new formula for folding the multiple peoples of the former USSR back into alliance.³⁵ Eurasianism, expressed in multiple ways, appealed to people of various ethnicities, including both supporters and opponents of dismemberment of the Soviet Union. In the 1990s, when Muslim activists were creating organizations and parties, Eurasianism intersected with aspirations for Islamic authority. Both "-isms"—Islamism and Eurasianism—raised the possibility of cultural allegiances that reached beyond Russia's borders.³⁶ As leaders of the former Soviet republics, reconfigured after 1991 as sovereign states, jockeyed for influence, image, and desirable connections in a post-communist world, Eurasia entered the vocabulary of high politics.³⁷

The first political leader to propose a multistate configuration of post-Soviet Eurasia was Nursultan Nazarbaev, the president of Kazakhstan.³⁸ In the 1990s Nazarbaev glided smoothly from the perch of communist party boss in the Kazakh Soviet Socialist Republic into the leadership of independent Kazakhstan. On March 29, 1994, he announced his plan for a "Eurasian Union" in a speech to professors and students at Moscow State University.³⁹

---

35. An example is Eduard Bagramov, a high-ranking specialist on nationality affairs who founded the journal *Evraziia: Narody, kul'tury, religii* (Eurasia: Peoples, Cultures, Religions) in 1993: Laruelle, *Russian Eurasianism*, 84–85.

36. On the multiple, and ephemeral, Islamic and Eurasian parties and movements, see Laruelle, *Russian Eurasianism*, 145–70. The Islamic Party of Rebirth, formed in 1990, opposed the breakup of the USSR. Its goal was an alliance of Russian and Islamic states against the west; ibid., 146–47.

37. The term Eurasia was also taken up by academics who studied Russia from abroad in the 1990s. Area studies centers, obliged to drop Soviet from their names, sought to extend their field of research beyond Russia and into the non-Slavic terrain of the former empire. See Stephen Kotkin's jaunty treatment of this phenomenon in his article, "Mongol Commonwealth? Exchange and Governance across the Post-Mongol Space," *Kritika: Explorations in Russian and Eurasian History* 8, 3 (Summer 2007): 487–531.

38. On Nazarbaev's version of Eurasianism, see Wanda Dressler, "L'identité eurasienne kazakhstanaise, nouveau pivot d'une géopolitique eurasiatique en Asie centrale," in Wanda Dressler, ed., *Eurasie: Espace mythique ou realité en construction* (Brussels: Etablissements Emile Bruylant, 2009), 264–83; Laruelle, *Russian Eurasianism*, 176–87.

39. For the speech, see N. Nazarbaev, "Evraziiskii Soiuz neobkhodim: my prosto obrecheny doveriat' drug drugu," pp. 32–38 in N. A. Nazarbaev, *Evraziiskii soiuz: Idei, pratika, perspektivy 1994-1997* (Moscow: Fond sodeistviia razvitiiu sotsial'nykh i politicheskikh nauk, 1997).

Nazarbaev began with the acknowledgment that a first attempt at post-communist alliance had been ineffective. Anticipating the dissolution of the USSR, Soviet party chiefs had hastily configured the Commonwealth of Independent States (CIS) in the fall of 1991. The structure was supposed to facilitate coordination of policies after the republics of the USSR became independent. The association's name in both Russian and English recalled the British Commonwealth.[40] But this first effort at reorganized and shared sovereignty had not been successful, Nazarbaev regretted. He called instead on the post-Soviet leaders to join "a completely new association."[41] In his Moscow talk, Nazarbaev appealed repeatedly to the long-term friendship and cooperation between Russia and Kazakhstan, recalling with affection the "spirit of united community, brotherhood, and unselfish help" that had benefitted Kazakh students and his nation.[42] He expressed his dismay at the fall of the USSR and his concern to reestablish stability and unity in post-Soviet space.[43]

Introducing his Eurasian project, Nazarbaev referred positively to another association of states as a model. Nazarbaev looked to the European Union as an example of the unifying process—"confederalization"—essential for survival and progress in a world of rapid technical developments and economic competition. He argued that the countries of the post-Soviet space were well prepared to work together; their shared past—their "forms and mechanisms of communication and rule, their common mentality"—had prepared them for "community."[44] In June 1994, Nazarbaev put meat on the

40. Eleven republics had signed on to this association by December 1991. Mark Galeotti, *The Age of Anxiety: Security and Politics in Soviet and Post-Soviet Russia* (New York: Longman, 1995), 148–52; Stephen Kotkin, *Armageddon Averted: The Soviet Collapse 1970–2000* (New York: Oxford University Press, 2001), 109–10.

41. Nazarbaev, *Evraziiskii soiuz*, 32. For an attentive analysis of this speech, see Luca Anceschi, "Kazakhstani Neo-Eurasianism and Nazarbayev's Anti-imperial Foreign Policy," in Mark Bassin and Gonzalo Pozo, eds., *The Politics of Eurasianism: Identity, Popular Culture and Russia's Foreign Policy* (London and New York: Rowman & Littlefield, 2017), 286–88.

42. Nazarbaev, *Evraziiskii soiuz*, 32.

43. Two years later, in a long report to the Academy of Social Sciences of the Russian Federation, he acknowledged how painful the "fall of our united country" had been: Nazarbaev, *Evraziiskii soiuz*, 274.

44. Ibid., 34–35.

bones of this idea with a proposal issued in Almaty, at the time Kazakhstan's capital, for a new integrative association with the provisional name of the Eurasian Union.[45]

Nazarbaev's draft document set forth "principles of unification" and the arenas where collective policy should be made—economy, science, culture, education, defense, and ecology. His proposal addressed future members' predictable worries about their independent status. Members would have to support the principles of non-interference in internal affairs of participating states, to respect "sovereignty, territorial integrity, and inviolability of state borders," to refrain from "economic, political and other forms of pressure in [their] interstate relations," and to cease military actions among themselves. The Eurasian Union would have a parliament, a council of foreign ministers, an executive committee, as well as a council (*sovet*)[46] on culture and other collective bodies. Crucially, a commission on economic matters would set up, among other institutions, the union's "International Investment Bank." Defense policies included the formation of "collective peacekeeping forces" that would "extinguish conflicts inside member states and between them." All Eurasian states, with the exception of Russia, would be "non-nuclear." Addressing another sensitive issue, Nazarbaev proposed that the official language of the union would be Russian, "alongside the functioning of national legislation on languages." As for citizenship: a visa regime would be required for relations with non-union countries, but a person living inside the Eurasian Union who changed countries would "automatically receive citizenship in the other country."[47]

Nazarbaev, it seems, was the first politician—and intellectual—to offer a formal proposal with a legal framework for a Eurasian polity. His "document"—in effect a constitutional proposition—and his speech testify to the anxieties of formerly communist chiefs who had suddenly been deprived of Soviet protection and economic integration after 1991. Nazarbaev's pragmatic institutional focus, his ideas about layered citizenship, his concern to avoid economic

---

45. Ibid., 44.

46. The Russian word *sovet*, written in English as *soviet*, means council, and was part of the official name of the USSR (Union of Soviet Socialist Republics).

47. Nazarbaev, *Evraziiskii soiuz*, 44–50.

imbalances echo Senghor's proposals for the creation of Eurafrica in an earlier post-imperial moment. The citizenship Nazarbaev envisioned was similar to the "superposed nationality" proposed for the French Community in 1959 and the superposed citizenship of the European Union after 1993 (chapter 2).

Like Senghor four decades earlier, Nazarbaev was acutely aware of the economic risks of independence. He was clear about the dependence of his country on Russian commercial connections: Kazakhstan's oil and its consumer goods had to be transported through newly internationalized borders. Nazarbaev's suggestions for a capital for the Eurasian Union were "cities at the crossroads of Europe and Asia," but his examples were Kazan and Samara— both on the Volga and both in the Russian Federation. Back in Almaty at a press conference in June 1994, the head of Nazarbaev's information apparatus hastened to reassure the audience that Nazarbaev's proposal was "in no way about the re-establishment of the USSR."[48]

There were no takers in the 1990s, despite Nazarbaev's unstinting advocacy for a Eurasian Union.[49] It suffered the same fate as Nkrumah's 1958 proposal for a United States of Africa (chapter 3). As president of Kazakhstan, however, Nazarbaev could make good on his idea for a Eurasian university.[50] While economic and strategic concerns constituted the main themes of Nazarbaev's Eurasian initiative, he did not neglect to mention his familiarity with the works of the Eurasianist founders of the 1920s and Lev Gumilev.[51] In 1996, Nazarbaev inaugurated the Lev Gumilev Eurasian National University in Astana; the city was converted

48. Ibid., 48, 51. This volume of Nazarbaev's speeches and documents includes reactions in the press.

49. See Nazarbaev's many speeches from 1994 through 1997, published in his book, *Evraziiskii soiuz*. Union, the name used by both the first communist leaders (Soviet Union) and French politicians (French Union), retained its international appeal at the time; see the European Union, founded in 1993, and the African Union, declared as a goal in 1999 and inaugurated in 2002.

50. See his speech of September 20, 1994 at a conference on "Eurasian Space: Integration Potential," in Almaty: Nazarbaev, *Evraziiskii soiuz*, 97–98.

51. See his answer at a Moscow meeting of academic and political organizations on October 22, 1994: ibid., 144. An essay on the "history and practice" of Eurasianism by a Moscow-based sociologist is included (454–476) in Nazarbaev's book of speeches: I. B. Orlova, "Evraziistvo—Istoriia i praktika."

into Kazakhstan's capital the following year.⁵² Nazarbaev reached beyond the former Soviet border to collaborate with Turkey in supporting the International Hoca Ahmet Yesevi Turkish-Kazakh University. Located in southern Kazakhstan in the city of Turkistan, described as the "historical center of science and culture in Central Asia," Ahmet Yesevi University hosts an active Eurasian Research Institute.⁵³

Nazarbaev and other former communist leaders of former Soviet republics could advertise their Eurasian credentials through articles in *Literaturnaia Evraziia* (Literary Eurasia), a journal edited by Timur Pulatov, a Tajik writer originally from Uzbekistan.⁵⁴ As the journal title indicates, post-Soviet Eurasianism was not confined to the politics of state-building: writers and artists found inspiration in the wide world of cultural affinity visible through a Eurasian lens. In cultural centers and universities founded or transformed after 1991, historians, linguists, and other scholars could re-center their research and publications away from the imperatives of a Moscow-centered and, in the eyes of some, Eurocentric academy. Russia's "regions" became validated topics of historical study. A major Moscow publisher inaugurated a new series on the "Outskirts of the Russian Empire" in 2007, followed by an officially sanctioned project dedicated to Gumilev, "The Polycultural Space of the Russian Federation in Seven Books" in 2013.⁵⁵ The collapse of the USSR had opened up criticism of Russian centralization and

---

52. On the university, see Laruelle, *Russian Eurasianism*, 178–79; Dressler, "L'identité eurasienne kazakhstanaise," 270–71. Earlier in Soviet times, a highly politicized study of ethnicity had prepared the way for such initiatives: Laruelle, "The Concept of Ethnogenesis in Central Asia." Nazarbaev's move of the capital to the north and a more central location in the country demonstrated his break with the Soviet past. Astana was renamed Nur-Sultan to honor Nazarbaev when he officially retired as president in March 2019. On Astana, see Geograficheskaia entsiklopediia, https://dic.academic.ru/dic.nsf/enc_geo/617, accessed January 27, 2022.

53. On the Akhmet Yesevi University, see Dressler, "L'identité eurasienne kazakhstanaise," 271, and the institute's website: https://www.eurasian-research.org/our-university/, accessed February 24, 2023.

54. Laruelle, *Russian Eurasianism*, 85.

55. "Ot redkollegii serii," *Sibir' v sostave Rossiiskoi imperii* (Moscow: Novoe literaturnoe obozrenie, 2007), 5–8; *Kul'tura Sibiri*, Book IV of *Polikul'turnoe prostranstvo Rossiiskoi Federatsii v semi knigakh* (St. Petersburg: Petropolis, 2013). The latter series was published with the support of the Ministry of Education and Science: *Kul'tura Sibiri*, 2.

imperialism, undermining the stark dichotomy between the capital cities and the "rest"—provinces, peripheries, or other kinds of inferior outsides—that had so thoroughly imbued Soviet literature and scholarship.[56]

The former (Russian/Soviet) empire could even be re-mapped eastward: very far east by enthusiasts of the "inner Asian" regions of the Russian Federation who saw the Altai uplands or Lake Baikal as geographic and spiritual heartlands of Eurasian space.[57] Other theorists focused on the Urals, no longer to be described as the border between Europe and Asia but rather as a region of dynamism, enterprise, and multiculturalism essential to the formation and salvation of the Russian state. In his twenty-first-century writings and on Russian television, the novelist Aleksei Ivanov designated the Urals as an area whose "genetic code" (echoes of Gumilev) allowed people of different ethnicities to live together in harmony and to build on their ancient heritage of connections across the steppe.[58]

Ivanov was one of several novelists writing in Russia who took Eurasian themes in multiple directions.[59] In the last years of the twentieth century and in the 2000s, the Orientalist fascinations of the early twentieth century that had seemingly disappeared in Stalinist times reanimated Russian-language literature in sometimes fanciful, sometimes sobering fashion.[60] Kazakh writer Olzhas Suleimenov had paved the way in Soviet times with his two-part

56. On the emergence and significance of the "provincial" in nineteenth-century Russian literature, see Anne Lounsbery, *Life Is Elsewhere: Symbolic Geography in the Russian Provinces, 1800–1917* (Ithaca, NY: Cornell University Press, 2019).

57. Caroline Humphrey, "'Eurasia', Ideology and the Political Imagination in Provincial Russia," in C. M. Haan, ed., *Postsocialism: Ideals, Ideologies and Practices in Eurasia* (London and New York: Routledge, 2002), 265.

58. See the fascinating discussion of Ivanov's work in Clemens Günther and Svetlana Sirotinina, "Beyond the Imperial Matrix: Literary Eurasianisms in Contemporary Russian Literature," in Friess and Kaminskij, *Resignification of Borders*, 73–81. Nazarbaev, too, used Gumilevian vocabulary. For an example, see his reference to the "genes" of Kazakstanis in his 1994 Moscow speech: Nazarbaev, *Evraziiskii soiuz*, 34. Note as well that the term Kazakstanis could be interpreted as a civic, not ethnic, identifier.

59. On Eurasianism in Russian literature and film, see Edith W. Clowes, *Russia on the Edge: Imagined Geographies and Post-Soviet Identity* (Ithaca, NY: Cornell University Press, 2011), especially 1–18, and 165–71.

60. On Orientalism's effervescence in early twentieth-century Russian literature, see Michael Kunichika, *Our Native Antiquity: Archeology and Aesthetics in the Culture of Russian Modernism* (Boston: Academic Studies Press, 2015).

manifesto in the form of a novel, *Az i Ia*, published in 1975. Writing in Russian, Suleimenov sublimed Trubetskoi's linkage of Turkic and Slavic languages into a Eurasianist revision of Russia's origin myth and an attack on Eurocentric linguistics. The book angered both Soviet academics and political authorities and was banned for a decade.[61] But in the 1990s, Suleimenov was back in high regard and even in office in Kazakhstan's first post-Soviet parliament. Nazarbaev referred to Suleimenov reverently in his 1994 Moscow speech,[62] and adroitly managed to redirect the celebrated writer out of electoral politics and into Kazakh diplomacy.[63]

Novelists responded to the Eurasianist revival variously, on occasion with mockery.[64] Some writers engaged the dilemma posed by Trubetskoi—what united people across Eurasian space? How could Slavs, Turks, and all the others live together harmoniously, not just in a re-imagined past, but in the future? Soviet education in the Russian language and Soviet training in Russian high culture had created the conditions for artistic expression before 1991; without this framework, it was not clear if meaningful connections among diverse populations could be sustained. The unsettled postimperial conditions of the 1990s inspired writers, artists, scholars, as well as overtly political activists to search for cultural and spiritual ways forward, a trajectory similar to that of Eurasianism after

---

61. Harsha Ram, "Imagining Eurasia: The Poetics and Ideology of Olzhas Suleimenov's AZ i IA," *Slavic Review* 60, 2 (Summer 2001): 289–311. Ram links Suleimenov to Trubetskoi and Jakobson's linguistic publications but emphasizes connections to the theories of the Soviet academic N. Ia. Marr and the Russian poet Velimir Khlebnikov. See also Günther and Sirotinina, "Beyond the Imperial Matrix," 71, and Laruelle, *Russian Eurasianism*, 172–76.

62. Nazarbaev, *Evraziiskii soiuz*, 37.

63. After 1995, Suleimenov served as Kazakhstan's ambassador to Italy, Greece, and Malta; beginning in 2001, he was the country's permanent representative at UNESCO: https://web.archive.org/web/20160313050436/http://unesco.natcom.kz/ru/index.php?option=com_content&view=article&id=3&Itemid=10, accessed February 23, 2023. After Nazarbaev's downfall in 2022, Suleimenov was unanimously elected president of the new party, "People's Congress of Kazakhstan": https://zonakz.net/2023/02/04/predsedatelem-partii-narodnyj-kongress-kazaxstana-izbran-olzhas-sulejmenov/, accessed February 23, 2023.

64. Works by Victor Pelevin and Vladimir Sorokin can be read as parodic and critical responses to political Eurasianism: Günther and Sirotinina, "Beyond the Imperial Matrix," 69. On Pelevin and Sorokin, see Clowes, *Russia on the Edge*, 68–95, 165–70.

the fall of the earlier Russian empire, but with far greater impact on multiple publics.[65]

Alexander Dugin: The Geopolitics of Empire

The most well-known and influential of the Russian Eurasianists of the 1990s and 2000s, or neo-Eurasianists as some prefer to call them, was Alexander Dugin.[66] Dugin entered the unruly political scene of the late 1980s as an activist connected to raucous nationalist and anti-semitic groups. Before the fall of the Soviet Union he was in contact with new right and traditionalist intellectuals and activists in western Europe, among them Alain de Benoist and Jean Thiriart.[67] He founded his own printing house during perestroika and in 1991 published a monograph entitled *Mysteries of Eurasia*.[68]

During the turbulent 1990s, Dugin tried to create Eurasian-oriented alliances first with the Russian Communist Party and later with Eduard Limonov's National Bolsheviks; both efforts foundered.[69] In 1995, Dugin ran for election to the Duma as a National Bolshevik and lost decisively. He subsequently focused on developing

---

65. See Günther and Sirotina, "Beyond the Imperial Matrix," 81–91.

66. On Dugin, see Laruelle, *Russian Eurasianism*, 107–44; Andreas Umland, "Formirovanie fashistskogo 'neoevraziiskogo' intellektual'nogo dvizheniia v Rossii. Put' Aleksandra Dugina ot marginal'nogo ekstremista do vdokhnovitelia postsovetskoi akademicheskoi i politicheskoi elity (1989–2001gg.)," trans. A. Kaplunovskii, *Ab Imperio*, 2003, 3: 289–304; Jafe Arnold, "Mysteries of Eurasia: The Esoteric Sources of Alexander Dugin and the Yuzhinsky Circle," Research Master's Thesis, University of Amsterdam, the History of Hermetic Philosophy and Related Currents, Department of History, European Studies and Religious Studies, 2019; Charles Clover, *Black Wind, White Snow: Russia's New Nationalism*, new ed. (New Haven, CT: Yale University Press, 2022); Yves Hamant, "Le Néo-Eurasisme dans la Russie contemporaine," in Dressler, *Eurasie*, 114–26; Romain Goguelin, "Le Néo-Eurasisme, une géopolitique de l'opposition," in Dressler, *Eurasie*, 127–37; Clowes, *Russia on the Edge*, 43–67.

67. Laruelle, *Russian Eurasianism*, 126–29. On Dugin's connections with nationalists and neo-conservative theorists in Europe, see Marlène Laruelle, "Dangerous Liaisons: Eurasianism, the European Far Right, and Putin's Russia," and Anton Shekhovtsov, "Alexander Dugin and the West European New Right, 1989–1994," both in Laruelle, *Eurasianism and the European Far Right*, 1–31, 35–53.

68. Aleksandr Dugin, *Misterii evrazii* (Moscow: Arktogeia, 1991); Arnold, "Mysteries of Eurasia," 60–67.

69. On Dugin's connections with Russian parties and groupings, see Laruelle, *Russian Eurasianism*, 108–109.

his influence where it counted—in the reconfiguring but powerful elite circles of military and other makers of Russian domestic and international policy.[70] He ramped up his publishing activities and became an astoundingly prolific author and editor.[71]

Dugin's presses re-published multiple editions of the early Eurasianists' works, turning once unknown and forbidden texts into classics for post-Soviet readers.[72] In his commentaries, Dugin introduced Trubetskoi and Savitskii as the "father-founders" of Eurasianism. Of the two, he preferred Savitskii: his formulations of the movement's principles were "sharper, clearer, more audacious" than those of his "colleague." Trubetskoi was a "pure intellectual, not inclined to political activism," while Savitskii was the "first Russian geopolitician in the full sense of that word."[73] Savitskii had used the term geopolitics in "Geographical and Geopolitical Aspects of Eurasianism," an essay that Dugin located in the Russian state archives. The word meant a lot to Dugin, and he used it twice in the title of his 1997 statement of purpose, a 600-page volume with the catchy title, *Foundations of Geopolitics: The Geopolitical Future of Russia*.[74]

The book was intentionally both provocative and didactic. Dugin defined geopolitics as a "world view of power, the science of power and for power." The book's purpose was to be a "handbook" for those who make "global (fateful) decisions—such as the

70. As Laruelle puts it, his goal was to be "counsel to the prince": Laruelle, *Russian Eurasianism*, 109.

71. On Dugin's enormous oeuvre, see Wikipedia's count. A December 2022 article on Dugin lists twenty-two titles in Russian, with many translations: https://en.wikipedia.org/wiki/Aleksandr_Dugin.

72. Dugin's publications included recovery of Nikolai Alekseev and his writings: Nikolai Alekseev, *Russkii narod i gosudarstvo* (Moscow: Agraf, 2003). Alekseev, a lesser known member of the first Eurasian generation, had published on political theory while living in Europe. His major statement on governance was published in New York in 1955: *Ideia gosudartsva: Ocherki po istorii politicheskoi mysli* (New York: Izdatel'stvo imeni Chekhova, 1955).

73. Aleksandr Dugin, "Posleslovie," in Petr Savitskii, *Kontinent Evrazii* (Moscow: Agraf, 1997), 434, 436–37, 444. This volume, printed by one of Dugin's publishing houses, and compiled by him, is described as the first collection of Savitskii's writings to be published in Russia: Savitskii, *Kontinent Evrazii*, 4–5.

74. *Osnovy geopolitiki: geopoliticheskoe budushchee Rossii* (Moscow: Arktogeia, 1997). The volume contains Savitskii's essay, mentioned above: Petr Savitskii, "Geograficheskie i geopoliticheskie osnovy evraziistva," 507–14.

formation of alliances, the beginning of wars, the enactment of reforms, structural transformations of society, the introduction of massive economic and political sanctions, etc."[75] Citing Savitskii's idea of place-development as well as multiple European theorists (Halford Mackinder among them), Dugin transformed Trubetskoi's plea for a revolution in consciousness into a demand for Russian power in the world. Space mattered for Dugin, but his emphasis was not so much on geography's impact on cultural formation as on the "new big space" where superpowers clashed.[76]

Political theorists will hear echoes of Carl Schmitt in this approach, and indeed Dugin included an article by Schmitt in *The Foundations of Geopolitics*. Schmitt's phrase "a planetary confrontation between East and West" figured in this essay;[77] Dugin later tweaked it into his "planetary duel between Atlantic USA and Russia-Eurasia."[78]

Buttressed with maps, diagrams, and excerpts from the so-named "classics of geopolitics,"[79] Dugin's text hammered home a transmuted variant of Eurasian theory. Rather than Europe—Trubetskoi's Romano-Germanic formula—Eurasia's enemy had become the United States and its Atlantic allies. In a more radical shift, Dugin turned the anti-imperialism of the early Eurasianists into an explicit assertion of empire as the appropriate form of power. Dugin rejected the very notion of nation-state, which he sneeringly called the "state-nation."[80] The appropriate political form for any self-respecting power was empire.

75. Dugin, *Osnovy geopolitiki*, 13–14.
76. Ibid., 82–90 (Savitskii), 43–50 (MacKinder), 414 (big space).
77. Ibid., 526–49. This section of Dugin's book is a Russian translation of Carl Schmitt, "Die planetarische Spannung zwischen Ost und West," from Piet Tommissen, ed., *Schmittiana-III* (Brussels, 1991). No pages provided.
78. This phrase is from Dugin's update—*Geopolitics of the Postmodern*—to his 1997 text: Aleksandr Dugin, *Geopolitika postmoderna: Vremena novykh imperii. Ocherki geopolitika XXI veka* (St. Petersburg: Amfora, 2007), 9.
79. Dugin, *Osnovy geopolitiki*, Part VII, pp. 489–549, contains excerpts from Halford Mackinder, Petr Savitskii, Jean Thiriart, and Carl Schmitt. Jean Thiriart was a Belgian political theorist who collaborated with the Nazis during World War II and later advocated various plans for a European superpower. Dugin's text purportedly reproduced Thiriart's "letter to German readers" from December 1982, entitled "Superhuman Communism": 515–25, 574. On Thiriart, see Laruelle, *Russian Eurasianism*, 128–29.
80. Dugin, *Osnovy geopolitiki*, 194.

Russia had been imperial from its earliest days, Dugin insisted. Since the eighteenth century, its leaders had defended the empire's structure and principles against the inroads of European state-nation thinking. It was only at the start of the twentieth century that Russia had made concessions to the European state-nation model, and the result was catastrophic—revolution. The Bolsheviks subsequently rebuilt a "Soviet empire," rendered stable under Stalin, but undermined under Brezhnev by bureaucratic structures typical of state-nations. Russians themselves were "people of Empire," and their fate depended on facing "geopolitical reality" and building a "New Empire." This new empire "must be Eurasian, span a great continent, and in the future, the World."[81]

Dugin's tirades against American hegemony and his design for Russian-Eurasian empire spoke to wounded post-Soviet egos in the unruly and uncertain 1990s. *The Foundations of Geopolitics* provided a charter for recovering Russian power on the space of the former Soviet empire and beyond. One chapter was devoted to the ominous topic of the "near abroad," described as a "geopolitical problem." People of the former Soviet bloc and other countries on Russia's borders had to face the imperatives of big-space politics: either become a colony of the United States and its "one worldism" or join with a great power that offered an alternative. That would be Russia's Eurasian empire.[82]

Ukraine figured in Dugin's analysis as a potential client of the Atlantic enemy and a threat to Russia. "Ukrainian sovereignty is a phenomenon so negative for Russian geopolitics that it, in principle, can easily provoke an armed conflict," he wrote in 1997.

> Total and unlimited control ... over the entire length of the Black Sea coast—from Ukrainian to Abkhazian territory—is an absolute imperative of Russian geopolitics.... The northern coast of the Black Sea must be exclusively Eurasian and subordinated to the central control of Moscow.[83]

---

81. Ibid., 193–98, 211–13.
82. Ibid., 419–38.
83. Ibid., 348–49.

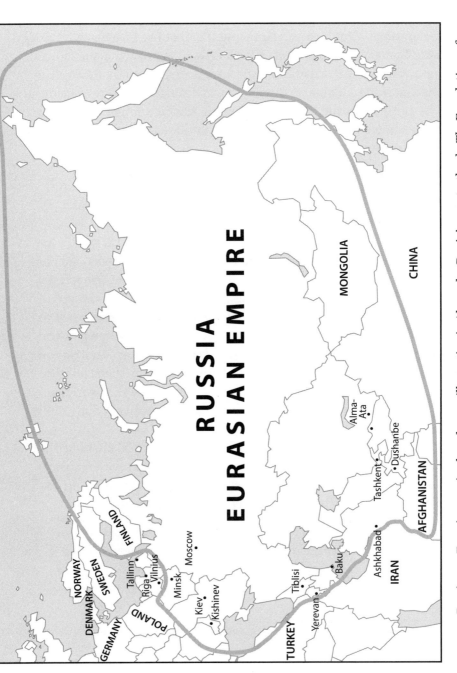

MAP 4.1. Russia as a Eurasian empire, based on an illustration in Alexander Dugin's 1997 textbook, *The Foundations of Geopolitics: The Geopolitical Future of Russia*

Belarus was also to be integrated into Russia. To enforce the "internal" consolidation of Russia's multinational space, ethnic Russians ought to be encouraged to migrate into Tatarstan. This would reinforce Russia's presence in an area whose Muslims enjoyed cultural connections with Turkey, with its threatening linkages to the western enemy.[84]

Dugin's propositions, like those of the early Eurasianists, seemed to contain ambiguities about the relationship of Russia to Eurasia. As if to answer the doubts of devotees of Russianness, the Russian idea, and other varieties of Russian ethnic politics, in 2002 Dugin published a paperback primer entitled *Eurasian Path as National Idea*. Here he declared that "every people, every state has a National Idea," but that in Russia this idea was in a "transitional stage." Soviet Marxism no longer stood up to the geopolitical situation and a new purpose had to be found. The book spelled out Dugin's program for what he called Russia's Eurasian future—its economic structures (similar to Savitskii's continental plans), its exchange connections (a customs union), its legal system (differentiated by ethnicity and religion), its culture ("conservative pluralism"), its religion ("new traditionalism" for both Orthodoxy and other religions of Eurasia). The book could be a handy guide for those worried about their "national identity."[85]

Dugin's pronouncements on the "religious identity of Russia" followed closely the early Eurasianists' elevation of eastern-style Orthodoxy. The core faith had been established a millennium earlier when "our people ... took up the mission of the Christian faith." Leaping over the inconvenient Kievan Rus', Dugin noted the achievements of the Muscovite "period," including the establishment of the Patriarchate, when Russia became the "greatest Orthodox power." Like Trubetskoi, he found the church schism of the 17th century "sad," but gloried in how Russian people had remained "deeply Orthodox," despite persecution." These comments recall

---

84. Ibid., 375–77 (Belarus), 330–31 (Tatarstan).

85. Aleksandr Dugin, *Evraziiskii put' kak Natsional'naia Ideia* (Moscow: Arktogeia-Tsentr, 2002), 3, 5, 87–131. Part I of the book is entitled, "What Is Russia? Sources of National Identity." See the chapter headings for the repeated use of "identity" (*identichnost'*), 11, 133–35. This term, lifted from western usage, gained popularity in Russia in the 1990s.

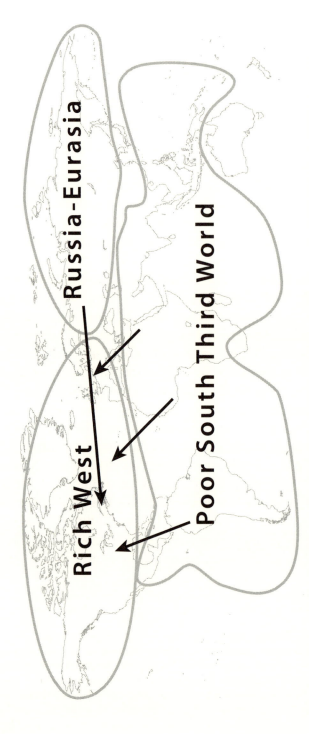

MAP 4.2. Alexander Dugin's image of geopolitical revolution, world map and labels based on illustration, "Geopolitical Revolution against Planetary Domination of the West Based on a Union of the Poor South with Russia-Eurasia," in Dugin's 1997 textbook, *The Foundations of Geopolitics: The Geopolitical Future of Russia*

Savitskii's interest in the Old Believer priest Avvakum (chapter 1). Dugin was himself associated with the Old Believer sect; his self-imagery evokes the authority and features of the rebellious true-believer of the seventeenth century.[86]

Ever attentive to the latest fads in western scholarship, in 2007 Dugin published an updated version of his textbook under the title *Geopolitics of the Postmodern: The Time of New Empires. Outlines for the Geopolitics of the Twenty-First Century*. The subtitles pointed the way forward in a new age of empires and geopolitical struggle. Correcting Samuel Huntington, whose "clash of civilizations" theory had attracted many Russian intellectuals, Dugin asserted that the major divide was not between the west and the rest or Atlantic order and world chaos, but a confrontation of two different world orders, "each with its own structure, own values, own ideals and methodologies"—the Atlantic project and the Eurasian project.[87]

Within a decade, Dugin achieved something no Eurasianist had accomplished before—the insertion of his theories into the mindset of the Russian administrative elite.[88] *The Foundations of Geopolitics* had been published in 1997 with the support of Russia's major military academy; it was subsequently used at many universities and institutes.[89] In 2012, Dugin boasted that he was "slowly, gradually, but steadfastly advancing to [his] goal" and that "academics, businessmen, industrialists, officials in powerful [security] ministries and departments, religious people . . . administrators,

---

86. Dugin, *Evraziiskii put'*, 42–44. Arnold, "Mysteries of Eurasia," 82, 88–89; Laruelle, *Russian Eurasianism*, 124; Clover, *Black Wind, White Snow*, 230–31.

87. Dugin, *Geopolitika postmoderna*, 18–19; Samuel Huntington, *The Clash of Civilizations and the Remaking of World Order* (New York: Simon & Schuster, 1996). On Huntington's appeal, see Laruelle, *Russian Eurasianism*, 93, 119. In the United States and much of the world, Huntington's arguments generated strong criticism.

88. For opposing analyses of Dugin's influence, see Andrey Tolstoy and Edmund McCaffray, "Mind Games: Alexander Dugin and Russia's War of Ideas," *World Affairs* 177, 6 (March /April 2015): 25–30, and Kirill Kalinin, "Neo-Eurasianism and the Russian Elite: The Irrelevance of Aleksandr Dugin's Geopolitics," *Post-Soviet Affairs*: 35, nos. 5–6 (2019): 461–470. Dugin's website is open for perusal in Russian, English, and many other languages: http://www.4pt.su/en, accessed December 9, 2021. His Eurasianism has morphed into what he calls "the Fourth Political Theory."

89. On Dugin's association with the military, see Clover, *Black Wind, White Snow*, 201–206.

journalists and oil merchants, and . . . a thick layer of the counter culture" were part of the "Eurasian current in contemporary Russia."[90]

Despite these proprietary claims, other intellectuals had contributed to the surging popularity of Eurasian ideas. In 1998, a sociologist, I. B. Orlova, produced her own textbook under the auspices of the Russian Academy of Sciences. Her *Eurasian Civilization: Sociological-Historical Retrospective and Perspective* was aimed at "sociologists, historians, political scientists, and a wide circle of readers, not indifferent to Russia's fate."[91] Eurasianism was discussed and debated in university fora. In 2002, Moscow's Friendship of Peoples (formerly Patrice Lumumba) University issued a volume entitled *The Eurasian Idea and the Present* that explored the concept's history, its philosophical merits, and its contemporary significance.[92]

The interest in Eurasianism was fed by multiple editions of Gumilev's works. By 2004, Airis Press had published nine volumes of his essays, books, and interviews.[93] A Gumilev encyclopedia (704 pages) appeared in 2013, in time for the "twentieth anniversary of the Eurasian idea of Kazakhstan's president, N. A. Nazarbaev."[94] Savitskii was rescued from oblivion and honored; in 2018 a compilation of his essays entitled *Scientific Tasks of Eurasianism* included extensive excerpts from his correspondence with other Eurasianists and a worshipful tribute to his poetic and humanistic endeavors.[95]

---

90. Aleksandr Dugin, *Putin protiv Putina: Byvshii, budushchii prezident* (Moscow: Iauza-Press, 2012), 25.

91. Orlova, *Evraziiskaia tsivilizatsiia*. t.p. verso. The book is copyrighted by the Academy's Institute of Social-Political Research.

92. *Evraziiskaia ideia i sovremennost'* (Moscow: Izdatel'stvo Rossiiskogo universiteta druzhby narodov, 2002). The volume contains an article analyzing the "contemporary literature on the assumptions of Eurasianism" (G. V. Zhdanova, "Sovremennaia literatura o predposylkakh evraziistva, 253–62) as well as a review of Orlova's textbook (A. V. Semushkin, "Proshloe i nastoiashchee evraziiskoi tsivilizatsii," 263–66). Orlova's reviewer expressed his doubts about her "well-meaning confidence" that the Eurasian idea was an "undisputed means" to address "all our social ills," but still found the book deserving of "attention and . . . recognition": Semushkin, "Proshloe i nastoiashchee," 266.

93. See the listings in Gumilev, *Chernaia Legenda*, backmatter.

94. This was the dedication of the volume: Gumilev, *Entsiklopediia*, 5.

95. Savitskii, *Nauchnye zadachi evraziistva*. See the essay in this volume by K. V. Ermishina, "Petr Nikolaevich Savitskii: Zhiznennyi i tvorcheskii put'," 7–61.

A New Emperor

The Eurasian influence in Russia political theory and aspiration in the twenty-first century undermined the European orientation of most reformist politicians in the last years of the Soviet Union.[96] A favorite slogan of Gorbachev had been "Our Common European Home"; Boris Yeltsin, Russia's first post-Soviet president, had pursued amicable alliances with western leaders.[97] But Vladimir Putin, Russia's de facto and mostly de jure president since 2000,[98] repositioned Europe as Russia's enemy. Putin was not a Eurasianist from the start; his ideological re-orientation was gradual, as he tended to the challenges of ruling the Russian Federation.

The structure of post-Soviet Russia after 1991 was, like that of the USSR, federal, this time made explicit in one of the state's two official names: Russia and the Russian Federation.[99] Following mergers and annexations, by 2010 there were eighty-three "subjects" in the Russian Federation—regions, republics, territories, autonomous districts, and federal cities. Most are named for the majority ethnic group in their territory. But the number of ethnicities in the federation far exceeded its component units: the 2010 census included data on 193 distinct nationalities.[100] In the absence of the Communist party's control over political levers throughout

---

96. On the European orientation of Russian intellectuals in the second half of the twentieth century, see Eleonory Gilburd, *To See Paris and Die: The Soviet Lives of Western Culture* (Cambridge, MA: Harvard University Press, 2018).

97. On Gorbachev's and Yeltsin's transformation of foreign relations, see Stephen White, *Russia's New Politics: The Management of a Postcommunist Society* (Cambridge: Cambridge University Press, 2000), 215–28.

98. Putin was President of the Russian Federation from 2000 to 2008, and again from 2012 to the present. In 2008, having abided by the constitutional limitation of the president's time in office to two terms, Putin became Prime Minister while Dmitrii Medvedev served as president. In 2021, the constitution was amended to allow Putin to be reelected for two more six-year terms.

99. The surely purposeful ambiguity of the dual nomenclature is declared in Article 1 of the country's constitution: "The names 'Russian Federation' and 'Russia' shall be equal": http://www.constitution.ru/10003000/10003000-3.htm, accessed September 1, 2021.

100. *Itogi Vserossiiskoi perepisi naseleniia 2010 goda* (Results of the All-Russia Census of the Population 2010). Federal'naia sluzhba gosudarstvennoi statistiki, 2001–2013. Vol 4, section 3, Naselenie po natsional'nosti i vladeniiu russkim iazykom, pp. 25–28: https://web.archive.org/web/20220411051753/https://www.gks.ru/free_doc/new_site/perepis2010/croc/vol4pdf-m.html, accessed February 23, 2023.

the country and its once inspiring ideal, Russia's leaders faced an old dilemma: how to ensure loyalty and inspire affinity in this highly diversified and nominally federalized structure.

A major imperative was countering the centrifugal pressures released by the engineered dismemberment of the USSR.[101] Putin's policies toward the typically diverse but atypically wealthy Republic of Tatarstan illustrate his evolving approach to this problem. In Tatarstan, a unit within the Russian Federation, the majority ethnic group in late Soviet times had been Russian, but after 1991 the balance tipped gradually to Tatar. In 2020, the republic contained eighty-eight national groups; its inhabitants spoke many languages—Turkic, Finn-Ugric, Altaic, as well as Slavic—and belonged to Muslim, Christian, and other confessions.[102] After an outburst of Tatar nationalism in the early 1990s, Tatarstan's leaders developed their own variant of multiethnic reconstruction, insisting on multi-lingualism and religious pluralism. The republic's ministries supervised extensively multicultural programming in education and the arts. To be a Tatar citizen, one did not have to be a Tatar.[103]

That was the ethnic part of Tatarstan's civic self-definition; it was combined with an ambitious assertion of leadership in Muslim affairs. While Tatarstan's authorities emphasized their respect for multiple confessions, they also promoted the republic's capital, Kazan, as the new center of Islam in the Russian Federation and as a node of connection to the greater Muslim world. The ancient city of Bulgar on the Volga, where, according to legend, the khan had adopted Islam in the tenth century, was excavated, renovated,

---

101. Among other studies of the end of the USSR, see Serhii Plokhy, *The Last Empire: The Final Days of the Soviet Union* (New York: Basic Books, 2014).

102. *Itogi Vserossiiskoi perepisi naseleniia 2010 goda* (Results of the All-Russia Census of the Population 2010). Federal'naia sluzhba gosudarstvennoi statistiki, 2001–2013. Vol. 4. Section 4. Naselenie po natsional'nosti i vladeniiu russkim iazykom po sub'ektam Rossiiskoi federatsii (Population according to nationality and command of Russian language of the subjects of the Russian Federation), pp. 29–141: https://web.archive.org/web/20220411051753/https://www.gks.ru/free_doc/new_site/perepis2010/croc/vol4pdf-m.html, accessed February 23, 2023.

103. Katherine E. Graney, *Of Khans and Kremlins: Tatarstan and the Future of Ethno-Federalism in Russia* (Lanham, MD: Lexington Books, 2009).

and memorialized.[104] The "Spiritual Administration of the Muslims of Tatarstan" claimed authority in the republic and beyond.[105] Tatarstan's elites deployed their Islamic credentials to initiate economic connections with Islamic powers outside Russia and to influence domestic finance and banking practices.[106] In Tatarstan, the worlds of Islam, Eurasia, and Russian empire intersected.[107]

In the early post-Soviet years, the republic's leaders—ethnic Tatars and veterans of compromise with Soviet power—carved a significant if slippery slice of sovereignty out from the weakened Russian state.[108] They did not ratify the Russian Constitution drafted in 1993 and insisted on drawing up bilateral agreements with Moscow. But after Putin's accession to power in 2000, Tatarstan's sovereignty shrank. Under pressure from the central administration, the Tatar Republic's constitution was pulled into line with the constitution of the Russian Federation. By 2005, ninety-nine of the Republic's laws on economic, political, and cultural matters were changed to match Russia's legislation.[109] The republic's decision to reintroduce the Latin alphabet for written Tatar was sacrificed to the Russian Federation's insistence on Cyrillic.[110] In 2007, Tatarstan lost the

104. Victoria Abakumovskikh, "The Development of Islamic Economic Politics in the Republic of Tatarstan: Combining Religious Ethics with Geopolitical Strategy," in Friess and Kaminskij, *Resignification of Borders*, 127–28.

105. On the politics of the multiple "Spiritual Administrations" of Muslims in Russia after 1991, see Gulnaz Sibgatullina and Michael Kemper, "The Imperial Paradox: Islamic Eurasianism in Contemporary Russia," in Friess and Kaminskij, *Resignification of Borders*, 101–18, and Renat Bekkin, "The Central Spiritual Administration of the Muslims of Russia (TsDUM) and Its Strategy of Subordinate Partnership in Dialogue with the Russian Orthodox Church," *Context* 4, 2 (2017): 7–28.

106. Abakumovskikh, "The Development of Islamic Economic Politics in the Republic of Tatarstan," 125–45.

107. Marlene Laruelle interprets the Islamic theories of Tatar activists as a non-Russian Neo-Eurasianism: Laruelle, *Russian Eurasianism*, 162–69.

108. On Tatar responses to the collapse of the Soviet Union, see Jane Burbank, "Eurasian Sovereignty: The Case of Kazan," *Problems of Post-Communism* 62, 1 (2015): 1–25. Tatars were active in Soviet politics from the time of the Bolshevik revolution; as communist officials, they were subject to multiple purges and executions: John M. Romero, "Rethinking Political Repression in the Tatar Republic, 1917–41," *Kritika: Explorations in Russian and Eurasian History* 22, 4 (Fall 2021): 841–64.

109. I. R. Tagirov, *Istoriia natsional'noi gosudarstvennosti Tatarskogo naroda i Tatarstana* (Kazan: Tatarskoe knizhnoe izdatel'stvo, 2008), 446.

110. On the sequence of alphabets used for Tatar, see F. S. Safiullina, *Tatarskii iazyk na kazhdyi den'* (Kazan: TaRIKH, 2001), 3.

right to levy its own taxes.¹¹¹ Similar adjustments to the laws and authorities of other "national" units of the Russian Federation were made as Putin clawed power back under top-down and centralized control.¹¹²

For Tatarstan, there were carrots accompanying Putin's stick. Putin supported the proposed millennium celebration of Kazan's founding—a controversial project because it made Kazan older than Moscow—with funds for Kazan's new metro and costly festivities.¹¹³ Appearing at the 2005 celebration, Putin opened his speech in Tatar and presided over a special "Kazan" session of the Russian Federation Council alongside Tatarstan's long-standing strongman, Mintimer Shaimiev. This vision of friendly collaboration appeared to validate both the cooperative relations between Russia and the Tatar Republic and its multiculturalist Eurasian-style policies. Advisors in Kazan boldly described their approach as the Tatarstan model of "tolerance and respect for all languages, cultures, and confessions."¹¹⁴ A statue of Lev Gumilev was erected in central Kazan during the millennium festivities.¹¹⁵

---

111. Tatarstan balked at implementing a Russian law ratified in 2021 that would remove its leader's official title of "President." This battle was also eventually lost, to the great regret of many. See Leyla Latypova, "Russia's Tatar Minority Mourns Loss of Regional Presidency," *The Moscow Times*, August 4, 2022.

112. See, for example, the complaint of people from the Republic of Sakha, geographically the largest unit of the Russian Federation, citing their loss of rights in 2009: "An Appeal from Representatives of the Republic of Sakha (Yakutia) to the United Nations Office of the High Commissioner for Human Rights (OHCHR)," *Cultural Survival*, November 29, 2022, https://www.culturalsurvival.org/news/appeal-representatives-republic-sakha-yakutia-united-nations-office-high-commissioner-human, accessed February 21, 2023.

113. Kate Graney, "Making Russia Multicultural: Kazan at Its Millenium and Beyond," *Problems of Post-Communism* 54, 6 (November–December 2007): 17–27. On the political controversies over the date of Kazan's founding, see Fred Hilgemann, *Le Tatarstan: Pays des musulmans de Russie* (Paris: Editions Autrement, 2007), 12–13. On the history of Kazan under Russian imperial rule, see Matthew P. Romaniello, *The Elusive Empire: Kazan and the Creation of Russia, 1552–1671* (Madison: University of Wisconsin Press, 2012) and Danielle Ross, *Tatar Empire: Kazan's Muslims and the Making of Imperial Russia* (Bloomington: Indiana University Press, 2020).

114. Rafael' Khakim, *Ternistyi put' k svobode (Sochineniia. 1989-2006)* (Kazan: Tatarskoe knizhnoe izdatel'stvo, 2007), 364. On Tatarstan and the question of sovereignty in Russia, see Burbank, "Eurasian Sovereignty," 1–25. On Khakimov as a theorist of pluralistic Islam, Tatar nationalism, and non-Russian Eurasianism, see Laruelle, *Russian Eurasianism*, 164–67.

115. Laruelle, *Russian Eurasianism*, 163–64. Laruelle considers Tatarstan the "locomotive of non-Russian Eurasianism," 162.

FIGURE 4.1. Monument to Lev Gumilev in Kazan, Republic of Tatarstan, Russia. *Source:* Deposit Photos. Photo by yulenochekk.

Carved on it was Gumilev's declaration to a Tatar newspaper in 1990: "I, a Russian person, have my whole life defended Tatars from slander."[116]

Putin's demonstrative celebration of Tatar history and culture signaled his embrace of multiethnicity as an essential component of Russian governance. During Putin's first presidential terms, there were other signs that he was leaning in a Eurasian direction. He visited the Lev Gumilev University in Kazakhstan repeatedly, and was awarded an honorary professorship in 2004.[117] In a speech to the faculty and students on October 10, 2000, Putin celebrated Gumilev as a great scholar of Eurasianism, whose historical work "confirmed the idea of eternal commonality, the interconnectedness of the peoples inhabiting the vast expanses of Eurasia: from

---

116. Interview republished in Gumilev, *Chernaia legenda*, 182, from the articles originally published in *Sovetskaia Tatariia*, September 29, October 6, 13, 20, 27 and November 3 and 17, 1990.

117. https://enu.kz/en/about-enu/enu-faces/index.php?sphrase_id=352710, accessed December 9, 2022.

the Baltic and Carpathians to the Pacific Ocean." Putin went on to praise Nazarbaev's persistent pursuit of a Eurasian union, crediting him with initiating the formation of a Eurasian Economic Community. The presidents of Russia, Kazakhstan, Belarus, Kyrgyzstan, and Tajikistan met in Astana that day and signed an agreement establishing their economic alliance.[118]

Dugin, who also received an honorary professorship at Astana,[119] was delighted with Putin's pivot to Eurasia. Putin's speech at the Munich Security Conference in 2007 was a "turning point in Russian history," Dugin exalted. The Cold War had not ended in 1991; Russia was back in. At Munich, Putin had called out the aggressive one-worldism of the United States and NATO—"not our partner, but our enemy"—and put Russia on a "path to geopolitical revolution." In Dugin's eyes, Putin had become the "man of fate," comparable to "de Gaulle, Churchill, Stalin."[120]

Dugin credited Putin with achieving six (out of twelve recommended) "heroic feats" in his first twelve years of leadership. One of these achievements was "giving the green light to the integrationist projects of the CIS," including his "support for the Eurasian idea" at the Gumilev University in Astana. Feat number six was that Putin "wrote the thesis of a 'multipolar world' into the conception of National Security of the RF [Russian Federation], which means in practice the juridical recognition of Eurasianism as the basic international strategy of Russia."[121] Dugin was also gratified by Putin's assertions of direct control over the administration throughout the Russian Federation, especially the replacement of elected officials with people appointed by the "Center."[122] The Russian people appreciated paternalistic, monarchistic authority, "trusted Putin,

---

118. http://kremlin.ru/events/president/transcripts/21625, accessed February 14, 2023. On this speech, see Hamant, "Le Néo-Eurasisme dans la Russie contemporaine," 122.

119. https://enu.kz/en/about-enu/enu-faces/index.php?sphrase_id=3527109.

120. Dugin, *Putin protiv Putina*, 73–81.

121. Ibid., 14–15. One of Dugin's pet formulas, reprised by Putin, is the "multi-polar world," set against the west's monolithic pretense. See Dugin's radio interview in 2002, "One Polarity and Multipolarity, How Many Poles Does the World Need?": Dugin, *Geopolitika postmoderna*, 177–86. The term took hold in Russian political discourse at about this time: Ray Silvius, "The Embedding of Russian State-Sanctioned Multipolarity in the Post-Soviet Conjuncture," *Globalizations* 13, 1 (2016): 7. doi: 10.1080/14747731.2015.1102944

122. Dugin, *Putin protiv Putina*, 15.

FIGURE 4.2. Vladimir Putin, President of Russia, and Nursultan Nazarbaev, President of Kazakhstan, at a meeting on February 27, 2017. *Source:* Website of the President of the Russian Federation.

and recognized his right to decisive action and demanded that he use this right." It was up to Putin to buttress his power with this "mandate for a revolution in conciousness," wrote Dugin, echoing Trubetskoi.[123]

---

123. Ibid., 78–81. The text continues: "We are dealing with a kind of 'plebiscitary authoritarianism' when monarchic rule becomes the voluntary covenant with the popular

Signaling his departure from off-limits western values, Putin began to give a Eurasianist treatment to his descriptions of Russian culture.[124] In speeches for both internal and external consumption, Putin emphasized the need for a "new national idea" that could not be copied from abroad. Addressing the Valdai Forum in 2013, he proclaimed that "extreme, western-style liberalism" was "far from reality." Similarly, a return to Soviet ideology or a conservative idealization of pre-1917 Russia were inadequate. Citizens had to be able to "identify with their own history, values, and traditions," and this required recognition of our "multi-ethnic character." Calling this multiethnicity into question, or exploiting nationalism and separatism, would mean, he echoed Gumilev, "that we start to destroy our own genetic code."[125]

In this 2013 speech, Putin repeatedly stressed his and Russia's devotion to its own version of multiculturalism:

> This multiculturalism and multi-ethnicity live in our historical consciousness, in our spirit and in our historical makeup. Our state was built in the course of a millennium on this organic model.... [The] state civilization model . . . has always sought to flexibly accommodate the ethnic and religious specificity of particular territories, ensuring diversity in unity.[126]

Russia has outdone the west in protecting minorities, Putin insisted. In contrast to the Europeans' struggles over multiculturalism: "Over the past centuries in Russia . . . not even the smallest ethnic group has disappeared. And they have retained not only their internal autonomy and cultural identity, but also their historical space." Moreover, "Christianity, Islam, Buddhism, Judaism and other religions are an integral part of Russia's identity," and the Russian Constitution defends the right to freedom of conscience for all.[127]

---

masses (80)." This theme harks back to an oft repeated interpretation of Russian political institutions: the tsar rules unilaterally but with the assent and will of the Russian people.

124. See hostile reactions to Putin's "Eurasianism" in 2012: https://newsland.com/user/4297767027/content/evraziistvo-gosudarstvennaia-ideologiia-putinskoi-rossii/4426513.

125. "Meeting of the Valdai International Discussion Club," President of Russia official site, http://en.kremlin.ru/events/president/news/19243.

126. Ibid.

127. Ibid.

Putin claimed Eurasia as the "major geopolitical zone" where these values could be defended on an even larger scale. The Eurasian Economic Union was to be built on the "principle of diversity"; it is to be a "union where everyone maintains their identity, their distinctive character and their political independence."[128] This program took many pages from Gumilev's book—the notion of a Russian genetic code, the creation of a super-ethnos that would unite multiple groups, the organic growth of a civilization, the antipathy toward other civilizations—without an inkling of the ethnic decline that Gumilev had also theorized. As this re-imagined cultural unity transgressed Russian borders and extended into international politics, Putin's Eurasianism, like that of both Trubetskoi and Dugin, morphed into a prospect of imperial enlargement. This tendency became reality in 2014 with the duplicitous annexation of Crimea and the instigation of war with Ukraine in the Donbas. Crimea was made into a republic of the Russian Federation (like Tatarstan) and its capital city, Sevastopol, became a "federal city" (like St. Petersburg).[129]

Eurasianism for the People

In the second decade of the twenty-first century, the anti-westernism developed in Dugin's publications and Putin's speeches became a persistent theme of official Russian media. Eurasianism was put on full display in the massive exhibit, "Russia, My History," installed since 2017 in dozens of cities across the Russian Federation.[130] Gumilev is highlighted as a historian and philosopher in the exhibition's multi-media reconstructions of the past. The Mongols are no longer the source of Russian backwardness; instead it is Europe that has assaulted Russia and its people repeatedly.

128. Ibid.
129. "Putin Signs Law on Reunification of Republic of Crimea and Sevastopol with Russia," TASS, 21 March 2014, https://tass.com/russia/724785, accessed September 1, 2021.
130. Karen Petrone, "The 21st-century Memory of the Great Patriotic War in the 'Russia—My History' Museum," in David L. Hoffmann, ed., *The Memory of the Second World War in Soviet and Post-Soviet Russia* (Abingdon, OX and New York: Routledge, 2022), 340–60. Petrone identifies twenty-three locations where the exhibit had opened at the time she was writing. These comments are also based on Jane Burbank's visit to the museum park at St. Petersburg in March 2018.

The executed Romanovs are presented as martyrs, victims of yet another dangerous European import—Marxism. The expansion of the empire is shown as grand and life-enhancing for its subjects. Their diversity is highlighted in folkloric glory.[131]

The re-imagination of post-Soviet Russia is a high stakes effort, in which leading political figures and scholars collaborate and compete.[132] Vladimir Medinskii, Minister of Culture from 2012 to January 2020, produced a "Plan for a State Cultural Project" that explicitly located Russia's "unique civilizational identity" in a global struggle for power. In his telling, both the communist revolution of 1917 and the "Liberal-Western path" of the 1980s and 1990s were attempts (failed ones) to change Russia's "cultural-civilizational identity." Western-style "multiculturalism" and "tolerance" are to be rejected as the state takes up its task of carrying out a "unified state cultural policy."[133]

The flexible capacities of the Eurasian tradition figured in Putin's official declarations about the Russian annexation of Crimea in 2014. Dugin welcomed the assault and became an obsessive advocate of military action in Ukraine. His calls for more violence against Ukrainians led to his dismissal from the Department of Sociology at Moscow State University.[134] The annexation, for Dugin, was the third landmark—after the successful second Chechen war and the 2008 war with Georgia—on Putin's path toward

---

131. Sergei Khazov-Cassia and Robert Coalson, "Russian 'History Parks' Present Kremlin-Friendly Take on the Past," Radio Free Europe/Radio Liberty, October 13, 2019, https://www.rferl.org/a/russian-orthodox-church-gazprom-history-parks/30214143.html, accessed May 24, 2021.

132. Dugin gnashed his teeth over the qualities of Putin's advisors, decrying the perfidy of a "fifth column" inside Russia—"westernizers, liberals, networks of agents of influence of the USA": Aleksandr Dugin, *Novaia Formula Putina: Osnovy eticheskoi politiki* (Moscow: Algoritm, 2014), 170.

133. From Medinskii's program, cited in *Izvestiia*, April 10, 2014, https://iz.ru/news/569016, accessed April 17, 2019. Shortly after Russia's invasion of Ukraine in February 2022, Medinskii was appointed head of the Russian delegation for negotiations over the war: https://www.rferl.org/a/russia-ukraine-talks-belarus/31727584.html, accessed February 23, 2023.

134. Vadim Rossman, "Moscow State University's Department of Sociology and the Climate of Opinion in Post-Soviet Russia," in Laruelle, *Eurasianism and the European Far Right*, 55, 71. Rossman describes Dugin's efforts to embed himself and his ideas in this department.

"freedom" of Russia as a "great sovereign power" in a multipolar world.[135] Speaking in March 2021 by video conference with "representatives of society of the Republic of Crimea and the federal city Sevastopol," Putin adroitly integrated Crimea into Russian history well before its first annexation by Catherine the Great in 1783. No, according to Putin, the critical date was the putative baptism of Prince Vladimir as a Christian in 988 in the ancient city of Chersones, next door to Sevastopol. This event made Crimea the "cradle of our spiritual self-awareness." From that time began the "creation of one Russian nation from the many Slavic tribes that lived on this territory."[136]

Putin conveniently cut off his chronological story at that point, skipping any reference to Kievan Rus', the Mongol Crimean Khanate, or other awkwardnesses. Lest his audience imagine that he was taking an exclusionary nationalist and/or Christian perspective on culture, Putin responded to a Tatar questioner that Crimea was a multinational space. His version of affiliation was both layered and paternalistic:

> It is important that all people who live in Russia in general ... and Crimea specifically—the multinational territory of Crimea—feel themselves on their land as if really in a homeland [*rodina*]. And that they help each other, feel the support of their neighbors, no matter to what confession they belong. That they feel their common homeland—is Russia which relates to all citizens of our country as to its own children.

Putin went on to say that he "regularly attends ... religious institutions, Orthodox, Muslim, Jewish and those of our other confessions." In response to questioners, he supported construction of cultural "hearths" for all of Russia's many cultures.

---

135. Aleksandr Dugin, *Ukraina: Moia voina: Geopoliticheskii dnevnik* (Moscow: Tsentrpoligraf, 2015), 309.

136. This citation and all others from the Crimean speech of March 18, 2021, can be found on official site of the President of Russia: "Vstrecha s obshchestvennost'iu Kryma i Sevastopolia," http://kremlin.ru/events/president/news/65172, accessed June 1, 2021. Catherine also made an ideological claim to Crimea based on the idea that the Scythians who dominated the area were in fact Russians: Erik Martin, "In Between (Eastern) Empire and (Western) Universalism: Eurasian Space and Russian Identity in the Émigré Discourse of the 1920s: N. S. Trubetskoi and M. I. Rostovtsev," in Friess and Kaminskij, *Resignification of Borders*, 24.

In these remarks on Crimea, Putin made a point of contrasting Russia's treatment of its populations to conditions in the United States. While Russia incorporated the natives of Siberia, the Americans carried out a genocide of Indian tribes; the United States suffered the "cruel, long, terrible period of slavery," leading to the injustices of the present, expressed in the "Black Lives Matter movement." Again echoing Gumilev, Putin insisted that Russians are "different people, we have a different genetic and cultural-moral code." Just how far back in time Russia's history extended was not addressed with precision in Putin's 2021 video conference. He avowed, in response to a request for support for scientific projects, that "in general this territory was developed by our ancestors in pre-historic times, even when they weren't called our ancestors. But they were our ancestors. Huns and Scythians and other peoples and so on; these were also our ancestors." Russia, it seems, could put all the peoples who ever lived in Crimea into its multiethnic composition.

A year later, Putin extended this argument to all of Ukraine and ordered his army to make it come true, but with a deadly twist on one of those peoples. Putin's speech on February 21, 2022 asserted that Ukraine had joined the "Euroatlantic"; its spurious statehood would not be recognized; and survivors of the "special military operation," suitably selected, would rejoin their Russian "compatriots."[137] It was left to commentators in the official press to spell out Russia's genocidal program for the rest.[138]

Eurasia, Russian-Style

In post-Soviet Russia, Eurasia has reemerged as an exploitable "-ism" for the twenty-first century. Trubetskoi's anti-European stance stressed Russia's amalgam of Eurasian peoples; Gumilev provided a "scientific" explanation of where ethnic groups came

---

137. "Obrashchenie Prezidenta Rossiiskoi Federatsii," February 21, 2022, http://kremlin.ru/events/president/news/67828.

138. See the genocidal proposal, "What Russia Should Do with Ukraine," written by a historian and published on an official Russian site: Timofei Sergeitsev, "Chto Rossiia dolzhna sdelat' s Ukrainoi," RIA Novosti, April 5, 2022, https://ria.ru/20220403/ukraina-1781469605.html.

from and how they developed. Savitskii called for transcontinental unity against European sea-based empires; Dugin outlined plans for a Russia/Eurasia that could stand up to its global enemies. Eurasianism's anti-western bluster combined with its premise of paternalistic governance and validation of the distinctive culture of each component group has something to offer to both the top and bottom stories of politics and culture. It survives, with official approval, in the latest variant of Russian empire.

What enabled the reinvigoration of Eurasia in its twenty-first-century variant, in strong contrast to the other transregional movements discussed here? For one thing, Eurasia had a foundation in a resilient imperial culture. In the late twentieth century it provided a language for leaders of different ethnic origins who had worked together in the past, representing regions that had been part of the Russian and later Soviet empires. Unlike Eurafrica or Afroasia, Eurasia was not about creating a new political space, but redefining an old one. The game of devolving certain elements of sovereignty was a well practiced one, for leaders both of units internal to the Russian Federation and of new states in Russia's near-abroad. The new Eurasia did not attempt to repudiate empire as a form of state, and instead accented spatial and civilizational continuity.

Eurasia's possibilities involved more than elites and more than the recent past. Trubetskoi's contention that a shared Eurasian tradition could become the basis for a reanimated Russian polity was prescient: people across most of the post-Soviet space reverted after 1991 to forms of social organization that were familiar to them and, excluding the western edge of the USSR, to their neighbors as well. That familiarity was based on centuries of history in a space with a long tradition of putting multiple peoples and cultures together under a superior authority.[139] The khan, the tsar, and the emperor preceded Lenin and his successors; these paramount leaders had worked with intermediaries who claimed to intercede for the welfare of their own dependents.

---

139. See Jane Burbank, "All Under the Tsar: Russia's Eurasian Trajectory," in Yuri Pines, Michal Biran, Jörg Rüpke, and Eva Cancik-Kirschbaum, eds., *The Limits of Universal Rule: Eurasian Empires Compared* (Cambridge: Cambridge University Press, 2021), 342–75.

These arrangements offered a means to connect different groups. Federation became the name; the challenge was maintaining the supreme leader's control over individuals who could speak for and to "their" people. Russian as well as many Central Asian and Caucasian authorities proved more accommodating to devolved, but supervised, sovereignty allocated on "national" principles than most of the elites promoting Eurafrica and Afroasia had been. Unlike Eurafrica, which was premised on the extension of democratic principles through continental connections and Afroasia, which presumed the sovereign equivalence of the liberated states of Africa and Asia, Eurasia presumed neither democracy nor equivalence and did not take on the burden of establishing those principles.

Nor did Eurasia set forth an agenda for economic development and social reform. Savitskii, Nazarbaev, and Dugin articulated the need for a common economic space, but the questions of Russia's relationship to its socialist past, to the liberal capitalism that western economists pressed for the 1990s, and to the inequities and injustices of Russian-style capitalism in the present were for the most part left in abeyance. Eurasianist ideology could float over an incoherent economic structure that inspired the ambitions of capitalists, but kept them subject to discipline from the top. As he sought to overcome the humiliations of Soviet decay, Putin found in Eurasianism an appealing replacement ideology. Its foundation in shared values across cultures over a big space overrode any residual Marxist obligation to attend to economic institutions.

Eurasia, unlike Eurafrica or Afroasia, dealt explicitly with confessional pluralism. Religion was seen as an issue that had to be prominent in politics. Perhaps because communists had tried to destroy religion or at least keep it in check,[140] the post-communist leaders of the Eurasian revival highlighted their respect for religions, all of them. Eurasianism, as Putin stressed, meant not just religious tolerance, but commitment to religious traditions as pillars of Russia's multicultural order.

---

140. Victoria Smolkin, *A Sacred Space Is Never Empty: A History of Soviet Atheism* (Princeton, NJ: Princeton University Press, 2018). On the complex religious tactics of the officially atheist state, see Kathryn David, "Galician Catholic into Soviet Orthodox: Religion and Post-War Ukraine," *Nationalities Papers* 46, 2 (2018): 290–300.

Eurasianism draws on the past to project a future. In Putin's vision, the deep past is providential, but history has to be handled gingerly. The trick is keeping the Bolshevik project at arm's length, denouncing the Leninist version of federalism, while refusing examination of the crimes committed in the name of Soviet communism. Russian leaders want to revitalize and revise appropriately long historical continuities rather than mythologizing revolution as the previous regime had done. One episode of Soviet geopolitical triumph has been retained—victory in World War II. This was what made the USSR a superpower. Enhanced with updated communications technology, spread through textbooks, and enforced with controls over the historical record, the battle against Nazism has been turned into the slogans of undeclared, genocidal war against Ukraine.

Is the programmed attempt to eradicate Ukrainian culture, people, and sovereignty, to make Russians and Ukrainians "one people, one whole," consistent with Eurasianist ideas? It may seem odd that Putin is trying to exterminate a people that appear to be ethnically closer to Russians than almost all other groups in the "near abroad." But Eurasianists even early in the twentieth century were hostile to Ukrainian claims for recognition as a distinctive nation. For Trubetskoi and Savitskii, Ukraine was a "problem"; their idea was that Ukrainian elites should join the hegemonic Russian top story, ditching their language and local allegiance for immersion in a higher cultural world. As Gumilev had pointed out, some ethnic groups can merge and create a more powerful super-etnos. Dugin's emphasis was, as ever, on geopolitics. Ukraine was a threat to Russia because Ukrainians had sided with the west. The issue was not ethnic difference, which Eurasianists in principle should respect, but the political allegiance of people who should have been more like Russians. Ukrainians' support for democracy and Europe was a threat to the core values of Russia/Eurasia. As such they have to be eliminated. In Putin's variant, Russia has to push the western enemy and its moral corruption out of Ukraine. Then the "big space of geopolitics" can extend itself, with its pluralistic Eurasian inclusivity, outward in other directions.

CHAPTER FIVE

Reflections

TO REFLECT ON the "post-imperial" is to evoke aspirations, not an actuality. Imperial ambitions and imperial institutions have not disappeared from the world.[1] The turmoil of two empire wars in the twentieth century provoked new ways of thinking about politics and inspired hopes of transforming a world dominated by a small number of states presiding over diverse and subordinated populations. Imperial elites sought to adjust their mechanisms of domination, while Japanese, Soviet, and fascist regimes developed their own versions of empire. These efforts at imperial recovery and reconstruction were challenged by mobilizations for world-wide communist revolution, claims to citizenship rights and political equality within existing empires, attempts to construct federations of different peoples within or outside of imperial structures, and designs for creating an independent state for each self-defined people.

The expanding number of states in the decades after World War II seemed to signal the triumph of the last of these alternatives. But to describe the pathway from empire to nation-state as linear and inevitable is to ignore the complexity of how empires came apart

---

1. In the winter of 2023, Timothy Garten Ash opined that if Russia's aggression in Ukraine could be thwarted and Ukraine, along with Moldova and Georgia, integrated into western institutions, this would spell the end of Russian empire, and "for the first time in European history, we would have a fully postimperial Europe—that is, a Europe with neither overseas nor land empires." "Ukraine in Our Future," *New York Review of Books*, February 23, 2023. As of this writing, Ash's comment is clearly more aspiration than actuality.

and the multiple possibilities for post-imperial transformations. Even at the height of violent and nonviolent struggles against imperial power in the 1950s, some of the most militant political actors in the colonies were looking beyond the nation-state to forms of integration and common action, achieved horizontally with other states emerging from colonial rule or vertically with the rich and powerful or through a combination of the two. Such efforts persisted into the years when the sovereign nation-state seemed to have become the international norm.[2]

With the collapse of communist domination in eastern Europe in 1989 and of the Soviet Union in 1991, another wave of states became full-fledged, autonomous members of the international community. Many observers at that time believed that they were finally living in a world of equivalent states, most of which shared in the norms of liberal democracy and participated freely in the movement of people, commodities, and ideas across state borders and across continents.

Yet in the twenty-first century, the stability and legitimacy of a world order based on national sovereignty is threatened by efforts, including war, to expand or restore imperial power, the inability of the international system to respond effectively to global problems like climate change and poverty, and tensions within many states—rich as well as poor—between the democratic ideal that self-determination seemed to imply and the ability of many elites to monopolize power within the bounded national sphere. Some of the critiques of the national order of things that scholars offer today were anticipated by anti-imperialist activists in their own times.

Our focus on a range of political ideas about a future after empire does not imply that these projects provided convincing solutions to economic inequity, social discrimination, political disempowerment, or interstate aggression. Democracy, humanity, and justice were indeed the concern of many anti-imperialist activists, but some were advocates for an ethnically, racially, or religiously

---

2. Some scholars of international relations have questioned the discipline's tendency to see today's world as a "monoculture of sovereign states," pointing to the heterogeneity of types of political units and of populations within states. See for example Andrew Phillips and J. C. Sharman, *International Order in Diversity: War, Trade and Rule in the Indian Ocean* (Cambridge: Cambridge University Press, 2015), 1 quoted.

homogeneous society and some cared little for institutionalized guarantees of human rights or democratic principles. Many of the first rulers of newly independent states were intent on ensuring their positions against all challenges. At the same time, the strongest states of the world found ways to exercise power or influence in what had been the colonial sphere.

Issues such as these were objects of debate over the course of the twentieth century. Intellectuals and activists addressed the question of how large, how inclusive, and how uniform units of political belonging should be. To some, the large scale of empire—if stripped of hierarchy and discrimination—seemed to offer possibilities for political, economic, and social progress that separate, smaller political units might not. For example, after the successful campaign in 1946 for the extension of French citizenship to the overseas territories, representatives of the people of French Africa sat in the French National Assembly, the French Senate, and the Assembly of the French Union. Following independence, the people of those territories might be represented in the institutions of their respective nation-states, but they no longer had a voice in French or European institutions. Other experiments in supranational federation at the time of decolonization—in East Africa and the West Indies, for example—opened alternatives that were later closed down as elites acquired an interest in their territorial bases.[3] There would be further experiments in regional alliances, common markets, and interstate organizations—the Southeast Asia Treaty Organization, the Economic Community of West African States, the Common Market of South America (Mercosur)—but they would be built on territorial nation-states, not on layered forms of sovereignty.

A world system based on mutual recognition of national states left the enforcement of rights—including those regarded as "universal"—to those states, whose rulers might or might not respect those rights. Nationalized sovereignty meant that citizens were in a position to make claims for economic and social resources only within their

---

3. The exclusion of possibilities in the transition to independence is emphasized by Malika Rahal, "Empires," in Martin Conway, Pieter Lagrou, and Henry Rousso, eds., *Europe's Postwar Periods 1989, 1945, 1918: Writing History Backwards* (London: Bloomsbury, 2019), 145.

states, even though the "national economy" was a fiction that did not represent the way that markets for resources and capital actually worked and did not take account of the history of extraction and exploitation that had shaped life and death in colonial territories. The new states could ask for aid; neither they nor the people they claimed to represent had a recognized entitlement to it.

The breakup of the Soviet Union in 1991 left in place the Russian Federation, shorn of fourteen former units of the USSR. For a time, Russia's leaders promoted a version of post-imperial federalism. But the relationship between imperial and post-imperial can be two-directional. The internal units of the Russian Federation have since 2000 become increasingly subject to centralized and authoritarian rule, losing the ability to elect their leaders and to control the allocation of their resources. To the countries on Russia's borders that gained independence in 1991, Putin's war with Georgia, support for separatists in Moldova, and no-holds-barred assault on Ukraine and its people send a strong signal that expansion into the "near abroad" is Russia's chosen way for the future.

Of the three transcontinental projects described in this book, Eurasia is the only one that remains politically viable today. It is also the most frankly imperial, revealed starkly in the vicious Russian invasion of Ukraine in 2022, but also in the Russian Federation's internal politics. Eurafrica, in contrast, offered the possibility—however difficult to achieve—of turning a colonial relationship into a democratic political entity. Afroasia promised to bring about greater equality among the states of the world, old and new, ex-colonizers and ex-colonized. Neither proposal succeeded in its own terms.

All three projects rejected the claims to cultural or civilizational superiority that were intrinsic to European empire in its heyday, acknowledging to varying degrees the spatial expansiveness and cultural diversity that connections across continents enabled while at the same time attempting to transcend the hierarchy and domination of imperial rule. The unraveling of colonial empire in the 1950s and the collapse of Soviet empire in 1989–91 produced possibilities for reimagining political space but also constraints on fitting bold new alignments into a world order that was reshaped as each subordinated territory, in turn, acquired independence.

However much the development of capitalism on a global scale was entwined with the extension of European empires overseas, capitalists learned in the 1950s and 1960s that they could live quite well without colonial empire. In the French case, as Denis Cogneau has shown, some French corporations had profited from the colonies in the twentieth century, whatever the benefits and costs of colonial ventures to the overall French economy. The large public investment made after 1945 created opportunities for French firms, and many of these businesses favored the retention of the colonies even when the pressures for decolonization mounted in the 1950s. Nonetheless, French capital adapted effectively to decolonization, and the years 1945–75 were a time of economic growth and improving welfare in France, as they were in much of Europe.[4] It was also a period of increasing wealth and corporate power in the United States and a time when the claim that communism would triumph economically over capitalism began to lose credibility, setting the stage for the Soviet elite's disillusion with the communist system.

From the mid-1950s to the mid-1970s, political leaders in African, Asian, and Latin American states, as well as a range of international political organizations, tried in various ways to come to grips with the fact that political liberation had not meant economic liberation. They were met with a strong reaction from wealthy states, international financial institutions, and corporate interests. The platforms of sovereignty and membership in the United Nations made challenges to economic structures possible, but the divergent interests and conditions of states made it difficult for the Afroasian or Tricontinental movements to face down their powerful opponents.

National independence gave governments responsible to their citizenry the possibility, if they so chose, to put money into education, health care, and social services that colonial governments had ignored until late in the imperial game. Independence also offered elites new opportunities to accumulate wealth. National sovereignty became a claim against renewed efforts at imperial

---

4. Denis Cogneau, *Un empire bon marché: Histoire et économie politique de la colonisation française, XIXe–XXIe siècle* (Paris; Seuil, 2023), 398–400.

aggression, even if international recognition of the principle did not deter Russia from a full-scale invasion of Ukraine in 2022.

Russia's war on Ukraine deepened Ukrainians' identification with their nation, but it did more than that. Ukrainians had taken to the streets in the early 2000s to contest corruption and to demand democratic procedures and economic justice from their leaders. The country was open to lively debates over history, language, and church politics, and the meaning of national belonging in a multiethnic, multiconfessional state. In the 2013–2014 Maidan movement, the long-term tension between Ukraine's two external orientations—with Russia or with western Europe—snapped; the Russian-oriented president was driven out of the country.[5] This civic mobilization and Russia's brutal response in 2014—in Crimea and the Donbas—highlight the persistent conflict between national and imperial claims. Ukrainians were defending a state's right to choose its economic and political connections. Although the "western" bloc was slow to appreciate the strength of Ukraine's commitment to its integrity and chosen alignments, Putin's war helped to convince the European Union and NATO that their supranational ties were in the interest of all their member states. What is at stake in the war is indeed national sovereignty, but also values and connections that transcend the nation-state.

Sovereignty can also be used to exert imperial power, as the People's Republic of China does in its persecution of Uyghurs in western China, the Turkish government in regard to Kurds, or Israel in relation to Palestinians. These governments push aside questions about human rights that members of the international community raise. Strong states have arrogated to themselves the right to judge whether the regimes of weaker states have the right to stay in power, as did the United States in Iraq in 2003. Imperial claims with a pseudo-historical basis can serve an expansionist purpose, such as the attempt to establish a "Greater Serbia" at the expense of Bosnia and Kosovo in the 1990s. But small states have also shown their ability to act against large ones: Vietnam against the United States, Ukraine against Russia.

5. Serhii Plokhy, *The Gates of Europe: A History of Ukraine*, rev. ed. (New York: Basic Books, 2021), 325–40.

What is to be gained by reflecting on the ways in which people in the past imagined different forms of politics that they thought might address questions of social justice, economic power, and cultural expression? Could recognition of these efforts to find alternatives to the normalized places of both empire and nation-state in world politics help us move out of the sense, complacent or despairing, that today's political structures were inevitable and that their continuity is inevitable too? Can we take a cue from the debates at Bandung in 1955 that affirmed the importance of national independence but sought forms of collective action beyond the nation-state? The following pages reflect on the significance of the three projects, each a plan for transforming or adapting global power relations, for thinking about political relationships in the twentieth and twenty-first centuries.

Out of Empire, or Not

The starting point for Eurasian, Eurafrican, and Afroasian projects in the twentieth century was empire. Of the three, one remained fixated on a redesigned but overtly imperial framework—Eurasia. Eurafrica represented an attempt to maintain a vertical relationship between France and Europe, stripped of its hierarchical dimensions. Afroasia posited a radical alternative, a horizontal relationship among ex-colonial states that would become a force for global economic and political equality.

Eurasianists, both early and late, argued that a transcontinental realm could protect and invigorate an array of different peoples under the supervision of paternalistic authority. Senghor's vision of complementary civilizations in Europe and Africa was buttressed by a strategy to bring the two together, combining horizontal and vertical solidarities. His proposal for layered political and administrative structures—ex-colonial territory, African federation, French confederation, Eurafrican polity—was a plan for transforming ideals into institutions. Afroasian solidarity emerged as a rejection of imperial power, and with the successes of struggles against colonialism turned into a collective effort of independent states to transform global economic and political institutions.

None of these projects precluded recognition of "national" sentiments, but all of them addressed these sentiments in relational terms—one could attach oneself simultaneously to different communities—Serer, Senegalese, African, French, and Eurafrican; Kazakh, Russian, and Eurasian; Vietnamese and Afroasian. Affinity did not necessarily assume homogeneity. Eurasianism drew on a collectivity that accepted difference; Eurafrica posited complementarity between different civilizations; Afroasia set forth a political project that crossed lines of cultural difference. They differed in their approach to religion. Eurasianists insisted that religion was an essential basis of affinity even when people's beliefs differed; Eurafricanists and Afroasianists tended to avoid rather than confront tensions among Christianity, Islam, Hinduism, Buddhism, and other religions.

Eurafricanists and Afroasianists were deeply skeptical of European claims to embody universal values, but leaders of these projects asserted demands based on universal rights: the right of equal people to choose their form of government, to profit from the natural resources of their territories, to develop culture in different ways. Eurasianists rebuffed universalistic reasoning and claim-making altogether. The Eurasian cultural mosaic was, so the argument went, distinct from and superior to Europeans' aggressive insistence on a single set of values for all. Against the Eurasianist theory of clashing cultures, Ukraine's leaders defend universal rights, accusing Russia's military of crimes against humanity.

These conflicting positions recall Savitskii's critique of Trubetskoi, whose impassioned argument for the integrity of different cultures failed to address the need for political power to defend that integrity (chapter 1). Likewise, the Afroasian movement's critiques of European cultural domination masquerading as universality has not been enough to overturn the economic and political—and cultural—might of "western" capital or "western" states. Eurafricanists' vision of cultural complementarity, shared governance, and redistributive economic policy could not overcome the ability of European states to decide what they wanted to share or redistribute. What has most acutely challenged that nexus of "western" dominance has been rival combinations of economic, political, and cultural power, notably that of China and Russia, evoking "Asian" or "Russian" values and mocking any notion of human rights. Today's Eurasianists—notably Dugin and his followers—have stripped the earlier Eurasianists' critique of the west of its humanistic values and turned the theory into an assertion of imperial power.

Advocates of Eurafrica forced intense debates about how institutions configured in imperial conditions could manage issues of cultural difference and economic inequality and address divisions of race, class, and gender. They confronted a fractured French political arena in the mid-twentieth century that included not only advocates of a less hierarchical form of imperial politics, but also defenders of old-style colonialism and elites who saw France's future interests in European terms. French political leaders who accepted—for reasons of state—the need for a more inclusionary citizenship had not necessarily discarded the racial and cultural prejudices well rooted in French society. In the end, the argument over Eurafrica exposed the limits of the agenda of France and its European partners: they were not willing to pay the bill to bring France's former colonies in Africa out of the poverty that was rampant there after more than sixty years of colonial rule.

By the 1950s Afroasianists were buoyed by the first wave of states emerging from colonial rule and winning, in international public opinion, the moral argument they had long been making against colonialism. New states sought to turn their political freedom into economic and cultural liberation; they provided platforms for activists and social movements to challenge western hegemony. Intellectuals from Africa and Asia have had a durable influence on intellectual and cultural life in Europe and North America as well as in the "Third World." But by the end of the 1970s, Afroasian projects for transforming the global political economy were blocked. The weak, even acting together, could not overcome the strong; they needed the strong too much.

Eurasia emerged as the Russian empire collapsed, but with deep roots in that empire's practices. Neither the early Eurasianists nor the latter-day ones wanted to devolve power away from the imperial leader. They developed an alternative ideology for a vast area where central power and cultural differentiation were widely accepted. A tsar, general secretary, or president could make vertical connections through intermediaries to people of various religions and ethnicities, allocate rights and privileges differentially, and not worry about commonality or equality. As Vladimir Putin consolidated his power in the Russian Federation in the 2000s, he could draw on traditions of centralized authority from the tsarist and Soviet periods while claiming that the unity-within-diversity of Eurasian culture offered more sustenance to Russia's people than the individualism, universalism, and arrogance of the "Atlantic" powers.

Putin's ambitions extended beyond Russia's borders, but could empire be put back together in a Eurasian form? After 1991, the former Soviet republics were all sovereign entities, each with its own mix of national sentiment and civic reconstruction. As in other post-imperial contexts, political leaders were inclined to defend their interests and independence even as Russia flexed its economic and military muscle. The Baltic states joined NATO as soon as they could. Ukraine's turn to Europe triggered Putin's war, but of all the states that had earlier been part of the Soviet empire, only Belarus, its dictator dependent on Russian force, voted against the UN's resolutions condemning Russia's aggression.[6] Post-empire is a volatile condition.

Trajectories

It is tempting to see Eurafrica, Eurasia, and Afroasia as doomed from the beginning—as false starts in a world of national states, exploitative economic structures, and unredeemable histories of racial prejudice. This interpretation assumes that whatever has come to be in the present was inevitable and glosses over the efforts of innovative thinkers and skillful politicians of earlier times. But to understand how the world has come to take the shape it now has, we should consider the possible alternatives as they existed for people who were trying to make the future but did not know what it would be. The three narratives presented here take us back in time,

---

6. See the votes on the resolutions of March 2, 2022, October 22, 2022, and February 23, 2023: UN Digital Library, https://digitallibrary.un.org/record/3959039, https://digitallibrary.un.org/record/3990400, https://digitallibrary.un.org/record/4003921, accessed March 4, 2023. Apart from Belarus and Russia, the other thirteen states either voted "yes" or "abstain" or did not vote at all. The vote of February 23, 2023 on a resolution that included a "demand" for complete withdrawal of Russian military forces from Ukraine in its internationally recognized borders was 141 in favor of the resolution, 7 against, 32 abstentions, 13 nonvoting. For the text of this resolution, see https://daccess-ods.un.org/tmp/2481989.26448822.html, accessed March 4, 2023.

to follow step by step what political scientists call "path dependence": to understand how historical conditions and actions at one time produced consequences that shaped the possibilities and constraints of each subsequent moment. We can shift the focus from looking for causes abstracted from time to examining sequences and conjunctures.

Take the case of Eurafrica. How did Africa and France end up in 1960 separated into fifteen states in sub-Saharan Africa and one in Europe (retaining a few component parts around the world), when hardly any leader of stature from those regions in 1945 and few in 1955 sought such an outcome? One can look at the paths taken and not taken from both African and European angles. Senghor pushed his African colleagues to federate among themselves before they became independent, but his plans ran up against politicians' vested interests in the territorial constituencies they had been developing since the first elections with significant African participation in 1945, based on regions designed by the French government around colonial borders. Slow and partial concessions by France of authority to the leaders of political parties in each territory deepened these interests.

Moreover, the French government was wary of aggregating demands. In 1956, power over most internal affairs was devolved to elected governments in each separate territory, bypassing the inclusive administrative units of French West and Equatorial Africa set up more than a half-century earlier. Until the very eve of independence, Senghor kept trying to line up support for an African federation that would be a part of a French confederation and a participant in whatever Eurafrican structures were negotiated. Eurafrica offered the possibility of scaling up this layered version of inclusion and sovereignty, but the rejection of France's African territories as active participants in the European Economic Community relegated them to second-tier, powerless status. As Guinea, the truncated Mali Federation, and the rest of France's African territories took different paths into self-government and adopted different economic policies, the possibilities of unity in French Africa, the French Community, and Eurafrica fell apart together.

From the vantage point of leaders in European France, the postwar trajectory was marked by shifting goals and possibilities.

An ambitious vision of European Union in which French colonies might be included, first discussed in the late 1940s, became a narrowly defined European Coal and Steel Community in the early 1950s and then a European Economic Community of six members, with France's African territories relegated to "associate" status. From there, European leaders' conception of Europe slowly expanded to include more member states, and planners returned to political as well as economic integration. The upshot was the creation of the European Union in 1993 and later a common currency and the Schengen system of border controls.

The debates over Africa's place in European integration during the 1940s and 1950s overlapped the uncertainty and conflict over overseas territories' place in French institutions. French elites, unable after World War II to maintain the subordination and exploitation of colonized people as before, faced choices between incorporating the colonized fully into the French political and social system at a high cost, fighting endless colonial wars, or turning the colonial project into something else. French leaders tried for years to keep their European and African options open. Africans had made clear that they would not be the "dowry" in a marriage of European partners. When France and its would-be European partners balked at the cost of including African territories in their integrative project in the mid-1950s, Africans had less incentive to overcome their differences with France and each other over how to structure a federal or confederal successor to empire. This sequence brought most leaders in France and French Africa to a parting of the ways that they only belatedly came to accept.

Both the diminished threat of one European empire dominating others and the demise of Eurafrica made possible a more national France and a more European Europe. France, no longer trying to hold together a differentiated polity created by colonization, could make its own decisions about the allocation of aid to former colonies and the terms on which citizens of those states would be allowed to work in or immigrate to France. By the 1980s, a significant part of the population of the French Republic was espousing a view of Frenchness that excluded the descendants of North and sub-Saharan Africans whom France had once tried to hold within a French polity.

Eurasia, Eurafrica, and Afroasia all began in opposition to Europe's domination of world politics, and each was stymied, in different ways, in the pursuit of post-imperial supranational formations. Meanwhile, Europe developed its own project, the European Union. The reconstruction of Europe is both a remarkable departure—built on negotiations, arguments, and compromise—from a long history of conflict and war, and a process that has been far from smooth. Today, politics in European institutions may appear chaotic—a hazard of transparent democracy—and at times it may seem that Europe is being run by bureaucrats in the face of public indifference. But especially since the overt war on Ukraine began in February 2022, the European Union has come to resemble what the current generation of Eurasian ideologues is railing against—a political entity capable of acting as a "bloc" hostile to Russian interests and actions. The EU's messy politics and its defense of humanitarian principles, the rule of law, and space for dissent contrast strongly with the authoritarianism of Russia's imperial revival. The EU is still an open-ended political experiment. It is not clear that the project has captured the political imagination of most people living on the continent, nor that the union has the will to defend social protections as readily as it defends commercial interests, nor that it can withstand attacks from participating elites whose autocratic, illiberal, or nationalist conceptions go against the collective endeavor.

In developing supranational institutions and defining a supranational citizenship, the EU drew on some of the ideas associated with Eurafrica but within strictly European boundaries. Subsequently, the EU erected barriers against immigrants or refugees coming from outside, including former colonies of European states. The same restrictions did not apply to Ukrainians fleeing from Russia's assault on their country. In the context of war on Europe's eastern edge, the EU has shown that it is willing not only to act collectively but also to cooperate with the United States despite rivalries in the economic domain. The EU and Eurasia serve as clashing models for other supranational political endeavors that look beyond the nation-state.

Afroasian aspirations, like Eurafrican plans, were caught up in a sequence of events that set different territories on different trajectories. Anti-imperialism between the two world wars was a politics of movements, of activists across borders. Colonial empires withstood these challenges for a time and were more decisively threatened by new imperial formations—Nazi Germany, Japan, and the USSR. The debacle of World War II damaged the winning empires as well as the losers and set the stage for multiple trajectories: from empire to independent state beginning in India (1947) and Indonesia (1949), imperial reform followed by negotiated independence in most of French Africa in 1960, tortuous paths through political conflict to eventual independence in British Africa (Ghana 1957, Nigeria 1960, Zambia 1964, Zimbabwe 1979), successful wars of liberation in Vietnam, Algeria, and Portuguese Africa (1954, 1962, 1974). The Bandung Conference of 1955 was an attempt to intervene in these transitions to independence. Ex-colonial states, acting together, wanted to accelerate the end of colonial rule in territories still under European domination and to challenge the remaining economic and political power of the imperial states.

What gave the Afroasian movement its strength in the mid-1950s and 1960s was also the movement's constraint: territorial sovereignty. State leaders had power at home and voice in the UN and other international organizations, but their influence derived from territorialized, and in theory nationalized, power. Although activists tried valiantly to put together a global movement against what some critics called neocolonialism, they ran up against both the resources of their foes and the strengths and vulnerabilities of the ruling elites of the Afroasian states. Potential allies in labor movements and socialist parties in Europe and the civil rights movement in the United States concentrated on winning or defending gains within bounded spaces and were divided over the question of pushing for social justice on a global scale. Ex-colonial states themselves followed different routes, some toward industrialization and rapid economic growth, others to repeated economic and political crises or stagnation. The ruling elites of Afroasian countries did not necessarily act in accordance with the democratic and egalitarian ideals Afroasian movements had espoused. The corporations, international financial institutions, and states of the capitalist world were able to stand up to the challenges of communism, OPEC, and the NIEO and offer a coherent worldview of a market-based world economy. After 1991, the triumph of corporate capitalism was a victory of ideology as well as realpolitik.

Eurasianism first emerged among intellectual exiles from Bolshevik Russia in the 1920s. The early Eurasianists repudiated communism but not the multicultural composition of the Russian state and society. Rejecting what they considered the imperious claims to universality of "Germano-Roman" culture, Eurasianists insisted that the heritage of the Mongols as well as the eastern variant of Christianity offered cultural inclusivity and social coherence to the people of the vast transcontinental region, united under the authority of a patriarchal ruler and an elite aware of the sensibilities of the populace.

When Europeans and Americans in the 1990s proclaimed the triumph of seemingly liberal capitalism and formally democratic politics, part of Russia's elite recoiled from the prospect of a unified world. Imbued with what has been called "imperial innocence,"[7] many Russians resented their loss of superior status both inside the formerly Soviet space and beyond. Promoting revival of Russia as a global power, a new generation of Eurasianists vaunted the recognition of multiple religious traditions inside a single polity over the secular and, in their view, exclusionary and morally perverse political culture of the west. The posture of civilizational difference, combined with the advocacy of multipolarity was both a defense and a threat. With democracy challenged worldwide in the 2000s by the Orbans, Erdogans, Modis, Trumps, and Xi Jinpings, and with liberal capitalism confronted by China's authoritarian version, Eurasianism provides a plausible coherence to claims that the new Russia stands for a viable alternative.

The Eurasianism of the 1990s and 2000s combined the multi-storied cultural constructions advocated by Trubetskoi in the 1920s, Savitskii's continentalism, the super-etnos theory of Gumilev, and Dugin's "traditionalism," "multipolarity," and "great space" geopolitics. It did not speak clearly about economics. As erstwhile party officials conducted privatized takeovers of state enterprises in their own unleashed interests, Eurasianism's inclusivity could be

---

7. Botakoz Kassymbekova and Erica Marat, "Time to Question Russia's Imperial Innocence," PONARS Eurasia Policy Memo No. 771, April 2022.

highlighted in contrast to the selfishness of neoliberal economic policy and its exploitation of the fragmented nation-state system. The Eurasian Economic Union piloted in 2015 could eventually, in principle, rival the European Union. At the very least, it would not be bogged down by democratic ideals. Following a brief interlude of multiparty democracy after 1991, Russia has returned to the rule of the great leader, an idea advocated by the Eurasian theorists.

Eurasianism remains a doctrine well absorbed by much of the Russian political and military elite, but many Russians who welcomed the political and economic liberties they acquired after 1991 have risked their freedom, their livelihoods and possessions, and their lives to sustain a struggle against a repressive regime. In the 1920s, Eurasianism developed among exiles from Soviet Russia; in the 2020s, many Russian citizens who have exiled themselves reject the version of Eurasianism now on offer. The war on Ukraine awakened sensitivity to Russian privilege vis-à-vis non-Russians, both in the Russian Federation and in the Soviet past. Academics and others who call for "decolonizing" Russia[8] castigate elites for their racist and civilizational arrogance—the kind of imperialism that the early Eurasianists claimed to reject.

Just how far Eurasianist politics can be extended is still in question. The war on Ukraine opened up more than one crack in Putin's version of Eurasian solidarity. Military defeats in the first year of the war energized Russian nationalists who call loudly for crushing both internal and external enemies. The extensive use of troops from outlying, non-Russian regions on the war's deadly battlefields can turn simmering discontent into anguish and anger in these soldiers' exploited homelands.[9] Many states that were formerly

---

8. For examples, see Botakoz Kassymbekova, "On Decentering Soviet Studies and Launching New Conversations," *Ab Imperio* 2022, 1: 115–20 and the forum "Decolonization in Focus," held at the Center for Russian, East European and Eurasian Studies at the University of Pittsburgh in February and March 2023, sponsored by Association for Slavic, East European, and Eurasian Studies and fourteen area studies centers: https://www.ucis.pitt.edu/creees/decolonization-in-focus, accessed March 3, 2023.

9. See the protest to the UN from Yakutia: "An Appeal from Representatives of the Republic of Sakha (Yakutia) to the United Nations Office of the High Commissioner for Human Rights (OHCHR)," *Cultural Survival*, November 29, 2022, https://www.culturalsurvival.org/news/appeal-representatives-republic-sakha-yakutia-united-nations-office-high-commissioner-human, accessed February 21, 2023. For a judicious survey of

Soviet republics take in Russian citizens fleeing conscription. Estonia, Latvia, and Lithuania vociferously defend their independence and their choice for European and Atlantic alliances. Ukraine fights for its own post-imperial future. Putin's war on Ukraine has undermined projects for unification of the "near abroad" under the Russian umbrella.

The transformation of colonial empire into nation-states in the 1960s and that of the Soviet Union into the Russian Federation and a group of formally national polities in the 1990s was facilitated by the new states' compatibility with globe-spanning capitalism. Corporations were well equipped to work with a world of nation-states: they could operate around the world, investing or not as they chose, negotiating with vulnerable states to allow for favorable operating conditions, weak labor regulation, and the right to repatriate profits. In Asia and Africa, much of the work of pushing people into commercial networks—and in some cases concentrating landownership in a small number of hands—had been done under colonial regimes. As former communists in Russia, Eastern Europe, China, and elsewhere took over ownership of the means of production from the state, economic conflicts involved different but interconnected capitalisms, not capitalism and radical alternatives.[10]

In the last decades of the twentieth century, multinational corporations, the United States, and the former imperial powers could pursue their interests in accord with the dual fictions of a world of equivalent nation-states and free markets. Yarimar Bonilla points to the parallels between the freeing of slaves in the Caribbean and elsewhere in the nineteenth century and the freedom of the decolonized state in international relations:

> The freedom of emancipation became equated with the freedom of the market, the right to work, and the naturalization of a desire for material rewards from toil. In a similar fashion, postcolonial sovereignty

---

views from one of the most mobilized regions, see Sam Breazeale, trans., "'Do You Know Why the Ukrainians Are Mad at Us?' How the War in Ukraine Has Changed Dagestanis' Views of the Russian Army," https://meduza.io/en/feature/2023/02/18/do-you-know-why-the-ukrainians-are-mad-at-us, accessed March 3, 2023.

10. On where and how property ended up after 1991 in Russia and Ukraine, see Jessica Allina-Pisano, *The Post-Soviet Potemkin Village: Politics and Property Rights in the Black Earth* (Cambridge: Cambridge University Press, 2007).

became equated with the right to a passport, a flag, a stamp, a coin, and the formation of a native state. It also became associated with a restrictive ideology that suggests that national borders can and should serve as containers for homogenous content.[11]

Elites would continue to vie for power within those national units, while the wealthier parts of the world could distance themselves from the constraints that poverty, underdeveloped infrastructure, and indebtedness placed on their poorer neighbors' possibilities for economic progress.

After empire, the smooth operation of capitalism met with obstructions, exacerbated by tensions in interstate relations and conflicts inside the new states, but these problems appeared, at least to business leaders, to be manageable, even exploitable. The hierarchies and inequities of global capitalism did not mean that it was a closed or uniform system. South Korea, Taiwan, and Singapore offered models for routes out of colonial empire toward integration into global commercial networks and national prosperity. Political reforms that might have challenged a capitalist world order—the New International Economic Order notably—were deliberately and decisively removed from the realm of realistic possibility.

Meanwhile the state with the oldest ongoing imperial tradition, reworked into an amalgam of communist ideology with top-down administrative and political control, had broken out of its economic constraints. China's version of far-flung, energetic, and informed capitalism proved able to combine commercial connectivity with political closure. The upshot of these trends is extreme inequality both within states and among them. As a report in 2022 from leading economists concluded, "Global inequalities seem to be about as great today as they were at the peak of Western imperialism in the early 20th century."[12]

---

11. Yarimar Bonilla, *Non-Sovereign Futures: French Caribbean Politics in the Wake of Disenchantment* (Chicago: University of Chicago Press, 2015), 13.

12. Lucas Chancel, Thomas Piketty, Emmanuel Saez, and Gabriel Zucman, *World Inequality Report 2022* (Cambridge, MA: Harvard University Press, 2022), 5. Since World War II, global inequality has been a source of anxiety and controversy, even though in much of this period (especially since the 1970s) inequality has become more extreme. Christian Olaf Christiansen and Steven L. B. Jensen, "Introduction," in Christiansen and Jensen, eds.,

The World Is Not Flat

The end of colonial empire might at first appear as the triumph of a horizontal conception of world politics: the equivalence of each people represented by a state they could see as their own. But if the crises of colonial empire put an end to the formal organization of power along vertical lines—colonial ministries, governors-general, governors, provincial commissioners, district officer, or their equivalents in organization charts—it did not install a definitively horizontal structure of power, either within states or among them. Sovereignty mattered—client states could shop for patrons for example—but it did not put an end to asymmetrical power relations.

Most present-day political systems contain a mix of horizontal elements—the voting citizen, constitutions recognizing equal rights—with vertical ones—patronage, unequal resources to contest elections. Anticolonial movements challenged the vertical structure of imperial power. African leaders saw in Eurafrica the possibility of using the horizontal power of citizenship and African unity to give Africans a clear and open voice in inclusive political institutions. Behind the Afroasian movement was the aspiration for a more horizontal politics on a world scale. Eurasianists, in contrast, sought to revivify a vertical version of politics and thereby claim a place in a world divided into rival civilizations and power blocs.

Although advocates of Eurafrica and Afroasia were not able to bring about the more horizontal relationships across continents that they sought, activists in many countries and regions continue to clamor for the voices of citizens to be heard. Although beaten back, protest movements challenged Putin's authoritarian rule after the contorted elections of 2011. The political mobilization in Ukraine that brought about a regime change in 2014 and the election of President Volodymyr Zelensky on an anti-corruption platform in 2019 were strong challenges both to Putin's strategy and to Eurasianist ideology, all the more powerful because it emerged in the overlapping cultural terrains of Russia and Ukraine. The

---

Histories of Global Inequality: New Perspectives (Cham, Switzerland: Palgrave Macmillan, 2019), 16, 20.

post-Soviet regimes in Belarus and Kazakhstan faced massive protests in 2020 and 2022, respectively.

Many countries, especially in Africa, were not able to develop or sustain the means to fulfill the mythical deal of liberal democracy: that states would provide an adequate level of protection and services, and citizens—not just a narrow elite—would accept the social order. By the late twentieth century, the inability of poor states to maintain the liberal bargain was catching up with the rich states. Facing highly mobile capital, offshore finance, and the relocation of jobs to places where labor had the least protection, states in the industrial countries were under pressure to limit wages and social benefits, and many economists and political theorists were justifying these measures on the basis of free-market ideology. In the twenty-first century, political mobilization of discontent took the form not only of attempts to remedy poverty or maintain social benefits, but of xenophobic movements that blamed deteriorating welfare on foreigners and immigrants and sought the recreation of a fictive self-contained national body politic. The politics of far-right movements reflects the problems of economic inequality and social dislocation; it does not solve them.

The national framework of politics remains compelling even though populations are generally more mixed, more mobile, and more open to change than that framework would suggest. The illusion of sovereign equivalence—political horizontality—coexists with the ability of capital to operate on a worldwide scale, while attempts at making verticality work for the poor, in the form of economic development programs, run into both the constraints of economic power and an ideological edifice constructed around the individuality of the economic actor and the autonomy of the individual state.

Do the histories of Eurasia, Eurafrica, and Afroasia mean that there are no alternatives to our fragmented system of state sovereignty cross-cut by the economic and ideological power of global capitalism? Or that we must keep thinking about new alternatives, bearing in mind that some projects for political restructuring in the past came closer to being realized than we might remember and not in the ways their creators expected? The compromises made during one phase of post-imperial reconfiguration in the 1960s and another in the 1990s did not produce durable solutions to basic problems. In our connected and unequal world, the questions of what kind of political transformations can be imagined and what kinds of transformations can be implemented have not gone away.

ACKNOWLEDGMENTS

THIS BOOK is based on research and reading that each of us began long ago and on years of conversations with colleagues in many fields of study and from many countries. Jane Burbank began studying Eurasianism in the 1970s while working on what became her book on Russian intellectuals' reactions to the Russian revolution. Frederick Cooper came to appreciate the possibilities of Eurafrica while doing research, beginning in the late 1990s, on citizenship questions in France and French Africa. Years later, we became intrigued by the comparison of Eurasia and Eurafrica. We gave joint talks on this subject at the European University Institute in Florence in 2014 and at NYU Abu Dhabi in 2015. Comments we received on these occasions convinced us to pursue this topic. Fred shared his early thoughts about Eurafrica with the History Department at Harvard University in 2018, and Jane spoke on Eurasianism in lectures on the 100th anniversary of the Russian revolution at Princeton University, Sciences Po Bordeaux, the Jordan Center at New York University, and other venues. The joint effort took on a new dimension after we gave a lecture on Eurasia and Eurafrica at the University of Turin in 2019. Our hosts, Federica Morelli and Alberto Masoero, encouraged us to complete the triangle by bringing in Afroasia.

After our stimulating discussions in Turin, we set to work on an article on all three transcontinental movements of ideas and politics. In pursuing this direction, we acquired a large debt to the scholars who have produced a rich literature on Afroasian political movements. During home isolation caused by the COVID pandemic, we realized that the article had exploded into a book. Months later, we sent a first draft to our friend and colleague Marina Mogilner, who delicately suggested additions and changes. We tried out a second draft of the book at a series of four workshops at the University of Naples in May–June 2022. We want to thank Olindo De Napoli, his colleagues, and their students for their commentaries; these became the basis for the next round of revisions. During the summer of 2022, we spent a month at the University of Konstanz, where numerous conversations with Manuel Borutta, Andreas Guidi, and their colleagues gave us ideas and encouragement. In September 2022, we led a workshop focused on the introduction at Yale University. Our host Lauren Benton offered her ideas on the text and the broader issues involved.

All along the way, we profited from the insights of friends and colleagues who shared their work and ideas with us. Here we want to acknowledge a few of the people who helped us extend this text beyond our usual research domains: Asli Iğsiz, Müge Göçek, Mrinalini Sinha, Saliha Belmessous, Sharad Chari, Andrew Ivaska, and Lynn Tesser. We thank Giuliana Chamedes for sending us parts of her forthcoming book project and for commenting on parts of ours.

John Burbank and Pam MacEwan took the time to read and make suggestions for the introduction. Marek Eby was a great help to us in many ways. He gave us insightful comments on the manuscript, saved us from several embarrassing errors in three languages, and pointed us to new sources.

During the last stages of working on this book, Priya Nelson went beyond the duties of an editor with her ideas for revising the manuscript. Emma Wagh of Princeton University Press provided generous assistance in arranging for maps and images and in putting together the manuscript. Shane Kelley drew excellent maps. Karen Verde helped us through the copyediting process. We appreciate Chris Ferrante's remapping of political space in his cover design.

Over the years, we have received generous assistance from archivists and librarians in many locations. Our special thanks and thoughts go to the National Archives of France (Paris, later Pierrefitte) and Senegal (Dakar), the Archives d'Outre-Mer (Aix-en-Provence), and the Bibliothèque Nationale de France, the New York University library, Widener Library, Columbia University library, as well as many other collections in France, Germany, and Russia. We greatly appreciate the contributions of the library personnel of New York University, including the librarians and IT specialists who work behind the scenes to make the web accessible to the New York University community, especially important during the pandemic years. Our special thanks go to Alla Rachkov, specialist on Slavic materials at NYU, who shares our interest in the Russian emigration and managed to locate many of the Eurasianists' original texts. Alexandra Shpitalnik of NYU's Jordan Center for Advanced Study of Russia helped us out at critical moments. Translations from the Russian and French, unless otherwise noted, are our own.

We think with great pleasure of the many friends, family members, colleagues, teachers, and students who for decades have enriched our lives and work.

New York, March 2023

INDEX

Page numbers in *italics* denote figures.

Abidjan-Matin (newspaper), 135–36, *135*
Aboitiz, Nicole CuUnjieng, 158
Ad Hoc Assembly, 118–19
affinity: Afroasia and, 27–29, 187–88, 268–70; Eurafrica and, 27–29, 89, 93, 97–99, 268–70; Eurasianism and, 28–29, 81, 93, 235–37, 247–48, 268–70; Pan-Africanism and, 155–57; Pan-Asianism and, 157–60. *See also* culture and civilization; horizontal solidarity; vertical solidarity
Africa: decolonization of, 2–3; democracy in, 281; migration from, 147–48, 219–20. *See also* Afroasia; Eurafrica; *specific countries*
African diaspora, 96, 147, 155–57, 168, 189n90, 199
African National Congress (ANC), 137, 192–93
L'Afrique: Champ d'expansion de l'Europe (Guernier), 93–94
Afroasia: concept and origins of, 2–11; affinity and, 27–29, 187–88, 268–70; China and, 157–62, 165, 168, 174–75, 182–84, 186, 198; Cold War and, 174, 178–82, 184, 197–98, 202, 207–8; communism and, 6–7, 8, 13; compared to Eurafrica and Eurasia, 4, 7–17, 24, 28, 89, 93, 95, 116, 128, 136, 152, 234, 259–60, 265–76; culture and, 14, 187–88; current status of, 265–68; Eurocentrism and, 3, 9; federalism and, 34; historical setting of, 36–44; imperial origins of, 17–24; imperialism and, 268; nationalism and, 161–65, 174–77, 200, 205; New International Economic Order (NIEO) and, 187, 203–20, 275–76; Non-Aligned Movement (NAM) and, 174, 183–87, *185–86*, 205; political, economic, and cultural connections and, 13–17; present and future of, 217–20; racial solidarity and, 191–95; social and economic inequality and, 26, 180, 209–20, 280, 281; socialism and, 8, 189, 275; sovereignty and, 11–13, 22–24, 31, 169, 172–78, 183–87, 190–91, 199–202, 275; Soviet Union and, 181–82, 187–88; spatial configuration of, 29–30; trajectory of, 271–72, 274–76; United States and, 178–80; unity and disunity in, 196–202; vertical and horizontal solidarities and, 25–26, 34–35, 176–77, 268, 280. *See also* Bandung Conference (Afro-Asian Conference, 1955)
Afro-Asian Conference. *See* Bandung Conference (Afro-Asian Conference, 1955)
Afro-Asian Peoples Solidarity Organization (AAPSO), 9, 187
Afro-Asian Writers Bureau, 9, 187–88
Ake, Claude, 188n89
Akhmatova, Anna, 225
Alekseev, Nikolai, 239n72
Alexander I, emperor of Russia, 47
Alexander the Great, 229
Algeria: Bandung Conference and, 173–74; Casablanca Group and, 17, 200–201; citizenship and, 100–101; European integration and, 129–30, 131, 144; G-77 and, 210n144; hirak movement in, 220; Non-Aligned Movement (NAM) and, 184, *186*, 205; plans for Bandung 2 and, 196–97; sovereignty and, 196–97
Algerian War (1954–62), 105–6, 125–27, 128–29, 140–41, 170, 275
All-African Peoples Conference (Accra, Ghana, 1958), 199–200

[287]

Amery, Leo, 93n6
Amin, Samir, 188n89
Amrith, Sunil, 178n65
anarchism, 160
Anderson, Benedict, 26–27, 164
Angola, 184
anti-imperialist and anticolonial movements: Bandung Conference and, 173–74, 275; communism and, 154, 160–64; democracy and, 263–64; discourses and boundary-crossing networks of, 154–71; European integration and, 112; impact of World War I on, 39–40; impact of World War II on, 168–71; internationalism and, 161–64, 191–95; Islam and, 160, 168; New International Economic Order (NIEO), 187, 203–20, 275–76; Pan-Africanism and, 155–57, 165, 168, 217–18; Pan-Asianism(s) as, 155, 157–60; racial solidarity and, 191–95; self-determination principle and, 154–55; socialism and, 169, 198–99; Tricontinental Conference of Solidarity of the Peoples of Africa, Asia, and Latin America and, 205–7. *See also* nationalism
anti-Semitism, 86, 229
Apithy, Sourou Migan, 117, 118, 122, 123
Arab Spring, 220
Ash, Timothy Garten, 262n1
Asian Relations Conference (Delhi, 1947), 168–69
Asian-African Legal Consultative Committee, 187
Asiatic Labour Congress, 159
Assembly of the French Union (Assemblée de l'Union française), 105
Association of Southeast Asian Nations, 198
Aubame, Jean-Hilaire, 120n94
Augustus, Roman emperor, 46
Australia, 21
Austria-Hungary, 18–19, 37–38
autocracy, 18, 274, 276–77, 280–81
Avvakum, 87, 243–45
Az i Ia (Suleimenov), 236–37

Baathists, 198–99
Bagramov, Eduard, 231n35
Bandung Conference (Afro-Asian Conference, 1955): anti-imperialism and, 173–74, 275; breakthrough and limitations of, 6–7, 9, 14, 171–78, *173, 175*, 217–18, 219; China and, 6–7, 174, *175*, 182–83; Eurafrica and, 130; Non-Aligned Movement (NAM) and, 205; plans for Bandung 2 and, 186, 196–97; post-Bandung spirit and, 178–91; race and, 191
Bangladesh, 216
Barnett, Michael, 165
Barry, Diawadou, 132
Bartol'd, V. V., 48n12
Bauer, Peter, 213
Bedasse, Monique, 192n100
Belarus, 243, 271, 281
Belgium, 118, 121–22, 129–33, 147–48
Ben Bella, Ahmed, 196
Ben Khedda, Youssef, *186*
Benoist, Alain de, 238
Biafra, 195
Blok, Aleksandr, 49–50
Bolshevism, 4, 41–42, 49–50, 56, 68–70, 77, 160, 241
Bonilla, Yarimar, 278–79
Bosnia, 267
Botz-Bornstein, Thorsten, 93
Boumediene, Houari, 210n144
Brandt, Willi, 212–13
Briand, Aristide, 93n6
British Commonwealth, 4, 21–22
British empire: anticolonial movements and, 112; citizenship and, 21, 166, 170 (*see also* British Nationality Act (1948)); federalism and, 103; impact of World War I on, 39–40, 43; World War I and, 19. *See also specific colonies and territories*
British Malaya (1826–1957), 170
British Nationality Act (1948), 22n22, 147n126, 170
Bromlei, Iuliian Vladimirovich, 230n30
Brown, Megan, 129n87, 138
Buddhism, 160
Burke, Roland, 23n24, 215
Burton, Antoinette, 191
Byrne, Jeffrey James, 184, 186, 196, 207n136

Cabral, Amilcar, 206
Cameroon, 100, 104n26, 106n29, 170
Campbell, Horace, 201n125
Canada, 21
capitalism: anti-imperialism and, 161–64, 168, 182, 188, 204; communism and, 3, 20, 181, 260, 266, 275–76; development economics and, 204–5; imperialism and, 20, 266; international order and, 3, 138–39, 180–82, 205, 212–17, 221, 260, 265–66, 275–76, 279, 281; nation-states and, 31, 35, 151, 266, 278–79; in post-Soviet space, 221, 260; Trubetskoi on, 52–53. *See also* New International Economic Order (NIEO)
Casablanca Group, 17, 200–201
Casely-Hayford, J. E., 32n40
Catherine the Great, empress of Russia, 49, 66
Catholicism, 124
Central African Republic, 216
Césaire, Aimé, 95, 176n60, 199n118
Chari, Sharad, 10
Chatterjee, Partha, 176n61
Chechen Republic, 256–57
Chelishchev, Petr, 59, *60*
China: Afroasia and, 154, 157–62, 165, 168, 174–75, 182–84, 186, 198; Eurasia and, 6, 53, 57, 61, 75, 88; rival empires and, 40, 48. *See also* People's Republic of China
Chinese Communist Party, 162
Chinese diaspora, 150–60
Chinese empire, 18–19, 157
Chinggis Khan, 70–79, 88, 229
Christianity: anti-imperialist and anti-colonial movements and, 160; Eurasianism and, 64–67, 71, 72–75, 77–79, 82, 84–85, 86–87, 243–45, 260, 276; Grand Princedom of Moscow and, 46; Russian empire and, 46–48; Savitskii on, 86–87; Trubetskoi on, 65–67, 71, 72–75, 77–79, 82, 84–85
Christiansen, Christian Olaf, 24n25
Churchill, Winston, 110, 179
citizenship: British empire and, 21, 166, 170 (*see also* British Nationality Act (1948)); Eurafrica and, 148–52, 170;

European Union and, 273–74; French colonial empire and, 18, 22n22, 90, 100–101, 102–9, 116–20, 139–45, 170, 264; nation-states and, 262–68; in post-Soviet space, 233–34; Russian empire and, 18–19
civil service, 107–8
civilization. *See* culture and civilization
Clavin, Patricia, 36
Cogneau, Denis, 108n31, 266
Cohen, Jean, 116n49
Cold War, 197–98, 207–8
Collins, Michael, 200n121
Colombo Powers, 171–72. *See also* Bandung Conference (Afro-Asian Conference, 1955)
Comintern (Communist International), 42, 160
Common Market (European Economic Community, EEC), 90n2, 110, 129–33, 196, 209, 273
Common Market of South America (Mercosur), 264
Commonwealth of Independent States (CIS), 232
communism: Afroasia and, 6–7, 8, 13, 198; anti-imperialism and, 154, 160–64; Bolshevik Russia and, 42; capitalism and, 3, 20, 181, 260, 266, 275–76; Eurafrica and, 136–37; Eurasianism and, 3, 261, 276; internationalism and, 189, 217–18; Padmore and, 156; post-Soviet Russia and, 2; Trubetskoi on, 70, 76–79, 84; United States and, 179, 266. *See also* People's Republic of China
Communist International (Comintern), 42, 160
Communist Party (China), 162
Communist Party (USSR), 41–42, 68, 181, 222, 224n5, 225, 231, 238
La Condition Humaine (newspaper), 98n14
Congo, 118, 130, 179, 195
Congress of Black Writers and Artists (Paris, 1956), 188, 199n118
Congress of the Peoples of Europe, Asia, and Africa (Puteaux, 1948), 169

Cook, Mercer, 199n118
Côte d'Ivoire, 152, 200–201
Coudenhove-Kalergi, Richard von, 91, *92*, 93, 95, 110, 164
Crimea, 51, 54, 78, 255–58, 267
Cuba, 205
cultural relativism, 53
culture and civilization: Afroasia and, 14, 187–88; Eurafrica and, 89, 114, 123–24; *Exodus to the East* (1921) manifesto and, 59–68; imperialism and, 265; Pan-Asianism and, 157–60; Putin on, 254; Savitskii on, 55–59, 86–87; Senghor on, 13, 14, 28, 95–97, 103, 114, 123–24, 268; Trubetskoi on, 13, 33, 51–53, 55–56, 62–68, 75–79, 82–85, 87, 88, 93, 157, 240, 276
Curzon, George Nathaniel Curzon, Marquess, 42n61
Czechoslovakia, 181

Davis, Angela, 192
Davis, John, 199n118
Debré, Michel, 140n114
Defferre, Gaston, 120–21, 123n73, 124–25, 131, 143
democracy: in Africa, 281; anti-imperialism and, 263–64; capitalism and, 3; Eurafrica and, 119, 138–39, 260, 265; Eurasianism and, 3, 35, 260, 276; European Union and, 274; in Hungary, 223; politics of, 34–35; in post-Soviet space, 221, 223; Russian Federation and, 277; Senghor on, 98–99; Trubetskoi on, 62–63; Ukraine and, 261, 267
development (economic): Afroasia and, 24, 172, 180–84, 197; as colonial project, 40, 90, 107–8, 170; Eurafrica and, 107–9, 117, 121–33, 136, 139, 141, 149–52; Eurasia and, 71, 260; international institutions and, 207–10, 212–14, 218–19; as post-colonial goal, 35, 207–12, 218; Savitskii on, 56–59, 69. *See also* New International Economic Order (NIEO); place-development
development economics, 204–5
Dia, Mamadou, 142, 151

Diagne, Souleymane Bachir, 176
diaspora (African), 96, 147, 155–57, 168, 189n90, 199
diaspora (Chinese), 150–60
diaspora (Indian), 158, 166–67, 169
diaspora studies, 193
Dietrich, Christopher, 210
Dinkel, Jürgen, 217n159
Diop, Ousmanne Socé, 122
disarmament, 184
Donbas, 255, 267
Du Bois, W.E.B.: Pan-Africanism and, 155, 168; on race and imperialism, 171, 176n60, 191, 192, 193
Dugin, Alexander: Eurasianism and, 11n7, 13–14, 20, 238–46, *242*, *244*, 252–58, 259, 260, 269–70, 276; "great space" politics and, 30n36; Putin and, 252–58; on religion, 243–45; on Ukraine, 241, 256–57
Duranti, Marco, 215
Dutch colonial empire, 39–40, 103, 170
Dutch East Indies, 170

East Germany, 181
Economic Commission for Latin America, 203
Economic Community of West African States, 264
economic sovereignty, 210–11
Egypt: anti-imperialist movements and, 154, 198–99; Bandung Conference and, 172, *175*; Casablanca Group and, 17, 200–201; independence of, 43; Non-Aligned Movement (NAM) and, 184, *186*; Radio Cairo in, 189–90; Soviet Union and, 181; Suez Canal and, 127, 179, 187. *See also* Nasser, Gamal Abdel
emigration/émigrés (Russian), 50, 53–54, 61, 69, 81, 86, 163, 227n19
empire: capitalism and decolonization in, 266, 279; concept of, 17–19, 167; federalism and, 32–33, 102–4, 111, 164, 273; inter-empire cooperation and, 38, 91, 94, 148, 153, 162; restoration of in Eurasianist politics, 2, 6, 68, 234, 240–41, 245, 256, 259, 270–71; as

starting point for Eurasia, Eurafrica, and Afroasia, 3–8, 17–24, 36–44, 46–49, 89–95, 99–102, 154, 157, 165–67, 170–71, 218, 236, 240–41, 259, 262, 268. *See also* British empire; France and French colonial empire; Mongol empire; Russian empire

Eritrea, 2, 195

Eslava, Luis, 177n64

Esperanto, 20

Estonia, 278

Ethiopia, 43, 195

ethnic diversity, 223–30

Ethnogenesis and the Biosphere of the Earth (Gumilev), 228–29

ethnography, 224–30

etnogenez (ethnogenesis), 224

Eurafrica: concept and origins of, 2–11, 89–99, *92*; affinity and, 27–29, 89, 93, 97–99, 268–70; citizenship and, 148–52, 170; compared to Afroasia and Eurasia, 4, 7–17, 24, 28, 89, 93, 95, 116, 128, 136, 152, 234, 259–60, 265–76; culture and, 89, 114, 123–24; current status of, 265–68; democracy and, 119, 138–39, 260; Eurocentrism and, 3, 94; European integration and, 5, 90–92, 110–39, 144, 149–51, 273–74; Françafrique and, 145–47; historical setting of, 36–44; imperial origins of, 17–24; imperialism and, 268; migration and, 147–48, 219–20; nationalism and, 93, 94, 98, 106n29, 143; political, economic, and cultural connections and, 13–17; post–World War II debates on, 109–10, 148–49; social and economic equality and, 8, 89, 98, 106–8, 149–51; sovereignty and, 11–13, 22–24, 116–20, 122–23, 133–34, 139–45, 146–47, 272–73; Soviet Union and, 116, 136; spatial configuration of, 29–30; trajectory of, 271–74; vertical and horizontal solidarities and, 25–26, 34–35, 125, 135–36, *135*, 138, 143–44, 148–49, 268, 280. *See also* Pan-Africanism; Senghor, Léopold Sédar

L'Eurafrique, notre dernière chance (Eurafrica, our last chance) (Nord), 110

Eurasia: concept and origins of, 2–11, 45–51; compared to Eurafrica and Afroasia, 4, 7–17, 24, 28, 89, 93, 95, 116, 128, 136, 152, 234, 259–60, 265–76; current status of, 265–68; democracy and, 260; Eurocentrism and, 3; historical setting of, 36–44; imperial origins of, 17–24; imperialism and, 268–71; nationalism and, 61–64, 79–82, 87, 93, 248, 254; origins and use of term, 50; political, economic, and cultural connections and, 13–17; Senghor on, 116; sovereignty and, 4–5, 11–13, 22–24, 258–61; spatial configuration of, 29–30; trajectory of, 271–72, 274, 276–78; vertical and horizontal solidarities and, 25–26, 34–35. *See also* Eurasianism

Eurasian Civilization (Orlova), 246

The Eurasian Idea and the Present (Kirabaev et al.), 246

Eurasian Path as National Idea (Dugin), 243

Eurasianism: affinity and, 28–29, 81, 93, 235–37, 247–48; vs. Bolshevism, 68–70; *Exodus to the East* (1921) manifesto and, 59–68, *60*; in post-Soviet space, 10, 182, 221–22, 230–38, 246, 258–61, 276–77, 280–81 (*see also* Dugin, Alexander; Putin, Vladimir); religion and, 64–67, 71, 72–75, 77–79, 82, 84–85, 86–87, 243–45, 260, 269, 276; Russian émigrés and, 10, 50–51, 53–54, 68–69, 81, 86, 87–88, 276 (*see also* Savitskii, Petr; Trubetskoi, Nikolai Sergeevich);

Eurocentrism: Afroasia and, 3, 9, 176; Eurafrica and, 3, 94; Eurasia and, 3, 41, 61–62, 87, 235, 237; imperialism and, 31; Soviet Union and, 41; Trubetskoi on, 51–53, 61–64, 87

Europe: communist bloc in, 263. *See also* Eurafrica; Eurasia; European integration; *specific countries*

"Europe and Eurasia (On Trubetskoi's Brochure 'Europe and Humanity')" (Savitskii), 54–59

Europe and Humanity (Trubetskoi), 51–59, 87

European Coal and Steel Community (ECSC), 110, 121–22, 124–25, 273
European Court of Justice, 23
European Defense Community, 122
European integration: Common Market (European Economic Community) and, 90n2, 110, 129–33, 196, 209, 273; Eurafrica and, 5, 90–92, 112–39, 149–51, 273–74; European Coal and Steel Community and, 110, 121–22, 124–25, 273; France and, 89–90; Great Britain and, 90n2, 121, 129; post-World War II debates on, 110–12
European Union (EU), 93n6, 110, 144, 273–74
European Union of Federalists, 111
European Youth Campaign, 123–24
Evans, Martin, 125n77
Evraziia (journal), 231n35
Ewing, Cindy, 171, 174n56
Exodus to the East (1921), 59–68, *60*

Fakhri, Michael, 177n64
Falola, Toyin, 220n164
Fanon, Frantz, 14, 176n60, 193, 206
fascist Italy, 19, 43, 94
federalism: Afroasia and, 34; as alternative to empire, 32–34; British empire and, 103; Dutch empire and, 103; French Community and, 141–42; French Union and, 102–6, 116; Houphouët-Boigny on, 115–16; nation-states and, 264; Pan-Africanism and, 199–201; Russian Federation and, 33–34, 247–52, 265; Senghor on, 20, 32–33, 98–99, 103–6, 113–15, 272; Soviet Union and, 1–2, 5, 33, 222; Touré on, 115–16. *See also* European integration
Fédération des étudiants d'Afrique noire en France (FEANF), 115n46
Florinskii, G. V., 59
Foccart, Jacques, 145n121
Foundations of Geopolitics (Dugin), 239–46, 242, 244
Françafrique, 145–47
France and French colonial empire: anticolonial movements and, 105–6, 112, 126–27, 170, 275; capitalism and decolonization in, 266; citizenship and, 18, 22n22, 90, 100–101, 102–9, 116–20, 139–45, 170, 264; Eurafrica and, 89–99; European integration and, 5, 8, 89–90, 112–39, 144; migration and, 147–48; sovereignty and, 139–45; Suez Canal and, 127; welfare in, 106–7, 150, 266; World War I and, 19, 39–40; World War II and, 99–100. *See also* French Union (1946–1958); *specific colonies and territories*
France Outre-Mer (journal), 134n100
FRELIMO, 192–93
French Community (Communauté française, 1958–1995), 140–42
French Indochina, 39–40, 90, 100, 102–3, 105–6, 170. *See also* Vietnam
French Union: citizenship and, 102–9, 116–20, 170, 264; European integration and, 112; federalism and, 102–6, 116; labor and welfare in, 106–7; origins and structure of, 4, 100–102; Senghor on, 116–18; sovereignty and, 122–23; territorialization and, 107–9, 138
Front de Libération Nationale (FLN), 125–27, 129, 196

Gabowitsch, Mischa, 50n18
Gandhi, Mohandas, 165–66, 176n60
Garavini, Giuliano, 209, 216n157
Garvey, Marcus, 156
Gaulle, Charles de, 103, 140n114, 141–42
"Geographical and Geopolitical Aspects of Eurasianism" (Savitskii), 239
Geographical Specificities of Russia (Savitskii), 69
geopolitics, 10–11, 15, 88, 238–45, 261, 276
Geopolitics of the Postmodern (Dugin), 240n78, 245
Georgia, 256–57, 265
Gerits, Frank, 180n69, 184, 200n122
German colonial empire, 18–19, 37–38
Germany: European integration and, 110, 121–22, 129–33; France and, 90. *See also* East Germany; Nazi Germany
Getachew, Adom, 199–200, 200n121, 217
Ghadar movement, 158–59

Ghana, 17, 170, 200–201, 202, 216, 275.
    See also Nkrumah, Kwame
Ghana Broadcasting System, 190
Glaser, Antoine, 147n125
Gorbachev, Mikhail, 247
Goswami, Manu, 161
Grand Princedom of Moscow, 45–46
Great Britain: European integration and, 90n2, 121, 129; migration and, 147–48; neoliberalism in, 213–14; Suez Canal and, 127. *See also* British empire
Group of 77 (G-77), 6, 208–17
Guadeloupe, 101
Guatemala, 179
Guernier, Eugène Léonard, 93–94, 109–10
Guevara, Che, 192, 206
Guinea, 17, 140, 141, 152, 200–201, 272
Gumilev, Lev Nikolaevich: Eurasianism and, 223–30, 234–36, 246, 258–59, 261, 276; Nazarbaev and, 234; in post-Soviet space, 258–59; Putin and, 250–52, *251*, 254–55, 258; Tatars and, 251; Tatarstan monument to, 250–51
Gumilev, Nikolai, 225
Guomindang (GMD), 158, 161
Guyana, 101

Hansen, Peo, 89n1
Harper, Tim, 164
Hayek, Friedrich von, 213
hirak movement, 220
Ho Chi Minh, 102–3, 160, 163–64, 179
horizontal solidarity: Afroasia and, 34–35, 176–77, 268, 280; Bandung Conference and, 176–77; Eurafrica and, 34–35, 135–36, *135*, 138, 144, 280; Eurasia and, 34–35; imagination and, 27; nation-states and, 263; New International Economic Order (NIEO) and, 211, 214–16; present-day political systems and, 280–82; Senghor on, 25–26, 97–99, 114, 180n69, 202, 268; sovereignty and, 281–82; Trubetskoi and, 64
Houphouët-Boigny, Félix, 33, 114–16, 130, 141, 143, 151
human rights: Afroasia and, 269; anti-imperialism and, 263–64; colonialism and, 218; Eurafrica and, 269; Eurasianism and, 269; New International Economic Order (NIEO) and, 215; in post-Soviet space, 223; sovereignty and, 22–24; violations of, 267
Hungary, 223
Huntington, Samuel, 245

identity: concept of, 27–28; Eurasianism and, 81, 243, 254–57; Pan-Asianism and, 157–58. *See also* affinity
identity politics, 28n30
Imagined Communities (Anderson), 26–27
immigration, 21, 143, 146–48, 156, 166, 169–70, 202, 219, 273–74, 281
imperialism: Afroasia and, 268; capitalism and, 266; culture and, 265; Dugin and, 240–46, *242*, *244*; Eurafrica and, 268; Eurasia and, 88, 221–22, 268–71; Eurocentrism and, 31; impact of World War I on, 39–44; nationalism and, 20–22; pathway to nation-state from, 3–11, 30, 153–54, 177, 218, 262–68, 278–79; in post-Soviet space, 221–22, 258–61; religion and, 20; Russia and, 235–36, 277; Savitskii and, 57–58; Trubetskoi and, 75–79, 87. *See also* anti-imperialist and anticolonial movements; *specific colonial empires*
In Search of the Imagined Tsardom (Gumilev), 230
Indépendants d'Outre Mer (Overseas Independents), 113–15, 117–18
Independent Commission for International Development Issues, 212–13
India: anti-imperialist and anticolonial movements and, 39, 158–60, 161–62, 165–66; Bandung Conference and, 172, 174; China and, 198; citizenship and, 21; federalism and, 32; independence of, 170, 275; Nagaland and, 195; Pan-Asianism and, 158–60; partition of, 168, 198; poverty in, 216; Soviet Union and, 181; Tibet and, 165. *See also* Nehru, Jawaharlal
Indian Council of World Affairs, 168–69
Indian diaspora, 158, 166–67, 169

Indian National Congress (INC), 21, 32, 158, 161, 166
Indochina, 39–40, 90, 100, 102–3, 105–6, 170. *See also* Vietnam
Indonesia: anti-imperialist and anti-colonial movements and, 39–40; Bandung Conference and, 172, 174n56; independence of, 170, 275; Soviet Union and, 181; United States and, 179
International African Service Bureau, 156
International Colonial Institute, 39
International Court of Justice (ICJ), 23
International Criminal Court (ICC), 23
International Labour Office (ILO), 94, 209
International Monetary Fund (IMF), 12, 215–16
internationalism: Afroasia and, 189; anti-imperialism and, 161–64, 191–95; communism and, 189, 217–18; Eurafrica and, 94; European integration and, 111; France and, 124–25; Pan-Asianism and, 159; roots of, 36–37. *See also* League of Nations; United Nations (UN)
Iran, 179
Iraq: Baathists in, 198–99; independence of, 43; mandate system and, 38, 154; United States and, 3, 267
Ireland, 43
Islam: in Algeria, 127n81; anti-imperialism and, 160, 168; Eurasianism and, 60, 73, 231; fear of, 221; Grand Princedom of Moscow and, 46; imperialism and, 20; in post-Soviet space, 231, 248–50; Putin and, 254, 257
Islamic Party of Rebirth, 231n36
Israel, 127
Israeli–Palestinian conflict, 267
Italy: colonialism and, 19, 43, 94; European integration and, 121–22, 129–33; migration and, 147–48
Ivan IV, tsar, 46
Ivanov, Aleksei, 236

Jakobson, Roman, 69, 237n61
James, C.L.R., 192
James, Leslie, 200n119

Japan and Japanese colonial empire, 18–19, 40, 159, 275
Jensen, Steven L. B., 24n25
Jonsson, Stefan, 89n1
Jordan, 198–99
justice, 3, 12–13, 218, 263–64. *See also* human rights

Katanga, 195
Kazakhstan, 231–35, 252, 281
Keita, Modibo, 142, *186*
Kenya, 2–3, 166–67, 170, 201–2, 212n149
Kenyatta, Jomo, 168
Khlebnikov, Velimir, 237n61
Khrushchev, Nikita, 181, 225
Kievan Rus', 45–46, 71
Kimani, Martin, 2–3, 201–2
Kisukidi, Nadia Yala, 146
Klimke, Martin, 207
Kojève, Alexandre, 126n80
Kondakov, Nikodim, 48–49
Korea, 154, 159. *See also* North Korea; South Korea
Kosovo, 267
Kropotkin, Peter, 160
Kurdistan, 195
Kurds, 38, 267

Labonne, Eirik, 110
labor, 31, 39–40, 87, 105–8, 150, 159–60, 181–82, 194, 214, 275, 278
Labour Party, 111
Lake, Marilyn, 167n41
Lal, Priya, 212n149
Lamanskii, Vladimir, 50n18
Laruelle, Marlène, 230n30
Latin America: Afroasia and, 9–10; Group of 77 and, 6, 208–17; New International Economic Order (NIEO) and, 187, 203–20, 275–76; Tricontinental Conference of Solidarity of the Peoples of Africa, Asia, and Latin America and, 9, 205–7, *206*; United Nations and, 9–10, 207–11, 266
Latvia, 278
Lawrence, Mark Atwood, 205n134
League against Imperialism, 14, 161–62, 217–18

League for Coloured Peoples, 156
League of Nations, 38, 93n6, 94, 100, 165. *See also* mandate system
Lecaillon, Jacques, 119n62
Lee, Christopher, 178n65
leftist movements, 114–15. *See also* communism; socialism
The Legacy of Chinggis Khan (Trubetskoi), 70–79, 88, 227
Lenin, 1–2, 41–42, 181
Lev Gumilev Eurasian National University, 234, 251–52
liberalism, 138–39
Libya, 17, 130, 200–201
Ligue Universelle pour la Défense de la Race Noire (Universal League for the Defense of the Black Race), 156
Lihau, Marcel, 137
Limonov, Eduard, 238
Lisette, Gabriel, 132n93
Literaturnaia Evraziia (journal), 235–36
Lithuania, 278
Louis, Wm. Roger, 180n68
Louro, Michele, 165n33, 177–78
Lumumba, Patrice, 179
Luna 2 (space ship), 227n17
Luxembourg, 121–22, 129–33

Mackinder, Halford John, 15, *16*, 50n18, 59–60, 240
Macron, Emmanuel, 145–46
Maidan movement, 267
Malaka, Tan, 163–64
Malay culture, 158
Malaysia, 198, 216
Mali, 17, 142–43, *186*, 200–201
Mali Federation, 142, 272
mandate system, 38, 42–43, 100, 101, 154, 165
Marr, N. Ia., 237n61
Martinique, 101
McCann, Gerard, 197
Medinskii, Vladimir, 256
Medvedev, Dmitrii, 247n98
Mercosur (Common Market of South America), 264
migration and migrants, 60, 93, 146–48, 151, 166, 169, 182, 219–20, 243
Milford, Ismay, 189, 190–91

Mohammad, 229
Moldova, 265
Mollet, Guy, 111, 124–25, 126–27, 131, 136, 143
Mongol empire, 70–75, 78–79
Mongols, 5, 41, 45–49, 57, 64–65, 70–79, 227, 230, 255, 257, 276
Monnerville, Gaston, 120n94
Monrovia Group, 17, 200–201
Morocco: Bandung Conference and, 173–74; Casablanca Group and, 17, 200–201; conservative monarchical regime in, 198–99; French Union and, 100; independence of, 127
Moses, Dirk, 215
Moussa, Pierra, 126
Moyn, Samuel, 23n24, 208n138
Mozambique, 182, 192–93
Münzenberg, Willi, 161
Muslim League, 168
Mussolini, Benito, 94. *See also* fascist Italy
Mysteries of Eurasia (Dugin), 238

Nagaland, 195
Napoleonic Wars, 37
Nasser, Gamal Abdel: anti-imperialist socialism and, 198–99; Bandung Conference and, 172, *175*; death of, 197; Non-Aligned Movement (NAM) and, 184, *186*; Radio Cairo and, 189–90; Suez Canal and, 127, 179
National Association for the Advancement of Colored People (NAACP), 171, 192
National Constituent Assembly (Assemblée nationale constituante), 101–2
nationalism: Afroasia and, 161–65, 174–77, 200, 205; Bandung Conference and, 174–76; Coudenhove-Kalergi on, 93; Eurafrica and, 93, 94, 98, 106n29, 143; Eurasia and, 61–64, 79–82, 87, 93, 248, 254; imagination and, 26–27; imperialism and, 20–22; importance of, 20, 26–27, 30, 93; in India, 162; internationalism and, 36, 162–64; Pan-Asianism and, 158; Russian émigrés and, 87–88; Senghor and, 98, 177; in Soviet Union, 229; Trubetskoi on, 61–64, 79–82, 84–85, 93

nationality, 10, 141–43. *See also* citizenship
nation-states: Afroasia and, 152; alternatives to, 4–5, 12, 17, 19–20, 30, 152–54, 157, 176–77, 240–41, 263, 267–68, 274; capitalism and, 31, 35, 151, 266, 278–79; Dugin on, 240–46; Eurafrica and, 119; France as, 148; international order and, 3, 186–87, 200, 215, 218, 221–22, 241, 264, 277–78; pathway from imperialism to, 3–11, 19, 30, 153–54, 177, 218, 262–68, 278–79; in post-Soviet space, 221–23
NATO (North Atlantic Treaty Organization), 1, 2, 271
Nazarbaev, Nursultan, 231–35, 237, 246, 252, *253*, 260
Nazi Germany, 19, 94, 275
négritude movement, 95, 165
Nehru, Jawaharlal: anti-imperialism and, 162, 168–69; Bandung Conference and, 172, 174; death of, 197; Pan-Asianism and, 158
neoliberalism, 213–15
Nesiah, Vasuki, 177n64
Netherlands, 112, 121–22, 129–33. *See also* Dutch colonial empire
New International Economic Order (NIEO), 187, 203–20, 275–76
New Zealand, 21
Nguyen Ai Quoc (later Ho Chi Minh), 102–3, 160, 163–64, 179
Nigeria, 170, 195, 200–201, 202, 275
Nkrumah, Kwame: anti-imperialism and, 168, 206; Bandung Conference and, 172; coup d'état against, 197; Eurafrica and, 137; federalism and, 199–200; nation-state and, 5, 30; Pan-Africanism and, 137, 168, 199
Nolan, Mary, 207
Non-Aligned Movement (NAM), 9, 174, 183–87, *185–86*, 205
Nord, Pierre, 110
North Atlantic Treaty Organization (NATO), 1, 2, 271
North Korea, 216
North Vietnam, 182
Northern Ireland, 43
nuclear disarmament, 184
Nyerere, Julius, 192, 200, 212n149

Offner, Amy, 204n131
Ogle, Vanessa, 214
oil, 128–29. *See also* Organization of Petroleum Exporting Countries (OPEC)
oil crisis (1973), 215–16
"On racism" (Trubetskoi), 86
"On the Ukrainian Problem" (Trubetskoi), 81–85
OPEC (Organization of Petroleum Exporting Countries), 209–10, 212, 215–16, 275–76
Organisation commune des régions sahariennes (OCRS, Common Organization of Saharan Regions), 128–29
Organization of African Unity, 201–2
Organization of Petroleum Exporting Countries (OPEC), 209–10, 212, 215–16, 275–76
Organization of Solidarity with the Peoples of Africa, Asia and Latin America (OSPAAL), 205–7
Orientalism, 236–37
Orlova, I. B., 246
Ottoman empire, 18–19, 37–38

Padmore, George, 156–57, 168, 193, 200n119
PAFMECA (Pan-African Freedom Movement of East and Central Africa), 190n95
Pakistan, 168, 198
Palestine, 184, 198–99, 205, 267
Pan-Africanism: as anti-imperialist movement, 155–57, 165, 168, 217–18; culture and, 14–15; federalism and, 199–201; nationalism and, 20; sovereignty and, 199–202
Pan-Arabism, 14–15, 20, 155, 190
Pan-Asianism(s), 14–15, 155, 157–60
Pan-Europa, 91–93, 110
Pan-Islamism, 155
Pan-Slavism, 14–15, 20, 155
Paris Peace Conference (1919–1920), 36
Parti Africain de l'Indépendance, 115n46
peasants, 27, 161, 194, 203
Pedersen, Susan, 38
Pelevin, Victor, 237n64

People's Republic of China: Afroasia and, 6–7, 13, 182–84, 186, 191, 196, 198, 211; anti-imperialism and, 154, 161–62; "Asian values" and, 223, 269; Bandung Conference and, 6–7, 174, *175*, 182–84; economic power of, 7, 35, 278; India and, 198; Pan-Asianism and, 157–60; plans for Bandung 2 and, 196; Uyghurs and, 267. *See also* China
Permanent Mandates Commission (PMC), 38, 165. *See also* mandate system
permanent sovereignty, 211
Perroux, François, 136
Peter the Great, emperor of Russia, 46–47, 65, 76
Philippines, 159n18
Pineau, Christian, 133, 139
place-development, 57, 69, 227, 228
Pleven, René, 134
Portugal and Portuguese empire, 179–80, 275
post-colonial studies, 193
post-colonialism and post-socialism, 10
Prague Circle of linguistic theorists, 51, 86
Prashad, Vijay, 191
Prebisch, Raúl, 203–5, 209
Pugachev, Yemelyan Ivanovich, 66
Pulatov, Timur, 235
Putin, Vladimir: authoritarian rule of, 280–81; Dugin and, 252–58; Eurasianism and, 10–11, 248–58, 260–61, 270–71; Gumilev and, 224, 251–52; invasion of Ukraine and, 1–3, 12, 198, 201–2, 258, 262n1, 265, 266–67, 271, 274, 277–78; photograph of, *253*; Tatarstan and, 249–51

Quenum-Possy-Berry, Maximilien, 132

Rabemananjara, Jacques, 188
racial solidarity, 191–95
racism and racial discrimination: African diaspora and, 147–48; anti-imperialism and, 165–67, 171; Asian-African relations and, 165–67, 191, 194–95; Bandung Conference and, 173–74; Pan-Africanism and, 155–57; in Russian Federation, 29; in Soviet Union, 29; Trubetskoi on, 86; United States and, 179, 192
radio, 189–91
Radio Cairo, 189–90
railroads, 128
Ram, Harsha, 237n61
Ranger, Terrence, 193
Rassemblement Démocratique Africain (African Democratic Assembly), 114–15, 132n93
Raza, Ali, 167
Reagan, Ronald, 213–15
religion: Afroasia and, 158, 269; anti-imperialist and anticolonial movements and, 160; Eurafrica and, 269; Eurasianism and, 64–67, 71, 72–75, 77–79, 82, 84–85, 86–87, 243–45, 260, 276; Grand Princedom of Moscow and, 46; imperialism and, 20; Savitskii on, 86–87; Trubetskoi on, 65–67, 71, 72–75, 77–79, 82, 84–85. *See also specific religions*
Republic of Kazakhstan, 231–35, 252
Republic of Sakha (Yakutia), 250n112
Republic of Tatarstan, 243, 248–52, *251*
Réunion, 101
Reynolds, Henry, 167n41
Rhodesia, 21–22
Rhythms of Eurasia (Gumilev), 230
Rice, Luisa Claire, 109n33
Riurik, 46
Robinson, Ronald, 180n68
Rodney, Walter, 188n89, 192, 193
Romulo, Carlos, 172–73, 174–75, 176–77
Roosevelt, Franklin D., 179
Roy, Franziska, 167
Roy, M. N., 160, 163–64
Rozen, Viktor, 48–49
Russia. *See* Bolshevism; Grand Princedom of Moscow; Russian empire; Russian Federation; Soviet Union
Russian empire: citizenship and, 18–19; end of, 68; Europe vs. Asia and, 46–51, 88, 241; federalism and, 33; Mongols and, 45–49, 70–79; post-Soviet reimagination of, 255–59, 270–71; Trubetskoi on, 66, 74–77; World War I and, 19, 41–42

Russian Federation: annexation of Crimea and, 256–58; autocracy and, 276, 277, 280–81; democracy and, 277; federalism and, 33–34, 247–52, 265; imperialism and, 269–71; invasion of Ukraine and, 1–3, 12, 198, 201–2, 258, 262n1, 265, 266–67, 271, 274, 277–78; official names of, 247; racism and racial discrimination in, 29; sovereignty and, 222–23, 259–60. *See also* Putin, Vladimir

Russian Orthodox Church: Russian empire and, 46–48; Savitskii on, 86–87; Trubetskoi on, 66–67, 71, 74–75, 77–79, 82

Russian Thought (journal), 54–59

Rwanda-Burundi, 130

Sahara, 128–29
Sakha (Republic of Sakha; Yakutia), 250n112
Sauvy, Alfred, 17n13
Savin, Leonid, 50n18
Savitskii, Petr: on culture, 55–59, 86–87; Dugin and, 239–40, 243–45; on *Europe and Humanity* (Trubetskoi), 54–59; on "geopolitics," 88; Gumilev and, 226–28; on place-development, 57, 69, 227, 228; in post-Soviet space, 246, 259, 260, 276; Trubetskoi and, 71, 75, 86–87, 269; on Ukraine, 86–87, 261
Schmitt, Carl, 240
Schuman, Robert, 121–22, 125–26, 143
Scientific Tasks of Eurasianism (Savitskii), 246
"Scythians" (Blok), 49–50
self-determination, 36, 62, 154–55, 174–75. *See also* nation-states
Sen, Tansen, 158
Senegal, 142–43, 151, 152, 200–201
Senghor, Léopold Sédar: Bandung Conference and, 177; Coudenhove-Kalergi and, 95; on culture, 13, 14, 28, 95–97, 103, 114, 123–24, 268; European integration and, 112–15, 120, 123, 131–32, 133–34; federalism and, 20, 32–33, 98–99, 103–6, 113–15, 272; French Community and, 141; life and career of, 95; Mali Federation and, 142; on nationalism, 98; Nazarbaev and, 233–34; Pan-Africanism and, 199n118; photograph of, *96*; on political affinity and solidarities, 25–26, 97–99, 114, 143, 180n69, 202, 268; as president of Senegal, 151; on territorialization, 107; Trubetskoi and, 64, 85, 95, 99n17

Serbia, 267
Shaimiev, Mintimer, 250
Shankar, Shobana, 195
Sheehan, James, 11
Shepard, Todd, 146n123
Shivji, Isa, 188n89, 193
Sidel, John, 163
Singapore, 216
Sissoko, Fily Dabo, 132, 133
Slavs, 47, 64–65. *See also* Pan-Slavism
Slobodian, Quinn, 138, 213
Sluga, Glenda, 36
social movements, 217–18
socialism: Afroasia and, 8, 189, 275; anti-imperialism and, 169, 198–99; Eurafrica and, 136; European integration and, 111; in France, 111, 120–21, 124–25, 126–27, 136; New International Economic Order (NIEO) and, 212–13; Tricontinental Conference of Solidarity of the Peoples of Africa, Asia, and Latin America and, 205–7; Trubetskoi on, 52–53, 77
Socialist Movement for a United States of Europe, 111
solidarity. *See* horizontal solidarity; racial solidarity; vertical solidarity
Soloviev, Vladimir, 48n11, 49
Somalia, 130, 216
Sorokin, Vladimir, 237n64
Soustelle, Jacques, 136
South Africa: Afroasia and, 192–93, 194; Bandung Conference and, 173–74; British Commonwealth and, 21; Eurafrica and, 137; Non-Aligned Movement (NAM) and, 184; poverty in, 216; sovereignty and, 202; United States and, 179–80
South Korea, 216

South Sudan, 2, 195
Southeast Asia Treaty Organization, 264
sovereignty: Afroasia and, 11–13, 22–24, 31, 169, 172–78, 183–87, 190–91, 199–202, 275; Algeria and, 196–97; anti-imperialism and, 169; Eurafrica and, 11–13, 22–24, 116–20, 122–23, 133–34, 139–45, 146–47, 272–73; Eurasia and, 4–5, 11–13, 22–24, 258–61; French colonial empire and, 101–2; human rights and, 22–24; Latin American countries and, 203–4; as layered, 11–12, 22, 95, 99, 116–20, 122–23, 133–34, 141–43, 199, 233, 257, 264, 268, 272; nation-states and, 262–68; New International Economic Order (NIEO) and, 210–12; Pan-Africanism and, 199–202; in post-Soviet space, 221–23, 231–35, 249–55, 259–60; Russian invasion of Ukraine and, 1–3, 12; Senghor on, 99, 116–18, 133–34; United States and, 22; vertical and horizontal solidarities and, 281–82. *See also* citizenship; federalism; nation-states
Soviet Union: Africa and, 151, 181; Afroasia and, 9, 13, 20, 41, 70, 81, 116, 181–83, 187–88, 211; China and, 7, 183; as empire, 19, 33, 41–42; ethnic diversity in, 70, 222–30; ethnography in, 224; Eurafrica and, 20, 136; Eurasianism and, 20, 70, 234–35, 259; European empires and, 181–82; federalism and, 1–2, 5, 10, 33, 222, 232, 247; plans for Bandung 2 and, 196; Putin on, 1–2; racism and racial discrimination in, 29; World War II and, 261, 275
Stalin, 181
stikhiia (spontaneous, elemental being), 67
student movements, 114–15
Subaltern Studies, 193
Sudan, 142, 195
Suess, Eduard, 50n18
Suez Canal, 127, 179, 187
Sukarno, 172, 174n56, 179, 197
Suleimenov, Olzhas, 236–37
Sun Yat-Sen, 157

Suvchinskii, P. P., 59
Syria, 38, 154, 198–99

Tagore, Rabindranath, 158
Taiwan, 216
Tamzali, Abdennour, 122
Tanganyika Broadcasting System, 190
Tanzania, 183, 192–93, 194, 212n149
Tatars, 73, 78, 249, 251
Tatarstan, 243, 248–52, *251*
Teitgen, Pierre-Henri, 107–8, 133
territorialization, 107–9, 138
Thatcher, Margaret, 213–14
Thiemeyer, Guido, 129n87
third world, 4, 17, 174, 177, 180, 186–88, 193, 197, 205–9, 212, 214, 217, *244*, 270
Thiriart, Jean, 238, 240n79
Tibet, 165
Tigray, 195
Tito, Josip Broz, 184, *186*
Togo, 100, 104n26
Toman, Jindrich, 51n21, 86n126
Touré, Sékou, 115–16, 151–52
trade unions, 77, 105, 108n31, 150, 161, 212–13, 217
Treaty of Rome (1957), 129–33, 149
Tricontinental Conference of Solidarity of the Peoples of Africa, Asia, and Latin America (Havana, Cuba, 1966), 9, 205–7, *206*
Trubetskoi, Nikolai Sergeevich: affinity and, 81, 93; on anti-Semitism, 86; on Chinggis Khan, 70–79, 88, 229; on communism, 70, 76–79, 84; Coudenhove-Kalergi and, 93; on culture, 13, 33, 51–53, 55–56, 62–68, 75–79, 82–85, 87, 88, 93, 157, 240; Dugin and, 239–40, 243, 253; on Eurocentrism, 51–53, 61–64, 87; *Exodus to the East* (1921) manifesto and, 59–68; Gumilev and, 227–28; on identity, 81; Jakobson and, 69; multistoried house metaphor by, 99n17, 276; on nationalism, 20, 61–64, 79–82, 84–85, 93; photograph of, *52*; in post-Soviet space, 222, 258–59, 276;

Trubetskoi, Nikolai Sergeevich (*continued*)
Prague Circle of linguistic theorists and, 51, 86; on religion, 65–67, 71, 72–75, 77–79, 82, 84–85; on "Romano-Germanic" culture, 51–53, 55–56, 62, 77–78, 87, 217–18, 240, 276; Savitskii and, 54–59, 269; Senghor and, 95, 99n17; Suleimenov and, 237; on Ukraine, 261
Tsiranana, Philibert, 140
Tunisia, 100, 127, 173–74
Turkey, 195, 235, 267

Uganda, 194, 212n149
Ukraine: democracy and, 261; Dugin on, 241, 256–57; Eurasianism and, 261; Maidan movement in, 267; Russian invasion of, 1–3, 12, 198, 201–2, 258, 262n1, 265, 266–67, 271, 274, 277–78; Savitskii and, 54, 86–87; Trubetskoi on, 81–85; Zelensky and, 280
union: use of term, 3, 100. *See also* European integration; French Union (1946–1958)
Union des Populations du Cameroon, 106n29
unions, 77, 105, 108n31, 150, 161, 212–13, 217
United Nations (UN): Afroasia and, 9–10, 12, 178, 207–11, 266; colonialism and, 176, 179–80; Eurafrica and, 12; Eurasia and, 12; Latin America and, 9–10, 207–11, 266; Non-Aligned Movement (NAM) and, 184; Russian invasion of Ukraine and, 2–3, 201–2; Universal Declaration of Human Rights (1948) and, 23
United Nations Conference on Trade and Development (UNCTAD), 209
United States: Afroasia and, 178–80; Bandung Conference and, 174; capitalism and decolonization in, 266; civil rights movement in, 170–71, 192, 275; colonialism and, 179–80; Dugin and, 240; Eurafrica and, 136–37; invasion of Iraq and, 3; Iraq and, 267; neoliberalism in, 213–15; plans for Bandung 2 and, 196; Putin and, 258; sovereignty and, 22; Suez Canal and, 127; Vietnam and, 267, 275
United States of Africa, 137, 199, 234

Universal Declaration of Human Rights (1948), 23
Universal League for the Defense of the Black Race (Ligue Universelle pour la Défense de la Race Noire), 156
Universal Negro Improvement Association, 156
universal rights. *See* human rights
Uyghurs, 267
Uzoigwe, Godfrey, 202

Verdery, Katherine, 10
Vernadskii, V. I., 228n24
Vernadsky, George, 227–28
vertical solidarity: Afroasia and, 34–35, 176–77; Bandung Conference and, 176–77; Eurafrica and, 34–35, 125, 135–36, *135*, 138, 143–44, 148–49, 268; Eurasia and, 34–35; imagination and, 27; nation-states and, 263; New International Economic Order (NIEO) and, 211, 214–16; present-day political systems and, 280–82; Senghor on, 25–26, 97–99, 114, 143, 180n69, 202, 268; sovereignty and, 281–82; Trubetskoi and, 64, 85
Vichy regime, 94
Vietnam: communism in, 179, 182, 198, 205; First Indochina War and, 105–6; France and, 100; independence of, 102–3; United States and, 267, 275. *See also* Ho Chi Minh

Wallerstein, Immanuel, 193
Wang Hui, 157–58, 198n116
Washington Consensus, 218
welfare, 106–7, 150, 266
Wells, H. G., 70n79
West African Student Union, 156
West Germany, 110, 121–22, 129–33
Westad, Odd Arne, 180
Windrush generation, 170n47
workers. *See* labor
World Bank, 12, 209, 218
World Health Organization (WHO), 209
World Trade Organization (WTO), 11
World War I, 19, 36–37, 39–40
World War II, 9, 99–100, 168–71, 261, 275

Wrangel, Pyotr Nikolayevich, 54
Wright, Richard, 199n118

X, Malcolm, 192
xenophobia, 147–48, 281

Yeltsin, Boris, 247
Younis, Musab, 157
Yugoslavia, 183, 184, *186*

Zachariah, Benjamin, 167
Zambia, 183, 275
Zanzibar Revolution (1964), 195
Zelensky, Volodymyr, 280. *See also* Ukraine
Zhou Enlai, 174, *175*
Zielonka, Jan, 144n119
Zimbabwe, 275
Zolberg, Aristide, 115n47

A NOTE ON THE TYPE

THIS BOOK has been composed in Miller, a Scotch Roman typeface designed by Matthew Carter and first released by Font Bureau in 1997. It resembles Monticello, the typeface developed for The Papers of Thomas Jefferson in the 1940s by C. H. Griffith and P. J. Conkwright and reinterpreted in digital form by Carter in 2003.

Pleasant Jefferson ("P. J.") Conkwright (1905–1986) was Typographer at Princeton University Press from 1939 to 1970. He was an acclaimed book designer and AIGA Medalist.

The ornament used throughout this book was designed by Pierre Simon Fournier (1712–1768) and was a favorite of Conkwright's, used in his design of the *Princeton University Library Chronicle*.